W9-AEX-642

WITHDRAWN

Gramley Library
Salem Academy and College
Winston-Salem, N.C. 27108

SOUTHERN LITERARY STUDIES

Fred Hobson, Series Editor

Winner of the Jules and Fi

PEGGY WHITMAN PRENSHAW

Composing Selves

SOUTHERN WOMEN AND
AUTOBIOGRAPHY

Louisiana State University Press

Baton Rouge

Gramley Library
Salem Academy and College
Winston-Salem, N.C. 27108

Published by Louisiana State University Press
Copyright © 2011 by Louisiana State University Press
All rights reserved
Manufactured in the United States of America
First printing

Designer: Laura Roubique Gleason
Typefaces: Minion Pro, text; Mrs. Eaves, display
Printer: McNaughton & Gunn
Binder: Dekker Bookbinding

LIBRARY OF CONGRESS CATALOGING-IN-PUBLICATION DATA
Prenshaw, Peggy Whitman.
  Composing selves : Southern women and autobiography / Peggy Whitman Prenshaw.
    p. cm. — (Southern literary studies)
  Includes bibliographical references and index.
  ISBN 978-0-8071-3791-8 (cloth : alk. paper)
    1. Women—Southern States—Biography—History and criticism. 2. Southern States—
Biography—History and criticism. 3. Autobiography—Women authors—History and criticism.
4. Autobiography—Southern States—History and criticism. 5. American prose literature—
Women authors—History and criticism. 6. American prose literature—Southern States—
History and criticism. I. Title.
  PS366.A88P74 2011
  818'.503099287—dc22

                                                      2010047344

The paper in this book meets the guidelines for permanence and durability of the Committee on
Production Guidelines for Book Longevity of the Council on Library Resources. ∞

To my son Rick and daughter Penelope
and to Eric, John, and David

Contents

Acknowledgments

Some ideas first proposed in "The True Happenings of My Life: Reading Southern Women's Autobiographies" in *Haunted Bodies: Gender and Southern Texts,* edited by Anne Goodwyn Jones and Susan V. Donaldson, University Press of Virginia, are substantially developed in this book. Major sections of my afterword to the University Press of Mississippi's 1999 edition of *Southern Belle* are incorporated in the commentary on Mary Craig Kimbrough Sinclair. For the commentary on Marjorie Kinnan Rawlings, I have drawn briefly upon an early essay, "The Otherness of Cross Creek," *Marjorie Kinnan Rawlings Journal of Florida Literature* 4 (1992). For my discussion of Eudora Welty's conceptualization of the writer's life, I have taken up ideas only implicitly suggested in "Fevered Desire and Therapeutic Gaze in Welty's World," in *Eudora Welty and the Poetics of the Body,* published by the *Presses Universitaires de Rennes* 5 (2005), but more fully developed in "Eudora Welty and the Writing Life," *Eudora Welty Review* 2 (2010). I have drawn heavily upon my essay "Elizabeth Spencer's Literary Landscapes," *Southern Quarterly* 47 (2010), for the commentary on Spencer. Permissions for use of this material have been granted by the publishers.

For significant support during the early stages of this project, I am grateful to Louisiana State University, especially to the faculty of the Department of English and to Dean Karl Roider of the College of Arts and Sciences. I should also like to acknowledge the contribution of Mary Frey Eaton and family in the establishment of the Fred C. Frey Professorship in Southern Studies, which I was privileged to hold. During my tenure at LSU, I also had the assistance of a group of able graduate students and the generous and supporting friendship of my departmental colleagues.

More recently, I have had a gratifying appointment at Millsaps College as the humanities scholar in residence. In addition to my research, I have come to know a number of bright, intellectually curious undergraduates in the classroom and have greatly enjoyed the companionable association of faculty colleagues. I should like to acknowledge the valuable support that Millsaps has given me.

Composing Selves

I

Region, Genre, Gender

In September 1932 Mary Hamilton, a woman from the backwoods of the Mississippi Delta, posted an extraordinary letter to her young friend, Helen Dick Davis, a thirty-two-year-old writer living at the time in the little sawmill town of Philipp, Mississippi. Davis had come to know the frail Mrs. Hamilton, who was then sixty-five, as the mother of her friend Edris and, more importantly, as a rich repository of stories of the clearing and settling of the Delta over the half-century span of her life there. Convinced that Hamilton's vivid tales of floods and cyclones, escaped convicts, and "feuds to the death" should be preserved, Davis urged her to write them down, "if only," she said, "as a record for her children and grandchildren."[1]

Mary Hamilton complied with a few short sketches written with pencil on tablet paper. These were enough, however, to intensify Davis's determination to urge upon her the writing of a book-long personal narrative. Understandably, Mary Hamilton demurred. Unlike her young friend, who had a degree in journalism from the University of Wisconsin, Hamilton was neither a writer nor an educated woman. Besides the sketches she had done to please Helen Davis, she had otherwise in a lifetime written only a few letters. Nonetheless, in early fall 1932 she wrote Davis that she would undertake the project. She begins her letter: "This is the first day I have sat up and I am going to write you the very first one, my best friend. I am convinced I am a selfish old lady, and it was a dream I had yesterday morning convinced me" (xvii).

She goes on to describe a remarkable vision. In the dream she is with Helen Davis's two children, picking lilies, handing all the flowers to them until she tires, telling them: "You get no more, children. This last is mine." Punishment for her "selfishness" comes immediately in the figure of a snake's head, but she is spared and the children resume laughing. She concludes her letter with her interpretation of the vision:

> I can't help believing that my little friend Nick, himself so lately from the Beyond, by coming to me in my dream and laughing at my selfishness, has given me courage to work on to the end of the trail. I believe that I have been spared to gather for myself that last and largest white lily, the writing down in a book the memories of a lifetime.
>
> So I will write down for you the true happenings of my life, and if I succeed all honor goes to Nick. I can hardly wait till I get home to start work and to see you. (xix)

Hamilton's elaborate rationale—or rationalization—for the writing of her life narrative, finally published in 1992 as *Trials of the Earth,* is a clear indication of her resistance to the self-aggrandizement, or "selfishness," that autobiographical writing represents in her early twentieth-century world. Even when the writing is focused not upon the self but the self's surround—the family, the neighbors, the workaday world, as Mary Hamilton's book is—the southern woman writing autobiography is ever mindful of the risky exposure she incurs in asserting a self in print. The constraints against public display that had been felt generally by nineteenth-century European and American women, especially intense in the American South, had hardly moderated in the early twentieth century. For women, honor and good name and "selfhood," such as might be confirmed by one's society, were attendant largely upon a woman's acceptance of a private—not public—domain. The act of expressing herself in public in writing, of intruding the female self upon the male-dominated turf, meant risking her standing in her family, the approval of her neighbors and church— indeed risking her acceptance by the community at large. Even a backwoods woman like Mary Hamilton had to invoke a divine revelation and offer a confession of selfish transgression to justify to herself her "right" to write the story of her life, to use her time in self reflection rather than in productive domestic duties, to claim the attention of readers who were remote, unknown, and more powerful than she.

Trials of the Earth has epitomized for me a genre of writing that I began to read with great interest some years ago. An autobiographical text, it poses an array of theoretical and interpretive problems leading directly to issues of authorship, discourse communities, the fashioning of a narrative persona, female identify formation, regionality, access to institutions of literary culture, and many other related issues, all of which have come broadly to engage both general readers and literary scholars. Indeed, today everyone seems to be writing about—or writing—personal narratives, especially those presented as memoir.

The current interest in autobiography owes to many influences—to a society that prizes individualism and the individual's right to define and explain the self in writing, to a deep-rooted history that has long held confession to be good for the soul, to a contemporary culture that has validated therapeutic self-analysis, to readers who seek accessible, linear stories written in what is usually a style of traditional realism (unlike much modernist and postmodernist fiction), and to culture watchers who are drawn to the life histories of men and women of widely diverse backgrounds, many of whom have heretofore been largely invisible in the literary culture. There is also the long-standing practice of historians and readers of history of seeking out the testimony and documents of eyewitnesses to lived experience. And finally, not to be discounted, life stories attract us curious, social beings who are ever alert to uncovering the "story behind the story," to hearing the particulars, the anecdotes, the gossip attached to a life-revealed-as-text, to parsing explanations of motives and interpretations of consequences, to enriching our own experience and knowledge of the world through reading the "I" witness account of one willing to share her story with us.

My first serious encounter with life writing came years ago in preparing for a women's studies course that involved a wide array of regional life writings—letters by southern women, their diaries, memoirs, oral histories, autobiographies, as well as fiction that had demonstrably autobiographical material. When I read Mary Chesnut's Civil War commentary, I confronted many of the theoretical issues that have grown immeasurably more complex and engaging over the past quarter century: the nature of the literariness and historicity of personal writing; the categorizing definitions and distinctions attached to differing forms of life writing (e.g., diary, memoir, autobiography), and a concomitant hierarchy of literary status typically associated with these forms—the diary or memoir regarded as less literary than the autobiography, for example. Early on, I observed that women's personal narratives tended toward the "lower," episodic, and fragmented forms.

Also growing in nuance and complexity in recent years have been the understandings, partly informed by the social and biological sciences, of the psychological and physiological impediments to "truth telling" and thus to the credibility of the narrator and the reliability of human memory. Readers may not question Mary Hamilton's intention to tell the truth about her life, may indeed be fully drawn into the "felt life" that she creates in her narrative of the Mississippi backwoods. But in this age of multiplying and varying witnessed reports of life events, not to mention our awareness of the mind's susceptibility to false memories (even of autobiographers' deliberate deceptions), we nowadays tend to read more mindful of personal writing's limits than credulous of its sweeping representativeness. And yet, despite the inescapable mediation—the filtering, the constructedness—of life writing, the reader and the autobiographer still come to it expecting some level of nonfictive truth telling.

Among other consequences, the steady undermining of reading personal writing as a record of unmediated experience has added further complications to the historian's attempt to discover historical truth. In 1981, I was particularly struck by C. Vann Woodward's frustrated search for an appropriate title for Mary Chesnut's edited and recomposed diary of her experience during the Civil War, a discomfiture he himself acknowledges and explains in his introduction to the edition that he entitled *Mary Chesnut's Civil War.* That book, together with the women's literature course, parted a curtain for me upon an engaging field of inquiry, one that connected textual analysis with women's life stories and southern regionalism.

This present study of autobiographical writings by women of the American South thus comes from a long-standing scholarly interest, aided and abetted by my own southern female roots. What I undertake in the following pages is an exploration of autobiography, women narrators, and "southernness," and the ways in which regionality, gender, and genre are experienced, enacted, and thus made visible in a variety of life writings by southern women. Although my readings of texts by several black writers, as well as those by the more numerous white writers, take into account the complex racial context in which they conceptualize the self and compose their work, I have been more interested to discover what commonalities mark their work as "southern," "female-authored," and "autobiographical."

Of the substantial library of available published texts, I have focused upon those by writers who grew up in the South during the years following the Civil War and into the first third of the twentieth century, that is, writers who did not directly experience the Civil War or slavery. The journals and diaries recounting life stories preceding and during the war years, as well as the narratives of emancipation, are understandably preoccupied with the extraordinary events of war and the trauma of slavery. The Civil War texts have received extensive commentary in recent years by such scholars as Drew Gilpin Faust, Elizabeth

Fox-Genovese, Marilyn Mayer Culpepper, George Rable, Catherine Clinton, Nina Silber, and many others who have greatly extended our understanding of this period and these women's writings. Harriet Jacobs's *Incidents in the Life of a Slave Girl,* in particular, has elicited not only the impressive research of Jean Fagan Yellin, who edited the text, but the wide-ranging study of a host of other scholars as well.

My purpose has been rather to read texts that reflect the experience of women who came to adulthood in the period one might designate late southern Victorian, the years between 1865 and 1930s. Assuming the years of one's girlhood to be a defining period for her socialization, or acculturation, I have located my attention upon writers who came of age as part of the several generations preceding and following the turn of the twentieth century. The dates of composition and publication of the texts I discuss, however, span the full twentieth century, from Belle Kearney's *A Slaveholder's Daughter* published in 1900 to Elizabeth Spencer's *Landscapes of the Heart* and Ellen Douglas's *Truth: Four Stories I Am Finally Old Enough to Tell* in 1998.

Let me acknowledge here at the outset the thorny complexities of chronology, of time and age referencing in writing about autobiography—the near impossibility of linear time framing. One reads a text that at the outset, at least, represents an imaginative journey backwards in time—a looped recollection by the contemporaneous narrator who re-members or reconnects her present self to her past experience. Even as she moves imaginatively toward and into a recreated earlier time, she is always the self who is writing, an older self, whose more mature age, life experiences, and contemporaneous historical moment at the time of composition shape her perspective upon the past. Belle Kearny was thirty-seven in the late 1890s when she composed *A Slaveholder's Daughter,* Elizabeth Spencer and Ellen Douglas both seventy-seven when their books were published at the end of the twentieth century, although in the case of Spencer's book some sections had been written years earlier and then edited or rewritten for the memoir. Acknowledging the problematic chronologies that operate in autobiography, I nonetheless have tried to locate the present study with reference to a defined historical period, choosing texts for analysis by autobiographers who came of age during Reconstruction and in the late nineteenth and early twentieth centuries.

The years that marked the South's transition from Victorianism to modernism in intellectual thought—the years of Reconstruction, New South industrialization, World War I, and the Great Depression—are years that incorporated many

cultural commonalities, despite the social tensions and economic transformations occurring throughout the period. Whether one regards the post Civil
War period as characterized chiefly by continuity in cultural values and social
practice with the antebellum past, as W. J. Cash maintained from his vantage
seventy-five years after the war, or by discontinuity with that past, as C. Vann
Woodward argued in his 1951 *Origins of the New South*, the several generations
following the Civil War clearly represent a time of vast readjustment for the
South. In coming to terms with defeat and reunion, the region struggled to re-
define its role and place within the nation.

After the immediate social upheaval and economic collapse that followed
upon the April 1865 surrender, it was poverty that constituted the single most
unifying feature of the South over the next half century, indeed, until after
1945. Woodward remarks that "no ruling class of our history ever found itself
so completely stripped of its economic foundations as did that of the South in
this period" (29). In the effort to reestablish a viable economy, the New South
advocates, who argued for diversifying the old agricultural, largely one-crop
economy by developing manufacturing and mining and other commercial enterprise, did not always fully acknowledge or perhaps comprehend to what extent social change would inevitably accompany economic change. Gaines M.
Foster has written that the "ghosts of the Confederacy" often emerged in the
ways in which these progressive supporters of business affirmed their loyalty to
the southern past by honoring traditional values of order and stability. At the
same time they could express impatience, even scorn, for the footdraggers who
clung to the past and resisted change (80–81). The Victorian constellation of
values—social stability, industrial progress, moral standards, genteel manners,
religious devotion and tolerance, scientific inquiry and advance—were values
fraught with potential for inconsistency and contradiction, no less so in the
South than in England and the American Northeast, whose experience of Victorianism somewhat preceded that of the South's.

In *The War Within: From Victorian to Modernist Thought in the South, 1919–
1945,* Daniel Joseph Singal views the cultural tension between Victorian and
modernist cultures to have been "fiercest" in the South, partly because it was
late in making the transition and so had something of a predecessor's "script"
to follow and partly because it was so regionally self-contained (8–10). Singal
locates in the idealized aristocratic gentleman who figured centrally in the an-
tecedent Cavalier myth of the South—a "myth" discussed in great detail by
W. J. Cash, W. R. Taylor, and others—the origins of the New South's model
capitalist. "A person of impeccable character, he was said to be ambitious but

not acquisitive; energetic, but not predatory; competitive, but never cutthroat. Unlike his northern counterpart, he was a man who subscribed fully to the paternalistic code, who opened factories primarily to provide poor whites with employment, and who cared deeply about their welfare. He was a philanthropist first and a capitalist second" (22–23). Of course, the Fugitive Agrarians of *I'll Take My Stand* gave short shrift to this remaking of the old benevolent aristocrat into the paternalistic manufacturer. In his opening essay, "Reconstructed but Unregenerate," John Crowe Ransom found it easy to define "the malignant meaning of industrialism" as "a program under which men, using the latest scientific paraphernalia, sacrifice comfort, leisure, and the enjoyment of life to win Pyrrhic victories from nature at points of no strategic importance" (15).

Laura F. Edwards has observed that for women the ideologies of domesticity and merit could be employed to maintain much of the old social order while displaying a commitment to change. Conservative white men and women espousing these ideologies could "obscure and justify the glaring inequalities that actually structured post war society." She notes that their well-appointed houses required more than beneficent character, but they could very well expect responsible character to be inferred from such possessions. The "white elite, holding up their particular aspirations as the 'natural' goals of all men and women," could thus justify the poverty and social status of the have-nots as the consequence of immorality and irresponsibility (110–11).

The modification that I would suggest in these descriptions of the high Victorian ideals of the New South white male and the elite white couple's cultivation of respectability is that the responsibilities for business success and for social sensitivity and selflessness were divided significantly along gender lines, with white women carrying much of the load for displayed selflessness. Nonetheless, one cannot gainsay the many public declarations of the manly chivalric ideal, well exemplified in one instance by Joseph Cumming, a Confederate veteran from Augusta, Georgia, in speeches he made throughout the 1890s. In her study of the impact of the Civil War upon gender relations in Augusta, Lee-Ann Whites cites Cumming's sentiments (e.g., "the term that most characterizes the representative southerner . . . is chivalry" [Whites 223]) as indicative of the rhetoric of the day. One need hardly add that the African American role in this word play was that of servant-laborer, a subservient ward of the chivalrous gentleman.

The divided ideals, even contradictions, of New South goals have stimulated much scholarly interpretation. One question that has provoked considerable debate, especially in recent decades, is why postbellum white women devoted themselves so ardently to memorializing the defeat of the Confederacy, to institutionalizing commemorations of a "Lost Cause." This is an important question for this study of women's autobiography because it foreshadows the divided impulses of many of the writers who are the subjects of this book. Gaines Foster discusses a range of explanations. For example, women were entreated to devote themselves to the rehabilitation of the veterans' broken bodies and spirits, to sustain their sense of manhood, to reestablish patriarchal authority. Their efforts in behalf of honoring the defeated men, both the dead and the survivors, doubtless owed to the war rhetoric of loyalty, bravery, and heroism, but their restorative efforts derived also from their own self-interest. To the extent that there was any hope of reestablishing normalcy, to regaining security if not privilege, that hope for the memorialists seemed to lie in restoring the old order's male dominance (28–35).

In "'You Must Remember This': Autobiography as Social Critique," Jacquelyn Dowd Hall reexamines the origins and consequence of Lost Cause memorializing through the lens of Katharine DuPre Lumpkin's *The Making of a Southerner* and the lives of her parents and sisters, Elizabeth and Grace. She shows that it was the decline of the patriarchal father's status that so imperiled the restoration of the Lumpkins' South, that is, the old social order. William Lumpkin was the son of a planter family who married well and had every expectation of the manly role Singal describes. For him, living in a kind of exile from his former state, the Lost Cause ideology offered some restitution of status and elite respectability. As Hall observes, his role in the memorial movement "gave him stature in his children's eyes; their participation, in turn, demonstrated his success as a father." The social aspirations of the wife and daughters of the household were linked to his patriarchal restoration. "The pageantry of the Lost Cause and the social relations of the family reinforced one another. Each cultivated race, class, and regional loyalties where they could grow most virulently: in the hearts of vulnerable and idealistic children" (446).[2]

In *Civil Wars: Women and the Crisis of Southern Nationalism,* George C. Rable also writes of women's readiness to enshrine the soldiers' sacrifice, even as they repressed the reality that the men had failed as "invincible protectors of their homes." Reading their memorializing efforts as principally an effort to escape despair and the "troublesome present or uncertain future," Rable concludes that "the ladies of the Lost Cause managed to forget the unseemly parts—especially conflicts within the Confederacy—and eventually rewrote the history of the war" (236). Their efforts, he suggests, whether regarded as a flight of mythologizing fantasy that sought to restore the past or a realistic but despairing attempt to wring some self-respect from defeat, were socially retrogressive.

In her influential 1990 essay, "Altars of Sacrifice: Confederate Women and the Narratives of War," Drew Gilpin Faust argues that, as the Civil War progressed, many women became increasingly disillusioned as their homes and families were threatened, if not devastated, and these changing sentiments had an adverse effect upon the progress of the war effort. At the conclusion of her later monograph, *Mothers of Invention: Women of the Slaveholding South in the American Civil War,* Faust considers the impact of women's attitudes upon the postbellum commemoration of the War. Like Foster, Jones and Rable, she acknowledges the widespread support of white women for Lost Cause devotion and fund-raising, noting their obvious intentions to further societal rehabilitation by way of a reestablishment of the patriarchy. Why would these women work so assiduously to embed their future in a defeated social order? Even among educated women who were later to work publicly for temperance and even suffrage, there was the "almost inexplicable paradox," as Faust observes, of progressivism and reaction. It is in the exigencies of maintaining race and class hierarchies that she finds the explanations of why white women were unwilling to challenge male dominance. Finally, "in ladyhood southern white women accepted gender subordination in exchange for continuing class and racial superiority" (247). In Faust's recent *This Republic of Suffering: Death and the American Civil War,* she further amplifies her analyses of the ways in which the catastrophic war forced upon southern women new roles and new rituals, which were designed to persuade themselves and the nation that the war was fought by brave, noble men, was a worthy cause, even if lost, and in the end led to a New South. Thus they gave voice to their suffering and regret as they acknowledged a new era that was coming into being.

The "paradox" of the late nineteenth and early twentieth-century white southern woman as a figure moving illogically toward both tradition and change is a subject that has been widely addressed in late twentieth-century scholarship and continues to garner lively scholarly research. The starting point for Jean E. Friedman's research was an effort to understand why the southern women's reform movement began belatedly and progressed so gradually. As she explains in her introduction to *The Enclosed Garden: Women and Community in the Evangelical South, 1830–1900,* she came to understand the directive role of the southern community in shaping women's lives—and, further, to see the community as defined by evangelical beliefs that ordained traditional gender roles for women. Family groups, brought together in the rural South through evangelical networks, were the primary social structures, Friedman maintains. She concludes that family loyalties, family connections—the constraining power of kinship networks—delayed modernizing influences in the South, including changes in roles that confined women almost wholly to the private sphere.

In *The Southern Lady: From Pedestal to Politics 1830–1930* (1970) and, especially, in the more recent *Natural Allies: Women's Associations in American History* (1992), Anne F. Scott traces the complex growth of women's organizations in the nineteenth and early twentieth centuries, first taking up those in the South and later casting her analysis nationally. She notes that the projects and policies the women's groups supported often served as "a kind of early warning system, recognizing emergent problems before they were identified by the male-dominated political process" (2–3). Scott, Friedman, and other historians have shown that the movement of southern white women into public activism almost always began with their involvement in church-related activities. The missionary societies were frequently the seedbeds for temperance work and for the kind of social-gospel outreach that characterizes much Progressive Era social reform in areas such as public health, prisons, and child labor. In *The Power of Femininity in the New South,* Anastatia Sims, writing of women's organizations and politics from 1880 to 1930 in North Carolina, observes that "when North Carolina women translated private domesticity into public housekeeping they contributed to a redefinition of the proper role of government" (3) and, of course, to a redefinition of the proper role of a lady. Women drew upon Lost Cause mythology and the antebellum ideal of the lady in their efforts toward social rehabilitation, Rebecca Montgomery writes, and thus connected their New South activism to the South's cultural past. "They were not so much public mothers as public 'mistresses' of a public 'plantation'" (181).

Marjorie Spruill Wheeler's study of the women's suffrage movement in the South also addresses the influence and persistence of deeply rooted traditional gender roles (as well as white supremacist political structures) upon efforts to win women the right to vote. Wheeler shows that suffragists' tactical considerations focused upon a local and state political arena that was typically defined by racism, and, indeed, many suffragists were themselves committed to white supremacy. Because the defense of whiteness so much turned upon the "protection" of pedestaled ladyhood, even active suffragists took the public forum proclaiming their dependence upon their white male protectors. As we will see, the overlapping and segregating systems of gender and race, so powerfully active in the nineteenth- and twentieth-century South, bear directly upon the "I" constructed by southern women in their presentation of self in autobiography.

Belle Kearney devotes the first half of *A Slaveholder's Daughter* to proving that her behavior and social ideas are the logical and ethical consequences of her southern upbringing. In her memoir, *Southern Belle,* Mary Craig Kimbrough Sinclair recounts her long and politically active life with socialist husband Upton Sinclair, much of it spent in southern California, as that of a "helpmate" grounded in southern-lady tradition. Even Elizabeth Spencer in the 1998 *Landscapes of the Heart* goes to great lengths to show that her independent streak is a deeply rooted southern tradition, unmistakably modeled for her by her maternal grandfather, John Sidney McCain.

In thinking specifically about the aftermath of the Civil War and its consequence for both the psyches and the social roles of white women, Drew Faust identifies a "conflicted legacy," the result of their shaken confidence about what lay within their power to control, about the advantages of female independence and the dependability of male support (*Mothers* 256). For public-spirited women who looked most determinedly backward to the past, their Lost Cause efforts allayed some of their anxieties by assigning them a role in the rehabilitation of the defeated men and the restoration of patriarchy. LeeAnn Whites does not, however, find these effects sufficient to explain the fervor or the discovery of authority and self-validation that characterizes the female memorialists. In *The Civil War As a Crisis in Gender: Augusta, Georgia, 1860–1890,* Whites develops her thesis that, in advancing the Lost Cause, white women gained social and political power. And, indeed, one finds in the Lost Cause movement the same effect Scott notes in her analysis of women's organization. In organizing a public cause, circulating petitions for public sites, raising funds, responding to queries and criticism in published statements, even the most socially conservative women established a new and expanded public space for their ideas and activity. In much the way conservative women in recent times have advanced their power by leading public causes to defend traditional "family values," southern white women pressed their initiative by claiming the war was fought to protect the home and family. The common soldier, who owned no slaves, had fought not for economic well-being, as had the materialistic Yankee, so the social narrative went, but to defend the hearth.[3] The preeminent motive for the war came thus to be the domestic arena, with a consequence in later years for an "ever expanding public domesticity, in the schoolroom, in the childcare centers for working women, even to the organized effort to curb men's drinking in the WCTU"

Gramley Library
Salem Academy and College
Winston-Salem, N.C. 27108

(Women's Christian Temperance Union). Ironically, as Whites notes, the "very persistence of a backward-looking memorial movement" spurred the somewhat retrograde Victorianism of the New South. Rather than a wholly modernist social order grounded in individualism and free labor, the New South economic initiative proceeded alongside an "expanded Confederate community," Whites argues, which was asserted and validated in the public mind by the memorial organizations (212–13). The "divided mind" of the New South described by Woodward in *Origins of the New South,* by the historians cited above, and by many others is, as we see, thus confirmed but modified when one examines the influence of women upon the social order.

Despite noticeable moves by women into the public arena to support Confederate memorials, the temperance movement, or women's suffrage, the expectation of southern society during the years framed by the Civil War and World War II was nonetheless that women's roles and behaviors were to be defined by family obligations and domestic duties. Elizabeth Fox-Genovese has made this point in much of her scholarship devoted to southern women.[4] In *Gendered Strife and Confusion: The Political Culture of Reconstruction,* Laura Edwards links the family centeredness that defined the role of white women during the period of Reconstruction to the antebellum period. She notes, however, that the family values "took on a new meaning and urgency for elite white women after emancipation, when the basis of their status had disappeared." Domesticity offered the agency for reestablishing identity and status (130). Indeed, even the work outside the home, to the extent that it was available and passed muster as "respectable"—principally school teaching for upper-class whites—or, in fact, the domestic service of many black women (or even field work of white and black tenant farming women) was expected to be undertaken in support of the family. The public space claimed by women or allotted to them by the larger society was still woefully narrow. As we have seen, for a woman like Mary Hamilton, even claiming the public space of writing one's own life story seemed transgressive and required the approval of divine authority.

In recent decades scholarly study of southern women's history has grown steadily, as evidenced by the books just cited. We have now a much more detailed, evidentiary record and interpretation of the social conditions of southern women's lives than we had at mid-twentieth century. Whereas Woodward rarely even mentioned women in the 1951 *Origins of the New South,* for example, a shelf of books on southern women has been published in the last quarter century. As historian Anne F. Scott has shown, not only were women's lives omitted in most of the traditional historical studies devoted to war, diplomacy, and politics, and economic and intellectual history overall; they are fairly invisible even in early to mid-twentieth-century studies of plantation and home life during the Civil War (*Making the Invisible* 173–258).[5] Only a very few studies before 1970, most notably Julia Cherry Spruill's *Women's Life and Work in the Southern Colonies* in 1934, had turned their focus upon southern women. But with the 1970 publication of *The Southern Lady: From Pedestal to Politics,* Scott galvanized a new direction in southern studies scholarship. The expanding body of study of white women of the North, such as Barbara Welter's *Dimity Convictions: The American Woman in the Nineteenth Century* (1976), Nancy Cott's *The Bonds of Womanhood: Woman's Sphere in New England, 1780–1835* (1977), and Carroll Smith-Rosenberg's *Disorderly Conduct: Visions of Gender in Victorian American (1985)* was relevant, but often only tangentially so to the lives of nineteenth-century southern women, especially those of the antebellum, slaveholding era.

The 1980s produced further important additions to the gathering of primary materials and scholarly analysis of the antebellum history of southern white and black women. Suzanne Lebsock, Jacqueline Jones, Catherine Clinton, Jean Friedman, Elizabeth Fox-Genovese, Steven Stowe, George Rable, and many others published books and articles that vastly extended our understanding of antebellum social history generally and women's experience in particular. Subsequent scholarship continues to elucidate this era of southern history. Among this productive scholarship Sally G. McMillen has written of pregnancy and childbirth, Joan E. Cashin of the differing experiences of men and women emigrating to the southern frontier, Victoria Bynum of "unruly women," and Christie Farnham has drawn upon letters of teachers and students to explore the extensive higher educational system available to elite white women. Equally active have been these and other scholars' research and analysis of the lives of women of the postbellum South. As will be evident, their work deeply informs this study of autobiographical writing.

In contrast to the writing of southern women's history, which has been most active in the past quarter century, literary study of southern women writers, especially individual studies of such writers as Kate Chopin, Ellen Glasgow, Katherine Anne Porter, Zora Neale Hurston, Flannery O'Connor, and Eudora Welty, has occupied critics since the heyday of the New Criticism of the 1940s and 1950s. In *Tomorrow Is Another Day* Anne Goodwyn Jones analyzes the fiction and literary careers of seven writers—Augusta Jane Evans, Grace King, Kate Chopin, Mary Johnston, Ellen Glasgow, Frances Newman, and Margaret

Mitchell—particularly in regard to the conceptualizations of southern woman-hood expressed in their lives and work. Throughout the 1980s and 1990s the expanding literary criticism published as articles, monographs, and essay collections significantly heightened the visibility of the contributions of southern women to American literary and cultural history. One notable gap addressed by Sarah E. Gardner in *Blood and Irony* is the body of Civil War literature by southern white women. Gardner illustrates not only the "transformative impact of the Civil War on southern women's historical imagination," she demonstrates the "continuing dialogue between interpreters and interpretations of the Civil War," one manifestation of which was the contribution of the narratives to the creation of the Lost Cause mythology (4–5).

In the vanguard of recent literary study of southern women's fiction is Patricia Yaeger's *Dirt and Desire: Reconstructing Southern Women's Writing, 1930–1990.* Aiming to redirect literary commentary from long familiar propositions about southern regionalism and character, Yaeger posits "more dangerous, up-to-date, culturally acute terms" for approaching these writers, examining black and white women writers "using similar rubrics to map out the regional geographies that they do and do not share," and challenging the "Faulkner industry" by showing what he misses and what writers like Alice Walker or Eudora Welty show readers "of the ways race functions in the non-epic everyday" (xv).

In 1997, when Anne Goodwyn Jones and Susan V. Donaldson edited *Haunted Bodies: Gender and Southern Texts,* they wrote in their introduction that reading southern texts, indeed, reading the "South," through the lens of gender is absolutely necessary to an understanding of the region and the texts. In doing so, one finds in place of "the monolithic images of the conservative, hide-bound, isolated South" a region that has steadily renegotiated stereotypes of manhood and womanhood, a "radically unstable region" always in touch with and influenced by the shifting gender definitions in the rest of the nation and world, as well as with shifts driven by local cultural and economic changes (16–17).

The evidence of tension between stereotypes and actual lives is nowhere more apparent than in the autobiographical writings of southern women. Perhaps more explicitly in diaries and journals not intended for public display, but also in memoirs intended for publication, writers give unmistakable voice to the lies and limits of idealized womanhood and, perhaps to a lesser extent, the coerciveness of the male-dominated culture that isolated white women on an illusory pedestal. Although in the years prior to the arrival of the new historicism in literary study these life writings were studied principally by historians, they now occupy a central role in cultural studies in the humanities and many areas of social science.

Surveying southern women's autobiographies of the nineteenth century, one finds that most life writing may be identified within one or another vein of a rather narrow tradition that is chiefly concerned with recountings of daily life shaped by the southern agrarian or plantation economy. There are Caroline H. Gilman's *Recollections of a Southern Matron and a New England Bride* (1838) and later Elizabeth Pringle's *A Woman Rice Planter* (1961), portions of which were printed in the *New York Sun* between 1904 and 1907 under the pseudonym of Patience Pennington. Joan E. Cashin has edited an extensive selection of antebellum documents, principally excerpts from letters and diaries by white women of property-holding families throughout the South, that reveal the resources and, especially, the constraints that marked the lives of even these rather privileged women. *Our Common Affairs: Texts from Women in the Old South* provides a synoptic view of women's family concerns and duties, which exhaust nearly all their waking hours, although there is a wealth of comments about their female friendships and their response to slavery and the gathering political hostilities threatening the South. In *An Evening When Alone,* editor Michael O'Brien brings to print the journals of four single women writing from 1827 to 1867: Elizabeth Ruffin of Virginia, an unnamed governess who wrote of her experiences in Natchez, Jane Caroline North of South Carolina, and Ann Lewis Hardeman, who lived and wrote of a life almost wholly controlled by the extended family she faithfully served in Mississippi. Extended journals of many pages and composed over a number of years, like that of the Georgia writer Ella Gertrude Clanton Thomas, which was edited by Virginia Ingraham Burr and published as *The Secret Eye,* anticipates many of the memoirs of a half century later that are my focus in the present study. The manipulations and equivocations in Thomas's report of her experience, combined with her pressing, urgent resolve to write candidly, seem to respond to various contradictory pressures: a stern self-judgment that required some mitigation of perceived misdeeds or wrong thinking; a consciousness of her children as readers of the journal; and a sense that she was, in effect, composing her case before God. In these several respects she often adopts a kind of coded language that allows her to tell the "true happenings" while still keeping up appearances, maintaining her dignity, and, perhaps, buffering self-exposure by means of self-deception.

The years after 1865 saw the publication of numerous journals and memoirs giving documentary and emotional records of women's Civil War experience.

Certainly, one of the most famous of these was Chesnut's, which appeared initially in 1905 as *A Diary from Dixie, as Written by Mary Boykin Chesnut, Wife of James Chesnut, Jr., United States Senator from South Carolina, 1859–1861, and Afterward Aide to Jefferson Davis and a Brigadier General in the Confederate Army.* The journals of Sarah Morgan, Kate Stone, Julia Le Grand, Phoebe Pember, and major sections of Grace King's *Memories of a Southern Woman of Letters,* as well as countless others, compose a rich history of Confederate women's narratives of war. These autobiographical writings have long served historians as primary sources for analysis of the Civil War period, but there is now also a growing body of research by scholars of southern women's history who read these texts as primary sites of women's experience, revealing not only of the Civil War story but of women's history broadly situated in American and in feminist studies. The anxiety, devastation, and loss brought on by the war are reflected in details of the 1861–65 period, but these writers also sought to portray and preserve the antebellum era for their children and posterity. The memorialist, elegiac vein is widely represented and may be seen in such work as Susan Dabney Smedes's *Memorials of a Southern Planter* and Constance Cary Harrison's *Recollections Grave and Gay.*

A sharply different kind of published autobiography is the emancipation, or slave, narrative, perhaps best represented by Harriet Jacobs's *Incidents in the Live of a Slave Girl,* which also draws upon the Victorian domestic novel in the author's characterization of the pseudonymous narrator, Linda Brent. Another widely read narrative, reprinted in 1988, is that of Elizabeth Keckley, *Behind the Scenes, or Thirty Years a Slave and Four Years in the White House.* The tradition of the slave protest narrative is modified and continued in the later accounts of racial discrimination experienced or witnessed and recounted by such writers as Anna Julia Cooper in *A Voice from the South,* Anne Moody in *Coming of Age in Mississippi,* and Mary Mebane in *Mary* and *Mary Wayfarer.* Related to these works are such books as Katharine DuPre Lumpkin's *The Making of a Southerner* and Lillian Smith's *Killers of the Dream,* subjects of discussion in later chapters, who write of their journey from racial innocence to an awareness of the racism they come to recognize as permeating not just their homeland but their own families. Fred Hobson refers to these accounts as conversion narratives, noting their ancestry in religious confessionals of an even earlier American literary tradition, as well as their affiliation with the slave narrative. In *But Now I See: The White Southern Racial Conversion Narrative,* he discusses autobiographies by Lillian Smith, Katharine Lumpkin, and Sarah Patton Boyle, as well as texts by male writers, and briefly remarks in conclusion upon later narratives by southern women that focus in some significant part upon race, autobiographies by Virginia Durr, Ellen Douglas, Elizabeth Spencer, Margaret Bolsterli, and Mab Segrest.

By far the broadest segment of autobiographies by southern women is that of writers who have had professional careers as writers and who compose life narratives that not only describe events and people of their experience but also explain how and why they came to be writers. In the twentieth century, there are autobiographical texts by Ellen Glasgow, Marjorie Kinnan Rawlings, Zora Neale Hurston, Lillian Hellman, Katherine Anne Porter, Lillian Smith, Bernice Kelly Harris, Mary Lee Settle, Eudora Welty, Elizabeth Spencer, Ellen Douglas, and others of their contemporaries, as well as a growing number of personal narratives by a younger generation of southern women writers. In *Feminine Sense in Southern Memoir,* Will Brantley focuses upon Smith, Glasgow, Welty, Hellman, Porter, and Hurston in a study that gives both insightful biographical commentary and an analysis of the texts as expressions of the writers' life themes of willed independence and racial and political tolerance.

My interest in this book is to read some of these and other selected texts individually, as well as to discover among them what connections and commonalities emerge that deepen our understanding of the autobiographers' sense of "southernness," or lack thereof, and what they understood or assumed being "southern" represented as an identifying characteristic. The overriding concern, though, is to understand their strategies—that is, their motives for composing a self in writing—and their tactics, the devices and rhetorical moves they employ in articulating a self.

Perhaps the most salient feature of southern women's autobiography is its indirection. Indeed, from the outset of much recent feminist critical and theoretical analysis of women's writing, the observation that understatement and obliqueness characterize women's autobiographical writings in general often has grounded subsequent discussion. In her introduction to the 1980 *Women's Autobiography: Essays in Criticism,* Estelle C. Jelinek notes that women tend to write of their girlhood and adult experience in an objective, documentary fashion, and that "they also write obliquely, elliptically, or humorously in order to camouflage their feelings," a technique, she adds, "used to play down their professional lives" (15). In the same year, Mary G. Mason in an essay *in Autobiography: Essays Theoretical and Critical,* an early and influential collection edited by James Olney, notes the recurrent practice of women autobiographers to focus their attention not upon themselves but upon others who figured prominently in their experience. Discussing four early English and American autobiographies, she concludes that "the self-discovery of female identity seems to acknowledge the real presence and recognition of another consciousness, and the disclosure of female self is linked to the identification of some 'other.'" She goes on to observe that, judging from the autobiographies of Dame Julian of Norwich, Margery Kempe, Margaret Cavendish, and Anne Bradstreet, the recognition of another consciousness seems "to enable women to write openly about themselves" (210).

After the interval of some several centuries, it may seem anomalous to find among the southern autobiographies of this study very nearly the same features of indirection that Mason describes—and, yet, perhaps it is not so surprising, considering the traditionalism and societal stasis that marked the South after the Civil War. The circumspect southern female narrator does not gaze into a mirror and report what she sees; rather, she gazes through a window and implies (rather than materializes) a self through a process whereby the self is deflected or triangulated. The formation of self flows outward, arising from the act of creating relationships with the world, a relational self. In *One Writer's Beginnings* Eudora Welty devotes the first three chapters to her parents, suggesting the many ways in which her sense of self derived from the shaping influence of family. She ends her autobiographical excursions at the beginning point of her professional career, the point at which she had "found a voice." That voice will be most fully expressed in the fiction, but even in the fiction (or especially in the fiction, as Welty would hold), life's impact is oblique. It is important to acknowledge that the reticence one notes among women writers of the generations about which I speak is only in part attributable to the constraining pressure women feel from a traditional society that circumscribes their public activity. More significant, especially for those autobiographers who as writers of fiction have long grappled with the effort to articulate truths of the human heart, is the conviction that truths of the self (or of others) are elusive, often inchoate, inevitably relational and disbursed among the self's connections with its surround.

Among many feminist and poststructuralist critics who have pointed out the consequence for female autobiographers of occupying the periphery on the gender status map, Bella Brodzki and Celeste Schenck write of the near impossibility of the female autograph's functioning as a mirror of the self. Whereas the male tradition of life writing may assume a life story as exemplary, universal, representative of the larger community, female writing practice is denied such assumption. "No mirror of *her* era, the female autobiographer takes as a given that selfhood is mediated; her invisibility results from her lack of a tradition, her marginality in male-dominated culture, her fragmentation—social and political as well as psychic" (1).

One finds an illustration of a male writer's easy conflation of his life story with the history of his culture in the 1954 essay, "Mississippi," which William Faulkner wrote for *Holiday* magazine. Merging invented characters and events with historical figures and sites plotted upon the state's geography, much as he does in his fiction, he inserts autobiographical surrogates who are, sequentially, "the boy" and "Mr. Bill." This character's perspective defines and encompasses the whole of Mississippi, every section of the state, and, with only a slight extension, the whole South, though he refers to his home in Oxford and the surrounding counties as most personally "his." Noel Polk characterizes the essay as Faulkner's "attempts to grapple with the specifically local problems and pressures his native land had caused for him, and of his reconciliation with past and present Mississippi" (9).

By contrast, when the native of nearby Carrollton, Elizabeth Spencer, writes of her Mississippi background, her gaze does not sweep from Memphis to the Gulf of Mexico, except to position Carroll County on the map. The operational distance she describes stretches only from her home in town to the nearby plantation that was home to her mother's family. In the brief page and a half chapter entitled "The Town" in *Landscapes of the Heart,* she describes an isolated country town that tightly circumscribed her daily life but nonetheless provided ample sights and people to feed a lively imagination. "You reached town by tunneling slowly on dusty gravel roads, worn down into deep roadbeds." The last public transportation "through" the town was the stagecoach to Natchez, later "the Trailways bus would detour off the highway and stop on the courthouse square. . . . It is a spread-out town. . . . You can never see it all at once" (6–7).

In a narrative like Mary Hamilton's, a story composed by a woman with little education and a life of hard physical activity, who had no expectation of writing such a narrative until the encouragement from Helen Davis, one is not surprised to find a story relentlessly devoted to accounts of husband, children, cooking, farming, surviving—details of the outer world, not of inward self. Hamilton gives a radical example, in fact, of a "self in hiding," to use the phrase introduced by Patricia Meyer Spacks in her essay published in the Jelinek collection. As we have seen, Hamilton invokes a vision of children, lilies, and serpent to authorize her taking up her pen. Even so, in her letter to her friend, she also asserts a creator self, albeit one posited obliquely in religious symbolism and cloaked in the rags of apology and denial. This self is of course an old woman who, in surveying her life experience, assumes that whatever claim to notice and worth she can rightfully make resides in the account of the survival skills she brought to her roles as mother and wife throughout a harrowing life in frontier country.

The Mary Hamilton who is the letter writer reminds us that the referentiality of the text always hangs upon the writing self. The aging Hamilton interpreted a dream as an assignment to write, with some degree of collaboration with Helen Davis she undertook the writing of the autobiography so as to address the values she assumed justified such life telling, and she selected, consciously or unconsciously, those memories that would accomplish her purpose. "I woke with a start," she writes. "Was I going to die? Was that snake head that just grazed my finger, Death? I lay awake thinking about my dream, and when the late mail that day brought your letter to Edris I felt sure that my dream meant something and I had been spared for some purpose" (xix).

On the face of it, Hamilton's story is not written for the purpose of self-reflection, for an understanding and analysis of how the life she has led has produced the person she is at the time of her writing. And above all, it is not a meditation upon the nature of that writing self, that crippled sixty-five-year-old woman facing death directly. Typifying many personal narratives by women, especially those by women who are not professional writers, her book issues from a construction of the self that lies between individualism and community, to invoke a paradigm that Elizabeth Fox-Genovese has widely employed in her studies of American women's culture. In *Feminism without Illusions: A Critique of Individualism,* she points out that "feminist knowledge of self as 'one' and as 'many' carries an edge that male individualism lacks" (231). Hamilton's autobiography is filled with accounts of lumbering camps, her work in the field, her piloting a ferry boat, keeping a rough backwoods home for an English-born husband who refused to be served the pork and corn foods of the Mississippi Delta, supporting siblings and neighbors, above all, bearing children—nine children, four of whom would die in infancy or childhood. Her story is presented to her reader as a recollected narrative of what happened to her and decidedly not as the active recollecting of a dominating consciousness. In so writing it, she reminds one of predecessors and contemporaries who likewise recount life narratives with their female selves firmly effaced. Such texts have raised questions for literary scholars, historians, and psychologists, indeed for the arts and social sciences generally, particularly in the early days of the recent flowering of autobiographical theorizing. How should one classify such texts as *Trials of the Earth?* The naming or categorizing by genre matters because in part it determines how we read the texts.

To understand more fully the issues at stake in the affixing or withholding of the designation "autobiography" in describing personal or life writing, one may consider one of the best known and most widely analyzed cases among nine-teenth-century texts by southern women, the journal of Mary Chesnut. In 1982 Yale University Press published C. Vann Woodward's 886-page edition of *Mary Chesnut's Civil War.* Two earlier, shorter editions published in 1905 and 1949 with the title *A Diary from Dixie* had made portions of the Chesnut journal widely available—and widely admired. Edmund Wilson wrote of the journal in his 1962 study of the literature of the Civil War, *Patriotic Gore,* that it "is an extraordinary document—in its informal department, a masterpiece." He notes that "the very rhythm of her opening pages at once puts us under the spell of a writer who is not merely jotting down her days but establishing, as a novelist does, an atmosphere. . . . " In fact, he finds the Chesnut journal "much more imaginative and revealing than most of the fiction inspired by the war" (279–80).

With the more recent research of Woodward, Elizabeth Muhlenfeld, and other Chesnut scholars, we now have an expanded understanding of Ches-nut's composition of the journal.[6] To begin with, the journal, or diary, as it was known to the public in the 1905 and 1949 versions, was composed twenty years after the recorded events actually took place. Chesnut did keep a diary during the Civil War years, 1861–65, but the wartime diary differs greatly from the re-vised version of 1881–84. Woodward acknowledges that "the dating of the man-uscript will inevitably raise questions among historians about the use of her writings and the way historians have used them extensively in the past. The bare fact of date of composition," writes Woodward, "certainly changes the preva-lent conception of the work and removes it from the conventional category of 'diary'" (xvi).

Indeed, threading throughout Woodward's introduction to this impressive, fascinating book is his puzzlement over what exactly its nature is and how to as-sess and understand, as he says, "the character of the art involved." He writes: "The importance of Mary Chesnut's work, of course, lies not in autobiography, fortuitous self-revelations, or opportunities for editorial detective work. She is remembered only for the vivid picture she left of a society in the throes of its life-and-death struggle, its moment of high drama in world history. . . . The

enduring value of the work, crude and unfinished as it is, lies in the life and reality with which it endows people and events and with which it evokes the chaos
and complexity of a war'" (xxvii).

For clarity and ease, Woodward adopts the practice in his introduction of
referring to Chesnut's 1880s version as a "book" and to the 1860s version as a
"journal." His quandary over what finally to call this text is reflected in the title
he gave it: *Mary Chesnut's Civil War.* Clearly, he values it chiefly as a source of
information about the times, not as a literary creation in which a woman creates a self/ herself by way of recounting her story of the Civil War. And yet, there
is some recognition of the literary and autobiographical purposes in that title.
Interestingly, in a 2008 study of the uses the historian may legitimately make
of memoirs and other autobiographical writings, Jennifer Jensen Wallach contends in *"Closer to the Truth Than Any Fact"*: *Memoir, Memory, and Jim Crow*
that the expressive, literary qualities of a text do, in fact, deepen rather than bias
our historical understanding of the past.

By and large autobiography has been regarded, at least until poststructuralist and feminist theoretical revisions, as the prose form least susceptible to
the craft of the literary artist, especially so for those autobiographical works
that aim to depict faithfully the facts and events of the life witnessed. Here the
writer appears to be at the mercy of the record, rather than being the maker of
it, subservient to the chronicle of events that is to be told. For this reason scholars prior to the 1980s typically sought to differentiate autobiography from diary
or memoir or journal, naming as *autobiography* what they regarded as the more
crafted and serious form, in which the development of the self is the chief object of attention, and naming as *memoir* the less deliberate, less artistic form, in
which the persons and events surrounding the self are witnessed, interpreted,
and recorded.

In a 1975 article, "Autobiography and Historical Consciousness," for example, Karl J. Weintraub insists upon the distinction between autobiography as a
reflection upon the inward realm of experience, and memoir as a record of the
external realm of fact. He argues that "real autobiography" is dominated by self-
consciousness, that it is most valuable when it focuses upon the character or
personality of the self. Weintraub writes that, by contrast, "the diary, the letter,
the chronicle, the annal have their value because they are but momentary interpretations of life; the premium for them lies in the function of faithful recording and not in the function of assigning long-range meaning." He concludes
that "autobiography and diary do not mix well" (827).

Elizabeth Bruss, in her 1976 study *Autobiographical Acts,* is less interested in

advancing guidelines for differentiating kinds of personal narrative than in lo-
cating the significance of autobiography in the acts of writing and reading, that
is, in the expectations or assumptions a writer or reader of a particular speech
group community brings to such acts. In fact, she finds "no intrinsically autobiographical form," although she does observe that the information and events
reported in connection with the autobiographer are asserted as "true" and are
expected to be regarded as true by the reader, who is free to "check up" on them.
One finds her point well illustrated by the public's response to the widely publicized deception by James Frey in his 2005 memoir, *A Million Little Pieces*. Readers from all camps, from Oprah Winfrey's Book Club to academic literary critics, seemed willing to forgive a reasonable lapse of memory but quite unwilling
to accept assertions of fact that turned out to be, upon checking, provably false.
Indeed, Nancy K. Miller reaffirms Bruss's point in "The Entangled Self: Genre
Bondage in the Age of the Memoir," observing that "genre is pretty intractable.
. . . Despite the slippage in terminology, and despite the ingenuity that writers
and artists deploy to deal with the autobiographical project that purports to
convey some aspect of a life story, when readers choose a memoir, they make
certain assumptions" (539). Bruss's advice to the reader, however, is to concern
oneself less with verifying "accuracy" than with interpreting the "clues" provided by the text for insights into the author's intentions and psyche.

   Clearly, the nature of the genre entails a "reading of the witness" in the same
act of reading the narrative. The narrator may be presumed to be reliable, but
the storyteller is engaged in composing a story and, further, may be long distanced from the feelings and events reported. This observation is well stated by
James Olney in his 1972 *Metaphors of Self*, in which he denotes autobiography
as, "intentionally or not, a monument of the self as it is becoming, a metaphor
of the self at the summary moment of composition" (35). Perhaps the most influential statement asserting that psychological and aesthetic patterns should be
the focus of autobiographical study, not facticity, was that of Georges Gusdorf,
in "Conditions and Limits of Autobiography," which was published in French
in 1956 and later translated by Olney and included in the collection *Autobiography: Essays*. Gusdorf held that the "literary, artistic function" of autobiography is "of greater importance than the historic objective function," that, in fact,
"autobiography is not possible in a cultural landscape where consciousness of
self does not, properly speaking, exist" (43, 30). In important respects, Gusdorf
anticipates Weintraub in defining autobiography as a sustained, self-reflective,
self-analytical narrative.

   I cite these works from the 1970s and earlier to suggest the relative agreement at the time among scholars, even among those with differing approaches and points of emphasis, that the forms and intentions of autobiography are signifiable, knowable, and located in a stable text. But then, of course, the floodgates of feminist and poststructuralist theoretical writings opened. In the past three decades there have been hundreds of articles and books written in this country, not to mention in Europe, by scholars of history, language and literature, communications, and the behavioral sciences on theories of writing and reading autobiography. And whereas before the 1980s there were very few Anglo-American studies devoted specifically to theories of female autobiography, or even general studies that included women to any significant degree, there has been a great proliferation of such books and articles since then. In a 1992 article in the journal *Women's Studies,* entitled "The Definitions of Self and Form in Feminist Autobiography Theory," Marjanne E. Gooze counts up and discusses a group of ten monographs and essay collections appearing in the 1980s that focus upon theories and practices of interpreting women's autobiographies. These include well-known collections of essays edited by Estelle Jelinek, Domna Stanton, Sidonie Smith, Shari Benstock, Bella Brodzki and Celeste Schenck, as well as monographs by Carolyn Heilbrun and Francoise Lionnet. Other scholarly studies of the genre and its reception follow apace. In *PMLA* in 2007, Nancy K. Miller writes that "whether the word enlisted to discuss the phenomenon is *genre,* or *category* or *classification,* it seems clear that autobiographical writing in the early part of the twenty-first century is posing sticky problems of reception" (539).[7]

More recently, Ben Yagoda has surveyed a great sweep of autobiographical writings in his *Memoir: A History,* noting many of the issues earlier scholars have discussed about the genre transformations that have occurred over time in narrative voice, subject material, motives for writing, and reader expectations regarding truth telling and fictiveness. He cites a vast range of texts from Saint Augustine's *Confessions* to James Frey's *A Million Little Pieces,* listing in an index well over six hundred "memoirs and autobiographies."

There seems to be no indication of waning interest in the theorizing of autobiography. At present, however, there does appear to be an expanding consensus about the complex nature of textual self-fashioning, originating as it does in memory, imagination, literacy, the historical moment, psychological conditions, and neurological processes, not to mention the constraints of textuality and the organizing power of narrative. About memory, recent scientific research shows increasingly the organic and environmental triggers that impinge upon functions of brain recall. One consequence is a heightened sophistication, if not skepticism, in current scholarship about literalist claims upon autobiography's facticity. And yet, everyone seems to go right ahead and presume, as Elizabeth Bruss predicted, some referentiality to "truth." Indeed, the writer Vivian Gornick in a 2001 article insists that the writer of personal narrative must "persuade the reader that the narrator is reliable. . . . In nonfiction the reader must believe that the narrator is speaking truth. Invariably, of nonfiction it is asked, 'Is this narrator trustworthy? Can I believe what he or she is telling me?'" (B7). Perhaps one can conclude on this point that, at the end of the day, the reader expects a good faith effort on the part of the autobiographer to tell her or his personal truth but recognizes that human truths are always glimpsed through interpretive filtering.

Another area of gathering consensus centers upon the definitions of the genre of autobiography, that is, about the kind of text the personal narrative is and the way in which it should or can be read—for aesthetic pleasure, psychological revelation, spiritual insight, worldly wisdom, historical or experiential detail, gossipy tidbit, straightforward voyeurism, or for any of the countless other reasons readers read books. The agreement about definition seems to be founded upon the principles of "agree to disagree," with every critic entitled to his or her own definition. The proliferation of terms used to designate autobiography offers the clearest evidence of the growing disaffection with delimiting definitions of the kind posited earlier by Gusdorf, Philip Lejune, Weintraub, and others. We now speak freely and often synonymously of personal narrative, memoir, life writing, diary, journal, autobiography, or autobiographical writing, even letter, sometimes making little or no distinction among these forms of writing. That writing (graph), by oneself (auto), about oneself (bio) may take a multitude of different forms seems to be the nondiscriminatory agreement. Some scholars go further, omitting textuality as a formal descriptor of life telling and including oral history, interview, and conversation in the genre of personal narrative.

One of the foremost scholars of autobiography, James Olney, takes up the matter of vexed terminology and definitions in *Memory and Narrative: The Weave of Life-Writing* (1998), concluding that he has "never met a definition of autobiography that [he] could really like" (xv). He goes on to observe, rather playfully, I judge, though still seriously engaging the definitional crux, that he is fond of the term "periautography" ("writing about or around the self") taken from an early Italian source, precisely because of "its *in*definition and lack of generic rigor, its comfortably loose fit and generous adaptability," meanings he also finds accommodated in the term "life writing." Determined to escape the arguments about whether to call a text an *autobiography, memoir, life narrative,* or *story*—since I find little actionable difference among the elastic terminologies employed by current genre theorists—I have used all these terms synonymously in this study.

These elastic and comprehensive definitions only defer, however, the ambiguities about text and narrator-self that literary scholars and historians confront at every turn in their reading of individual texts. What one finds is often an interplay between motives for reading and, in the case of scholarly research, disciplinary practice in approaches to texts. The uses of the text (the reader-response contingency, one might say) condition one's theoretical stance, disposing a reader variously to find and defend empirical information, psychological tracings of identity, aesthetic construction, or whatever. Olney's literary approach to his readings of St. Augustine, Rousseau, and Beckett in *Memory and Narrative* is explicitly to avoid foregrounding theory as an entry gate to the texts, following rather an inductive process of close reading that is informed by knowledge of the whole body of a writer's work and the cultural milieu from which he emerges and that he reflects in his writing.

The consequence of the many controversies and practices, agreements and disagreements about autobiography upon this study of southern women's life narratives is that they inescapably influence and hover around my discussions of genre, as well as gender and regionality. The ambiguities are further manifest in the differences among the texts I have chosen to discuss and in the range of inferences I draw from my reading of the texts. For example, most life writings by southern women are not "real" autobiographies by Weintraub's definition, nor are they aesthetically significant autobiographies by Gusdorf's definition. The characteristic approach for a female writer of the early and late nineteenth-century South, as well as for most of the twentieth century, as indeed for most women generally, has not been studied attention to and analysis of the self. Such an overt display of self would have been regarded as immodest, egotistical, and above all unladylike, thereby attracting hostile reaction and dismissal from many of the very audience one sought to address. Understandably, we find texts that focus attention not on the self but on the selves and events that surround the writer, and most typically in forms of diary, journal, memoir, day book, letters—those fragmented, discontinuous "lower" forms. My focus here, however, does not center upon diaries and journals but rather book-length texts written for an external audience, written with the expectation of publication. The differences between a holograph diary and a narrative composed for publication may be great or slight, but even if slight, the variation in the degree of self-exposure will likely be significant. To gauge the difference, one might consider the following: (1) the censorship the autobiographer imposes upon herself as she thinks of the diverse audience to whom she is submitting her life story—family, associates, other writers, the general public; (2) the demands that the composition of a narrative forces upon her decision about how to tell her story—how to give it sequence, connectedness, *meaning;* and (3), the involvement of editors and the publishers' staff in the production of the text, with their suggestions for revision, cuts, additions.[8] The diary may offer immediacy and less censorship by author or editor, but the published narrative gives us a writerly text, the autobiographer's art, and it places the life story in an expressive public context.

One of the generalizations that one may make with some assurance about these personal narratives of southern women, both the published and unpublished, is that the main thread of the life story does not run deeply into the self but outward into a network of relations through which the self is revealed. Even in sustained, lengthy narratives such as Mary Hamilton's or that of a public figure like Mississippian Belle Kearney's in *A Slaveholder's Daughter,* indeed even in the narratives of seasoned writers like Welty, Hurston, Rawlings, Spencer, and Douglas, the focus is not upon the individualistic or autonomous self but upon a relational self that emerges indirectly from the narrator's account of others. The critic Sidonie Smith, discussing at length the different societal conditions encountered by male and female writers engaged in the act of writing autobiography, attributes this relational self to an ideology of gender that idealizes the woman who is self-effacing, who has no public or heroic life but rather one of "fluid, circumstantial, contingent responsiveness to others." Such a figure, having no autonomy, has no "autobiographical self," Smith concludes (50). Feminist critic Susan Stanford Friedman in "Women's Autobiographical Selves: Theory and Practice" extends this critique of the autonomous, "heroic self," noting that "the individualistic concept of the autobiographical self raises serious theoretical problems for critics who recognize that the self, self-creation, and self-consciousness are profoundly different for women, minorities, and many non-Western peoples" (34). The recognition of the autobiographical narrator as a relational self is reaffirmed by virtually all feminist theorists of the genre. Nancy K. Miller, discussing Joan Didion's memoir, *The Year of Magical Thinking,* announces that "perhaps it is time to understand the question of relation to the other—to others—as being as important, foundational, to the genre as the truth conditions of the 'autobiographical pact.' Not the exception but the rule. Put another way, in autobiography the relational is not optional.

Autobiography's story is about the web of entanglement in which we find ourselves, one that we sometimes choose" (544).

The issue of what kind of self can claim exceptionalism amid a welter of gender, racial, and ethnic markings has devolved anew upon the Western male self, usually Caucasian, whose putative autonomy has often been regarded as a rather privileged, aggrandized self, one too often expressed through a kind of anachronistic posturing. He may even be a deflated Romanticized self, isolated from the compensating strength to be found in collective or relational identity. Predictably, such an egoistical figure cries out for theoretical and interpretive deconstruction, and indeed there is a growing body of commentary answering the call. Most notable is Paul John Eakin's lengthy discussion, "Relational Selves, Relational Lives: Autobiography and the Myth of Autonomy," in *How Our Lives Become Stories: Making Selves*.

Eakin revisits ideas about the author of autobiography, the singular "I" that he explored in two earlier books, asking, "Why do we so easily forget that the first person of autobiography is truly plural in its origins and subsequent formation?" His revisionary premise, announced at the outset, is that autonomy is a myth, that *"all* identity is relational," that autobiography criticism has yet to reflect the extent to which the self is defined in relation to others, and that the definition of autobiography must include the forms of life writing in which a relational self is displayed (43–47). Later, he suggests that "the old Gusdorf model" of the individualistic autobiographer ("the Marlboro Man") already would have likely been exposed but for attacks of feminist critics who, by opposing it, ironically maintained its currency. Eakin argues that the "criterion of relationality applies equally *if not identically* to male experience." His revisionist rejection of the assumption that the autobiographical narrator is necessarily an individualized, singular persona is unequivocal: "The fact that a case for it should need be made in autobiography studies shows just how profoundly the myth of autonomous individualism has marked the thinking of autobiographers and their critics, including resisting feminists, including myself" (50–51).

The central argument between the individualistic model and the relational model strikes me as having less to do with gender differences (which, notably, critics attribute to societal conditioning rather than to essentialized male/female nature) than with differing assumptions about the motives of autobiography and the nature of authorship. A reader may expect, for example, to find an authorial self who is knowable and known, such as St. Augustine, who plumbs self's memory of passions and senses in search of higher, godly understanding, as James Olney has observed (*Memory* 52, 79). Or one may expect, following Rousseau, to find the knowable and known author who seeks to evoke the empathy of the reader for the feelings the narrator reveals—and thereby win the trust and admiration of the reader. Or, a reader may anticipate an encounter with a modernist persona who undertakes in the act of writing to discover a self, to create a textual self more unified and stable than would ever be possible in life. And, shadowing behind such a textual self, one has to assume, exists an even more diffuse self who is not given shape in words—an organic self, variable and subject to forces early and late, within and without, especially by the family and childhood. This latter psychological-sociological-anthropological model, which has most interested feminist theorists, is of course not only the model of authorship and selfhood assumed by and characteristic of most contemporary literary theory but one especially well suited to the generic ambiguities of life writing.

The challenge to the solitary, autonomous image of the self has, of course, a long history in the world's religions and philosophies. In a short monograph first published in 1995, *Life in Common: An Essay in General Anthropology,* the political philosopher Tzvetvan Todorov offers an incisive survey of Western ideas about the solitary-versus-social origins and manifestations of the self. Focusing upon Rousseau as the transitional figure who established the preeminence of a social being, Todorov elaborates a view of human kind as originating in dependence upon the "other" and developing throughout life by means of complex interconnections with others. "The membrane that separates the self from others, the inside from the outside, is not airtight. Others are not only around us from the beginning, but also from the youngest age we internalize them and their images begin to be part of us. In this sense," he writes, "the poet is absolutely right: I is another." Seen as a social animal by the scientist, a language bearer of received words by the linguist, a socialized psyche by the psychologist, the human being barely emerges as an autonomous individual. Todorov insists that "the internal plurality of each being is the correlative of the plurality of people who surround him." Within that "plurality" we thus find the agency by which we situate ourselves in the world: "as soon as they are born, these images . . . will be projected outside onto their prototypes or onto other people, subsequently determining our perception of the outside world. The self is the product of others that it, in its turn, produces" (122). In the discussion of individual texts that follow, especially those of Belle Kearney, Mary Craig Kimbrough Sinclair, Katharine DuPre Lumpkin, Elizabeth Spencer, and Ellen

Douglas, one quickly comes to see that the connections between self, other, and text, issues of intersubjectivity and intertextuality, are inseparable from an understanding of motive, gendered personae, and voiced regionality.

The "relational self" as narrator of autobiography is a significant concept here because it best describes the personae of most southern women autobiographers. I would also note, however, that with the expanding definitions discussed above, the relational self has generally replaced the autonomous self in conceptualizations of identity formation and self-expression in life narratives. One outcome, of course, as we have seen, is that the distinction between "memoir" and "autobiography" has blurred, if not disappeared altogether.[9] Another development to come from the questioning of an autonomous male and relational female as the central binary of autobiography has been a broadening of ways to think about "relationality" and thus about the numerous overlapping categories of identity shapers—not only gender and family relationships but class and race, region, age, and education cohorts. The consciousness of self is engendered—and modified—by the gaze of the other, the acknowledgment and confirmation of the existence of the self. But let it be remembered that the gaze-formed self is not just the product of infancy but rather that the intersubjective collaboration is a lifetime project.

Using the term "geographics" to name an interdisciplinary field of identity studies that moves away from premises of "stable centers and cores," Susan Friedman "maps" a shifting in such studies, which she regards as a "discourse of spatialized identities constantly on the move." In her emphasis upon identity as a "historically embedded site," she addresses both her feminist and postcolonialist concerns not to define identity solely in terms of gender, which "reinscribes other forms of oppression by rendering them invisible" (*Mappings* 18–21). My own concern in this study of southern women's life writings is to read a variety of texts from a variety of perspectives and in so doing to know better the selves formed (and informed) particularly by gender and region during a certain era of recent history. Indeed, an understanding of the textualized self proceeds upon seeing the subject as a point of intersection between the composing writer and the world of historical circumstance.

On the matter of gender, studies of the history of women in the South—or broader studies that have included even the mention of women—were, as Anne Scott has shown, largely absent before the 1960s. Even rarer have been examinations of the ways in which women have experienced and defined "southernness" and expressed this regional identification in autobiographical writing.[10]

As I discussed at the outset, one of my own early impulses toward an effort to understand and articulate regionality was associated with a seminar devoted to studying women's literature from a regional perspective. And years earlier, I had written a doctoral thesis that attempted to analyze Eudora Welty's theories of place and her deployment of place details as key signifiers in her fiction. Both efforts led to many questions about the sources of cultural identity—and very few answers.

Of course, there is a vast and ever-growing library of scholarly investigation addressing in one way or another the "mind of the South," or, even more ambitiously, "What is the South?" Books, scholarly journals, conferences, societies, popular magazines, and more are devoted to ascertaining and characterizing, or assuming and displaying, "southernness." The judgment that the South represents a distinctive region of the United States, with a special history and a continuing sense of itself as a distinctive region, is generally accepted, despite the numerous demurrals and qualifications to the proposition of southern separateness. More to the matter is the pointed insistence by contemporary scholars of southern studies that the "South" is, and always has been, vastly more diverse, more comprehensive of racial, ethnic, and gender differences than was admitted, say, into the Fugitive Agrarian image of the region. Literary scholars, especially, have challenged long-established claims about the defining features of the South—notably Susan Donaldson, Anne Goodwyn Jones, Patricia Yaeger, Michael Kreyling, Suzanne Jones, among many others.[11] Certainly, my own thinking about how to recognize and argue the presence of southernness (or its absence) in the autobiographical writings I am reading is informed by this body of scholarship, as well as by the popular culture. But I have also been prodded in my thinking about gender and region, or regionality, by two propositions that sharply question whether most women have in fact written about or even experienced region in the ways that men have. The contrast of Faulkner's "Mississippi" and Spencer's *Landscapes of the Heart* cited above is an illustration of that difference.

In 1980, Richard King argued in *A Southern Renaissance: The Cultural Awakening of the American South, 1930–1955* that, with the exception of Lillian Smith, neither women writers nor black writers have been "concerned primarily with the larger cultural, racial, and political themes" that define the region in which he is interested, nor have they placed "the region" at the center of their imaginative visions (8–9). Since the book appeared in 1980, virtually every feminist scholar writing about southern women writers has rebutted the assertion, usually challenging King's definitions or unstated assumptions about

the meaning of "region." Susan V. Donaldson has written that King's assessment "would undoubtedly come as news to the host of white and black women
writers active in the South since the middle of the nineteenth century." Noting
that such writers as Louisa McCord, Harriet Jacobs, Augusta Evans, Anna Julia
Cooper, Katharine DuPre Lumpkin, Eudora Welty, and Zora Neale Hurston
have been "profoundly concerned about the nature of their culture," Donaldson
moves beyond the argument of "who speaks for the culture?" to question the
tactics of writing even revisionist literary history and definitions of the profession of letters in the South, concluding that these activities entail "exclusionary
strategies" that are "more compromising in nature than most students of the
region would care to acknowledge" (44–45).

In 1982, Elizabeth Hampsten, who had been engaged as I had been in conducting a study of women's literature from a regional perspective, published
*Read This Only to Yourself: The Private Writings of Midwestern Women, 1880–
1910*. From her survey and analysis of writings collected in North Dakota, primarily unpublished letters and diaries, she concludes that "what women—the
ordinary women whose casual writings I have been describing—have written
least about is the one subject that our schooling in literature has taught us to
expect writers to begin with: their place, locale, the landscape of wherever they
are" (29). She continues:

> These women's writings do not do that; their "place" is not where we had
> expected to find them. In much of this writing, for all its particularity, it is
> hard to tell (if the postmark is missing) where the writers are, for they do
> not bother to tell us in words we are used to. If there is something to be said
> for "regionalism" as a mode of literature, the term hardly applies, I find, to
> the private writings of ordinary women, and I think it is important to make
> a note of that when we describe their literature.
>
> . . . . History, topography, climate, and the like have, of course, had conse-
> quences for human nature. Pronunciation and word usages can be localized,
> as can some foods, games, jokes. But I do not think that these go as deeply
> into people's essential myths as proponents of regionalism think. As a prin-
> ciple in literary criticism, regionalism has largely misjudged and ignored
> the manners in which women have reported their sense of locale, and most
> of the time has imposed criteria that are alien to women's perceptions. (29)

As a case in point, Hampsten turns to the Fugitives and southern Agrarians—Ransom, Allen Tate, Robert Penn Warren, and others—and, drawing
upon Donald Davies's *Southern Writers in the Modern World* (1957), consid-

ers the "image of the South" as imagined by these writers. She is not persuaded that such a South, absent of blacks and women, as it effectively is in their conceptualizations, is an actual, material region. Then she goes on to observe that such definitions of regional cultural characteristics as those advanced by Davies (and the Agrarians) do not apply to women. Hampsten's remarks turn upon the meaning one infers from the term *region*. As a term that signifies the public, political, and commercial attributes of a physical jurisdiction, *regionality* has largely excluded women. In fact, Hampsten voices her objection to "applying regional criteria to women's experience because these have only reinforced women's already long and institutionalized disenfranchisement from culture, industry, and politics, and because no focus on regionalism takes into account women's observations as they have reported them" (31).

Hampsten's objections and King's definitions of region are related to a longstanding controversy about the practice of naming or categorizing certain writings as "regional" or as "local color fiction." Many critics have noted the gender-coded and trivializing implications of the term. For example, in *Resisting Regionalism: Gender and Naturalism in American Fiction, 1885–1915*, Donna Campbell explores the development of American literary naturalism as a masculinist counter tradition to realism and, especially, to "female-dominated local color writing" (5). And in a celebrated essay, "Place in Fiction," Eudora Welty famously dismisses the use of "regional" to describe writing—a "careless term," she says, "as well as a condescending one, because what it does is fail to differentiate between the localized raw material of life and its outcome as art. 'Regional' is an outsider's term; it has no meaning for the insider who is doing the writing, because as far as he knows he is simply writing about life" (*Stories, Essays* 796).

But once again the ambiguities of life writing, to the extent that it may be said to differ from fiction, mix the messages here because to some degree such writing does embrace the "localized raw material of life." The questions I put to the texts discussed in subsequent chapters have to do chiefly with the textual self, the narratized self, but answering the questions has undeniably to do with reading this figure (typically a "relational" figure) inferentially, through the narrator's depictions of the people, places, and events of her surrounding world. What I find is that most of these writers are not in the business of conceptualizing southern regionalism, Lumpkin and Smith being primary exceptions. The characteristics of southernness that are prominent in the narratives are geographical, culinary, and linguistic—remembrances of flora, food ways, speech patterns. In her foreword to *Trials of the Earth,* for example, Ellen Douglas especially notes Mary Hamilton's "evocation of the natural world she lives in—of the power of the river and of the wild lonely forests, still resounding with panther screams and the howls of wolves" (xii). Other recurring patterns in the autobiographies are associated with racial mores—the segregationist ordering of domestic and public settings—and close affiliations with the extended family. Ancestors living and dead are remembered and often discussed. Church going, mostly Protestant, is widespread and especially influential in some of the autobiographers' youth, although the direction they often take in maturity is away from spiritual matters and toward commitments to social justice, particularly in regard to racial justice and woman's suffrage.

Charles Reagan Wilson has identified a number of features often regarded as signifying southern culture, many of which are associated with the Civil War and some invented long after the historical period of their putative origin—the Confederate flag, the war monuments, the Lost Cause, memorialization of Robert E. Lee's birthday, a distinctive southern oratory, Greek Revival style architecture, the antebellum mansion (e.g., Scarlett O'Hara's Tara), and, from the white perspective, a black culture present in the background. Wilson also discusses the role of women in the "invention of southern tradition," ladies who were "artifacts of white power" (15).

Certainly, for many women—and for a few of the autobiographers of this study—class consciousness is expressed in terms of "southern ladyhood," a term usually applied to white women, though the image of the respectable lady is likewise found among descriptions of well-to-do black women. The lady has the respect of the community, and she is modest, deferential, well spoken, well dressed, well mannered, physically attractive, and, above all, loyal to family. Laura Edwards describes the ideal as one who "created a comfortable, cheery home to uplift the spirits of her family." She occupied a domestic sphere in which she was the preparer of appetizing meals, trusted companion of her husband, director of the children's moral, religious, and academic education" (130). As Edwards has noted, this version of domesticity for elite white women after emancipation was an expression of racial and class superiority.

Of course, these characteristics of the late nineteenth century "lady" are certainly not exclusive to the South. They also form the recognizable stereotype of the Victorian "lady." The autobiographers that I discuss in this book are all well aware of this idealized figure, Hamilton and Hurston no less than the privileged Craig Sinclair and Lindy Boggs. Although this image of the lady is typically coded in the region as "middle or upper class white," one also finds in elite black communities in the cities similar expectations of class markers, as illustrated in

Anna Julia Cooper's *A Voice from the South*. The authors of the life narratives considered here, however, uniformly present themselves as outliers to the lady tradition, having traits of ambition, independence, willfulness, intellectual curiosity, or simply a history like Hamilton's of hard physical labor. They marry a divorced man (Sinclair), or divorce an incompatible one (Rawlings), or never marry (Kearney, Lumpkin, Smith, Glasgow, Welty). They study medicine and go to China (Fearn) or pursue a career in nursing (Barber); they run for a deceased husband's Congressional seat (Boggs); they are outspoken foes of white supremacy (Durr). They present themselves as individualists—but not loners. They write of lives embedded in relationships that form the chief content of their stories—relationships for most of them that reflect a consciousness of living in a racially divided society,

What most distinguishes the region from other sections of the United States, I should say, what surely bespeaks "southernness" of this period, is the presence of large numbers of African Americans and Caucasians living side by side in complex social relationships, especially acute in the years after the Civil War and into the twentieth century. The distinctive racial makeup of the states of the Confederacy has exerted the most persistent marker of the region since colonial times and continues to do so into the present. John Shelton Reed has provided some of the most detailed sociological data available on the characteristics of the various groupings of southerners—by race, class, gender, geography, political affiliations, and so on. In his 1982 study of southern ethnicity, *One South,* he finds white southern identification to be significantly related to racial views. He poses a "cardinal test" of southernness and concludes: "Assuming that southern identification is not simply translatable as localism, we find no readily available theory to predict what its social correlates might be, and it seems to have few in any event. There is more reason to expect that it is associated with certain social-psychological measures—support for white supremacy and opposition to racial desegregation, in particular" (82–83).

Joel Williamson's comprehensive study of black-white relations in *The Crucible of Race* analyzes the shifting racial patterns in the years from 1887 to 1915 and later, showing the persistent connection between southern white identity and ideas about race. Whether the attitudes were informed by liberal or conservative or radical ideations of race, white southerners' consciousness of racial difference was constant. His helpful chart linking dates to prevailing ideas and behaviors reflects the varying levels over time of white accommodation to black southerners, as well as gradations of white fear, hostility, and violence (314–15).

Williamson underscores a point relevant to a study of southern women's auto-biographies, one many scholars of southern studies have asserted, that the absoluteness of racial roles is directly tied to the absoluteness of sex roles (497).

In her introduction to "Southern White Women's Autobiographies: Social Equality and Social Change," Jeanne Perreault follows the general view that the defining feature of southern society from Emancipation to the 1960s is "social inequality based on race" (32). In her 2008 *Contemporary Southern Identity,* Rebecca Bridges Watts posits a more comprehensive category as the defining feature of southern exceptionalism, a "concern for order." Her argument flows from insights such as Williamson and others have developed, as well as from her analysis of recent political leaders, who "chose to structure southern life by keeping its people divided . . . , principally according to race but also according to gender and socioeconomic status and often through some combination of these factors" (9–10). But, of course, the political leaders are rarely female. The concern for order that women typically express in life narratives is located in the family, the household, the farm, or the individual projects and careers they commit themselves to. Although the women considered in this study of southern autobiography are exceptional by virtue of undertaking to write a publishable life narrative, it should come as no surprise to find that they conform in many respects to the social norms of their time and place.

Finally, let me admit forthrightly that defining what social attributes are southern is an unavoidably circular enterprise, at least in part. One defines the characteristics one looks for as southern, finds them, and declares "southernness." Thus, risking some circularity, I would note that women growing up in a patriarchal South do often define their identities in terms of relationships with male members of the family and older females. Indeed, the relational self is the most familiar self one encounters in these texts. Educated and privileged white Mary Chesnut, Belle Kearney, and Susan Dabney Smedes in *Memorials of a Southern Planter,* no less than frontier woman Mary Hamilton and well-educated wives like Mary Craig Kimbrough Sinclair and Agnes Anderson, explicitly derive identity from fathers or husbands and define selfhood—that is, construct their subjectivity—in relation to family, especially to husbands' careers, and to community commitments, church, and local polity. Even Harriet Jacobs in *Incidents in the Life of a Slave Girl,* exposing as she does the abuse and oppression she suffered in the South and North during the antebellum period, constructs an identity that is interwoven not only with her family, but with her oppressors and the white Victorian standard bearers whose judgment of women rested largely upon sexual purity. We could say of her, too, that—indirectly, through the form of the sentimental novel that she employs, and directly, in her presentation of a "self" characterized as Linda Brent in the autobiography—she appeals to patriarchal sanction for the reforms she implicitly urges upon the patriarchs.

Considering the models of southern personality often characterized in academic and popular culture, one might conclude that "southernness" disposes both male and female autobiographers to experience and express a relational rather than an individualistic sense of self. J. Bill Berry persuasively argues this point in "The Southern Autobiographical Impulse," noting that since colonial times a southern mode of life writing produces a relational rather than an individualistic narrative. "The self has been a social one rather than an individual essence confronting the forest or a symbol of the American ideal." He argues that "the southern personal narrative is a conversation, often heated, within the self, between the self and the community, between the South and the country, and with those outsiders within, the other race" (13–14).

Bertram Wyatt-Brown's study of southern honor and Steven Stowe's study of patterns of intimacy and power in the nineteenth-century South both point toward the social, relational origins of southern identity. In her work on twentieth-century southern women's autobiographical and fictional writing, Lucinda MacKethan similarly identifies a sense of self that is grounded in social relationships. She outlines attributes of regionality that constitute "a southern way seeing," which she finds exemplified by the subjects of her study—Glasgow, Hurston, and Welty. This southern way of seeing comprises "first, respect for family as the heart of social order; next, the symbolization of the home as the locus of all inheritable values; third, the tension between hate and love for the father, who in the culture holds the power to define, to validate, to circumscribe, and to disinherit; and finally, acceptance of memory as the primary means of knowing" (23). The family, the home, the dominant male order—that is, a web of personal, relational affiliations—these are the chief components of the lives typically depicted by female autobiographers—and by southerners, male and female. Even professional writers like the three MacKethan discusses, writers who have cultivated a distinctive voice and style, reflect these patterns. Reading their texts calls upon the reader to engage selves that dissolve into other selves, protagonists who sometimes seem nearly invisible, and narrators who resist forthright expression, expressing intentions indirectly, even obliquely, but narrators who often demonstrate an acute political sense of the uses of language for winning approval of others and for influencing others' actions.

In the autobiographies by later professional writers, like the earlier narratives of Chesnut and Harriet Jacobs, or the autobiography of Belle Kearney, one reads personal writing that constructs the female self as connected in limitless ways with others. This self may be a contingent, uncertain, anxious being, especially when subjected to judgments according to male values of dominance and hierarchy, but the southern female self can also mirror great strength and resilience, supported precisely by the web of connections that constrain and define her identity.

2

A Feminist Life Narrative in a Traditionalist Society

BELLE KEARNEY

In many respects Belle Kearney's *A Slaveholder's Daughter* is a rhetorical maze, representing the differing directions and complex strategies one sometimes encounters in southern women's autobiographies, especially those that aimed in the late nineteenth and early twentieth centuries for a wide national audience concerned with public affairs. Standing at the intersection of so many cross-allegiances, Kearney took on the project of writing an autobiography because she was deeply committed to advancing the causes of temperance and woman's suffrage, but she clearly realized the minefield she had to cross to reach a sympathetic audience. One glaring obstacle to reaching a southern audience was the rural, dispersed population of the region, where book purchasers was not as numerous as in the cities. Historian Joseph Kett notes that in 1900 only 16 percent of the South's population lived in places with 2,500 or more people, compared to 40 percent in other regions. Only New Orleans, Louisville, and Memphis had 100,000 or more inhabitants (171).[1]

As a white southerner of a once slaveholding family, Kearney also had to appeal to a largely northern audience by disavowing slavery, even as she maintained her own deep reservations about African Americans' capacity to exercise responsible freedom and enfranchisement, reservations shared by most white southerners and, in fact, by many white northerners. She goes to great lengths to discuss "the Negro problem" in an expository style designed to demonstrate her knowledge of the societal conditions and policy debates of her time, as well as her commitment to the just outcomes (though limited, in her view) to be sought in progressive race relations, at least in her foreseeable future. She is faced with the dilemma of legitimizing and supporting her arguments for moral behavior and social justice, particularly as these are expressed later in the book in regard to temperance and suffrage. Furthermore, she must find a way to do so in ways that neither undermine her ethical stance nor betray her own racial views, that is, her need to disavow the slaveholding past without alienating her fellow southerners. Ghosts of the Confederacy were not just hovering over the South but actively intervening to assure an entrenched color line. This was, after all, the era of "Lost Cause" fervor for memorializing the Civil War—the Sons of the Confederacy was organized in 1896—and sectional sensitivities were still edgy, despite the efforts of the industrial North and South to "move on" beyond the Civil War. In addition to mollifying southern prickliness, Kearney, as a woman appealing to a genteel and largely religious group of readers, also needed to present herself as a public activist without arousing hostile dismissal. She might have easily been accused of overreaching the boundaries allowed to women by the tenets of the Christian church or by the Victorian standards of proper ladyhood espoused by the society at large. It was risky terrain.

Discussing southern and northern Progressives of this period, Kett identifies two constraints that characterized the situation of white women in the South. First, they had to confront the condition of southern ladyhood, which held them "unfit for the rigors of public life." Acknowledging Anne Scott's work, Kett writes that "before they could enter politics, they had to leave the pedestal." Second, observing that southern women had to "tread cautiously" on the subject of race, he precisely describes Kearney's situation: "Keeping quiet about race in the South in 1900 or 1910 meant not challenging the disfranchisement of most blacks (along with many whites) that had occurred during the late nineteenth century. With few exceptions, southern Progressives allowed themselves little more than a cautious accommodationism on racial issues" (170).

Kearney was thirty-seven years old when *A Slaveholder's Daughter* was published in 1900. Born in March 1863, she had known the Civil War only from the stories of her elders, but she knew all too well the hardships of poverty and lost opportunities that had come with Reconstruction. Even after her successful advancement as a leader in the Women's Christian Temperance Union (WCTU) and the women's suffrage movement, her vivid memory of the obstacles she had had to overcome possessed her as surely as did her ambition to further her social causes. The result is an autobiographical amalgam that is a memoir of her childhood, a story of a plantation family and the devastations of war, and a journey of the self toward maturation and discovery of social purpose. It is also a religious conversion narrative that harkens to a long tradition in American letters and, especially, to the testimonial writings and speeches of nineteenth-century

female activists who justified their work on behalf of temperance and other social reforms as religious crusades. The young-adult conversion that Kearney relates, for example, empowers her to formulate a God-directed mission that justifies her travel far from family and family duties. The last half of the book gives
account of this career, blending a narrative account of her speeches and travels
on behalf of the WCTU with an essayist's political and social commentary.

A Slaveholder's Daughter also provides a revealing illustration of a southern
autobiographer who represents her life as deeply enmeshed in the biographies of
others—intimate family connections as well as influential personages like Frances Willard and other associates from her WCTU and suffragist work. Kearney
in fact constructs a "relational self," a figure who typifies the autobiographical
narrators one finds in the subject texts of this study. Despite a considerable variety in life experience and the differences of class, age, and eras in which they
compose their narratives, these personae often identify their writings and their
lives as inseparable from the lives of others, especially family members and intimate associates. Further, some explicitly assert that they write only to serve
others. The ideology of female sacrifice of self that has been so much discussed
by scholars of women's history is evidenced everywhere one looks among life
writings by southern women who came of age in the late nineteenth and early
twentieth centuries. As we will see, even in highly atypical cases like Helen
Keller's *The Story of My Life* and the physician Anne Walter Fearn's *My Days of
Strength,* the protagonist of the narrative is as much a biographer of others as
the main character in her own life story.

In the effort to understand more fully the voices that narrate these texts, and
more generally the regional and gender inflections of these voices, it is helpful
to cast a backward glance, especially in the case of Belle Kearney. Her autobiography looks backward not only to an earlier half-century of plantation memoir and fiction, including the widely read *Uncle Tom's Cabin* and that novel's
rebutting southern counterparts, but to books such as Susan Dabney Smedes's
Memorials of a Southern Planter (1887) and Anna Julia Cooper's *A Voice from
the South* (1892). Smedes composes a memorial, chiefly narrative, to the mid-
nineteenth-century South and the white patriarchs who governed it, whereas
Cooper, in a series of essays that incorporate her personal experience, censures
the injustice that lay at the root of slavery and the racism that continued after
the Civil War to compromise the professed moral principles of southern (and
national) white supremacist society.

A brief consideration of these two predecessors gives one a better understanding of the autobiographical forms and rhetorical styles that a growing

tradition of southern women's nonfiction writings offered Kearney. The Smedes and Cooper books also suggest something of the expectations of the reading audience that Kearney could anticipate as she shaped her narrative to appeal to readers interested variously in history, plantation culture, religion, the hardships of Reconstruction in the South, and, especially, the women's temperance and suffrage movements.

When the first edition of Susan Dabney Smedes's *Memorials of a Southern Planter* was published in 1887, it found an audience already well accustomed to the "war" of plantation storytelling. Harriet Beecher Stowe had ignited the country's imagination and most of the white South's fury with her tale of Uncle Tom in 1852, the legendary consequence of which is repeated often in quotations of Lincoln's reference to her as the "little lady" who brought about the Civil War. Both autobiographical and fictional refutations of Stowe's depiction of slavery and plantation society would follow for a half-century and more. Indeed, the moral and social complexity of the slaveholding South and its descendants, both black and white, continues to deeply engage American storytellers. But the readers of the generation at the end of the nineteenth century, the sons and daughters who inherited the Reconstruction era, were seemingly tireless in their interest in the antebellum South. That most of the printing houses and bookshops were in the North, where book sales were largest, and even in England, where a large readership for American plantation stories could be engaged, undoubtedly influenced the southern writers' perceptions of their audience.

In *The Romance of Reunion: Northerners and the South, 1865–1900,* Nina Silber has shown that there was a lively market for books that embodied the South and North in characters of familiar romantic plots. Describing how "a sentimental rubric took hold of the reunion process," she writes that politicians, journalists, and financial leaders, as well as a general readership of middle- and upper-class northerners, "paid homage to a romantic and sentimental culture of conciliation that characterized the North-South relationship in the Gilded Age years." The gendering of the South as female, she maintains, had roots in the antebellum period. Abolitionist discourse, for example, isolated the South through a variety of metaphors that suggested all southerners, regardless of race or sex, were "weak, feminine, and out of control" (2–7). Despite some scholarly thought that even antebellum southerners associated the region with feminine imagery, Silber is not convinced, disputing the notion that "prewar southerners constructed a feminine self-image." Rather, they held "a distinctly southern view of masculinity, one that had very different attributes than the northern sense of manhood" (198–99, n. 9). These attributes might be expressed in admirable forms of civility, chivalrous deference to ladies, and nobility, but evidence of the lingering negative manifestation of these traits, the weak and feminized southern male, is hard to miss in such later fictional characters as Ashley Wilkes in Margaret Mitchell's 1936 *Gone with the Wind.*

Of course, Hollywood for years would take up the regional romantic plot in film, a good example of which is the 1938 *Jezebel.* Although the more familiar plot of the regional postbellum romance stars a romantic belle who wins the heart of a northern hero, the protagonist of *Jezebel* is the antebellum southerner who is defeated by her own vain excesses and finally brought to heel. The southern gentleman, played by Henry Fonda, is subjected to the willfulness and wiles of his betrothed southern belle (Bette Davis), marries a northern girl of sense and mature sensibility, and when "wounded" (i.e., infected) by yellow fever, finally redeems the scarlet jezebel. In a lush, sentimental scene with heraldic music rising, she rides from New Orleans in a wagon with the stricken, having at last given up her immature vanity and impetuousness, risking her life to aid him and the dying masses.

A firsthand account of life on the plantation, in its way as sentimentalized as the romantic fictions and later films, was what Smedes offered her readership in 1887. The recollection of the past as she saw it, or wanted to see it, was an ennobling story of a graceful, chivalrous, honorable society made even more so by the stature of a virtuous planter who brought justice and fair consideration to all in his domain—her father, Thomas Dabney. In some respects it anticipates *Gone with the Wind,* published almost fifty years later, especially in its account of Mammy Maria, the black woman who is largely in control of the household. Smedes states her motives for writing the book in a brief preface that reflects motives similar to those of many women who kept journals or wrote memoirs of the Civil War. It also anticipates the basic format of many of these books, which began as personal documents but would later be written or edited for publication. From the outset she establishes a requisite feminine modesty by asserting that she never expected to make public her personal life history but did so in order that the "memory and example" of her father's life might be preserved for his grandchildren, "who will come to mature years in a time when slavery will be a thing of the past." The stated motive is widespread among antebellum memoirs.[2]

Smedes then turns to the example her father gave to his family, which she portrays as that of "a good master," one who "cared for his servants affectionately and yet with a firm hand, when there was need, and with a full sense of his responsibility." Smedes thus intends to show that he was an honorable patrician, a patriarch willing to sacrifice himself for his charges—his slaves and his family. Finally, she returns to her modest claim that her decision to write the book is in no way a claim for attention to herself and her life story but rather the result of suggestions by friends that, "by laying bare much that is private and sacred" (lvii–lviii), she will have served the greater good of preserving for all a role model, as it were, of an honorable life well lived. The book is very much in keeping with its time, in its way cultivating that shift we see so clearly a little later in Lost Cause memorializing, which moves the focus of the Civil War from a defense of slaveholding to a defense of home, family, and "property rights" unfettered by the federal government.

Smedes's introductory lines are genealogical: "In the fair land of France the old Huguenot name and family of d'Aubigné still live." Although an English reviewer would later dispute Smedes's claim of a Huguenot ancestry that traced the American Dabneys back to the sixteenth century, Smedes devotes a ten-page introduction to details of the family tree, thus establishing an aristocratic bloodline. She begins chapter one with her subject, front and center, aligning him with America's foremost hero. "My father, Thomas Smith Gregory Dabney, was born at Bellevue, his father's country-seat on the Pamunkey River, in the county of King and Queen, Virginia, on the 4th day of January, 1798, and he used to tell us that he was two years in the world before General Washington left it" (3). What follows is a story devoted largely to family and plantation, as told by the dutiful witness Susan, the second daughter and eighth of the sixteen children born to Thomas and Sophia Hill Dabney.

Memorials of a Southern Planter takes place principally in Hinds County, Mississippi, where the Dabneys moved from Virginia in 1835. Smedes sketches a romanticized life filled with domestic kindliness, slaves who are loving and loyal to the Dabneys, political activism on behalf of her father's ardent Whig allegiances, and then the devastation of the war. In his sixties, Thomas Dabney sacrificed his ambition to join the Confederate forces to stay at home to keep the crops going and see to the well-being of his large family. After the war, faced with a great burden of debt he was determined to repay, the ever-honorable Thomas led the family in "rigid self denial." Smedes gives an example of the extremity of both their poverty and their father's chivalry in an account of his determination to take on the laundry chores rather than see his daughters brought "to the wash tub." With no sense of irony or self-consciousness about excluding African American women from her generic "woman," Smedes writes: "His chivalrous nature had always revolted from the sight of a woman doing hard work" (223). An impression of the tone and vocabulary of Smedes's writing is well communicated in her conclusion to the washtub story:

> This may give some idea of the labors, the privations, the hardships, of those terrible years. The most intimate friends of Thomas, nay, his own children, who were not in the daily life at Burleigh, have never know the unprecedented self-denial, carried to the extent of acutest bodily sufferings, which he practised during this time. A curtain must be drawn over this part of the life of my lion-hearted father! (223)

Smedes's *Memorials* went through eight editions between 1887 and 1914. It was published in England with much support from William E. Gladstone, who reviewed the U.S. edition in England and then helped negotiate an English edition, which was published in 1890 as *Life of Susan Dabney Smedes*. In his introduction to his 1981 edition of the book, Fletcher M. Green attributes the lackluster sales in England to the misfortune of its title, which he thought would have more profitably been *A Southern Planter*.

What can these alternate titles tell us about the literary market? About the expectations of the audience for whom Smedes wrote? And, most important, what do they show us of the social context in which a Susan Dabney Smedes formed a sense of self? It is doubtless naive to regard the "voiced" self in her book as a calculated mask devised to sell books (or even to assume a preexisting self formed and available for the narrative before she ever put pen to paper). She wrote her "memorial," I think we can say, mindful of her audience, who were variously partisan, nostalgic, genteel, religious, and culturally conservative, readers who had lived through the years of the Civil War and Reconstruction, readers especially in the North and abroad who were witness to the rapid changes brought on by industrialization. What she wrote was the story she could coherently construct from this social fabric for herself and her readers.

The lesson could not have been lost upon Belle Kearney, whose home in Madison County, Mississippi, was, incidentally, adjacent to Smedes's Hinds County. When Kearney took up her pen a decade later, she had a recent and near-at-hand model of southern autobiography that illustrated a variety of strategies for attracting a wide national audience. As a slaveholder's daughter, she could tell the "Old South" story passed on to her by her elders and, from her own experience, a story of the postwar wages of slaveholding—poverty and hardship visited not just upon the slaveholders but upon the descendants and the entire region. In the title and in her early chapters, she presents herself as "daughter," in the manner of Smedes's focus upon family, the plight of the South, and her loyal support of both. But whereas Smedes maintains her peripheral position throughout, ending her book with an account of Thomas Dabney's death and a maudlin story of the faithful Mammy Maria's death several weeks later of a grieving, "busted heart," Kearney enters her narrative explicitly by the end of chapter one, although as a protagonist continually bound to others' interests.

A different perspective upon postbellum southern history and a sharply different rhetorical model of autobiographical discourse by a southern woman, a discourse focused upon social reform in a manner that Kearney's book eventually aspires to, is represented in Anna Julia Cooper's *A Voice from the South by a Black Woman of the South,* published in 1892. Cooper, born in 1858 in North Carolina, the daughter of a slave woman and her white master, was a leading figure among black feminists at the turn of the century.[3] Not so visible an activist as Mary Church Terrell or Ida B. Wells, she was a respected intellectual, lecturer, and educator—for many years a principal and teacher at Dunbar High School in Washington, D.C.—and a leader in various women's organizations, including the Colored Women's YWCA, which she helped found. Although she does not present as memoir or autobiography the speeches and essays that compose *A Voice from the South,* she clearly calls upon her own experience to validate the portrait she draws of the black woman's status in society. The title of the book invokes the personal, but it does so to mark the departure point for the institutional and political reforms that Cooper was committed to advancing. One infers a certain deferential modesty in the title—"a voice," and the southern voice of a black woman at that—but a claim as well for authority that comes from direct witness of the "race problem" in the former slaveholding region. The rhetorical strategy that Cooper employs throughout the book in her arguments for reform is in many respects like Kearney's, although in *A Slaveholder's Daughter* Kearney writes a linear narrative in which she integrates life story and social argument.

Cooper's discourse is assuredly political. The opening chapter of *A Voice from the South,* "Womanhood: A Vital Element in the Regeneration and Progress of the Race," a paper delivered in 1886 at a conference of the black clergy of the Protestant Episcopal Church in Washington, D.C., calls for recognition and support of black women as key to racial uplift and to the betterment of American society generally. Clearly, she assumes a male audience, and an indifferent if not resistant one at that. Proceeding in straightforward fashion, she asserts propositions aimed at eliciting agreement from the audience—statements of conventional, noncontroversial values—and then deduces conclusions that she maintains are logical and inevitable, all the while steadily praising and commandeering the good sense, logical minds, and Christian grounding of her listener-readers.

The opening volley, for example, is a sharp contrasting of Christianity and Islam, the former furnishing society with an ideal of womanhood, Cooper argues, and the latter an image of woman "uniformly devoted to a life of ignorance, infamy, and complete stagnation" (9). She deftly acknowledges her audience as aligned with the Christian West, not the "Oriental countries," and thus allied with her in a view of enlightened womanhood. A second source of modern civilization's "noble and ennobling ideal" of women she identifies only as "perhaps" an influence—the chivalric traditions of European feudalism. Both Christianity and feudalism provide her with ample field of discussion for displaying her broad, impressive knowledge of history. At the outset, then, Cooper establishes a politic voice that is reasonable, deferential, and authoritative—clearly *a* voice rather than *any* voice from the South. She alternately addresses a national, interracial audience and a specifically African American one. For example, she speaks of the "American civilization" as not having yet reached the ideal society it espouses and then quotes the English historian Thomas Macaulay that one "may judge a nation's rank in the scale of civilization from the way they treat their women" (12). She also calls upon the general respect for the values of true womanhood, noting that mothers "first form the man by directing the earliest impulses of his character" (21). And then she turns to the black clergy, her immediate audience in 1886.

"A race is but a total of families" (29), Cooper asserts, beginning a peroration in which she positions the black woman as the maternal, and essential, guide to the "regeneration" of the race. Several times noting that African Americans were only "twenty-one years removed from the conception and experience of a chattel" (26), she implies a condition of immaturity that calls upon the offices and experience of the mothers of the race. Careful not to attribute immaturity to her audience (and readership), she points rather to the "homes, average homes, homes of the rank and file of horny handed men and toiling women of the South (where the masses are)" as those whose uplift depended upon black women. In perhaps the most famous line in the book, Cooper announces her justification for urging attention to the status of black women and especially to improved provisions for the education of young women. "Only the BLACK WOMAN can say 'when and where I enter, in the quiet, undisputed dignity of my womanhood, without violence or suing or special patronage, then and there the whole *Negro race enters with me*'" (31).

Subsequent chapters in *A Voice from the South,* one on the higher education of women and another on the status of women in America, extend Cooper's feminist arguments. She writes scathingly of what she sees as a pernicious influence of southerners throughout the history of the nation, she mocks white southerners' obsession with blood lines and genealogies, and she exposes the hypocritical demands for privilege by white southern *ladies,* a term she uses deliberately and for which she may be pardoned, she wittily notes, being a black southern *woman* (108). She also responds directly to the growing sentiment among many white suffragists that southern male voters could best be appealed to by arguing the "injustice" of the enfranchisement of black men but not white women, or by citing the need to negate black votes with enfranchised white female votes: "It is not the intelligent woman vs. the ignorant woman; nor the white woman vs. the black, the brown, and the red,—it is not even the cause of woman vs. man. Nay, 'tis woman's strongest vindication for speaking that *the world needs to hear her voice*" (121).

As many scholars have noted, even in her most impassioned feminist statements calling for gender reforms, Cooper maintains a tone and a vocabulary that at least on the surface signal to a male audience her acceptance of woman's role in society as remaining primarily in the woman's sphere of domesticity. Whereas Susan Dabney Smedes assumes a largely sympathetic audience for her portrait of a patriarchal South—or, perhaps one should say, an audience nostalgic and voyeuristic—Cooper's strategy assumes a male-dominated and resistant audience. She proposes her feminist reforms in an array of nonthreatening rhetorical ploys, beginning with her invocation in Part I, the "Soprano Obligato" of George Eliot ("Though I were happy, throned beside the king, / I should be tender to each little thing / With hurt warm breast . . . "). In the opening essay, initially composed as an address to a convocation of Episcopal clergy, she early makes a point of disclaiming her role as initiator of the cause of black women by lauding the leadership and prior publication of Dr. Alexander Crummell, whose pamphlet, "The Black Woman of the South," she cites as the work of a "Moses and the Prophets." There is evidence that the efforts at ingratiation hardly made a dent. In her introduction to the Oxford University Press edition of *Voice,* Mary Helen Washington notes that five years after the 1892 publication of Cooper's book, a group of black intellectuals, including Crummell, in organizing the American Negro Academy to promote literature, science, and art, limited membership exclusively to African American males. Washington also cites Frederick Douglass's dismissal at this time of any noteworthy female contributions to black intellectual history—doing so "in the very year that Cooper published *A Voice from the South.*" She writes: "When asked by historian M. A. Majors to name some black women for inclusion in Majors' biographical work on black women, [Douglas] responded: 'I have thus far seen no book of importance written by a negro woman and I know of no one among us who can appropriately be called famous'" (xl).

Despite Washington's conclusion that Cooper wrote "the most precise, forceful, well-argued statement of black feminist thought to come out of the nineteenth century," she finds Cooper's ideas diluted, or deflected, by the constraints of true womanhood ideology. Other scholars have read Cooper's voice differently, some detecting a current of ambivalence adroitly communicated, despite her seeming acquiescence to woman's place as a separate sphere. Others have read Cooper's deployment of true womanhood rhetoric as a thoroughgoing camouflage for her radical message.[4] At whatever point on the transparency-to-opacity scale one locates Cooper's communicated voice, there can be little disagreement that the voice *is* constructed to address a resisting reader who assumes a position of intellectual and political superiority.

By contrast, the welcoming climate in the 1880s, 1890s and 1900s for southern texts that nostalgically and sentimentally recalled "plantation days" and Civil War hardships is reflected in the popularity of "memorials" like Smedes's or the fiction of Thomas Nelson Page—and subsequently in a long line of life writing and fiction, as Nina Silber has shown. Even such African American writers as Charles Chesnutt found a ready audience for depictions of an antebellum South that readers seemed ready to regard almost as an exotic anachronism. Much of the fiction appeared in popular magazines, whose readership was a largely female audience whose lives were chiefly defined by domesticity and who enjoyed domestic romance, especially stories that also included a theme of North-South reunion. Thomas Nelson Page was the master of the form, as Grace King acknowledges in 1932 in *Memories of a Southern Woman of Letters:* "It is hard to explain in simple terms what Thomas Nelson Page meant to us in the South at that time. He was the first Southern writer to appear in print as a Southerner, and his stories, short and simple, written in Negro dialect, and, I may say, Southern pronunciation, showed us with ineffable grace that although we were sore bereft, politically, we had now a chance in literature at least" (377).

There was also a welcoming climate for accounts of a New South that was energetically committed to commerce and entrepreneurial activity—and that also managed to hold on to enough of its antebellum customs to entertain readers with its "charm." An especially revealing article, "Here and There in the South," which reflected the national predilection for reading the South as changed and yet unchanged, appeared in *Harper's New Monthly Magazine* in 1887. The author was Rebecca Harding Davis, who is known best for her *Life in the Iron Mills*. Davis composes an entertaining fable of a rail journey of an aging couple traveling to New Orleans for the 1884–85 Exposition. Although a Union supporter and "pastor of a church in western New York for forty years," Mr. Ely remembers with fondness a trip he had made to the South before the Civil War, and he is intent upon returning to view the remembered landscapes and people he had met. Other travelers from the North likewise hold stereotypical images of southerners, though not so admiring as Mr. Ely's. A "little ironmaker from Pennsylvania" knows that "the men spend their time in idling, dueling, and drinking. The women are merely lovely, helpless babies" (236). But at every stop along the way southern passengers boarding the train sharply contradict these wrongheaded assumptions—one Virginia plantation belle is reported as having "ploughed and dug until she was able to hire hands." Mrs. Ely finds that Lynchburg quite reminds her of Pittsburgh, and in all the cities they pass there are reports of vigorous industrialization. A young woman who in Mrs. Ely's eyes is probably "a teacher from Boston" turns out to be the daughter of the convivial Major Pogue, a former Confederate officer left penniless by the war who serves in the narrative as a kind of information officer of the New South.

Evidence of the old South sought by Mr. Ely is to be found in the small towns and countryside, where he spies "a picturesque old mansion, which seemed to him to embody all the tragedy of the departed South." There is also a mysterious stranger—"a typical Southerner at last," the travelers think—seeing in him a "haughty reserve." But "Dupre Mocquard," once a great plantation owner, turns out to be an overseer on one of his former estates, though he retains an "old-fashioned courtesy," according to Mrs. Ely, that "would become a deposed monarch." And though the Elys are pleased to hear a report that southern hospitable ways of visiting and hosting continue, Lola Pogue's sharp response is that the custom "keeps many a family poor, and makes life a tread-mill for most women." The point Davis makes throughout this genial satire is that the imagined old South in the late 1880s is as much an indulgence of the North as a defensive apology of the South. In both cases, she suggests, the reading audience is reluctant to let go its image of an exotic South.

In his history of the New South period, commenting upon the fiction of the time, Edward L. Ayers remarks that writers, "by and large, did not use fiction as smokescreens for a southern political agenda, but rather as a way to order and explore the events and forces that so affected their lives." We can read their work as an indicator of what Ayres calls "the elusive emotional geography of the New South" (339). Deeply felt conflicts about gender roles, familial duty, race, religion, industrialization, and regional identity are variously the subjects of Mark Twain, George Washington Cable, Kate Chopin, and others whose works we read today with special attention to the critiques they offered of their society. But the national audience of the 1880s and 1890s responded more to Twain's dialect humor than to his social critique; the southern audience gave cold reception to Cable's call for racial justice, and Kate Chopin's 1899 *The Awakening* found few sympathetic readers for Edna Pontellier's flight from stagnating domesticity.

How, then, would a writer like the Mississippian Belle Kearney, who had a reformist political message she wanted to advance in a book that she hoped would sell widely in 1900, construct a voice that had a chance at least of being heard, if not sympathetically received? In addressing temperance or suffragist supporters, she could be resoundingly direct, as she shows in a testimonial quoted by Josephine K. Henry in an 1895 article, "The New Woman of the New South," published in the social reformist periodical, the *Arena*. Henry cites a long list of similar statements by southern women explaining their support of enfranchisement. Kearney writes, "I want the ballot because I am a human being, and desire with my whole heart to stand before the law the equal of any other human being" (360). She clearly does not assume the same audience for *A Slaveholder's Daughter* as for the *Arena* article.

In the daughter-self Kearney constructs, she aims to bridge the chasm between the true womanhood ideals of purity, piety, and domesticity and her radical ideals of woman's political equality, and, in doing so, to convince her audience that her reform agenda constitutes no threat to civil harmony in either private or public spheres. Of course, her reach calls for a considerable rhetorical stretch, but there was no lack of models in the 1890s—nor in years following. In the widely read *Century Magazine*, for example, Wilbur Fisk Tillett of Vanderbilt University devotes much of his lengthy 1891 article on "Southern Womanhood as Affected by the War" to accounts of the expanded opportunities for education and employment for women, bolstered by excerpts from questionnaire responses by women young and old from across the South. In his conclusion, however, he celebrates such opportunities by reasserting the submissive, domestic southern lady ideal. "It is certainly an age that has witnessed great changes in the life, education, and labor of women everywhere," he writes, "and these changes have all been in the direction of enlarging the sphere of woman's activities, increasing her liberties, and opening up possibilities to her life hitherto restricted to man." Continuing his laudatory tone for the progressiveness of the times, he notes that "it is a movement limited to no land and to no race." And then, without transition, a sharp turn: "So far as this movement may have any tendency to take woman out of her true place in the home, to give her man's work to do and to develop masculine qualities in her, it finds no sympathy in the South. The Southern woman loves the retirement of home, and shrinks from everything that would tend to bring her into this public gaze" (16).

In reading life writings by southern women of the late nineteenth and early twentieth centuries, writings intended for publication, one does well to keep in mind the pressures of the receiving audience upon the sending voice. Indeed, the textualized self, as discussed earlier, is inevitably composed responsively, shaped by life experience, motives for writing, and the imaginative scope made possible by one's linguistic inheritance.

Belle Kearney was born on March 6, 1863, shortly after Lincoln's issuance of the Emancipation Proclamation on January 1. "Just two months and six days too late for me to be a Constitutional slaveholder," she writes (9). The hint of youthfulness and irony in this narrator's voice contrasts markedly with Smedes's more somber sermonic voice. But Kearny's strategy in composing her voice is to take every rhetorical advantage offered by the victim-speaking survivors of the war, such as Smedes's, to heighten the emotional appeal of her story and establish herself as a woman tempered by hardship and so steeled for the later arduous work of social reformer. The anonymous epigraph with which she opens the book makes the point explicitly, linking as it does the defeat of the South with the crucifixion story.

A land without ruins is a land without memories . . . without history. A land that wears a crown may be fair to see; but twine a few sad cypress leaves around the brow of any land, and be that land barren and bleak, it becomes lovely in its consecrated coronet or sorrow, and it wins the sympathy of the heart and of history. Crowns of roses fade—crowns of thorns endure. Calvaries and crucifixions take the deepest hold on humanity. (1)

What is most compelling about the narrator Kearney composes in this book is her constant maneuvering between a self that is an obedient, self-sacrificing daughter and sister, who always puts her family's interests before her own, and a self that is individualistic, ambitious, and determined to live in a larger world than the domestic sphere. Indeed, the persistent thread of the narrative is a plot that shows an intrepid Kearney, like a host of young heroines of nineteenth-century domestic novels, successfully embodying both selves. For example, even as a girl she comes to be something of the household manager. Her father, "injured and depressed by a frail constitution," and her mother, "a martyr to neuralgia," were further incapacitated by not knowing "how to work, nor how to manage so as to make a dollar, nor how to keep it after it was gained" (21). Her oldest brother dies at fifteen, her sister at twenty, making Belle the oldest child in the family. "When nine years old," she writes, I put my small 'shoulders to the wheel' to ease mother's burdens" (23–24). So it is that Belle serves as mother surrogate for three younger brothers and, later, for yet another baby born into the family—one not welcomed by any of the four older siblings.

It is in this section of chapter three that Kearney first uses the voiced "I," the reflective acknowledgment of the subject as the narrator. She recounts the scenes of her sister's marriage and death in an emotional but terse passage that says volumes about Kearney's perception of motherhood and her eventual choice to pursue a life of public activism over family service. "While my only sister was at college in Oxford, Mississippi, she formed a romantic attachment for a young University student, whom she married when she was but sixteen" (22). Belle was five years old when the wedding took place, the memory "indelibly impressed upon my mind," she writes. She describes the guests, "the handsome bridegroom, my lovely sister in her bridal robes, my head aching, and eyes swollen from much weeping, the good-byes, the roll of the carriage down the long avenue of cedars to the gate, the after-loneliness and gloom of the house." It is easy to read this figure as a model for William Faulkner's portrayal in *Absalom, Absalom!* of the child Rosa Coldfield, who similarly watches her sister Ellen's departure with Thomas Sutpen. Four years after the wedding, Kearney is led into the parlor to view her sister in her coffin—"the child-wife, just twenty years old, and the mother of two little daughters!" One presumes this childwife died in childbirth although Kearney offers no explanation of the death. It remains in the telling as mysterious as it was to the nine-year old witness, who notes only that "the iron entered my soul very early in this great battle we call 'life.' I looked about me with wide-open eyes, full of comprehension and a heart full of bitterness" (22).

Like Kate Chopin's Edna Pontellier, Belle well understands the limits that nature exacts upon female sexuality—a woman's freedom and, quite possibly, her life. Kearney never married, remaining a "daughter" throughout the book (and indeed until her death in 1939). She writes of party going and an active social life in her teenage years, though the account is absent any mention of suitors. In the story she tells of her youthful preparatory years outside the home, foremost are her earnest pursuit of an education and her renewal of religious faith in what she describes as a life-changing conversion experience. These details are crucial to establishing the intellectual and moral authority that she must claim later as a leader of temperance reform and woman's suffrage.

Thus it is that in the first part of the text she composes a *southern* memoir, one in which she focuses upon a broad spectacle of personal experience and social conditions endemic to the southern region: a portrait of defeat and impoverishment that calls out for social transformation, a family story of hardship and dutifulness, and also an analysis of the state of education and career opportunities for women (other than marriage and family) as she knew them firsthand. Her voice is alternately personal and detached, at times filled with emotion and revealing of inner desires, even confessions, and at other times systematically profiling crop acreage, demographics, tax incomes, and race relations in a journalistic third-person voice. What perhaps is most compelling about the Belle-protagonist of the early chapters is the inconsistency of voice and character. It is as if she is straining to appeal to a welter of differing audiences, pulled by competing models of identity that offer only the most complicated sort of merger. Remarkably, in most instances she is admirably adept at doing so, though the identity stretch exacted upon her may seem to some readers as more resembling that of an Augusta Jane Evans or E.D.E.N. Southworth heroine than that of a woman contending with real-life desires and compromises.

Here I think we find a rather clear example of what Susan Stanford Friedman has called the "geographics of identity." Noting that identity develops from the dialectic between difference and sameness, she observes that identity is constructed relationally through difference from the other. ("Identification with a group based on gender, race, or sexuality, for example, depends mostly on binary systems of 'us' versus 'them,' where difference from the other defines the group to which one belongs.") She observes that identity suggests sameness as well, "some form of commonality, some shared ground" (19). Kearney quite clearly claims commonality with the groups to which she belongs by birth: white southerners, specifically Mississippians, women, and the Kearney family. She also claims common ground with the WCTU, with progressive women committed to social reform, with Christians, and with humankind from distant places, whose welfare she comes to see as connected to her own. Although the universal experience of maturation virtually assures that one must make a transition from a childhood identity to an adult one, what we have in *A Slaveholder's Daughter* is not the story of such a transition but the story of an autobiographer in her mid-thirties trying as an adult to forge together textual identities that are in most cases acutely at odds. The dilemma for the Kearney-protagonist-self of the narrative is that the coherence and credibility that Kearney-the-writer is trying to create for the narrator is undercut by the great social distance between the competing identities, that of the traditional southern woman and that of the progressive or "new woman," which she herself often regards as a rebellious stance. The conflict between the writer and the character is exemplified in the pervasive alternations of voice.

One sees this pattern of shifting voice illustrated in the progression of the first twelve chapters, that is, in the "southern" sections of the autobiography. Here she wavers between idealizing her girlhood, the family, and her homeland and, on many grounds, condemning them, sometimes subtly but usually quite pointedly. For example, Kearney relates her miserable efforts at age nine at housekeeping and cooking, which devolve upon her whenever her mother's frequent illnesses befall. "If a low moan issued from mother's room early in the morning, my heart sank, for it boded no good to me" (24). The somber realism of Kearney's childhood plight as mother-surrogate quickly converts to sprightly domestic romance as an older Belle, derided by her brother for not knowing how to cook, strikes a bargain that illustrates both a native wit and her readerly precociousness. When he upbraids her ("I have no respect for a girl who is eleven years old and doesn't know how to cook), she offers an exchange of duties: "If you will cook every time mother gets sick, I will tell you one of Dickens' stories or one of Sir Walter Scott's novels as regularly as the nights roll around" (25). Kearney's dialogue is more reminiscent of such fiction than it is persuasive of remembered family conversation.

She is most authoritative and persuasive in her matter-of-fact first person reporting of a father, who, like Thomas Dabney, found the "postbellum world too much for him," a mother who was unrelievedly depressed and sickly, and a self who yearned for formal education and travel and, though never acknowledged, relief from the poverty and despair of the South she knew. Perhaps above all, she yearned for relief from what she clearly felt to be an imprisoning family—although the moment she realizes she has pictured them so, she commences an impassioned paean in respect of their various virtues and endearing qualities. As she recounts her despair at age fifteen when forced to leave school because money was scarce and, "besides, the boys were growing rapidly, and the oldest *must* be given at least one year at the University," she claims that 'it would have been sinful to upbraid father'" (40). In linking religious belief to the father's dominance, she bears out Marjorie Mendenhall's 1934 description of the postbellum family as "patriarchal by inheritance and the sanction of religion." In matters of great and grave decisions, "all final commands were made by the father or older brother" (95–96).

Quite clearly, as the older woman writing of her youth, Kearney does "up-braid" the father. She deeply resents the prejudice toward women, and the sharp irony in her comment about the favoring of boys' education intensifies in the following paragraphs, in which she berates the denial to women of any sort of remunerative work that would allow them to provide for their own education. "*I had never heard of a woman working to pay her way through school*," writes the older author Belle Kearney, and she goes on to emphasize the manipulative and hypocritical customs that oppressed her. "My family would have considered it an eternal disgrace for me to have worked publicly. . . . Household drudgery and public work were very different questions. The former was natural and un-avoidable; the latter was monstrous and impossible" (41). Her irony gives way to bitterness over the opportunities denied her, and she claims that among all "unhappy sights," the most pitiable is that of one who yearns for "better things than it has known, atrophying in the prison house of blind and palsied cus-tom" (41).

What is perhaps most instructive in reading Kearney's life story as a *south-ern woman's* autobiography is coming to see the weight of family in shaping the sense of self, to be sure, but also to see the dominating effect of the racial caste system upon the formation of racial and gender identities, especially those of white women. Scholars of African American studies, southern history, and American feminism have over the years analyzed the many ways in which the image of a "black menace" has been constructed within racist social institu-tions to justify white male power over blacks and white women. For women of Kearney's race and generation, who typically internalized many of these nega-tive images of blacks and thereby justified—validated—their complicity in their own limited freedoms, the "cognitive dissonance" that otherwise might have troubled the intellect was largely submerged in denial. So it is with Belle Kear-ney. And yet, the specter of racial oppression haunts her claims for gender jus-tice, for she is too intelligently reflective to bury her consciousness of the par-allels between the limited freedoms of blacks and those of white women in a patriarchal South.

In the passage quoted above, in which she grieves for those human beings who are "atrophying in the prison house of blind and palsied custom," Kear-ney ends the sentence—and the chapter, which is entitled "The Young Ladies' Academy"—with an implicit indictment of her society: "there is no one in the passing throng brave and great enough to break the bars and 'let the oppressed go free,'—into the larger liberty where God meant that all His creatures should *live* and *grow* and *shine*" (42). She follows this complaint and plea immediately with a chapter devoted to slavery, emancipation, and the societal changes brought by the Civil War. Her ambivalence about these changes and their consequences for "young Southern men and women" (e.g., "white" men and women) is acute. The liberation of 4 million slaves has eliminated not only the caste system (about which she voices many reservations throughout the book) but has also brought about an "amalgamation" of the middle and upper classes (about which she heartily approves). The blue bloods have been jolted from family-tree worship, and the middle class has come into its own, "equal to the emergency" of defeat and Reconstruction. She exults that her generation has learned that "work is honorable," that only through the "hard, earnest toil of hands or brain" will one succeed in the future, and she celebrates the end of the "unsafe and unnatural code of the manorial leisure of other days" that was abolished along with slavery. But the young self that Kearney portrays in the book cannot claim the empowerment that these changed circumstances and attitudes offer, for they were only to develop later, she writes, through "the slow growth of years" (43-44).

In chapter five, "Storms of the Soul," Kearney gives a vivid portrait of a self trapped in ambivalent emotions toward family and region and thus prevented from forming a workable identity. Jeanne Perreault writes of her self-presentation as "root-bound, not just with family and money and domestic spaces, but with the multiply dimensioned values, beliefs, and unconscious climate of [her] world" (32). Unable to secure an education, burdened with poverty, uncertain of her future, and having no one with whom she could discuss her spiritual questioning, the young Belle enters a period of dispiriting aimlessness. The older narrator formulates this experience as a decade-long travail of disbelief, in which the young woman comes "to despise Christianity" (46). Thus the narrator substitutes an estrangement from God for the disaffection from family and society that preceding chapters have portrayed as the experience of the adolescent and young adult. The narrative of spiritual confession and conversion offers familiar and safer ground for Kearney's interpretation of the crucial transition in her life when she comes to question the "prison house" that she was trapped in. One is reminded of Mark Twain's dilemma about what to do with Huckleberry Finn once he had completed his life-changing trip down the Mississippi and had watched his friend, the slave Jim, obtain his freedom. Twain, as we recall, sends Huck "out West," not back up the river to live among its prison-house society of racists and hypocrites. I think we have to read Kearney's escape not only as an inward, religious journey but, like Twain's solution for Huck, a passive opposition to the oppressive society.

Indeed, there are many overtones of *Adventures of Huckleberry Finn* (as well as the Brer Rabbit tales of Joel Chandler Harris and the southern romances of Thomas Nelson Page and other local color writers) that immediately come to mind in these early chapters, in which Kearney obviously intends to offer her firsthand witness of the South of her girlhood along with her later-aged commentary upon it. The Negro sermon rendered in dialect, as well as the account of the outlandish costumes of African American women, is clearly intended to add "local color." But as in *Huck Finn,* these light interludes constantly threaten to turn into serious matter. Describing the black woman's "natural love of dress," the narrator shifts suddenly from her position as privileged observer to that of an impoverished supplicant who, like Huck, has to swallow her white pride. She writes, "My desire for employment was so great, and there being no other opening, though it nearly crushed me, I swallowed my pride and asked the negroes to bring their sewing to me" (55).

At other points in the depiction of Belle's years of aimlessness, the narrator briefly takes up the theme of her southern-belle period, which is characterized by "society chat," "round-dancing, and card playing," and other sinful, time-wasting activities, according to her later judgment. For example, she ascribes a later fifteen-year stint of bad health to a profligate belledom, which had her going out in freezing weather in thin slippers and gauze dresses, dancing until fatigue overcame her, and then rushing out into the night with only a lace shawl covering.[5] The portrait perfectly anticipates Katherine Anne Porter's character in "Old Mortality," Miranda's Aunt Amy, the legendary belle whose similarly careless ways eventuate in her early death.

It is fascinating to follow Belle Kearney's efforts to portray a youthful self that is both rejecting and respecting of her familial and regional birthright. She is clearly a heart in conflict with itself, and the sections of the autobiography in which she grapples with the conflict—both in her depictions of the girl Belle and in the explicit comments and judgments the older writer-narrator makes upon her youthful experience—are by far the most compelling passages in the book. Her primary strategy is to show Belle as gamely trying to live by the traditional customs of her society but doing so with little success. The narrator, of course, identifies the failure as resulting from the spiritual emptiness of the belle's life, the dire burdens brought on by poverty and lack of educational opportunity, and, perhaps above all, the proscription against women's working outside the home.

A white woman's working for hire outside the home was regarded almost universally by white southern men as a shameful public declaration of the male family members' inability to support "their women." (One should also note that affluent black families likewise regarded the wife-homemaker as a significant symbol of class and economic success.) To Belle Kearney's credit, she does not attempt to soften the features of this social code that proved so restrictive of women's independence. There is hardly any way to overstate the frustration of many women in Belle's position, a woman of intelligence and ambition, reared in the land of the free and the home of the brave, whose economic well-being was tied utterly to the success, or failure, of her male supporters. In fiction, even delicate white Creole belles like Aurora and daughter Clothilde Nancanou in Cable's *The Grandissimes* (1885) are faced with choosing either an impoverished destitution, which nonetheless imparted a semblance of social status, or, if they dared, the loss of respectability by taking hired work. (They are, of course, "saved" by romantic heroes.) One of the blocks to Edna Pontellier's striving for freedom in Chopin's *The Awakening* is her realization that, lacking the talent and discipline to become an artist, there are no alternatives available to her other than dependence upon a husband or lover. The sole exception for most middle- and upper-class white women, at least those with some education, was teaching or writing, although even this path incurred some loss of status for the teacher and her male family members, being, as it were, a statement of financial need. Of course, there were a very few writers like Grace King, Ruth McInery Stuart, and Augusta Jane Evans who achieved both remunerative incomes and celebrated acceptance by genteel society, but their example of the successful working "lady" was hardly ordinary. It did represent, however, just the kind of strategic negotiation of a traditional and nontraditional life that so attracted Belle Kearney.

One of the fully dramatized scenes that Kearney creates in the book is one in which she informs her father that she intends to begin teaching. The dramatic emphasis marks the scene as a turning point in her determined rebellion against conventional domesticity. It is an emotionally charged moment, one the author Kearney signifies as the site of the young woman's courageous early steps toward a different way of life. "'But you forget,' he exclaimed, making a desperate effort to control the quaver in this voice and to hid the tremor of his eyelids that revealed the storm in his heart, 'you *forget* that I am able to give you a support. You forget that you are my only daughter'" (71). Kearney does not underplay but rather *overplays* her willfulness and rebellion. She does so in order to expose the taboo against woman's work as an example of a "palsied custom" that has overstayed its time and is ripe for reversal.

The limitations and barriers to female employment that so frustrated Kearney were especially oppressive in the South. In his 1892 *Southern Women in the*

Recent Educational Movement in the South, A. D. Mayo reported the figure of 346 paying industrial occupations available to American women. But for southern women, "even now there are not forty-six, possibly not twenty-five, outside a few localities, where a southern girl at home can make a respectable living in any way and, twenty years ago, school-teaching was certainly, even with its small compensation, the most attractive and reliable of the dozen uncertain methods of keeping the wolf from the door" (168).

With some recognition of the wolf at the door, one has to assume, Kearney's father acquiesces to her plan and simply watches as she transforms an upstairs bedroom into a schoolroom that, at the beginning, accommodates seven students paying in total a tuition of $12 a month. With her one brave stand, the fierce patriarchal opposition folds, exemplifying a model she doubtless hopes to impress upon her readers, especially any white patriarchs who happen to take up her book. Her father says "not one word. His courtesy was never at fault; besides, he had discovered in me a certain will-force, inherited from both 'sides of the house,' and an indomitable energy which he began to respect" (72). In a strategy she and many other female autobiographers employ, she attributes her assertive qualities to personality features inherited from the father, who is thus subtly, or not so subtly, pressured to admit and accept the patrimony evidenced in the daughter's actions.

Her mother she describes as "radiant with delight from the beginning"; her mother is the one who understands her "longings." Here the reader glimpses Kearney's recognition of her mother's own repressed longings for a life different from the passive, maternal one she has lived, a life she flees in depression and illness. Kearney thus justifies this early direction toward a teaching career—a decision that lays the foundation for her later choice to become a temperance and suffragist activist—not only as an act that rectifies palsied custom but as an enactment of her mother's repressed desires.

Throughout the book Kearney never relinquishes her self-image—or self-portrayal—as dutiful daughter. From time to time she acknowledges lapses in noticing the needs of her parents, but once these are identified, she immediately accepts responsibility for attending to them. In 1891, at a juncture when her father has been elected to the state senate and her three brothers are all occupied in business or college, a "presentiment" that her mother is ill "seizes" her as she is teaching in her public school classroom in the small town of Flora. Returning home, her intuition is confirmed, and she immediately arranges for a cook and a housekeeper—"never since that sad day has the home been without one" (83).

The clear pattern that emerges in Kearney's ordering of her life story is a linear account of the developing preparation of the young Belle for her later mission, preparation that entails dutifulness and courage to act. In this respect *A Slaveholder's Daughter* mirrors many features of the classic bildungsroman. But the linearity is disrupted by a transforming religious conversion that will send the reformed sinner out into the world to further God's crusades in whatever direction she is called. Then, as later autobiographers like Lillian Smith and Katherine DuPre Lumpkin would do more adroitly, Kearney modulates from personal maturation story to broader social critique and thereby identifies fields of service that constitute a manifest "call" for her service.

In key chapters nine through eleven Kearney describes three major social issues calling for response and reform: "educational matter," the "southern problem" (e.g., the racial problems of the South), and "the evolution of southern women." These chapters are mainly expository essays, resembling in form those of Anna Julia Cooper, with only occasional references to Kearney's own experience. They offer instead some somber, heavily researched reports of postwar social conditions. These outline quite clearly grounds for social activism, and they culminate in describing "the transformation," the religious experience that readied her for action. There is first the confession—details of the "embittered spirit" that had afflicted her for ten years—and then the conversion. Her Christian belief recovered, she writes that her spiritual hunger is fulfilled, her heart made peaceful, her "unrest stilled" (131). So she concludes the first half of the book that explains how she came from being slaveholder's daughter to a committed advocate of temperance and social justice for women.

In her excellent study of the rhetoric of the temperance movement, *Well-Tempered Women: Nineteenth-Century Temperance Rhetoric,* Carole Mattingly identifies a number of attributes of the movement that help explain why Belle Kearney and southern women generally would find the cause of temperance more congenial to their conservative traditional backgrounds than, say, the cause of suffrage. The pattern of development for many southern women activists was, first, involvement in church-affiliated foreign and home missions, notably Methodist Home Missions, and then work in temperance and other women's associations. This pattern is amply discussed and documented by historian Jean Freidman in her study of women in the nineteenth-century evangelical South and by Anne Firor Scott in *Natural Allies: Women's Associations in American History,* which gives a richly detailed account of women's voluntary associations, showing that reform agendas often began with church missions and grew into causes around which women organized themselves to effect public policy. In organizing to achieve some public good, women found a venue for their intellectual energy as well as a training ground for their entry into wider participation in public affairs. They also came to face more directly and politically the constraints of a male-dominated public arena and to organize for women's rights. In the South a commitment to woman's suffrage almost always developed by way of activity in church, then in temperance work, and then the more radical causes of suffrage or race justice, exactly the progression that Kearney exemplifies.

Such women were more often political pragmatists, however, than radicals. In fact, as Marjorie Wheeler so well documents in her study of the southern woman's suffrage movement, *New Women of the New South,* many white women maintained deep reservations about full black equality even as they worked ardently for female enfranchisement. Indeed, as Glenda Elizabeth Gilmore writes in *Gender and Jim Crow,* the issue of race dominated the North Carolina campaign to ratify the Nineteenth Amendment and the subsequent registration of women voters (203). In the development of the Women's Christian Temperance Union, there was ample allowance for southern organizations to maintain strict racial segregation through the separate departments of "Southern Work" and "Work among Colored People." Although some cultural historians today condemn such mixed progressivism as benighted or as timid temporizing, the fact is that social movements comprise a whole spectrum of belief and behavior, then as now. As we have seen, voices from the South had many reasons for seeking conciliation rather than confrontation. Ida B. Wells's famous quarrel with Frances Willard about the timidity of the WCTU in opposing lynching is an exception. Better known is the contrast between Booker T. Washington and W. E. B. DuBois, with the southerner Washington arguing that postbellum black education should consist in "practical knowledge" that built upon the slavery past, rather than aiming for intellectual knowledge that, in his view, would less well serve most African Americans of his time.

What approach best leads to an understanding of the beliefs and actions of one hundred years ago? A presentist judgment that their conciliatory language makes them "complicit in their own oppression" strikes me as too glib a dismissal. That the conception of self and the presentation of self that are embodied in so many earlier life writings of southern women are marked deeply by affiliation with family and a society whose values today one rejects is more a subject for inquiry and understanding than condescension. The conclusion that Mattingly reaches about temperance women strikes me as ethically rigorous and humane: "They were strong sensible women who recognized the real circumstances of their existence and strove, pragmatically, to improve life for themselves and others" (1). In consciously employing traditional definitions of femininity in the ways they spoke and dressed and even decorated their public meeting facilities, they served their cause. "Newspaper accounts reveal a generally more positive coverage for temperance women than for other woman's rights activists, reflecting the conciliatory and complex rhetorical approach taken by temperance women" (120). Mattingly persuasively argues that their temperate rhetoric was more deliberate strategy than timid masking.

In an essay on Booker T. Washington's 1901 autobiography *Up from Slavery* and Kearney's *A Slaveholder's Daughter,* William Andrews considers both texts as attempts "to articulate through their self-portraits a liberating standard for black manhood and white womanhood in their long-standing struggle with the white southern patriarchy." He reads both writers as seeking "negotiation, not confrontation," and as presenting themselves as "reformers *within* the South." But in so identifying themselves, he argues, they had to "affirm their southern reverence for honor, while finding a way to discount certain patriarchal traditions that would deny them an honored status in the South." He charges that the failure of both writers to forcefully oppose the racist white patriarchy of their day undercut their efforts at reform. In the effort to avoid alienating the powerful white fathers, they were effectively co-opted by them, he writes. "They want to reform the patriarchal order, while appealing to the patriarchy for sanction to do so" (86–91). I would offer a different reading of Kearney's situation and her narrative.

Kearney was committed to an ideology of women's civic rights, but she was not so much an ideologue or theorist as a politician who kept her eye steadily on her goal: winning full voting rights for women, as well as achieving a full slate of other reforms that she thought could be made possible by the ballot. Her political strategy was validated in her election in 1923 as the first woman to serve in the Mississippi Senate. A generation after the publication of *Slaveholder's Daughter,* Kearney was still working for reform, not radical change. Joanne Hawks and Mary Carolyn Ellis observe that women in southern legislatures in the 1920s "appeared to be content with the political structure that existed in the South—the one-party, white-dominated politics of the day. They focused primarily on need for improvements in the social sphere" (82). Reading today Kearney's position on African American suffrage and political participation in 1900, the heyday of Jim Crow in the South, one encounters views that we clearly mark as white supremacist. Perhaps it should come as no surprise that most of the white southern suffragists held such views, basing their strongest case for woman's suffrage on the injustice of black men's having the vote, with so much less education and potential civic engagement than white women. Indeed, they argued that only by giving women the vote could the "tainted" voting practice of blacks be effectively negated in the South. Wheeler's study of the leaders of the woman suffrage movement in the southern states gives a detailed history of these political strategies, which were formulated by northern as well as southern voting rights strategists.

There is another side to Kearney's unrepudiated affiliation with her traditionalist society. It is true that she wanted to win the favor of her audience, which certainly includes white patriarchs, though doubtless many more female than male readers. She wanted to win support for the causes she supported. She was also ambitious for a successful career as a reformer and as an admired professional lecturer. All these aims disposed her toward appealing to, rather than chastising, her readers. But even more at issue is her need as both Belle Kearney behind the text and Belle the character within the text to compose some thread of psychological coherence. It is necessary, for example, for her to justify her character and her motives as consonant with what she regards as the truest and deepest values inculcated in her by her family, especially her father. These values may have been falsified or deformed by "palsied custom" in the larger society, and even threatened within the family by conditions of poverty or misplaced pride, but the slaveholder's daughter had formed her character upon precepts learned in the father's house. Through modulations of tone and alternations between dramatic scenes and essayistic passages, however, what Kearney communicates is her ambivalence toward the contradictions in her family (and in the South) that she is unable to reconcile. Nonetheless, her insight into the experience of double consciousness comes across as seasoned and mature, rather than naive, as she registers and claims the complexity of the culture. She writes:

> Mother and father had reared me in a very liberal atmosphere concerning the intellectual and political status of women, for they were both advocates of woman suffrage; father was particularly ardent. He had often said that it filled him with humiliation to think that his wife and daughter were not his equals before the law. . . . Notwithstanding father's broad-minded position in the earlier days it did not occur to him that *his* daughter might desire to enter the field of active modern workers. That was "the pinch"; but since my way had been fought into public school teaching he had never opposed my progressive views nor interfered with my undertakings. By grad-

ual stages he became alive to every issue in which my interest was involved and did all in his power to further my projects. (108–9)

Daughter of a slaveholder, but an ardent supporter of equal rights (for white women) and for women's freedom of thought and expression, Belle Kearney lived the conflicts that so characterized the nineteenth-century South. Her sense of honor, worth, and self-respect was bound up with the father and the homeland, and to deny the bonds was to betray her own identity. Furthermore, as she well understood, it was politically advantageous to portray (or reflect) her embodiment of a true woman—or southern lady—so as to show that it was not in conflict with her commitments to social activism. In this regard, we see that the character-self in the text is very much influenced by the present consciousness of the author and, perhaps to a lesser degree, also by the audience she assumes she is addressing. But it is important not to infer that Kearney's effort to connect her reform ideology with the seemingly disparate values that she shares with her traditionalist family and southern society is a dissembling strategy.

Kearney's example prompts reconsideration of the nature of identity formation, memory, and the self-narration that is autobiography. In his discussion of the "relational self," Paul John Eakin calls upon the ideas of the psychologist John Shotter to describe how an individual is constrained to experience reality "very largely as it is constituted for us by the *already established* ways in which we *must* talk in our attempts to *account* for ourselves" (*How Our Lives* 62). An "I" subject is inescapably an amalgam of communal fields of social and linguistic acculturation, which is not to say that an individual has no autonomy but to remind one of the constraints upon that autonomy. As we will see in the next chapter, Helen Keller, deaf and blind from early childhood, was racked by the uncertainty of where the words—and thoughts—her teacher Annie Sullivan had given her ended and where the Helen-self began. As psychologist Mark Freeman observes in *Rewriting the Self: History, Memory, Narrative*, "In true poststructuralist fashion . . . Helen herself had raised the possibility that both the outer and the inner world were in some sense artifacts of words, of language" (225).

Furthermore, the "I" subject is continuously involved in rewriting the self-narrative, having not only new experience to integrate into one's selfhood but new perspectives that call for reinterpretation of one's life story. There is no access to memory except through one's present consciousness. Belle Kearney, a leader in temperance and suffrage movements, successful lecturer who has travelled far from her rural Mississippi home—activist "New Woman" in most respects—sits at her writing desk composing a narrative that includes a childhood oppressed with duties to serve her parents and brothers, a young adulthood repressed by constraining poverty and womanhood ideology, and a "belledom" of "round-dancing," and "card playing." How are these and the other experiences of her past to be interpreted so as to present a coherent narrative that eventuates in this woman at the desk? Freeman offers an interesting observation regarding the inevitable "rewriting" of the self. If one is composing a narrative reflecting the present self, that subject whose values, beliefs, worldview, and judgments have altered over time, whose *interpretations* of past events have changed, then it is "ipso facto the case that this cannot possibly be accomplished by recounting one's previous experience 'as it was.' . . . As a matter of course, it is a going-beyond what was, an attempt to situate the experience of the past in a comprehensive interpretive context, such that their interrelationship is made evident" (30).

Finally, not to be overlooked in considering the composition of autobiography are the demands made by the conventions of discourse, particularly written discourse, as Michel Foucault insists. The autobiographical self is a literary figure, composed of memory material to be sure, but finally artifice—and artifice that borrows greatly from a storehouse of precedent. As it often does, what comes to my mind is Eudora Welty's succinct statement of our place in the human chain—"We start from scratch, and words don't; which is the thing that matters—matters over and over again."[6] What Kearney shows us in full light is the process whereby the subject "I" partakes of the culture and then reproduces it. This point about the intersubjectivity and the intertextuality that are touchstones of lives and life narratives has been especially well stated by Tzvetan Todorov in his commentary on the construction of the self cited in Chapter 1. "The membrane that separates the self from others, the inside from the outside, is not airtight," he writes. From our youngest age we internalize the others around us, and "their images begin to be part of us" (122). As we will next see, the inseparability of the experience of language and the composition of self is strikingly illustrated in the life narrative of Helen Keller.

3

A Distanced Southern Girlhood

HELEN KELLER AND ANNE WALTER FEARN

The texts by Susan Dabney Smedes, Anna Julia Cooper, Belle Kearney, and others discussed in the preceding chapter are all distinguished by having subjects whose identity as southern women is pointedly expressed not only in the titles of their books but in the focus upon social attitudes and practices they explicitly associate with the South. In many respects, they explain, or imply, motives for writing about themselves that are located in memorialization, in condemnation of injustice, or in progressive reforms that are specifically attached to the region—or, in Kearney's case, some combination of these. They address audiences they assume to be wary, if not resistant, to female interventions in the public sphere, and they adopt a voice, even when advancing an impassioned argument, of deference, reasonableness, and modesty—a lady's voice. Belle Kearney, the determined and indefatigable activist, disclaims any desire for self-aggrandizement, portraying herself, at least overtly, as a dutiful daughter of God, her family, the South, and the nation, formed and guided by all these. The selfhood she composes in *A Slaveholder's Daughter* is that of a woman dedicated to the service of others.

Two quite different autobiographers, Helen Keller and Anne Walter Fearn, are instructive about other ways in which southern women during this period developed self narratives that decenter the self, composing stories of agency and courage but still deflecting acceptance and recognition of their personal power. Their life stories lead in the direction of the memoir, accounts of people and places that have arrested their attention and compose their memory. This is true even of Keller's later narrative, the more self-contemplative *Midstream,* which depicts an autonomous narrator who is nonetheless very much intertwined with the lives of others. The titles are telling, departing as they do from the third-person indirection of the books considered in Chapter 2. Helen Keller's *The Story of My Life* (1903) and *Midstream: My Later Life* (1929) and Anne Walter Fearn's *My Days of Strength* (1939) recount lives of women who, from an early age, undertook professional careers that set them worlds apart from most other southern women of their time. Both women depict themselves as fortuitously and almost accidentally discovering a sense of life direction—Keller being rescued from her blind-deaf isolation by teacher Annie Sullivan and Fearn by unexpectedly meeting a female physician whose example was a galvanizing model. For both women the South meant childhood and home place, but the impact of the region on their lives, though formative in significant ways, was finally tangential for them as adults. It is particularly interesting to see how often they invoke typical, even stereotypical literary images of the South to characterize their own experience of place and custom. Perhaps the most salient characteristic of these texts is the self-portrait they project of women who, as a matter of fact, understand and accept their equal needs for autonomy and connectedness. Elizabeth Fox-Genovese has observed that southern women have "wrestled with the claims of individualism and community for their self-representations, but they have not normally seen these claims as incompatible" ("Between Individualism" 36). The observation may somewhat describe Kearney's position, insisting as she does that she is equally serving self and community through her progressive reforms, but Keller's and Fearn's claims are different. Their defense of autonomy—or self-possession—is not at all apologetic or rationalized by careers that promise some betterment of the world, though they do pursue such careers. They rather take their separateness as a psychological (and for Keller, physical) inevitability, although they desire and value personal attachments. And Keller, with her extraordinary handicaps, engages deeply the broad existential question of self's essence and the permeability of boundaries between self and other—anticipating Tzvetan Todorov in questioning how much of the self is unoriginal, indebted to and even indistinguishable from other selves, who reflect and confirm one's conscious existence.[1]

Indeed, among all the autobiographies considered in this study, the most extreme case of blurring between the self and the social surround is represented in Helen Keller's *The Story of My Life*, first published as a series of magazine articles in *Ladies Home Journal* in 1902, when she was only twenty-two years old, and as a book in 1903 by Doubleday, Doran.[2] At this young age Keller became a national celebrity, esteemed for her remarkable acquisition of language after an illness that had left her without sight or hearing from the age of nineteen months. Although Keller's southern background seems to have played little part in the long career of writing and lecturing that occupied her until her death in 1968, it does appear in telling ways in the early autobiography. There were many other books to follow, including the second volume of autobiography, *Midstream* (1929), as well as early works like *The World I Live In* (1908) and the later *Teacher: Annie Sullivan Macy* (1955), which give an account of her relationship to the woman who figured as the central presence in her life. But *The Story of My Life* is of particular interest here for what it suggests about the way she perceived "southernness" as a young woman growing up during the final decades of the nineteenth century in Tuscumbia, Alabama. These were years in which her communication with others was limited for a time to bodily sensation and physical interactions with her family, and then later to linguistic formulations that principally came to her filtered through the fingers of Annie Sullivan.

Keller's dramatic experience of language, her realization that "w-a-t-e-r" spelled into the palm of her hand signified a world beyond herself, one she could call up, name and control with movements upon hands, triggered a miraculous birth of consciousness. Her discovery of the symbolic power of human language to bestow reflexive consciousness has inspired endless rumination and "mind experiments" among writers from Mark Twain to Walker Percy about the self and its dependencies and boundaries. For Percy, the ecstatic moment of Keller's discovery of symbolic language embodies the creation moment of human consciousness, the "breakthrough from the good responding animal which behaviorists study so successfully to the strange name-giving and sentence-uttering creature who begins by naming shoes and ships and sealing wax, and later tells jokes, curses, reads the paper . . . or becomes a Hegel and composes an entire system of philosophy" (35). Percy's emphasis in "The Delta Factor" falls mainly upon the unique nature of the individual, about whom "science cannot utter a single word," but Keller in her autobiographical texts is greatly more troubled by the seeming impossibility of individuality, or "originality." Even in his discussions of the "interpersonal process" essential to symbolic language (189–214), Percy tends to focus upon the gap between the "second person" who provides the stimulus and audience for one's words. But Keller's concerns, especially in *The Story of My Life,* are for the inescapable conjunction of the second person and the self. For her, the relational life, not the separate life, defined the self who communicates with others. Her questionings, like her life itself, take a quite different approach to the notion of an autonomous or individualist selfhood. Mark Freeman offers an instructive discussion in *Rewriting the Self* of the many ways in which Keller's story elucidates the symbolic power of language, the relationality of language, and the problematical constructions of originality and individual identity (50–80).

Helen Keller was born in 1880 in a little town in northern Alabama, the daughter of a former captain in the Confederate Army, as she writes in the opening chapter, and of a mother twenty years younger than he—a beautiful, educated woman described by Keller's biographer Dorothy Hermann as a "Memphis belle," though not a "dyed-in-the-wool Southerner" like her husband (6). When Keller comes to describe her family and home in *The Story of My Life,* she includes details of the early years when body language was her only mode of communication. Of course, her fluent English narrating those years issues from the education and perspective of the Radcliffe college student that she was at the time of composition. What we read, then, in these early chapters is a narrative that was *available* in language only later to the author—Keller was nearly seven years old when Anne Sullivan arrived in Tuscumbia to begin her language instruction.

Keller is circumspect in her claim of accurate remembrance, but she nonetheless writes a fairly vivid account of episodes involving family and servants in the house and around the farm, even of the time before she acquired language. A few years later in *The World I Live In,* however, she would write of the empty consciousness that marked this period.

> Before my teacher came to me, I did not know that I am. I lived in a world that was a no-world. I cannot hope to describe adequately that unconscious, yet conscious time of nothingness. I did not know that I knew aught, or that I lived or acted or desired. I had neither will nor intellect. I was carried along to objects and acts by a certain blind natural impetus. . . . I can remember all this not because I knew that it was so, but because I have tactual memory. . . . My inner life, then, was a blank without past, present or future, without hope or anticipation, without wonder or joy or faith. (113–14)

Over forty years after Annie Sullivan's arrival in her life, Keller would write in *Midstream* that she had "no vivid recollection" of her mother before her education began (216), an assertion that may be read as waning memory or, more reasonably, as an indication of how much Keller relied upon information formulated for her by others, both persons and books, for the 1902 text. She in fact does signal her anxiety about authenticity in the opening lines of *Story,* though she begins by suggesting that it is the trespassing upon sacred childhood rather than failing to possess original memory that most concerns her: "It is with a kind of fear that I begin to write the history of my life. I have, as it were, a superstitious hesitation in lifting the veil that clings about my childhood like a golden mist." But then she states her greater concern: "The task of writing an autobiography is a difficult one. When I try to classify my earliest impressions, I find that fact and fancy look alike across the years that link the past with the present" (3). Having issued the disclaimer, she goes forward, as all autobiographers do, to construct a self history that explains the life experience of the composing author—here, a blind and deaf young woman in college in Massachusetts in the late 1880s writing of how her life has been transformed from that of an afflicted child in Alabama into a budding national celebrity.

The two most characterizing features of the southern home Keller describes in *The Story of My Life* are the sensuous fertility of the place and the evidence, even to the blind and deaf Helen, of a racial color line. She reports in several poetic, even ecstatic, paragraphs a pastoral scene of fragrant roses, honeysuckles, "drooping jessamine, and some rare sweet flowers called butterfly lilies, because their fragile petals resemble butterflies' wings" (5). The names of flowers obviously come from the later "language world" that Annie Sullivan introduces. Linked to these floral images are recurrent recollections of her mother, to whose "loving wisdom," Keller writes, she owes "all that was bright and good in my long night" (9). Her elementary studies—in reading, geography, and history with Sullivan—she remembers most fondly for their associations with the aromatic outdoors: "All my early lessons have in them the breadth of the woods—the fine, resinous odour of pine needles, blended with the perfume of wild grapes" (34). The southern homeland is a balmy, maternal, feminized, and nurturing habitat—"Never have I found in the greenhouses of the North such heart-satisfying roses as the climbing roses of my southern home" (5). What Keller does find in the North, however, is intellectual experience and an anxiety or sense of risk that comes with the unfamiliar. In 1888 she travels with Sullivan to Boston to visit the Perkins Institution for the Blind and then to vacation on Cape Cod, where she discovers the ocean. Describing herself as an "inland" child, she is unaware of the vastness of the ocean and unprepared for the terror of being swept off her feet by billowing waves. Whereas the South is a region of great physical beauty, materiality, and sustenance for a youthful, bodily self, the North is the region of mind. (One finds here in Keller's characterization of the regions the same pattern of gendering of North and South that Nina Silber identifies in the late nineteenth-century texts that she discusses in *Romance of Reunion*.) Returning to Alabama in 1888, Keller later writes that she was aware that "the barren places between my mind and the minds of others [had] blossomed like the rose" (50). Her simile equates the pleasures of mind with those sweet fragrances so pleasing at home and carries the point that intellectuality and communication are as available to her as her acute sense of smell.

The chapters of *The Story of My Life* recounting the early years also include a provocative description of young Helen's caretaker Martha Washington, a black child several years older. At no time does Keller signal an awareness that the African American child bears a famous name. She introduces her simply as "a little coloured girl," "a constant companion" who understood her signs. "I seldom had any difficulty in making her do just as I wished. It pleased me to domineer over her, and she generally submitted to my tyranny rather than risk a hand-to-hand encounter" (11). A few pages later she tells a story of familiar childish mischief—cutting off hair—but in language and visual imagery that call to mind the racial stereotypes so frequently encountered in domestic novels, as well as in the popular media of the day. "Two little children were seated on the veranda steps one hot July afternoon. One was black as ebony, with little bunches of fuzzy hair tied with shoestrings sticking out all over her head like corkscrews. The other was white, with long, golden curls. One child was six years old, the other two or three years older. The younger child was blind—that was I—and the other was Martha Washington" (12).

It would be misleading to say that the nineteen-year-old Helen Keller who wrote these lines had thought deeply about race relations in the South or had consciously formed any sort of philosophy of societal organization. She was a college student in an English class, writing the required themes, when, as she relates in *Midstream,* she was visited by William Alexander of the *Ladies Home Journal* and informed that "Mr. Bok wished to publish *The Story of My Life* in monthly installments" (4–5). She was inexperienced and uncertain about her ability to carry off such a project, but the promised $3,000 was "magic," and she was assured that the themes she had already written would together make up half a book. She writes of the frenzied effort to furnish the copy on deadline and of the editing assistance she needed and got from professors at Radcliffe and editors of the magazine. She does not mention Annie Sullivan, who was always at her side during these years, nor does she say anything of the *Ladies Home Journal* audience that she was writing for. But all of these influences were in play as she composed the autobiography. I am reminded here of Richard Brodhead's observation in his discussion of the culture of letters in the nineteenth century that "writing has no life separate from the particularized mechanisms that bring it to public life" (5). Clearly, what brings this text to life is a multiplicity of intentions, some rather random circumstances of motive and choice of content, and a bevy of consulting editors. Placing the later text written when Keller was in her forties alongside this teenage one reveals an expected maturing of style and thought; the later text is quite different from the stock, formulaic material of *The Story of My Life.* Interestingly, *Midstream* does repeat and even enlarge upon the imagery depicting the South as sensuous and feminized, but Keller wholly supplants her casual, patronizing characterization of Martha Washington with explicit assertions of her commitment to social and economic justice.

By 1929 Keller had come to be known as an outspoken, even radical advocate for a great range of social reforms, not only support of programs for the disabled, with which she was most identified, but as a defender of racial equality, organized labor, access to birth control information, and even the Russian Revolution. Biographer Dorothy Hermann quotes a testimonial by W. E. B. Dubois in 1931 in which he commends Keller's advocacy for racial justice: "Helen Keller was in her own state, Alabama, being feted and made much of by her fellow citizens. And yet courageously and frankly she spoke against the iniquity and foolishness of the color line. It cost her something to speak. They wanted her to retract, but she sat serene in the consciousness of the truth she had uttered" (363). The reaction of Keller's family and many fellow southerners to her repeated defenses of her "crusades," such as the instance Dubois refers to, was often to attribute them to the influence of her "northern" teacher or to other "outsider" influences. Joseph P. Lash notes that her endorsement of the National Association for the Advancement of Colored People (NAACP) that appeared in the *Crisis* was reprinted in the *Selma Journal,* paid for by an anonymous "Alabamian" intent on exposing her perfidy. "The people who did such wonderful work in training Miss Keller must have belonged to the old Abolition Gang for they seemed to have thoroughly poisoned her mind against her own people" (qtd. in Lash 454). She makes clear in *Midstream* that she was aware of the likelihood of censure and of the readiness of her admirers to hold others responsible for views they found objectionable. "I have kept silence on issues that interested me deeply," she writes, "through the fear that others would be blamed for my opinions" (175).

Although Keller in middle age had clearly developed a more autonomous self than had the author of *The Story of My Life,* the crux of where self ends and the influencing other begins would prove to be a lifelong concern for her and one of the provocative biographical issues that so intrigued the general public. A traumatic incident related in the book encapsulates a problem, especially acute for her during her student years, that she feared would compromise all her striving to establish an original (or autonomous) voice in her writings. When she was eleven, she wrote a story, "The Frost King," which she presented as a gift to the director of the Perkins Institute for the Blind, Michael Anagnos. He was so pleased at the demonstration of Helen's giftedness that he published it in the alumni magazine and authorized reprints elsewhere.[3] When it came to light that the story replicated in plot and language a children's story by Margaret T. Canby, "The Frost Fairies," a messy and lengthy scandal ensued, eventuating in charges of deliberate plagiarism attributed mainly to Annie Sullivan, as well as Helen, who was thought less culpable. Together and individually they were interrogated in an official hearing by a panel of Perkins administrators, and in a vote of four to four, Helen was found innocent after Anagnos broke the tie in her favor. "The Frost King" episode left a permanent scar, a fear that she could never be sure that what she thought and wrote came from her own head. Clearly, she had heard Canby's story and had retained the details, but had almost certainly forgotten their origin and so had employed them as her own in a story she believed she had composed. In Lash's and Hermann's summaries of the claims and counter claims in the case, the charges seem finally to have had as much to do with attacks upon Sullivan as upon Helen. Hermann concludes that Sullivan had in fact read the story to her student but, when questioned, had lied about doing so. What Helen was left with was the uncertainty that "memory" could be relied upon to separate "fact from fancy."

When Keller published *The Story of My Life,* there were skeptics, such as the writer for *The Nation* who sharply questioned whether she might legitimately be said to be the author—or the authority—of the book. Her knowledge was all "hearsay knowledge." Even her sensations were "for the most part vicarious." The critic would have her come to know that "it is better to be one's self, however limited and afflicted, than the best imitation of somebody else that could be achieved" (qtd. in Hermann 136). Remarkably, the same charge was leveled—in almost the same words—by Judith Shulevitz in a 20 April 2003 column in the *New York Times Book Review.* Reading a recent edition of *A Story of My Life* edited by Roger Shattuck, she questions Keller's putting "what she has been told on the same epistemological plane as what she has learned through direct observation." Shulevitz wants, rather, to hear from the "real" Helen Keller. "What she knew of her own observation is exactly what we want to know from her." With no implied irony, she continues, " We want to locate the boundaries between what was real to her and what she was forced to imagine" (31).

Clearly, the language of Keller's text is often stilted and bookish, and it draws heavily in style and vocabulary upon the reading that formed so much of Keller's understanding of the world. Unarguably, it also owes a debt to her teacher. How much of the content, one asks, owes to Annie Sullivan's perceptions, judgments, and language? Who is the "real self" composing this life story? Helen made her book of the language she appropriated from others, but what autobiographer does not? "We start from scratch," we are reminded in Eudora Welty's aphorism, "and words don't." Even Helen's portrait of the Alabama of her own first-hand tactile experience draws upon familiar stereotypes of a South racialized and feminized (fertile, maternal, and visceral as opposed to intellectual). In her early years in Tuscumbia, Annie Sullivan often criticized the "untidiness" and "shiftlessness" of southern housekeeping—and of southerners generally (Hermann 61)—but little of this regional characterization or disdain shows up in Keller's account, which takes a more sentimental and poetic direction.

What one comes finally to recognize, and appreciate, in this autobiographer's story is the vast network of influence that so produces and constrains what we might call individualistic agency. Contemplating ideas that would be extensively elaborated by many later theorists, Keller expresses in unforgettable language the necessity of social interrelationship to the attainment of consciousness. She writes in *The World I Live In:* "When I learned the meaning of 'I' and 'me' and found that I was something, I began to think. Then consciousness first existed for me" (117). Toward the end of the book she returns to the origins of consciousness in her discussion of dreams. Here she writes of her "bodily sensations," which, though extremely acute, could not impart self-awareness. "They had little relation to each other, to me, or to the experience of others." Again, she concludes that the originary moment of self-empowerment is the realization that "I" can be formed and communicated in language's symbols. "Idea—that which gives identity and continuity to experience—came into my sleeping and waking existence at the same moment with the awakening of self-consciousness" (159). Beholding the other brings consciousness of self, she says, which inevitably leads back to one's searching for images of one's own emotions and sensations reflected in the other, and thus the hermeneutical circle is established.

The Helen Keller who wrote a second volume of autobiography in 1929 was a woman who had grown far from her southern roots during the years that marked her transformation into one of the most famous women of her time. She was a woman who had overcome severe, socially isolating affliction, a woman who was invited to visit Theodore Roosevelt in the White House, to appear on lecture platforms in cities and hamlets across the continent—a celebrity so large as to command invitations or visits from, by her own and others' account, virtually every other famous person alive. When she composed *Midstream,* she was about the age of Belle Kearney at the time she wrote *A Slaveholder's Daughter,* and her story resembles that of Kearney's in her emphasis upon her work and the travel associated with the work. What is unique to Keller is that, although she was tireless in promoting public acceptance and support for the blind, the appeals were part of the public performance of herself that was the way she made a living for her, Annie Sullivan, and other dependents. She says at one point that "people are not interested in what I think of things outside myself" (329).

Keller was a public oddity, a spectacle who went to Hollywood and played herself in a film about her life. From 1920 to 1924 she even performed on the vaudeville circuit. Annie Sullivan would first describe her early years and her education, and then Keller would come on stage, make a brief speech, which was articulate but marked by unnatural rhythm and pitch, and then answer questions. "Can you tell the time of day without a watch? Have you ever thought of getting married? Have you ever used a Ouija board? Do you think business is looking up? . . . Do you believe in ghosts? . . . Do you dream?" (*Midstream* 214). Her commodifiable "talent" was self-presentation, one that displayed to her audiences her mastery of language, a victory over bestial sensation and confirmation of the higher human capacity for sentient selfhood.

For Keller, gender, race, and regionality played a lesser part in her public identity than did "blind-deaf person who speaks, reads and writes." But the fact that she was a beautiful woman, especially as a young adult, with the gracious manners and expressions of a Victorian lady obviously enhanced her platform appeal. To correct a bulging eye, she had had glass eyes surgically implanted, a feature that many did not detect and regarded instead as unusually expressive eyes. Her own sense of her body image is quite negative, at least as she describes herself in the filmmaking episode. "Awkward and big," she writes, not like the graceful, "sylph-like" actresses. "I could not, like Ariel, 'do by spiriting gently'" (*Midstream* 187). But it was her manifest intelligence and use of language, not her body, that garnered attention, as she well understood.

Whenever she tired of performing this intellectual persona of Helen Keller, her thoughts typically turned to the South, or to the outdoors that she associated with her childhood home. Needing confirmation that "mankind is real flesh," that she was not a "shadow walking in a shadowy world," she sought retreat from the worrying world, from her work and obligations, by going to the little garden outside her home in New York. It is the resinous evergreens that comfort her, with their scent so like the pines she associates with Alabama: "As I walk round and round the green circle, rain-wet winds . . . send a spray of whispers thorough my mind—'Home!' 'South-land!' 'Mother,' 'Father' . . . The warm winds of Alabama flit between me and the years." Keller's reverie is of "coming home . . . to hide myself from work and cares behind the arras of your gay laughter!" (308). For her, the South is figured as a place of carefree youth and sweet sensations, a nurturing haven.

A large part of Keller's metaphor-made South is her mother, whom she describes admiringly, sometimes adoringly, but with intimations of disappointment and regret. She says of Kate Keller that she "never talked about herself," was "veiled" and "sensitive to the point of pain." By temperament she was "not domestic," Helen writes, but she applied herself to the management of a large demanding household and farm enterprise, including lard making. Helen notes that Annie Sullivan "often wondered how such a sensitive, high-strung woman could endure this sort of work; but my mother never complained" (219). She was an "omnivorous reader" and an "avid gardener," whose skill was particularly evidenced in her beautiful roses, flowers that powerfully informed Helen's early sensory experience and would later power her figurative vocabulary. But *Midstream* also hints of a complex, if not troubled, intimacy between daughter and mother.

Helen Keller early on, it seems, came to accept that her disabling illness was the central event in her mother's life. "After that," she writes, "life was never the same for her. It was as if a white winter had swept over the June of her youth; I know, although she never said it, that she suffered more through me than through her other children" (*Midstream* 127). The need to relieve her mother's pain by successfully making as normal a life for herself as possible was surely intense. Overcoming the blindness and deafness as a vindication of her mother's suffering clearly motivated Helen throughout her mother's life—she died when Keller was thirty-one. What Keller does not discuss but instead glosses over is the breach that, predictably, accompanied the education, travel, and celebrity that denoted success. Her idealized affiliation with her mother, complicated by her sense of obligation to remedy the depressive grief, seems to hold her in thrall to the relationship. She never married, and thus her primary family relations, with all the usual complicating emotions connected with family, were centered upon her siblings and her mother. For all her celebration of her fondness for family, which Keller associated with fragrant images and balmy winds, there is an undercurrent of sadness and tragedy.

One final point about Keller's relation to the South should be made. Despite her desire to please and honor her mother, she does not betray her public defense of social justice, even when her mother challenges those views. She records her admiration for her mother's knowledge and curiosity about the world, describing her as having "a Southerner's interest in politics"; she could "intelligently, brilliantly" discuss current events. Nonetheless, Helen's perspective upon these events had taken a decidedly different turn from her mother's over the years. Looking back, the daughter analyzes the divergence in extremely neutral terms, clearly trying to put the best possible light on exchanges that had surely been strained political quarrels. "After my mind took a radical turn she could never get over the feeling that we had drifted apart. It grieves me that I should have added to the sadness that weighed upon her, but I have the consolation of remembering that no differences could take away from us the delight of talking together" (220). For the author of *Midstream,* it was the idealized fragrant South of her mother's roses that she preferred to call up in her text. Olfactory sensation she was surer of getting right than she was an understanding of her mother.

When one asks after reading this midlife narrative where the points of emphasis and tension are, how the rhetoric is deployed and to what purpose, and what her assumptions are about truth telling, one begins to realize the overall obliquity of the text. Keller tells the truth but tells it slant in a mélange of genres that includes narrative, poetic reverie, Thoreauvian nature writing, impressionistic biographical profiles, literary commentary, short philosophical essays, a statement of her credo, a tribute to her mother, and, in the concluding chapter, a celebration of Annie Sullivan's presence in her life. What is especially remarkable, however, is Keller's pondering focus upon the elusiveness of selfhood and her insight that writing autobiography magnifies for the author the contingency and instability of identity.

She considers, for example, the inadequacy of narrative details to signify the "real self." Claiming not to have any gripping record to relate—no "great adventures," "thrilling romances," or "extraordinary successes," she has only "impressions and feelings" to offer in an autobiography (44–45). "But, perhaps," she writes, "our sensations and emotions are what are most worth relating, since they are our real selves." Of course, sensations and emotions must be communicated in words—metaphors of the self, to use James Olney's phrase—and the multiformed medley that Keller composes is clearly aimed at supplying as wide array of metaphors as she can imagine. Still, she is always aware of the gap between feeling and word, a distance that is further exacerbated by narrative's requirements to affix experience in a place and time that has already changed. How does one recover and write truthfully of a "truth" that has evaporated? Her statement of the autobiographer's dilemma is profound:

Time invariably disintegrates the substance of most experiences and reduces them to intellectual abstractions. Many of the poignant details elude any attempt to restate them. It is not merely the difficulty of recapturing emotions, it is almost equally difficult to define attitudes, or effects upon others. They are, as it were, in solution, or if they do crystallize, they appear different to the persons concerned. It seems to me, it is impossible to analyze honestly the subtle motives of those who have influenced our lives, because we cannot complete the creative process with the freshness of the situation clinging to it. (*Midstream* 148)

Keller's solution to the impossibility of writing one's life story, which she comes fully to understand in the process of her attempt, is to accept metaphor as offering the best possibility for an accurate image of the self. To make emotion as immediate as the odor of a rose is, of course, the work of the poet—and it is finally her ambition for poetic, imagistic truth that animates the text. "As I recall the Wrenthan [Massachusetts] years, they appear to my imagination surrounded by an aura of feeling. "Words, incidents, acts, stir in my memory, awakening complicated emotions, and many strings vibrate with joy and pain." She will depend upon the images to mirror truth. "I shall not try to resolve those experiences into their elements" (148), she concludes.

In addition to the limits of words, Keller is also mindful of the limitlessness of selves that makes one's presentation of a life story always partial, incomplete. "We are all complex. I wish I were made of just one self . . . which would move graciously through my autobiography." But like Walt Whitman, she declares herself to be a "multitude of egos," a person she cannot fathom. "I ask myself questions that I cannot answer" (333). And then there are also limits upon the perspicacity and sensitivity of the perceiving self, a point she makes with the example of her youthful ignorance, believing as she once did that "we were all masters of our fate." She had forgotten, she says, that "whatever character I possessed was developed in an atmosphere suitable to it. I was like the princess who lived in a palace all composed of mirrors, and who beheld only the reflection of her own beauty" (156–57).

Keller's wisdom and humility about the ineffable nature of selfhood—and her wariness about the possibility of saying truthfully that one can know or even possess oneself—are deeply situated in her disability. From at least as early as "The Frost King" embarrassment, she was keenly conscious –and chary—of the commingling of the outside world communicated to her through tactile sensation and books, especially books, and her own memories and thoughts. "I prefer to put quotation marks at the beginning and the end of my book and leave it to those who have contributed to its interest or charm or beauty to take what is theirs and accept my gratitude for the help they have been to me. I know I am not original in either content or form" (328).

Her disclaimer is not just a ladylike display of modesty; she understands that the payment due for her release from isolation into society is a lifetime obligation of acknowledging her connectedness and dependence—of acknowledging that she is a "relational self." The figure who most aptly embodies the "other" who must be claimed as part of oneself is, of course, Annie Sullivan, and it is with a tribute to her that Keller concludes the autobiography. Keller is quite alive to the paradoxes that emerge as she describes an independence and agency that she owes to Sullivan. "She was a delightful companion, entering into all my discoveries with the joy of a fellow explorer . . . explaining what I did not understand. And in those days there was scarcely a thing in the world I did understand." Sullivan had sat beside her through four years of college and with "supple speaking hand" had spelled out the lectures word by word. Keller writes simply, "Slowly, slowly, out of my weakness and helplessness she has built up my life" (344–47). As a metonymic of that external social world that frames and institutes human life, Annie Sullivan is sacralized as the "guardian angel." Only the unreflective and arrogant, Keller suggests, believe they alone construct their lives.

Another autobiographer who assumes her independence and writes such a self into existence, only to reveal that the contours and center of that life are mostly defined through its connections to others, is Anne Walter Fearn in *My Days of Strength*. A slightly older contemporary of Keller's, closer in age to Belle Kearney, Annie Fearn was born in Holly Springs, Mississippi, in 1865, just a month after Lee's surrender at Appomattox Courthouse. She came from a prominent family, having a lawyer father who was in her words the "ruling spirit" of Holly Springs and having grown up in a house known as the "Walter Mansion." By all accounts she was expected to follow the traditional domestic path for such a white southern girl. Instead, she graduated from Women's Medical College of Pennsylvania in 1893 and immediately set off to practice medicine in Soochow [Suzhou], China, and later in Shanghai, where, except for rather extensive travel, she resided for the rest of her life. Married for thirty years to a medical missionary, she pointedly defines her own medical practice as secular, not religious. She had one child, a daughter, Elizabeth, who died in childhood of amoebic dysentery. Over the span of a long life, Fearn was a curious and attentive observer of a foreign culture she came greatly to admire, as well as a dedicated physician who by her count delivered over six thousand babies during her long tenure of service. Witness to nearly a half century of Chinese social history and to the experiences of a life energetically and adventurously pursued, she died in 1939 while visiting a sister in Berkeley, California, just three weeks after the publication of her autobiography. According to an article in the *Memphis Commercial Appeal,* she was en route to her beloved Shanghai.[4]

In *My Days of Strength* Fearn writes quite explicitly from the perspective of her retirement, with a consequent motive and tone not so much interested in winning converts to any reform or even empathetic understanding as in sharing the vivid details of a foreign culture and an exotic life. This is a retrospective narrative that devotes two short opening chapters to the years prior to her leaving for China at the age of twenty-eight. (Although Fearn is scrupulous in registering dates throughout the text, the fact that on the first page she shaves two years off her birth date leads to some later confusions in dating.) From the third chapter, the three-hundred-page text is focused upon the hundreds of episodes that filled Fearn's busy medical practice and her travel in China and throughout the world, fifteen around-the-world trips in all. In a recent anthology of American women's autobiographies, editor Jill Ker Conway includes an excerpt from *My Day of Strength,* noting in the introduction that Fearn's "loving invocation of the sounds, colors, smells, and light of South China" constitutes some of the strongest prose in the book, showing "a sense of place never demonstrated for her Mississippi home" (527). I would say that her sense of home place is quite powerfully communicated through family relationships and cultural mores— less graphic and sensuous, to be sure, but perhaps even more deeply grounded in "place." I am reminded here of Elizabeth Hampsten's comment that the more estranged from place a woman feels, "the more she is apt graphically to inform others of her whereabouts" (226). But there is no gainsaying the preponderance of text devoted to China, which accounted for much of the book's appeal. The wide interest among American readers in Asia and in the state of world affairs generally in 1939, as well as the popularity of writers like the 1938 Nobel Prize winner Pearl Buck, who brought home to America the exotic foreignness of China, all helped bring *My Days of Strength* to critical attention, as did the able promotion of the Harper publishing house.

In her half-page review in the *New York Times Book Review,* Katherine Woods praised the book's engaging story of "an enterprising, public-spirited, indomitable woman who was born to be a Southern belle, scandalized the neighbors by going to medical school, and worked for forty years with unbounded vigor and resolution as a doctor in China" (9). Summarizing some of the memorable episodes in which Fearn describes the more alien customs she encountered, the reviewer concludes with praise of Fearn's dedication in her last years to breaking down cultural barriers among the diverse populations of Shanghai. "She was adding her tolerance and broad understanding to the genius for hospitality that was her natural heritage—she was a Southern belle." Harper's advertisement in the same issue of the *Review* touted the author as "the Southern girl who turned her back on society to risk her life—and save lives. . . . From palace to brothel Dr. Fearn saw all sides of life. Princesses and prostitutes, they all came to her for help—and became her lifelong friends" (11). The review in *Time* magazine began, "Popular, petite debutante daughter of a wealthy Mississippi plantation owner, Anne Walter annoyed her mother by studying medicine in San Francisco and Philadelphia" (95). The marketing cachet presented by an autobiographer who tells of being a belle who rejected belledom is everywhere obvious in the promotion of *My Days of Strength.*

Of course, the country was agog over belles in the late 1930s. *Gone with the Wind* ranked at the top of the bestseller list in 1936 and 1937 and premiered as a blockbuster film in 1939; Bette Davis was a bad belle who would not wear white, who gave her film audience the selfish vixen and a pale saint, and who was finally recuperated through her sacrifice to the yellow fever epidemic in *Jezebel.* The fascination with the belle, especially among women readers, was no new occurrence, going back to earlier novels, as Helen Papashvily discusses in *All the Happy Endings,* her 1956 study of nineteenth-century American fiction. She describes the belle—"her curls cascading over her shoulders, her hoops swaying, her voice fluting, her power and influence unobtrusive but supreme"—as "what every woman longed to be" (174–75). Later, Kathryn Seidel, in *The Southern Belle in the American Novel,* proposes that the belle came virtually to portray the South itself. "Early on, writers saw the belle as their ideal South, pure and noble," but she notes that "more self-conscious and critical modern southern writers use the 'darker' side of the belle—the repressed narcissism, etc.—to indict the Old South or to describe the New" (xiv). Laura F. Edwards makes an interesting connection between the Lost Cause mythologizers of the late nineteenth century, the era of Fearn's girlhood, and the Old South mythologizers of the 1930s. She argues that the elite white women who engaged in the Lost Cause inventive memorializing of a graceful and noble antebellum past "helped create the Old South of *Gone with the Wind,* with its mint juleps, fine houses, beautiful belles, kind masters, and happy slaves" (181).

Almost by formula, Anne Walter Fearn represents her girlhood of the 1870s and 1880s as a preparation for growing into a marriageable belle. Whether she was drawing upon an internalized narrative of her youth that she had long sustained or was imposing a narrative pattern that fit the image of herself that she constructed in the course of the book's composition during her early seventies, one cannot be sure. But reading her construal of the belle formula tells one a great deal of how she viewed the South and represented her identification as a southerner in this text. She opens the book with a dramatic account of herself as an eleven year old, a "small girl with cropped, curly hair . . . perched precariously on the edge of the veranda," watching her father reassure an anxious crowd of neighbors frightened of the yellow fever epidemic raging around them. It was her last sight of Harvey Washington Walter and her three grown brothers, all of whom died of the fever after she, her mother, and her younger siblings had been sent away to safer ground. What she records of that final memory of her father is a face and eyes that reminded her of "lions," full of "power and strength." Although unspoken in the text, it is her father who models for her the strength that she so much admires throughout her life and seeks to emulate. The bare-bones plot of the story she tells is of the journey she will make from that girlish onlooker to "the best known woman between Suez and the China Coast," as Carl Crow describes her in his introduction. Her belle beginnings make her transformation into a courageous, self-possessed woman, indeed into an extraordinarily active professional woman, all the more dramatic and appealing to her readers.

Fearn's portrait of the South during the years of the 1870s and 1880s, as well as her own life narrative, follows closely that of Belle Kearney. Her family is organized around the patriarchal figure of her father, and after his and the older sons' deaths, her distraught mother turns dependently to the husbands of the older daughters. It is finally with their help that "security and comfort" are regained. The prestige and influence of the family are reflected in the family mansion, a "red brick colonial house with octagonal towers on both sides," "huge Corinthian capped, fluted columns" and a wide veranda. Fearn even includes a page-long poem by one Genevieve Wilson Bartlett extolling the Walter House's beauty, its embodiment of "the gracious living of the South," and its occupants, "a virile race that calls it home" (5).

A pattern we have already seen in prior examples and will see repeatedly in later autobiographies is the depiction by these southern daughters of male forebears whom they portray as powerful and honorable men who, significantly, embody the very qualities that the writers claim for themselves and insist are duly continuous with the male ancestors. Although their own lives may seem to

contradict the ideal of a pedestaled and dependent southern woman, these writers argue that they in fact possess other traits just as demonstrably "southern"
and in some respects, though certainly not in respect of their work outside the
home, just as consistent with southern female roles. Fearn, for example, emphasizes her skill as a generous and hospitable hostess, qualities she invariably links
to her southern background. She is particularly adept at casting her youthful
self as a charming but capricious ingénue and then showing the joie de vivre to
be an empowering strength.

Her choice of a medical career comes about because she is eager to have a
"full life," as she says. She has engaged the social life of Mississippi and Memphis with great energy, having managed to have her debutante party at the governor's mansion in Jackson, despite the tight finances that put new clothes out
of reach. In the tradition of Scarlet O'Hara and a long ancestry of fictional heroines faced with hard times, she finds in an upstairs cedar chest "satins, brocades,
silks and velvets" that had been worn by her mother and older sisters. "These
were transformed into dresses for me and thus clad I went forth to conquer" (6).
But the life of social butterfly, an aimless life she thinks, lacks the verve and opportunity for adventure that she craves. In 1889, when she is twenty-four years
old, she suffers an attack of malaria and leaves the South to visit her brother in
San Francisco. Almost as dramatic as Kearney's religious conversion, which led
to her crusades for temperance and suffrage, is Fearn's meeting a woman physician on the train. This woman precipitates her decision to study medicine and,
along with other physicians she later meets in San Francisco, demonstrates that
one may be both a doctor who lives a full life, "fighting against great odds with
energy and courage," and a "fine, gentle, and sensitive" woman (11). An important influence upon the choice she made, Fearn writes in her old age, was her
assurance that as a physician she would not have to wear "gentlemanly attire"
or become a "coarse-grained freak," an assurance she is pointedly validating for
her reader.

However determinative of her future life was the chance meeting of the physician on the train, Fearn needs such a scene to furnish a dramatic turning
point in her progression from southern belle to practicing physician. A narrative requires a cause, or inciting action, that then resolves into an effect. Kearney's conversion episode, however true, or not, to life, is composed in the text
to provide a similar *narrative* function. Fearn's self-portrait of the young adult's
making life choices reveals only a little of the inner turmoil that the text implies. As she tries to separate herself from family and "southern tradition," she
also holds to the ideals of genteel ladylikeness she has been carefully taught. We

can see that a major emotional strategy is to identify with the father's dignity and sense of honor and to distance herself from a mother whom she characterizes as distraught and melancholy for years after her husband's death, and as inveterately inept in managing finances. In fact, it is only as an unsuccessful money manager that she claims to resemble her mother. But even here, Fearn proves the vice, at least as she possesses it, to be nearly a virtue, when years later, despite misgivings and warnings about shaky finances, she courageously persists in owning and running her own hospital in Shanghai.

Most of the details about her relationship with her mother imply tension and rebellion. Upon receiving Fearn's letter informing her of the proposed medical study, her mother wired back, "No disgrace has yet fallen upon your father's name. Should you persist in carrying out your mad determination to study medicine I shall never again recognize you as my daughter" (12). This opposition strengthened Anne's backbone. "That settled it," she writes, "I just had to study medicine." Although a few paragraphs later Fearn says she eventually won her mother over and, in fact, witnessed her joy and pride when word came that she had been awarded her degree, the dramatic and precise quoting of the telegram suggests a hurt that never quite healed.

It is easy to speculate that medicine attracted Fearn because of her traumatic witnessing of yellow fever devastation and her sense of powerlessness as a young adolescent to save her father and brothers. That experience undoubtedly was consequential for her in many ways. But the protagonist of *My Days of Strength* spends few words upon self-analysis or contemplative reflection about deep-lying motives and influences. As already mentioned, her narrative style is focused upon people and place details, succinctly plotted anecdotes, and episodes of life experience that place the reader behind Fearn's own curious and attentive eyes, watching a serial panorama unfold. We come to think of her affinity for medicine as a perfect fit, offering her a legitimate venue for an extremely active participation in the life around her. It was a sure anodyne for boredom and a palliative for the vast human vulnerabilities she had confronted as a child and would come to know even more deeply in China.

By the old definitions of autobiography, this book is obviously not one. Fearn not only materializes as a "relational self," she makes her own subjectivity secondary to the surrounding world of experience that her memoir narrates. We see her in the text as a participating actor, one who often starts a scene through her naiveté or curiosity. Where she goes, action follows. In a doomed but determined effort to bring sanitary practices into the hospital in Soochow—"to clean up the place"—she gains the nickname "Tai Foong," meaning a great wind or a small typhoon. She rarely speaks of books or writers, having little time for anything other than a busy involvement with patients, friends, travel, and, occasionally, her husband.

In 1896 in Soochow, Anne Walter met and married John Burrus Fearn, a medical missionary. He, too, was a Mississippian, and, although she had not known him earlier, she mentions that his sisters had been friends in her "long ago debutante days." He was a man who clearly held quite traditional views about the proper role of woman and wife. What was the attraction? She gives almost no details of their courtship, abruptly announcing at the beginning of a chapter entitled "My Marriage and Some Other Dramas" that, returning from a vacation to Japan after the exhausting year in Soochow, "the first thing I did was to fall in love!" (87). He was tall and handsome, she notes, but does not mention that she had just passed her thirtieth birthday. Indeed, the chapter is remarkable for all the gaps and interruptions in her account of the wedding, an omission that speaks volumes. She recalls that her "personal life at this time was more dramatic than ever before or since. Perhaps it is only the glamour that surrounds any young woman in love that makes the incidents of this period stand out with such startling vividness" (88). But she does not detail anything of this personal drama, elusively noting only that "work and courtship, tragedy and comedy were interwoven in all their varying moods." She proceeds to tell a story of several pages about the death of a patient in childbirth, an incident that brought "a period of depression and discouragement." Then, just as she is about to turn to the wedding, she delays, recalling a story about "an experience of mob fury." She had treated a woman with a cancerous throat, knowing that the condition was beyond help, only to be confronted by the angry family who claimed the "foreign woman doctor" had bewitched her. Finally, she returns to the wedding narrative:

> Then came the day of my wedding, the one day I can't remember much about. I only know that it was a day of confusion. I delivered four babies to inconsiderate Chinese mothers who might have had them one day earlier— or later—before I could rush into my wedding gown and down into the parlor of my house. There missionaries, doctors and other foreign friends from as far away as Shanghai had already gathered to witness the ceremony— a very pretty one I've been told. And it must have been, with the flowers and the green grass, the cherry and peach trees blossoming, and one stately magnolia in full bloom in the front yard. (94–95)

They went to Hangchow for their honeymoon before taking up work in adjoining hospitals. "The beginning of our life together did not give promise of a useful happy marriage," Fearn writes, attributing the division between them chiefly to his having "grown up in the church" and her having spent her time "in dancing and other pleasures." Rather than commenting directly on their marriage, she mirrors the tenor of their relationship in a scene that shows the friction. One morning during his insisted-upon routine of Bible reading, an "obsession" in her words, she is urgently called to the bedside of a woman awaiting a Caesarean operation. Trying to delay and obediently listen to five chapters of Isaiah, she finally springs up "tempestuously," crying, "I can't bear it! I wish I'd never seen the damned thing!" And she writes that she flung the Bible to the floor and rushed straight to the operating room (96).

Despite the paucity of detail, there is more than enough to indicate the disappointment of her marriage, although she depicts a more accepting and congenial relationship in later years. What is more noteworthy, however, is her proportional allotment in the life narrative to her personal life. Even the details about the birth, early years, and death of her beloved daughter Elizabeth are truncated and straightforward. There is a physician's control of sentiment ever present in the telling. Her rich emotional life remains largely implicit, not explicit, in this book.

Anne Fearn's gaze is directed almost always upon her work, an attribute we find among autobiographies by women who have led activist lives but rarely find among professional writers. This is a point to be considered in greater detail in later chapters. For Fearn, adversities were to be overcome with busy strength, not analyzed or memorialized. Perhaps the interior self is not so much concealed as simply marginal to the flow of events and the pleasures of activity. Perhaps. The interior self in this text, however, keeps sending out sounds of its presence like Jane Eyre's nemesis imprisoned in the attic.

Her self-presentation as a youthful belle in the opening chapters occludes a variety of miseries that leak out later in the text. A bout of "confluent smallpox" as an infant left her with a severely pitted face, which brought childhood embarrassments that diminished as she grew older but never quite disappeared, it seems. The devastation of these scars, so inappropriate to a belle beauty, is mentioned but once, buried within an anecdote of her medical study days that is designed to show her courage and strength. She describes her dread when hearing the announcement of an upcoming lecture on smallpox, commenting that the word "smallpox" had always in the past made her faint. Nonetheless, the emphasis of the tale falls upon the encouraging support from her friend Dr. Sarah Poindexter, whose successful coaxing helps Fearn subdue her fear.

There were other physical infirmities, barely mentioned, that obviously affected her body image. As one sees from photographs, she had a drooping eyelid, quite apparent even in her student years, and she had a weak heart from a case of rheumatic fever. These are acknowledged, but it is a petite, curly-headed, vivacious girl who is foregrounded in the self-portrait of her youth. One might read this characterization as a conscious design to heighten the drama of the belle-to-doctor story, except for the fact that repression of emotional pain, or, for that matter, emotion of any sort, typifies Fearn's narrative. In this respect she is, of course, hardly atypical. The familiar pattern of "leaving oneself out," to recall a phrase from Mary Chesnut's journal, is evident among writings by women who grew up during the nineteenth century and the lingering Victorian era, as many feminist literary critics and historians have observed. Writing of British women novelists in *A Literature of Their Own* (1977), Elaine Showalter spoke of the "training of Victorian girls in repression, concealment, and self-censorship," which proved to be so inhibiting as they attempted to materialize feelings through images on the page (25).

Among southern autobiographers, Chesnut is memorable for words that so fully expose the suppression of "trouble." In the 1860s journal, she wrote a sentence she deleted in the later revised manuscript: "I wonder if other women shed as bitter tears as I." Behind the dissembling vivacity (a word that for me always calls up Tennessee Williams's Amanda Wingfield), lies an untold story, Chesnut confides. "Much they know of me—or my power to hide trouble—much trouble" (29). The tradition of the secret self's masking her troubles beneath a vivacious exterior seems to continue well into the present. Cherry Good, conducting a series of interviews with southern women in the 1980s, reports in "The Southern Lady, or the Art of Dissembling" the same language of concealment that Chesnut expresses. She quotes as a typical response the comment of one woman: "I grew up believing, though I could never have voiced it, that a woman might pose as garrulous and talky and silly and dotty, but at heart she was a steely, silent creature, with secrets no man could ever know, and she was always—always—stronger than any man. ('No, you don't have to let on about it,' my mother would advise me')" (75).

For all the brisk command of her life that Fearn implies in her autobiography, she also cues her audience to read the adversity and bouts of powerlessness and entrapment that she faced as a woman and as a human being subject to life's vicissitudes. For example, she describes the aftermath of her father's death, when she returned to Holly Springs with her mother and family: "Of our homecoming I cannot speak," adding later that it "was years" before they heard their mother laugh again" (2–3). As already noted, there is little detail of her unhappy marriage but ample clues to imply how unsatisfying and even rancorous it was.

Her daughter, born a little over a year after the wedding, brought much joy and seemed to make a family of the three of them. But Elizabeth, named for Fearn's friend, Dr. Elizabeth Yates, died in her fifth year in the arms of her mother, who was powerless to cure the ravaging dysentery. Telling the story of Elizabeth's death in one sentence, Fearn adds the ironic reflection that "ten years later Vedder discovered emetine as a specific cure for amoebic dysentery" (114). There is no mention of comfort from "Dr. Fearn," as she calls her husband, following the Victorian fashion, to be sure, but nonetheless creating a frosty, formal tone. Elizabeth's birth had been a difficult one, the marriage was strained, and there were no other children.

In June 1914, Fearn left China for an extended world trip with Elizabeth Yates and Yates's niece. At the outbreak of World War I, she attempted to enlist in England as an army doctor, was turned away, and tried again with the Red Cross in New York, only to be told that "men surgeons and women nurses could be accepted" (179). She returned then, to her husband in Shanghai, but was determined not to fall back into the "desultory" medical practice—and wifehood as well, one infers—that she had been trapped in during the prior seven years. Clearly, this period marks a new direction for her. With the purchase of a new car, she writes, her spirits "rebound," and, rejuvenated, she acts upon a long-held dream to own her own hospital. The account of her purchase of a lavish estate as site of what would become her sanatorium is voiced in excitement and joyful anticipation, more like a wedding story well remembered, one might say. She notes the very moment of her entering the new estate: "The Gereckes . . . moved out of the house at nine o'clock on the night of November 30, 1916. The next morning at dawn I moved in. My great adventure had begun" (185).

Fearn writes glowingly of "her hospital," a small institution she describes as like no other in the world, especially not like the Shanghai General Hospital, the largest hospital in the Far East, where her husband served as director. Happily engaged in her new enterprise as director of the Fearn Sanatorium, she describes the two of them as "friendly rivals." Her hospital catered mainly to foreign nationals, especially visiting Americans, and offered amenities that she describes as "extravagant"—cocktails for patients' visitors, food trays of polished silver plate with a vase of flowers, coffee and tea services of sterling silver, and a music room for violin and piano entertainment, when it was not serving as an emergency operating room. One of her foreign patients was Mississippian Estelle Oldham Franklin, who in a few short years would divorce husband Cornell Franklin and return to Oxford to marry William Faulkner. In 1923 Fearn delivered the Franklins' son Malcolm. In *Faulkner in Love,* Judith

Sensibar recounts that Estelle attended one of Shanghai's famous social gatherings that Fearn writes of in *My Days of Strength,* the 1922 George Washington Birthday Ball. Sensibar proposes that this may have been the occasion when the two of them first met. Although Fearn does not mention Estelle in her autobiography, Sensibar finds evidence to suggest that the two women, though differing by a generation in age, did become friends. She writes, "I suspect that Annie's marital and economic-professional self-reliance and assertiveness may have encouraged Estelle to write fiction—and perhaps even leave Cornell in November 1924." Some evidence of the friendship is suggested in Estelle's two anticolonial romances, which included incidents of Fearn's life. Further, Estelle's daughter Jill Faulkner recalled accompanying her parents to visit Fearn after she had retired and returned to Mississippi (340; 412–13).

The gratifying, all-consuming enterprise, the Fearn Sanatorium at 30 Pichon Loo, Shanghai, is ultimately jeopardized by John Fearn, although Anne Fearn describes his part with no recrimination. She had mentioned earlier, however, that "all of or married life was tinged by the merest shadow of a professional jealousy" (216). Her hospital had always had a tenuous financial standing, much of which she attributes to her own cavalier, or inept, financial sense. When the municipal council proposes a competing hospital, overlapping hers in its mission and situated close by, she concludes that the only course is to close her hospital. The management of the new municipal hospital is offered to her husband, "a great tribute to him and to his work," and she recalls that the hospital committee said that "he was the only man who could fill the bill" (259). Her softer tone surely owes in part to the circumstances of that period—John Fearn was ill, and dying, of Bright's disease even as he took on the job of opening and managing the new hospital. With his death the thirty-year marriage came to an end. In keeping with her long-established pattern of terse response, Fearn writes, "I cannot speak of the last days of his illness."

Anne Fearn was a disappointment to her husband; whoever it was he thought he was marrying turned out not to be his wife. "He condemned my lack of interest in the religious life," she says in a one-page summing-up of their life together," and he "felt that my independence was unbecoming to a woman" (261). With a forgiving understanding, though, she speaks of the "constant pull" in his life between an intolerant, "small-town Methodism" and the liberating influence of the actual life he chose to live. "China and Yazoo City were in conflict," as she succinctly puts it. His regard did matter very much to her, however. Like Henry James's Daisy Miller in her reproach of the cautious traditionalist Winterbourne, Anne Fearn makes no apologies for her independence or her failure to conform to his ideal of ladyhood, but she does express affection and regret. Concluding the brief retrospective upon their marriage, she enacts a final vindication of her contribution to it. At the end of his life, John Fearn was brought to her sanitarium, just days before it was sold. In a tribute that she casts as a dramatic line of dialogue, he at last pays homage to her strengths: "'I didn't approve of your opening this hospital, Annie, but as I lie here I keep thinking how thankful I am for the care and comfort that surround me, and that it's all due to you'" (261–62). As she does repeatedly, Fearn turns sorrow or failure into triumph, or, at least, into a satisfying resolution.

Of the many intriguing aspects of Fearn's self-narrative, one that is especially indicative of her physician's perspective is her stance of detachment from her own experience. She observes whatever circumstances or conditions confront her and then decides upon an action as if she were prescribing a therapy. Problems are treated, forgotten, or pushed deeply enough into memory to allow the busy life to flow forward. She responds to an enervating depression following the death of her husband and the sale of her hospital with travel that lifts her spirit, and she initiates a medical treatment to renew, literally, her flagging body. In Vienna she undergoes a thirty-day "rejuvenation treatment," administered by a well-known endocrinologist, which sends her home "a new person." She writes, "I took stock of myself. . . . My hair was still white as ever. I obviously was sixty and not sixteen, but my vitality and energy had increased, my blood-pressure had dropped considerably, and certainly my entire circulation had improved. . . . I would not now hesitate to call [this treatment] a true regeneration" (280–81).

Among the various narrative stances adopted by southern women autobiographers in their assessment of conflicting claims of self and society, Anne Walter Fearn is virtually unique in her possession of the self-assured equanimity with which she apprehends and lives out competing, often contradictory values and social roles. Eschewing "coarseness," she was also implacable in her determination to deliver good medical care to the waifs and prostitutes, the footbound, opium-addicted, and unclean who presented themselves to her. This lady doctor feminist at the end of her tale celebrates her great success as a hostess when she describes, in relatively lengthy detail, a dinner party she organized to honor Mrs. Theodore Roosevelt when she visited Shanghai. Indeed, it is her skill as a convivial diplomat in bringing together the Chinese and the foreigners that is the theme of Carl Crow's introduction. As Fearn describes the dinner party guests, however, she includes her satisfaction in remembering how many friendships "had their beginnings in a physician-patient relationship, many of them starting in my hospital" (296). Whatever memory is recalled, it is almost always looped around her self-image as a successful physician. The "lady" answers finally to the physician. Of Fearn's overt expression of feminist agency, I think one must conclude it is of a genteel, late Victorian hue. Relentless in her promotion of women's health and general well-being, she recounts story after story of the dire plight of Chinese women. Unlike her reticence about her own emotional travails, her rhetoric on behalf of her Chinese patients is unbridled: "So often they were pathetically hopeless. Day after day the women came to us with the same sad story. They told of the dreary monotony of their lives; they pointed in silence to their tiny tortured feet; they spoke with shame and helpless misery of the diseases that rendered them unfit for wifehood or motherhood, they related sorrows so deep that all the world seemed but a throbbing echo of their appeals for help" (58). We see in this passage her earnest addressing of gynecological problems, including female sexuality and venereal disease, but her language is evasive and euphemistic, although surely in keeping with the circumspection expected by the 1930s general reading public.

A more direct sign of her declared feminism is her admiration for the "extraordinary emancipation of the Chinese woman of the upper classes," which strikes her "forcibly" when she returns to Shanghai, having determined that her attempt to return to America and retire among her family was bringing her "no peace." She tells of meeting Lee Ya-ching, an aviatrix in the mode of Amelia Earhart, who only the year before the publication of Fearn's autobiography had been lost at sea during a widely publicized flight across the Pacific. Fearn's admiring profile of Lee Ya-ching portrays her as "typical of the modern girl of the new China," a young woman who thinks "a little" of her son and daughter but mostly of how she can serve her country. This story is the most consciously crafted episode in the book, with a dramatic *in media res* beginning, a harrowing accident—her fall from an airplane into San Francisco Bay and rescue by the instructor pilot—and a recapitulation of the young woman's extraordinary life story. Divorced from an oppressive elderly husband of an arranged marriage, holder of the first noncommercial pilot's license issued to a Chinese woman flier in China by the American Department of Commerce, a military nurse serving when war broke out in 1937, she is described by Fearn as "determined, dynamic, youthful and dainty in appearance, but adaptable and practical" (285). One recognizes immediately the appeal of this image, daintiness and all; it is Anne Fearn's ideal of a modern woman, the woman she has herself aspired to be.

To readers of the early twenty-first century, Fearn's feminine ideal, for all

its progressive enlightenment, may seem conflicted, or timid, in its deep attachment to Victorian ladyhood and its reverence for dainty beauty. Looking
back over Fearn's life, readers are also likely to notice unspoken assumptions
of cultural superiority in Fearn's account of the "delight" she took in Shanghai
and the great satisfaction she found in delivering medical care to the unsani-
tary and backward Chinese. Despite her background in biracial Mississippi,
she writes of African Americans only once, relating an episode from her early
medical training. She was invited to accompany "Dr. Joseph Price, a Southerner
and one of the world's greatest surgeons and obstetricians," in performing an
operation upon a patient who had refused to come to the hospital, "a Negro
woman somewhere in the slums." Fearn is startled when Price motions her to
his side to assist, and then later, still "carried away with excitement," she insists
upon seeing to the care of the patient overnight. About four in the morning, she
happens to glance at the window, only to be terrorized by a face peering in—"a
Negro, his face bestial, malignant. At once it disappeared. . . . Suddenly, I heard
steps on the stairs . . . and all the while I sat paralyzed" (17). Voicing the perennial and stereotypical fear of the southern white woman, Fearn thus portrays
her experience of absolute horror as imminent attack by a black man. Despite
many later experiences when her safety is at much greater risk, she does not
report—nor, one infers, experience—these events as so threatening or frightening as the spectral black face peering through the window. As it turns out, the
footsteps belonged to Dr. Price, whose face had been darkened by the night and
the windowpane. He had come to check on the patient and the attending Fearn.
She does not record any reflection upon the unwarranted fearfulness, although
one can infer that she cites the incident to suggest that one's "greatest fear" may
prove to be groundless. That this "greatest fear," which she invokes to illustrate
her point, is the very one so often advanced to defend white supremacy—the
threat of the black man's rape of the defenseless white woman—doubtless harkens to the era of her Mississippi childhood. In her telling of the episode, she
offers no retrospective interest in parsing the racialized fear. It still lies ready,
unmoderated, to come to mind and pen.

Interestingly, the point of Fearn's story has entirely to do with her account
of mentors who encouraged and supported her and of her own determination
and strength to succeed as a physician, even in a hostile, foreign world. She
does not explicitly take up the issue of black-white relations in her life story—
her awareness and negotiation of ethnic difference are focused upon Anglo-
Asian relations. Like Helen Keller, Fearn starts out from a position of nativist
white hegemony but becomes increasingly aware of the false sense of privilege

that Caucasian whiteness assumes. Still, even with a broadened worldview and a commitment to social justice, Fearn is finely attuned to class difference. She pays tribute to the young Chinese aviator's grace and dignified, aristocratic spirit of independence. She admires the noblesse oblige of the "three famous Soong sisters": Mme. Sun Yat-sen, Mme. H. H. Kung, and Mme. Chiang Kai-shek, whom she regards as "the acknowledged leaders of the new women of China" (288). And she sees her own role in the main as that of benefactor for the less fortunate.

It would be a misreading of Anne Fearn, however, to regard her as lacking in self-awareness. She values the self as it is realized and expressed in action, not contemplation. The Fearn-self of this text is an ego on the move, interwoven with people and events resurrected from memory and constructed from details witnessed and reshaped by the writer late in her life. With her enormous appetite for experience, she gives us an incredible range of self-portraits—from belle to grand dame hostess and, in all the years between, a hardworking physician, one who at the end of her active practice discovers she hasn't even owned a hat for seven years. Anne Fearn and Helen Keller voice selves that seem akin to Walt Whitman's songs of self, celebrating always outward movement, the will to embrace the world but, equally, to possess a separate self in that world.

4

Wifehood Narratives

MARY HAMILTON AND AGNES GRINSTEAD ANDERSON

Can't a woman stand a lot when she feels she is needed to take care of
someone she has grown attached to, or was it love? I wondered.
—MARY HAMILTON

As I look back, I wonder what held me there. Was it a belief in him that I
had never succeeded in shaking? Was it love?
—AGNES GRINSTEAD ANDERSON

One recognizes in the life writings of Helen Keller, Anne Walter Fearn, and
Belle Kearney, as well of autobiographers who preceded them, widespread evidence of the ways in which women of the late nineteenth and early twentieth
century South were socialized in a family-centered, patriarchal, and socially
conservative culture. Further, their stories illustrate the complexity of the narrators' separating a single consciousness from their communal surround. Well
into the twentieth century, even the most individualistic women had to contend
with a powerful model of ladyhood—that persisting pattern of "true womanhood," described by Barbara Welter, Nancy Cott, and other scholars writing in
the 1960s and 1970s of the nineteenth-century social ethic ordaining females
to be selfless and subordinate to the needs of others, especially those of the
family.

This ethic of domesticity also assumed a female sphere in the white South
that largely proscribed work outside the home or, for that matter, proscribed any
activity that would elicit public attention. We should not be surprised, then, to
find in these female life narratives a pattern of "other-directedness," the origins
of which may lie in earlier times but which continued to inform the autobiographies of women writing throughout the twentieth century. The discourse strategy that expresses most explicitly the code of self-effacement is the tendency

to displace the self in texts that focus outwardly upon people and events and that manifest "subjectivity" and "agency" obliquely through suggestion or implication. Some years ago, Patricia Meyer Spacks exposed such autobiographers as "selves in hiding," but it may be more useful to discuss them as "relational selves" who regard identity as intrinsically bound up in their social being, that is, inseparably connected to others.

Turning now to two autobiographers for whom the marital bond imparted perhaps the principal shaping force upon their sense of identity, we see how the pattern of obliquity and relationality is exemplified in what might be called the "wife-story." The texts are centered upon the wifehood of the authors, and in many respects they may be fairly described as biographies of husbands, the kind of narrative illustrated by the Smedes text's focus on the father. The story of Mary Hamilton, introduced in the opening chapter, and Agnes Grinstead Anderson's *Approaching the Magic Hour* (1989) give particularly revealing models of the type, with Anderson's wife-narrative beginning in the year, 1929, that Hamilton's concludes.

Hamilton's *Trials of the Earth,* composed in 1932–33 but not published until 1992, is an extraordinary account of the narrator's relentlessly demanding, pioneerlike experience, principally during the years of her marriage to Frank Hamilton from 1884 to 1914. In contrast to the booming industrialization and modernization going on in other parts of the country, Hamilton's northeast Arkansas and northwest Mississippi locale can only be described as a frontier region of barely settled wilderness. This is the region historian James C. Cobb has named the "most southern place on earth."[1] At the turn of the century, logging and stave-making employed the men who came to work the forests, living without their families and often in tents. One of the few families in the area, the Hamiltons lived in physically grueling and isolated conditions. "I think I was the very first white woman to cross Sunflower River coming into this country to live" (80), Mary writes, looking backward from the vantage of her mid-sixties. She has withstood nine pregnancies, the deaths of four children, marriage to an alcoholic and illness-plagued husband, and hard work of infinite variety—including cooking for large crews of men, sometimes as many as eighty, with only the most primitive resources to draw upon.

Mary Hamilton's story might well have been titled *My Days of Strength,* for her exertions for her family over her long life are unstinting and nearly limitless. Still, when she is encouraged by her educated young friend Helen Dick Davis to turn her wonderful tales of adventure and hardship into a written story of her life, she doubts that she has sufficient skill as a writer to do so. She is old and sick, preparing to die, she implies in a 1932 letter to Davis, but then she is unexpectedly persuaded to undertake the project. She recounts a prophetic dream that revealed to her, she says, that she was called upon for one last labor, the work of writing the story. It would be "selfish" of her to turn away from the task, she reasons, and so she promises Davis, "I will write down for you the true happenings of my life, and if I succeed all honor goes to Nick" (xix). Davis's young son had appeared to Hamilton as a messenger in her dream and thereby had in her view figuratively authorized the writing. She is thus exonerated from "selfishness," the recurring accusation against women who failed to put all others' needs before their own. She agrees to write her story only after she is convinced that God has sent her a vision instructing her to do so, that Helen Davis wants—and needs—her to write it down, that to shrink from the work would be reprehensible, and that her skill and memory bank of tales are sufficient, with Davis's help, to complete the task.

Hamilton's letter to Davis arrived in September; by the following spring in 1933 she had composed a manuscript of 150,000 words—about a third longer than the published text. The text that we have, *Trials of the Earth,* is centered upon Mary's years of wifehood, married to Frank Hamilton, an Englishman of mysterious origins who is more than ten years older than she. We learn from Davis's 1933 preface that Hamilton's first writings were "piecemeal," episodic remembrances of ten to fifteen pages composed on "cheap tablet paper." As she writes in a 1992 addition to the earlier preface, Davis, a journalism graduate of the University of Wisconsin, had come to know Hamilton when she and her husband Reuben Davis, also a writer and a farmer, moved to tiny Philipp, Mississippi. Listening to Hamilton's lively tales, Davis was fascinated by her life story.

Clearly, the Hamilton manuscript owes its existence to Davis, who provided the initial stimulus for the project, and owes its eventual publication years after its composition to an accident of discovery. Just before her death in February 1992, and in preparation for the publication of the book, Davis wrote an addendum to her earlier preface, explaining that "while working with Mrs. Hamilton I learned of a writers' competition sponsored by Little, Brown & Co., and we decided to enter her autobiography" (xx). She implies that the writing had begun before she knew of the contest, but it seems likely that the serious work of organizing and editing that she brought to the project was stimulated by the prospect of sorely needed prize money. In a journal entry dated 28 January 1931, Davis describes the conditions of the times: "An old Negro man came to the back door yesterday and said he and his wife have had nothing to eat but one rabbit in two weeks. They have made shoes of inner tubes . . . . This year, with banks breaking everywhere, most of the big delta land owners have no way of getting 'furnish money' to feed their labor, and the road is full of Negroes and whites looking for homes" (xxi). In fact, the Davises lost their own property and moved to North Carolina in 1936, returning to the Delta three years later. It was only then that Helen Davis learned of Mary Hamilton's death.

In her original preface, Davis explained that her role in assisting Hamilton had been entirely that of an editor. She was perhaps anticipating the judges' skepticism about the ability of a woman of Hamilton's circumstance and education to produce such a lively, well-written story. "I have edited it, worked over it with her, and guided her in her choice of material, but I have in no case added to nor changed what she wrote." Davis states that her "whole work" has been to "cut down." She writes, "The memories of the busy difficult days of her wifehood and motherhood have been minutely stored in her brain, as bees store honey, so that every smallest event of every day of her life is there: what they had to eat at each Thanksgiving dinner, what became of every neighbor they had in the wilderness of the woods. It has been my task to strain the comb of the honey, removing the less interesting material and leaving in the dramatic and moving events" (xix).

In assessing Davis's contribution to the authorship of Hamilton's life story, one must be satisfied to say that the version that was published is a wonderfully detailed, elucidating, evocative, and credible narrative of Mary Hamilton's life in the backwoods delta country at the turn of the century. Not only do we have Davis's account of their friendship and Hamilton's letter but also the 1992 addendum comprising excerpts from Davis's journal, other letters from Hamilton, and a verbatim transcript of Hamilton's holograph manuscript describing her childhood. As Ellen Douglas writes in her foreword, "It is indeed a miracle that all this rich material has survived" (x).

The question of the single-authored text no less than that of the autonomous life gives rise to many controversial and disputed issues, as we have already seen. In an extensive and sensible analysis of the "myth of solitary genius," Jack Stillinger argues for a more realistic recognition of the "multiple authors" that so commonly produce texts we think and speak of as single-authored, including autobiographies. He persuasively documents a historical record of editorial interventions that evince collaboration. One finds that the creation of a text typically owes not only to the "nominal author" but often as well to the contributions of "a friend, a spouse, a ghost, an agent, an editor, a translator, a publisher, a censor, a transcriber, a printer, or—what is more often the case—several of these acting together or in succession" (v). We are reminded that such collaborations can be shown to have occurred in numberless writing projects, from wife Harriet Mill's revisions of John Stuart Mill's *Autobiography,* to Maxwell Perkins's hand upon Thomas Wolfe's *Look Homeward, Angel* or Ezra Pound's upon T. S. Eliot's "The Wasteland."

In the case of *Trials of the Earth* what seems most to bespeak Davis's editing is the organization of a major three-part division; the chapter structure and titles; the heightening of a romantic plot focused upon Frank Hamilton's secret origins, presumably an aristocratic English family from whom he had long been estranged; a connecting theme of Mary's desire and search for a home of her own; and recurrent passages of well-formed, even novelistic dialogue. Davis corrected spelling (by her own admission and example, Hamilton was a terrible speller), punctuated, and typed the manuscript. In a journal entry from January 1933 she records a grinding schedule—"typing about four hours a day and working from two to three every night on this book which must be in by March first." She also adds that "Mrs. Hamilton is still here" (259), presumably writing or simply available for the editing in progress. Nearly sixty years later, when the faded carbon copy of the manuscript was discovered in 1991, boxed under the bed of Davis's granddaughter, "the yellowed pages crumbling," Davis remarks that she and her family read it "like archeologists examining ancient inscriptions." Although finding "troubling references to racial and ethnic minorities," she chose not to edit further but to let the manuscript go to press as an "authentic indicator of attitudes at that time" (xxi).

With Davis's able editing, Hamilton's episodic, busy, outward-looking narrative rarely reports the tedium of dailiness or wanders off into disconnected recollection. By contrast, when one reads, for example, the 1890–91 diary of Nannie Stillwell Jackson, who lived in Watson, Arkansas, just across the Mississippi River from the vicinity of the Delta where the Hamiltons were living at about the same time, one has to agree with editor Margaret Jones Bolsterli's warning that "the reader must be prepared to accept the sometimes tedious nature of reading about such a tedious existence." Nonetheless, the life Jackson describes, in which the high point of a day might be "a gift of a dish of greens or a pat of butter," is doubtless an accurate portrait "shared by millions," as Bolsterli observes (3). One is reminded here of the portrait of boredom and isolation in an Arkansas hamlet so memorably depicted by Mark Twain in *Adventures of Huckleberry Finn* (1885). The muddy streets and lanes described by the narrator Huck resemble closely the black "gumbo" that Hamilton struggled with across the river in Mississippi:

. . . they warn't nothing else *but* mud—mud as black as tar, and nigh about
a foot deep in some places. . . . You'd see a muddy sow and a litter of pigs
come lazying along the street and whollop herself right down in the way,
where folks had to walk around her, and she'd stretch out . . . whilst the
pigs was milking her, and look as happy as if she was on salary. And pretty
soon you'd hear a loafer sing out, "Hi! *so* boy! sick him, Tige!" and away the
sow would go, squealing most horrible. . . . Then they'd settle back again till
there was a dog-fight. There couldn't anything wake them up all over, and
make them happy all over, like a dog-fight—unless it might be putting tur-
pentine on a stray dog and setting fire to him, or tying a tin pan to his tail
and see him run himself to death. (Chap. 21, 118-19)

Another writer who registers the scenes of late nineteenth-century rural Arkansas is Octave Thanet, writing of her home state in two 1891 articles in the
Atlantic Monthly.[2] In the earlier essay, "Plantation Life in Arkansas," she describes a scene from her window: "a wide plain greening under the February
sun; fields with mouse-colored fences and freshly turned black furrows; away
in the distance, negroes and mules ploughing; down the lane, a belated cotton
wagon crawling to the gin, a few cows among the trees, a black pig here and
there rooting under the fences, and a dozen horses, with ragged saddles, tied to
the 'hitching-bar' under the great willow oak in front of the store" (32). The pastoral scene changes, however, when she turns to the lives of the black field workers and the white tenant renters, whose early marriages, she writes, are "a most
prolific source of poverty and unhappiness." Marriages of boys of seventeen and
girls of sixteen are common. "The women have a hard life, working in the fields
and in the house; they age early, and die when, under happier chances, they
would be in their prime." Thanet quotes an old planter's callous quip, meant
to emphasize the hardships the area imposed upon these families: "Why, right
down there I buried two or three wives, and four children, and a heap of niggers!" (46).

Recalling the vivid detail of a Twain or Thanet description in her accounts of
mud, snakes, floods, flowering trees, canebreaks, exploding boilers, gun fights,
fist fights, cock fights, and more, Mary Hamilton's story also gives the reader a
focused, sustained narrative. With Davis's editorial help, the 250-page book is
structured in a roughly chronological order and has two overarching themes,
which connect the multitudinous figures of Hamilton's scenes. Her narrative is
about being a wife to the enigmatic Frank Hamilton and endeavoring to make
a home for him and their children. Unlike other autobiographies, this one alto-

gether omits an account of the author's childhood, beginning instead with her family's move in the early 1880s from Missouri to northeast Arkansas when she was seventeen. Her father's untimely death, followed some months later by the deaths of her mother and oldest brother, leave her with the responsibility of caring for her younger siblings, a duty she can best discharge with the support of a husband. At age eighteen—and on page seven of the text—she marries Frank Hamilton, a man whom she hardly knows, but who has a job, has befriended the family, and is on the market for a wife who can relieve him from "boarding around from pillar to post." The story of her thirty-year marriage, which ends in 1914 with Frank's death, is effectively the whole of her autobiography. Although she lives for several decades afterward, she devotes one short, concluding chapter to subsequent events, mostly to give details about the families and occupations of her adult children.

What strikes one so forcibly about this thirty-year wifehood is how little Mary Hamilton expected of it and yet how totally defining and circumscribing it was of the life opportunities available to her. She entered into it for the simple reason that she felt responsible for supporting her orphaned siblings and acquiesced to her mother's dying advice to marry the support. "There was no word of love on either side," she writes. After thirty years of marriage and nearly twenty more of widowhood, she is still unsure, or unwilling to say, whether her marital relationship was one of "love" or just feeling she was "needed to take care of someone she [had] grown attached to" (29). So slight is Mary Hamilton's self-regard or apprehension of any prospect of individualistic self-determination that she never voices thoughts about possible alternatives to what she manifestly regards as her fate. Of course, at the time of Hamilton's writing, her choices have receded into the past, but even in her reflection upon that past, she dwells upon events, particulars of detail about the locations and constant relocations where she struggled to make a home. This is a narrative of action, not of contemplation.

One should note that Mary Hamilton's attitude toward marriage and her unequivocal acceptance of her "fated" role as wife and mother were in no way exceptional for her place and time, her sex, or social class. In his voluminous study of the "plain folk" of the New South period, I. A. Newby describes courtship conventions among poor whites, mainly sharecroppers and mill workers, as brief and noticeably lacking in overt expressions of attraction or even of emotion. He notes their extreme reserve in talking of their courtship and marriage: "Their discussions were summary to a degree that suggests indifference to the events themselves; and folks rarely mentioned the emotions those events involved" (288). Quoting responses of persons he interviewed, he nearly paraphrases Mary Hamilton. "I don't know as it was too young," one North Carolina woman says to him of her marriage in 1911 at the age of seventeen. "I could've waited a year or two and done a sight worse. Been married twenty-eight years and me and my man still get along." Newby wonders, as Mary does in her telling, "Was that a matter-of-fact evaluation or a way of understating a love deeply felt?" (288).

Although the Hamiltons occupy a slightly higher rung on the social ladder than the sharecroppers and millworkers, the customs that Newby identifies typify white southerners generally, at least rural and small town southerners—renters, farmers, skilled laborers, and merchants alike. Large families of closely spaced children were common, and women's principal concern from the time they were wed until old age was devoted to bearing and raising the children, as well as assisting in providing for them. Some of the mothers Newby interviewed clearly found childbearing and rearing greatly burdensome, and indeed childbirth was life threatening, but he notes that the validation women derived from motherhood was evident (296). The barren wife in the rural New South was as pitiable as the childless plantation wife, a condition Mary Chesnut ruefully describes in her Civil War narrative. Wives and children did not, however, occupy the center of the society. As Newby writes, "Folk society was man centered in appearance and ideal" (309), and we see the patriarchal dominance clearly in the example of the Hamiltons.

Always dictating the direction of Mary's itinerant life is Frank Hamilton, the husband who brings higher social status to the marriage. His characterization provides a suspenseful plot line that remains unresolved even at the end of his life. The accumulating clues spread throughout the book coalesce to depict a man estranged from an aristocratic English family, who came to America because he "couldn't stand petticoat government any longer" (9). After some years in the British military in India, which left him with serious permanent wounds, he flees family and Queen Victoria for the freedom of the United States. Before he arrives in Crowley's Ridge, Arkansas, he has already contracted lead poisoning in a mining venture in the West, and he has recurrent onsets of malaria and bouts of rheumatism in "spells that would last for days." For Mary, though, who nurses him through these old afflictions as well as all the accidents and new ills that befall him, including failed business ventures and financial collapse, the most troubling of his disabilities is his alcoholism.

Unlike many nineteenth-century autobiographers, Mary Hamilton does not disguise her husband's drinking by claiming he simply had an irritable or moody temperament. In her introduction to Ella Gertrude Clanton Thomas's journal, published as *The Secret Eye* in 1990, Nell Irvin Painter reads Thomas's concealments in her text as owing to ambiguous motives—partly to shield a family embarrassment from her readers, partly to evade her own long-standing denial. As Painter says, "leakage" and "deception clues" expose Thomas's secret, but whether deception or self-deception governs is impossible to decide (56). In Hamilton's forthright account, there is neither denial nor deception, although she does routinely put the best face possible on Frank's bouts of drunkenness. Forgiving, uncomplaining, even cheerfully positive about her life as she recalls it in older age, she attributes his drinking, as well as the disappointments and mental abuse she suffered because of it, to his physical pains. The threat of alcohol to the stability of the family, an argument that was the temperance movement's chief attack, was Mary's main worry. Even so, the harshest condemnations she makes are voiced in the dialogue of others, particularly that of the beloved daughter Nina, who on her deathbed says to her father: "When you come home tomorrow, and I can't come to meet you, because I'll be gone to heaven, will you promise to stop drinking so you can come to heaven, too?" (110).

Like many fictional heroines, Nina speaks words that eventually lead her father to sobriety, though not before many other ill consequences occur. This section of the autobiography strikingly dramatizes a conflict analyzed by Ted Ownby in his study of the culture of manhood in the rural South during the years 1865 to 1920, that is, the conflict between the family-values sentiments of evangelicalism, forcefully advanced by temperance supporters such as Belle Kearney, and the seemingly intractable male recreation that drinking represented (167–71). Shrewdly, as it turns out, Mary promised not to nag about the drinking nor, according to her late-age recollection, did she ever once confront him with a threat to leave him. Rather, when she speaks directly in the text of the consequences she suffered, she does so obliquely in language that is more reportorial than emotive: "I admired Frank . . . for he was honest, didn't gamble, and wouldn't tell a lie to anyone, unless it was me. He drank and made some bad trades while drunk, but when he saw things looking shaky, as they were now, he kept a pretty level head" (130).

One comes away from *Trials of the Earth* with the impression that Mary's "attachment" to Frank was grounded in her admiration for his dignity and independence, her respect for his knowledge of languages, good books, and distant countries, as well as for what she regarded as his honorable, manly integrity. She never mentions sexual attraction, or sexual relations at all, for that matter, which is in keeping with prevailing conventions about what could appropriately be voiced in life or, especially, in a life story written for others to read. But she is clearly proud of him as the father of her children. When he informs her at the birth of their first child that she will "have nothing to do" with the naming of the baby—or, as it turns out, with the naming of any of the eight others—she accepts his dictate. Taking the textual narrator as our authority, we see that she was convinced of his highborn bloodline, the truth of which he never wholly disclosed. Ostensibly, a main motive for her writing the autobiography was the prospect of having someone from his family recognize his story and so identity the "real" name of Frank and thereby share the rightful name of the family with her children. The dedicatory inscription reads, "To my husband's people whoever they are, and wherever they may be." From beginning to end, his story is presented as the dramatic, romantic one; hers is a tale of surviving.

Although Mary Hamilton never sees herself as heroic, but simply as facing what had to be endured, she strikes most contemporary readers as a woman of monumental strength, particularly in her effort to provide a home for her children. They live in a tent, a small cabin with a dirt floor, and later, at last, a house of their own. But that is destroyed in the 1897 flood, and when they finally again own a home and property, it again is lost, this time in a disputed legal claim. At Frank's death she is left with five children, the oldest of whom, sixteen-year-old Frankie, becomes the head of the family. After they have moved and paid freight costs for their few belongings, they have one dollar among them.

The importance of the extended family is a noteworthy aspect of Mary Hamilton's life. Time and time again she turns to brothers and especially to sisters for help during pregnancy and childbirth, for assistance with the care of the children and her heavy work load as a cook, for counsel and emotional support, and for much of the social interaction available to her. Jean E. Friedman's observation about southern families was never borne out more fully than in Mary Hamilton's life: "The importance of kinship cannot be underestimated in the Victorian South: it remained the vital connection, the difference between isolation and security" (3). But whereas the families Friedman writes about are seen to have social connections extended through their membership in evangelical churches, Hamilton has recourse to no such network. Her husband, a member of the Church of England, maintains an aloof distance from the Baptists, at least until his very last days. Although reiterating her religious belief throughout the book, with references to her readings of the Bible and such books as *In His Steps* ("What would Jesus have done?"), as well as accounts of her and the children's prayers, little Nina's piety, and her own abiding trust that events in life are God willed, Mary does not have the support of a church community, perhaps largely because of her itinerant existence.

Another distinct handicap she faces is that Frank brings no local family connections to the marriage, a situation hardly if at all mitigated by claims of "good blood." Writing of the political economy of this era's poor whites, for example, Jacquelyn Jones notes that families often depended upon connections with landed kin in order to accomplish their own advancement, that, in fact, "a lack of kin in an area could signify a household's particularly desperate situation" (209). Many times Frank's solitary status, along with his independence and unwillingness to seek the help of friends, leaves the Hamiltons vulnerable to hardship and disappointment. Still, Mary takes comfort in his putative bloodline, at least in her recollected account, and she finds great satisfaction in her children. At the end of the book, she asks "no better blessing from God than just to let me keep house for Bruce till I leave this world for a better one, if such can be, and I ask for nothing better to take with me than the memory of my life with Frank and the love of my children and grandchildren" (248). Her unmarried son Bruce is the one who most needs her, and it is with him that she spends her final days.

The portrait that emerges of motherhood in this autobiography is a vivid one not only of the pleasures children bring but of the untold rigors—and all too often the heartbreak—of childbearing. Mary Hamilton's nine pregnancies reflect almost exactly the range of experience that Sally G. McMillen describes in her study of motherhood in the antebellum South, except that Mary did not die while giving birth. One is reminded of the grave threats to women's lives in the unforgettable scene that Belle Kearney recounts, when she looked down upon the corpse of her twenty-year old sister, who was already the mother of two children. Hamilton's first child died in infancy of croup, long a common killer according to McMillen. She notes that the federal census of 1850 names the disease as causing the greatest number of deaths among children under the age of one (146). Mary's second child, born prematurely, died as a consequence of a disastrous journey that she undertook in obedience to Frank's insistence. Her third child, her beloved son Oswald, died when a physician accidentally administered strychnine poison along with the dose of calomel that was routinely prescribed for nearly every illness. Golden-haired Nina, according to Frank a virtual replica of the women of his family, died when she was six years old, perhaps the victim of malaria and its complications. Mary and Frank's fifth child survived through childhood, as did the four other children.

Mary narrates each account of pregnancy, including several extremely difficult and life-threatening experiences of childbirth, but she does so briefly and in a surprisingly unemotional way. As already noted, Nina's dialogue, narrated in the language of the sentimental novel—Stowe's handling of Little Eva's death in *Uncle Tom's Cabin,* for example—is one of the few passages saturated with sentiment. The really affecting moments in her accounts of her children come when she reports in a matter-of-fact manner that she had to sell her cows to buy school clothes (184) or that she had to keep a child out of school to help care for the toddler during yet another of her confinements. In true-grit fashion, she neither complains nor explains; she describes what she did, and had to do, to survive.

The self-portrait that Mary Hamilton composes in this book is stolid and unmindful of any life other than that of wife and mother. In many ways she is a fully vivified illustration of the hardscrabble life of a backwoods frontier woman. What is remarkable is that she inscribed this life in a formal autobiography. We have few such texts, explicitly composed with the aim of publication, by poorly educated, hard-working women in the rural South. There are diaries and private journals that were subsequently published, often posthumously, and a number of oral histories that have been recorded and transcribed over the years by interviewers, such as those of the WPA project of the 1930s.[3] But Mary Hamilton's book is exceptional in so richly furnishing the imagination of the reader with the felt life of what she knew firsthand. Her severely limited life choices, her unquestioning submission to her dominating husband, her social isolation, and the grindingly hard physical labor that she undertook for much of her life all suggest a woman who would not likely sit down to write an autobiography, and we must infer that Mary Hamilton would not have done so but for the insistence of Helen Dick Davis. Hamilton's life, destined otherwise to be invisible to later generations, is thankfully memorialized in this compelling book, for which we have both women to thank.

For all the autobiographer's and editor's efforts to make an interesting story of a marriage to a mysterious husband and the search for a home of one's own, I find more interesting and unexpected the revelations expressed in the various accounts of Mary's arduous but satisfying and self-validating work. She is a prodigious worker who derives as much sense of selfhood from her labors as Anne Fearn does from her medical practice or Belle Kearney from her temperance campaigns. Although she names her position in the world as that of wife and mother, her voice often expresses a confident, self-assured woman who possesses whatever may be required for survival. Shortly after her wedding, when she discovers Frank's drinking and the vulnerabilities it subjects him to, she declares that "she began to see he needed me far more than I needed him" (9), which is a rare statement for her, overtly independent and modestly self-praising.

Mary Hamilton's simple testimony of the skill and energy she brought to the daily work that sustained her and the family over the years bears out her early declaration of self-sufficiency. Six months after the wedding, for example, she is faced with running the kitchen for a boardinghouse that Frank has taken charge of. When the cooks all quit, she tells him that "if he would get me a pastry cook I would do the general cooking with Lucy [her sister] to help. We had a boy and girl to wait on tables, but even with that help, the cooking for eighty men was hard and the hours long" (11). She neither gets nor asks money of Frank until shortly before the birth of her first child, when she is faced with having to secure the baby's layette. Then, three weeks after childbirth, this time in an even more isolated boardinghouse serving thirty-five log drivers, Frank needs her to cook. A neighbor woman cares for her infant, bringing him to nurse every three hours. "I would be hot and tired and I was afraid my milk would be bad for him. She would bring him home at nine o'clock at night when I was through at the boardinghouse, and I could have my baby until four in the morning when I had to go back. It was hard on him and on me" (20).

Despite the burdens and deprivations of such work, Hamilton eventually tells of it in a spirit of victory. One of her most significant displays of enthusiasm comes in an account of a German cook who was employed briefly for one of their larger enterprises. Hamilton writes that he was the "finest cook I ever saw," and she recalls that she asked him to teach her: "We make plenty of money but can't save much; all I get out of it is a living and the pleasure of knowing how to cook and handle this work the easiest way. So if you just let me be your pupil, we will get along together fine" (122–23). She takes considerable pleasure in her reputation as a good cook and occasionally recalls compliments she received from the boarders. But her most victorious moments are those when she saves the family from financial disaster, such as taking on the "man's job" of clearing new land. With Frank off at a timber camp, Mary leaves the child Leslie to care for the babies while she works along side a sixteen-year-old hired boy to clear land, determined "to save our home if it killed me" (157).

When the home is eventually lost, she ratchets up her pace. Calling upon her family, the Hamiltons move to Lucy's husband's acreage near Parchman, the Mississippi state prison, and Mary begins a new routine:

> After my morning work of milking, churning, cleaning house, getting dinner and supper at one time, and cutting a dress for someone, I would help the children in the field all afternoon. Then I would come in at sundown and

milk, while Leslie finished supper. Bruce always had the wood and kindling in and water pumped for the stock and the house. After we ate supper—which was always a happy meal, to know our day's work was over—while the children did the dishes, I started making the dress I cut out that morning, and I never got up from the machine till that dress was finished. Every one I made meant a dollar cash, and that was mine. I wasn't supposed to put that in the living fund, but to do as I pleased with it. While we were making those crops I would make a dollar sewing almost every day. . . . [F]rom cotton-picking time till after Christmas I made an average of forty dollars a month sewing, at the rate of one dollar a dress; but in order to make my two dresses a day, I would have to sew till ten o'clock every night. (207, 210)

The social class markers that Hamilton attaches to her work are instructive about the status gradations she assumes to organize her society. Just as Belle Kearney noted, there was no limit to the drudgery that might be asked of a respectable woman and still not lessen her class status, or, more importantly, the status of her male protectors and family, as long as it was not performed for "wages." Even a woman as poor as Mary Hamilton is acutely sensitive to the taboo. Early in her marriage, for example, soon after the death of her first-born and at a time when Frank has left for Kansas City to look for work but has ended up instead in the hospital, stricken with one of his recurring illness, Mary faces destitution. Unpaid burial and other expenses are pressing, and she sells everything she owns—her watch, her rugs, the Brussels carpet that had been a wedding gift, even the prized quilts, feather beds, and pillows that in her view always signified a measure of her accumulated wealth. She answers an advertisement for a hotel cook in Imboden, Arkansas, and sets about earning "a man's wages." Although she defends this wage work as necessary at the time, it is clear that the memory of it is like a stain on her good reputation. "This is one chapter in my life I have tried to forget. Not that I am ashamed of it, I only did what any true wife would do, but just the same it is a part of my life not one of my children knows of, nor will unless they read of it here" (31).

Although there is much made in the South, and in studies of the South, of bloodlines as determinative of social class, when true cases are laid bare, one finds that the American predilection for wealth as the sufficient and necessary marker of class operates as surely in the South as elsewhere. Although Mary Hamilton's book, with the assistance of Helen Davis, reiterates the point of Frank's origins, the details of her life bear out the overriding effect of work upon her sense of identity and life success. As Elizabeth Hampsten observes

of the Midwestern farm women whose turn-of-the-century diaries she studied, women, as well as men, "define themselves in relation to the work they do"
(50). The implication of the term *working-class,* which typically is used to mean
working for wages, fits poorly the condition of hard-working rural women and
men—especially small land owners but also even sharecroppers—who differ in
their means of remuneration from, say, wage-earning mill workers. And non-
wage earning women, who today are still often referred to as "not working," are
seriously misrepresented by this common terminology. Hampsten attempts to
identify separately the women whose entire day is devoted to "cooking, cleaning, sewing, preserving, caring for livestock"—thereby reducing expenditures
and thus supplementing the family's income—from those women whose unem-
ployment brings value by demonstrating the prosperity of husbands, fathers,
and brothers (50). But among southern women—especially, though not exclusively, white women—the distinction is quite blurred.

Notably, Hamilton's dress-making work, which takes place in the home, is
an enterprise she describes with considerable pride. No confession or apologies are necessary. The fact that her lucrative business is built significantly upon
dress orders from black as well as white women, though, is a point that she
obviously regards as requiring some explanation, and she addresses it, just as
Belle Kearney does in *The Slaveholder's Daughter.* Hamilton says, in fact, that
she preferred to sew for the black women because she could "make two dresses
for the colored people as quick and easy as one for the white." All they asked of
her was that the dress fit, and "they were all sure pay and never came for their
dress without the cash" (210). Conscious reflection or content details about race
relations are relatively rare in this autobiography, although it is clear that racial
caste, not class, is the paramount division in the culture. Most of Mary's associations outside the family, other than those with whom she comes in contact
as cook, are white women who, like her, have accompanied husbands into the
backwoods lumber-related work. And there are few of them.

The final impression of Mary Hamilton that emerges from *Trials of the
Earth* is that of a pioneer, a woman on the frontier battling hunger and floods
and wolves and all else that threatened her family. The 1890s were especially terrible times for the rural South. C. Vann Woodward writes in *Origins of the New
South* of the "flood, drought, and plague" that competed with "debt, mortgage,
and bankruptcy" to make life miserable for farm families (270). The floods were
merciless, and one of the most dramatic scenes in Hamilton's book describes
the terrifying day and night she spent stranded on a tall, broad stump, holding
her little children close to her, above the rising tide waiting for rescue. Even the

forests were being depleted, exploited mainly by large northern land companies seeking maximum short-term profit. Faulkner's portrait of the disappearance of the Delta wilderness in *Go Down, Moses,* as Boon Hoggenbeck screams at the encroaching machines, is a fair depiction.

Although Mary Hamilton comes from this rural background and its hard-scrabble folk, we do not hear much of her story voiced in plain folk dialect. A few southernisms slip in—"fixing to," for example, and on occasion "niggers," though *Negro* and *Negroes* is the common usage throughout. The careful editing of Helen Davis, as well as the usual editing preparatory for publication, produces a text with standard spelling and grammar. Still there is no mistaking the ever-present, shaping southern frontier that so defines who this woman is. Along with the characteristic markers of geographic description and cultural details, however, we see that the core of her conscious self is the daily, local work of her life, much as we have seen in Anne Walter Fearn's quite differently situated but similar experience. The concreteness and event-laden action of this story rarely give way to ruminations upon the self or generalizations about the region.

Like the lives of the tenant farm women described by Margaret Jarman Hagood in her 1939 study, which she titled *Mothers of the South,* Mary Hamilton's story is about getting through each day.[4] Hagood praised the emotional maturity of the women she interviewed—their acceptance of economic hardship, their refusal to submit passively to it, and their dedication to a "constant output of labor" so their families could subsist. The generalization well fits Mary Hamilton, as does Hagood's observation that these women directed their attention to outward conditions, not to "inner goals demanded by inferiority feelings or other internal maladjustments." The self-reliant Mary, however, would likely have been puzzled by Hagood's conclusions that the environmental (or regional) determinism provided "no escape." Although Mary's experience exemplifies the sociological findings—poverty, poor education, isolation, and a "culturally inherited ideology [that] holds the mothers to their tasks and in their places with the sanction of God and the Southern tradition" (Hagood 76–77)—the self-image Hamilton portrays in *Trials of the Earth* is more self-determining than victimized.

It is well here to remember the empowering and transformational effect of writing one's life. Whatever one's experience has been, however random or imposed, scattered and seemingly disconnected, the writing inevitably imparts plot and pattern. First one thing happens, and then, we human beings so often reason, the next one follows somehow because of it. When Mary Hamilton writes a narrative of memory, she draws upon her present consciousness to adjudge and connect what have been the significant events and forces in her life. Her descriptions of her past impoverishment and isolation are informed by everything that has happened to her up until the time of her writing. And her inscription of her life narrative is subject to and shaped by the language available to her. The written life is a different order of being from the raw lived life. As Walker Percy writes, "There is a difference between the way things are and saying the way things are" (45). Even when the sentient self is trapped by cultural determinism and bound to place and the needs of others, the writing self determines how she will portray the protagonist of her narrative. In a sense, that composing self is a soul who selects her own society.

A generation after Mary Hamilton's trials in the Arkansas-Mississippi Delta, Agnes Grinstead Anderson entered upon a marriage in Ocean Springs, Mississippi, that would mold the rest of her life. Walter Inglis Anderson—brilliant but tormented artist, charismatic, demonic lover—was, as his wife remembers, "a painter always, a lover at times, a husband and father never" (128). During the spring of 1933 while the aging Mary Hamilton and Helen Davis were working tirelessly on the narrative they would submit to the Little, Brown contest, Agnes Grinstead, or Sissy, the name she was known by and uses herself in the text, wed Bob Anderson, as he was called, and commenced a life that eludes any easy telling or understanding. She does not stint in her descriptions of the anxiety and pain he brought into her life, nor does she temper her gratitude for the God-like lens he provided, giving her access to a magical, manifold world. The title of her book, *Approaching the Magic Hour: Memories of Walter Inglis Anderson,* announces her intention to inscribe her memory of a man whose artistry and life radiated significance and meaning for her. Her motive is quite explicit: to memorialize his achievement and his unique mind. By way of this memoir, she, who was witness, muse, faithful and supportive partner for thirty-two years of marriage, will set forth her interpretation of Walter Anderson's character and so explain, finally, why she stuck by him all those years.

Sissy Anderson began the writing in 1966, the year after her husband's death, and in over twenty years time had composed 1,800 typed pages. The 177-page published text owes to the able editing of Patti Carr Black, who had come to know Mrs. Anderson and the Anderson family during the years Black was the director of the Mississippi State Historical Museum. In the late 1970s, I had the good fortune to meet Mrs. Anderson and talk to her about the book project. At that time the bundle of manuscript pages was already voluminous. Fired up by my feminist interest in southern women's writings and spurred by the women's regional literature project mentioned earlier, I urged her during several different visits to Ocean Springs to think about the project as an autobiography, as about writing *her* life. She was adamant that her life was not the significant or exceptional one, except as she had contributed to her husband's ability to do his art and the extent to which she had occupied a vantage for knowing its depths and brilliance.

In the acknowledgments, Anderson attributes the publication of the text to the encouragement of family and friends, first of all, to her daughter Mary, "who took my random writings home and brought them back to say, 'It's beautiful. It's a book that must be.'" And of Patti Carr Black, she writes that she "has been to me as Maxwell Perkins was to Thomas Wolfe, my friend and mentor." Here again we encounter the process of collaboration in the transformation of a life into a text. Like Helen Davis, Black clearly gave advice about selection and organization of material, but unlike Mary Hamilton, Sissy Anderson drew upon an educational background that included study at age fifteen at the Lycee de Jeunes Filles at Versailles, a year at the Sorbonne, and four years at Radcliffe College. In the contrast between these two women, one is reminded of how elastic is the cultural stretch in the adjective *southern.*

In the biographical profiles of Walter Anderson and Agnes Grinstead that Black provides in the introduction, the central features of the families' background and education, highly atypical of Mississippi families generally in the early twentieth century, are briefly stated. Walter Anderson, born 1903, second of three sons, grew up in New Orleans, where his paternal and maternal families were well established. His mother, an artist who had studied pottery at Newcomb College, invited artists to visit and work at the family's summer home, a twenty-six-acre compound in Ocean Springs, where the Andersons moved in 1922. The oldest son Peter, with his mother's help, opened Shearwater Pottery there in 1928. The entry for Ocean Springs in the 1938 Works Progress Administration guide, *Mississippi: A Guide to the Magnolia State,* explains the pottery's name as that of "a variety of sea gull found on the Mississippi Gulf Coast." The products, "sold throughout the United States," are described as "distinctive in the originality of design and variety of glazes used," many of the designs being "objects familiar to the Coast—gulls, pelicans, fish, and crabs." The entry notes that "figurines of Negroes are notable for their humor, grace, and character" and that "the pottery is owned and operated by G. W. Anderson and his three sons" (292). There is no mention of Annette Anderson, the guiding light for the enterprise.

In his introduction to *The Horn Island Logs of Walter Inglis Anderson,* editor Redding S. Sugg Jr., writes that from the age of eight to fourteen, Walter attended St. John's School in Manlius, New York. He returned home to New Orleans at the outbreak of World War I and entered a local school, now Isadore Newman School, but in 1923 he returned to New York to study at the Parsons Institute of Design. The following year he entered the Pennsylvania Academy of the Fine Arts (12). He would later pursue his education under his own tutelage during travels in Europe, visiting architectural and historic sites across the continent. Afterwards, he returned to Ocean Springs to take up his life as an artist and, of necessity to earn a living, as a decorator-designer of objects produced at Shearwater.

Agnes Grinstead was born in 1909 in Gautier, Mississippi, to a wealthy family; her father was a lawyer-banker who had graduated from Harvard Law School. On account of his health, he came to the Mississippi Gulf Coast, where he met and married Marjorie Hellmuth. In 1919, the family moved to Pittsburgh. Patti Carr Black notes that during Agnes and her older sister's early childhood, "they spent their summers taking cruises from Mobile to New York and visiting relatives in Canada and Louisville, Kentucky" (x). After the move, they returned each summer to the family home, Oldfields, with its pecan and citrus orchards. It was here that Agnes met Walter Anderson during summer vacation just after her sophomore year at Radcliffe.

Photographs included in the book show one of Sissy in 1931, leaning against her convertible, surrounded by Hellmuth cousins obviously sharing a pleasant social time. She might remind one of Zelda Fitzgerald but for the rather shy and casual downward tilt of her head. Her demeanor suggests little interest in attracting attention to herself; rather, she shows the quiet self-possession that is evidenced throughout her writing. The wedding photograph is especially suggestive—even prophetic. Walter, dressed in white shirt and tie but absent a coat, stands stiffly, almost theatrically, his arm awkwardly extended to her. His body is turned only slightly toward her, though his head is more fully turned. His facial expression, not quite a smile, is taut, even tense, and his eyes are fastened upon her. In a gracefully draping afternoon dress, wearing corsage and hat and holding gloves, she smiles back at him with a pleased expression. Her whole body is turned toward him, and though her grasp of his arm seems light, she seems to be balancing his stiff figure. In fact, her posture, her clothes, her expression all bring softness and moderation to this photograph, relaxing the rigidity and tense self-certainty that flow from the figure of Walter Anderson.

That Sissy Anderson could so expressively capture the intricate weaving of this complex relationship in *Approaching the Magic Hour* is a measure of her own artistry. She is a gifted stylist, not just of standard expository prose but of a literary prose that is enriched by imagination, a command of vocabulary, and striking metaphor. Well realizing the potency of words—and images—to intensify experience and give it habitation in memory, she also understood the power of the journal and pen in imparting to the writer a sense of control and comprehension of life events. We learn from the editor's introduction that Anderson had a "life-long habit of keeping journals" (xi), which she periodically destroyed.

Despite her disclaimer of interest in composing autobiography, she does nonetheless, in the act of composing her memory of Walter Anderson, provide a "center of consciousness" in this text, quite like a Henry James character through whose view we see the story unfold. In the end, it is the seer herself, or himself, who is the central character most fully revealed. Yet also like a James figure, the narrator of *Approaching the Magic Hour* remains elusive. Her analysis of Walter Anderson seems so sure, her telling so straightforward, her revelations so candid, her tone so persuasively steady that the reader moves right along, asking few questions of this reliable narrator. But at story's end, one realizes that the most provocative character of this text is the storyteller, who has left most of the interpretation of her motives and actions to the reader.

As with Mary Hamilton's book, the focus is on the husband. Consistent with the book's subtitle, Anderson writes little of her background before meeting him, moving quickly by page five to her engagement in 1930 after her junior year in college, and then four pages later to her wedding in 1933 when she was twenty-four. The book ends with Walter Anderson's funeral in 1965 and a subsequent memorial visit by Anderson to Horn Island, the place that her husband had so often visited and painted and where he had studied nature, searching out "the rhythms of the universe," realizing, as he would write, the unity of all living things. It is from Walter Anderson's *Horn Island Logs* that she takes her title, *Approaching the Magic Hour.*[5] That his brilliance was captivating and unique, drawing her into his orbit like a polestar, is manifestly evident. But how is one to understand this process of lifelong gravitational attraction? What, finally, is her portrait of him? And what does it reveal of her, her voice?

Before searching the implications of Sissy Anderson's motives for writing, trying to analyze her interpretation of a life refracted through her view of her husband, perhaps one best begins by considering what she explicitly has to say. She opens her narrative in the summer of 1929 with her return to Oldfields, writing of "the wonderful feeling of contentment [that] began in Pascagoula as we crossed the long bridge over the marsh with its smells of salt and creosote." For her, as with Helen Keller, going south meant going home. "How I loved summers on the Mississippi coast!" she writes. From her sister Pat's excited talk of the Andersons, especially of Peter, the older brother to whom Pat would be engaged by summer's end, Sissy hears of Bob, whom Pat describes as "an artist—a *real* one." Having just decided to major in fine arts, Sissy is intrigued by the handsome, intense young man who more than returns her interest. The following summer, after Pat and Peter Anderson's wedding in the spring, Bob initiates a passionate courtship and asks Sissy to marry him. "He both fascinated and frightened me," she writes, adding that she was "emotionally very young" and "liked romance vicariously." Her description of his letters to her in Cambridge calls up a Cyrano-like passion and lyricism, whose directness she finds decidedly discomfiting. Her father, whom she calls "the kindest and most courteous man in the world," strongly objected to Walter Anderson and opposed the marriage. It is not until several years later, after William Grinstead has suffered a "mental collapse," that she marries Walter Anderson.

In the main, the Andersons' first three years of marriage resemble a pastoral idyll. To be sure, there were a traumatic wedding night and Bob's adamant insistence that he "did not want to have children, ever," a decision his wife neither shared nor accepted, except "temporarily," as she writes. Also casting a shadow were his frustration over having so little time for his painting and her guilt at his having to "struggle with the clay and the plaster and the kiln, the abominable business of making a living" (20). There was even the sad, untimely death of her mother. But their marital relationship during the years 1933–36 was predominately happy, so pleasurable and captivating that Anderson's recollection of this period—and her later hope of some measure of restoration—sustains her through the anxious, often dispiriting years to follow. Brief, it was time enough for her to find intellectual excitement, sexual passion, an endless adventure of spirit, and, most of all, evidence of the "tremendous creative surge that gave him his godlike quality" (20).

What would follow for her would be years of alternating reunion and threatening bouts of Bob's deepening mental illness. In 1937 she barely averted his attempt to kill them both when he pulled her toward an overpass, intending to plunge them onto the lane of an oncoming bus. At the Phipps Clinic at Johns Hopkins, where he was taken for treatment, he attempted to strangle her when he noticed her pregnancy during one of her visits. In these years of his most serious mental illness, two children were born, both adamantly rejected by a father whose delusions convinced him he was impotent. At a crucial turning point in his treatment, Sissy authorized the use of an experimental drug that would induce a chemical shock treatment, a decision that haunted her for years afterward. In the 1940s there was a tentative reestablishment of family "normalcy" back at Oldfields, when a third and fourth child were born, but in 1946 he left the family circle for what would be primarily a lifetime of solitude devoted to his art and study. Of this period, she writes that "he would not live with me, but he could not stay away. It was fifteen miles between Ocean Springs and Oldfields; his bicycle was his means of locomotion. He never came during the day, but he would arrive at midnight to sleep a part of the night and depart before dawn" (119).

Anderson took up the responsibility for her four children, supporting them by taking a teaching position in 1947 and accepting the continuing help of the Anderson families. She moved to Shearwater, closing Oldfields, which for her, during those few brief years in the early 1940s with her growing young family gathered round, would represent "halcyon days" that were never to be regained. For the nearly two decades that followed, she never gave up the promise of that better time, nor the deep, ineluctable connection she felt with her husband. "I could say that he was of little use to me, for he was more and more absorbed in his own world, but it would not be true. The minutes here and there that we managed to spend together meant everything to me" (130).

Even when Bob's visits to the family compound at Shearwater grew erratic and tense, with "increased drinking, increased smoking, and ceaseless painting," and even when his weeks on Horn Island, often in the severest weather, stretched into virtual seasons, Sissy maintained a "heart line stretched as strongly as a monofilament line." The petition for his safety that she uttered then, and that she revives and records years after his death, is "God in Bob, God through Bob, God over Bob" (149). She remained steadfast until the end, which came with his death in a New Orleans hospital in 1965 following surgery for lung cancer.

Is this a story of a woman's willing devotion of self to the higher calling of serving a man who, despite his mental illness, had extraordinary, godlike gifts? Are we reading an account of her self-fulfillment, of agency and empowerment that are realized and enacted because of, and within, this marital relationship? Realized in a spiritual bond? A passionately erotic bond? Is the reader to infer that her fulfillment as a wife came in the form of spiritual revelation? A tutelage in a unique, connected way of knowing the world? In market terms, could one say these remunerations were commensurate with her expenditures of love and caring support?

Or, is this a story of selflessness, self-lostness? Of an unspoken self-sacrifice that calls into question the affirmation that Anderson claims the relationship engendered? Could this book even be credibly read as an example of "marital Gothic," a term used by literary critic Michele Massé to describe a masochistic pattern in some nineteenth- and twentieth-century novels in which an innocent young woman sacrifices the self to a marriage seeking "voice" and "movement," only to discover psychic entrapment and physical threat? (20 ff.). Is this masochism denied or disguised by a self that finds gratification in renunciation and submission? One can make a case for most of these provisional readings based on textual evidence, for Anderson's complex marriage and richly lived life substantiate many, if not all, of them. The vectors of her mapping of this relationship go in many different directions.

First, if we are to understand how she comes to her judgments about her husband and her marriage—and her sense of self—we might consider the likely assumptions she held about the life choices that lay open to her as a young woman entering adulthood. Quite simply, she had been reared to be a wife and mother. The fine arts education at Radcliffe did not equip her for a job so much as it heightened her expectations for a successful and gratifying domesticity. Patricia Albjerg Graham, director in 1978 of the National Institute of Education, presents a revealing overview in *Signs* of the history of women in American higher education (759–73). She notes a persisting cultural view of woman's nature and her "proper role" in society as one hardly changed from the nineteenth century. "The feminine ideal—as opposed to the feminist one—that won such wide support in the early and middle years of the twentieth century was a constellation of virtues: youth, appearance, acquiescence, and domesticity." Even educated women were expected to foster "their natural predilection for acquiescence and domesticity." Graham quotes a woman reporter of the *New York Times:* "After four years of studying everything from ancient art to modern psychology, the average college girl views her future through a wedding band" (770).

One can hardly fail to see the striking parallel, as Graham points out, between the "modern" feminine ideal and the "true womanhood" virtues extolled in the nineteenth century—piety, purity, submissiveness, and domesticity. Little had changed. In the minds of many, this persistent ideal of womanhood simply strengthened the belief that these were the essential, natural qualities of women. The assumptions that one's life would be centrally devoted to being a wife and mother were even more deeply rooted in upper-class women, like Sissy Grinstead, than in women like Mary Hamilton, who knew that the hard work of subsistence living was as inevitable as the caring for husband and children. But even in Hamilton's life, we witness the taboo against a wife's working for wages, a prohibition felt most deeply by white society, but also evidenced in the class aspirations of the black middle class. The fierce disapproval of a "respectable" (white) woman's taking gainful employment and, especially, a wife's working outside the home, hardly differed from the cultural attitude that Belle Kearney had bemoaned in 1900. Still further enforcing the taboo in the 1930s was the calamitous effect of the Depression. Scarce jobs, it was argued, should go to married men who had families to support.

Obviously, if one's choice of a husband is to define who a woman is to become and what shape her life will take, the choosing is the paramount decision of one's life. This "universal truth" has been nowhere better explored than in the nineteenth-century fiction of writers like Jane Austen, the Brontës, Gustav Flaubert, George Eliot, Henry James, and others. We see repeatedly in their novels the search of young women for fulfillment in marriage, which is often launched as a search for, or, at least a hope for, a dashing romantic hero—indeed, often one with artistic aspirations. Anderson's own retrospective description of her younger self, caught up in the drama of courtship, resembles a naive heroine intrigued by the sensuality and adventurous promise of a passionate suitor. Bob Anderson, unlike anyone she had known in college, is "fascinating" and "frightening." Her vividly detailed account of his marriage proposal evokes the aura of romanticism that gripped her, awakened her, like a Sleeping Beauty opening her eyes to a prince.

In a few paragraphs describing the proposal scene, Anderson introduces most of the key elements that will play out in her long marriage to this man—the erotic allure, the protestations of love, the violence (self-directed in this passage), and the complicated thread connecting his romantic excess, his sexual urgency, and his potent, animated perception of the sensible world.

> One hot day when I was napping in the cool hall at Oldfields, my mother shook me awake. "Bob Anderson is coming up over the bluff from his boat." I heard Bob's voice, which was extraordinarily low, asking for me. When I went out, he invited me to go for a walk. As we set out, Bob dashed around the end of the house out of sight, then stopped so suddenly that I ran right into his arms. "I love you," he blurted out, "I want you to marry me."
>
> I was startled and backed away. He groaned and fell on the ground as if so weakened he was unable to stand. He beat his balled fists on the dirt.
>
> My heart was leaping about. What could I say? How could this be love? I had not even thought about such a thing. Suddenly he was on his feet again, coming close, pleading passionately. I turned and fled.

"I will. I will think about it," I promised.

We skirted the pond. Dragonflies were dipping about it. Some of them were coupled, and I blushed. "Is that what you're afraid of?" he asked. "I would never push you, never." Then, "The color! Look at the color of their bodies."

I had always loved the color of the dragonflies. We sat down on a little grassy bank at the end of the pond. He pulled out his sack of King Bee tobacco, a small book of Riz-La papers, rolled a cigarette, and handed it to me. Then he rolled another and lit them both. It was my first King Bee and I rather liked it.

We smoked in silence. Suddenly I smelled the odor of burned flesh. He had pressed the coal at the end of the cigarette against the flesh of his clenched palm. He never flinched. A terrible shiver went through me. . . . All summer he courted, now charming and winning, now tense and passionate. Each time we were together there were sparks. He seemed mysterious and unpredictable. (3–4)

Rachel M. Brownstein has written an insightful book about the interplay between heroines of marriage-plot novels and the idealized images that girls reading such novels internalize and seek to realize in their own lives. In the way that Anderson portrays the girl Sissy in this scene, an innocent, curious figure mesmerized by the seductive power of the hero, one is reminded of Brownstein's observations that "young women like to read about heroines in fiction so as to rehearse possible lives and to imagine a woman's life as important" (xxiv). That is, they are influenced by a cultural image, mirrored in fictional heroines, of a woman's desire to be powerfully loved by an extraordinary man and thereby to have her life transformed from a generic or even incoherent one into one of significance and singularity. Something like such a script seems to be directing Sissy's actions and emotional response in this scene.

Still, for all the flamboyant pull of romantic ideals, Anderson also reveals her uncertainties about the relationship, her sense of risk. When Bob abandons her in the woods one dark night in a blunt effort to "strip away" her fear of darkness, she is terrified. She runs in search of him, falling over briars and eventually landing in "an open grave," a detail heavy with suggestion of future calamity. Her comment about this early evidence of his stringent "instruction" characterizes the incident as a "metaphor of our lifelong relationship," but the implications she draws invert the images. She reads his intentions as beneficent and her own response as shortsighted. He wanted "desperately to give me his sense of wholeness in the universe . . . and make me see with my whole being, to give me inner light" (4–5). We see here a recurring pattern in the way Anderson narrates such episodes. First, there is some daring, often threatening, word or movement by Bob; then follows her response, often a pained or timid, or even frightened, misunderstanding of his intention. The resolution of the episode is expressed as a revision or correction of her misapprehension, which she is able to rectify because of his explanations or because she intuits his motives in some subsequent piece of work.

Although she acknowledges that her own nature is to prefer "quiet and tenderness," whereas he made for "violence and storms," she rarely accords her preferences an equal showing. In a late episode in the text, having returned from the hospital where her husband lies gravely ill to her comforting family and home, even to the added joy of a new grandchild, she challenges the values she attaches to her motherly and home-keeping pleasures. These she describes as a "hollow assumption of the role of Martha, busy about many things," which she locates in how she "pours herself" into the roles of "mother, grandmother, and schoolteacher" (168). It is manifestly obvious, however, that to the extent she has aimed for a wifely complementarity to her husband's artistic temperament, it has been as much or more the Martha that he needed as partner than a Mary. All along it has been her stable, being-there support that has sustained him, and never more so than as he lies in the hospital waiting for her arrival from Shearwater.

There are numerous examples in this memoir of Anderson's self-characterization—and even her prose—at war with some of her idealized images. For example, in her descriptions of the courtship period she employs distanced self-references and reflexive sentence patterns, exposing a wary youthful heroine. The elderly writer seems almost to signal this younger self to beware her actions, for she makes the young Sissy an onlooker to her own responses: "I heard myself agreeing to become engaged," she writes, like a sleepwalker. Many years later, in a tender scene in which she speaks of her great admiration for Bob's "wonderful and very painful gift" (You are "one with creation. You partake of it."), she afterwards takes him into her arms, inwardly asking herself why he could not be like other men. Then she adds, "I remembered that I loved him as he was" (155). There is ongoing in this textualized Sissy an internal monitor that continually reminds her of the role she is occupying in this drama. Formed partly upon a romantic ideal, partly upon a feminine ideal, and doubtless upon a deeply rooted loving attachment as well, this voice is full of ambivalence.

The wariness of the youthful object of Bob Anderson's desire ultimately gives way to his pleadings, but there were other reasons that move her along toward wifehood. Family circumstances also impinged upon her acceptance of his proposal, suggested by the fact that she does not agree to the marriage as long as her father is in full possession of his mental powers. Only after his breakdown and Mrs. Grinstead's decision to move with him permanently back to Oldfields does Sissy, at age twenty-three, go forward with the marriage. Her older sister was already married to Peter Anderson. The only unfinished business in this family circle was the transition of the younger sibling from daughter to wife.

Finally, considering the questions posed earlier about what kind of self Anderson portrays in her story of wifehood—affirmed and fulfilled or sacrificed—we are returned yet again to the maze of emotional paths that lead now in one direction, now another. In her conclusion there is no doubt at all that she regards her life with Walter Anderson in sacramental terms. She has been blessed, fulfilled, and the fulfillment she describes is essentially spiritual. On her visit to Horn Island after his death, for example, she celebrates his felt presence as a "man of light who translated into visual form the 104th Psalm, Ikhnaton's *Hymn to the Sun,* upon the walls of his house; this man whose heart actually beat faster at the words in Genesis, 'Let there by light': this man who pursued in myth and history the Sun God's presence; this man whose life's work is full of light." And then, in her next sentence, she encapsulates her sense of union with this deified man, both in life and death, with the terse assertion, "I was with him" (176).

Viewed in the realm of the personal, the day-in, day-out life of a married couple, one cannot help but register the writer's recurrent pain and loss, her expression in explicit narrative and implicit rhetoric of how much was denied her and what sacrifice of self and desire was required. At one point she candidly acknowledges the bargain she has struck. "Compared to the heights of creative experience, ordinary happiness, I think, can have little appeal. I had grown up in a family in which the creative act was the giving of oneself to others in ordinary human intercourse." She follows with the now-familiar self-reflexive pattern of stylistically distancing the authorial voice from the experiencing figure: "I perceived a willingness within myself to give up my own desires and longings for normalcy to nurture his creative nature" (40).

What follows is a characteristic expression of Anderson's resolute affirmation of the primacy of her husband's vision and his need: "The beauty he was able to interpret became the all-important thing in my life." If this "unusual relationship, filled with bliss and despair," exacted sacrifice, so be it. Looking beyond the personal, she finds the greater treasure in the "living synthesis" of the artist's engagement of life, which Walter Anderson left behind in his work (40–41). What is more, her role was not merely to make a sacrifice of self; it was actively to empower him as an artist. Writing of the period after he had left the family home, she concludes that her acceptance of his "apartness" and her willingness to continue the marital relationship on his terms had ultimately been essential to the most productive period of his artistry. "I believed," she writes, "that it was I who had released him to be himself" (137).

Anderson's judgment of the many menacing incidents when she faced a psychotic husband holding an ax or butcher knife or drawn fist, or even on a few occasions when in her presence he threatened the children or his mother, is that, despite the illness, she would not give up on him. "Quitting was sin," and, besides, she always believed that she could help sustain his stability enough for him to realize his extraordinary vision of the natural world in his art. She sought institutionalization for him when the threats were dire but did everything possible to give him freedom to travel and to work.

It is a great irony that this woman, socialized to be the daughter of a protecting father, spouse of a protecting husband, becomes the ultimate protector, even of her aging father as he moves toward senility. Almost from the beginning of her marriage, she realizes Bob's frustration at having to work as breadwinner and thus neglect his painting. Despite the social strictures, she considers looking for a job so as to relieve him. When she mentions her remedy, however, her sister insists that her taking a job would "make Bob feel like a failure." Too, as already noted, the opportunities for work in Mississippi during the worst of the Depression were almost nonexistent. R. A. McLemore reports in *A History of Mississippi* that the average teacher's salary in the state in 1932 was $414 per year, down from $637 three years earlier (99). Anderson did eventually enter the classroom, but only after Bob's hospitalization.

Her father's financial and emotional support offset some of the burden she felt, but increasingly these faded as his mental powers slipped away. The Andersons, too, were always a source of support. When the moment comes, however—when in 1940 she does finally accept, after her husband's several hospitalizations, that she must take control—it is she who organizes the family's move back to Oldfields, arranges for her father's care at the house with her, and sets about establishing a home for her children. This decisive action, more than any other, indicates the point at which she claims a necessary autonomy for her and her family's well-being.

One must acknowledge, as Anderson herself does, if only briefly, that this autonomy is partly made possible by the black caretakers who come to Oldfields with her. As is so often the case in stories of the white South, the black labor is nearly invisible and nearly always essential. "I found a good older woman . . . to cook. Her son, about sixteen, was old enough to be a house and yard boy. The farmer who lived in the tenant house there was a friend of many years' standing. Robert would help with Daddy" (82). Robert, whom she describes as a "friend from childhood," is at her side when she suffers a miscarriage, speaking in the text in a rare instance of dialect: "The doctor's coming soon. We be having you fixed up. Jes' you lie still. I take care of everything" (110). Although Anderson frequently creates dialogue for her and her husband's exchanges, as well as for some other figures who appear, her style in these is standard and rather formal. The composed dialogue, as in many autobiographies, often seems more like fictional dialogue than recalled conversation. In fact, the occurrence of dialogue in autobiography presents one of the sharp reminders that the narrative is a construction by the writer, not a slice of life being reenacted on the page. To the most literalist reader, the question arises of how the writer could possibly remember the exact words someone spoke years earlier. But of course memory is always an interpreter, not a recorder. The dialogue is no more or less imagined than any other feature of the prose. And the few slight lines of Robert's black speech imaginatively open up a space in the text through which we glimpse the strictly segregated South that formed the society in which the Anderson story unfolds.

The focus upon Walter Anderson that forms the core intention of this text gives rise to many gaps and omissions one might wish were more filled in to reflect the larger story of Agnes Grinstead Anderson and her time and place. But as we see in the metonymic passage of dialect above, as well as in the recurring self-reflexivity and various other recurring rhetorical displays earlier discussed, she does signify a more complex view of her story than the delineation of her husband. The overriding pattern that she would have us read is the story of a magical being, but the more gripping tale is imagining what it was like for her—and would be like for anyone—to live in the presence of magic. It is the wife's tale that calls up our empathy.

There are two aspects of the wife's tale that, by way of concluding this discussion, I want to consider briefly. Both of these narratives invert the customary hero's centrality to the tale. In reflecting upon Sissy Anderson's role as protector and Bob's role as genius requiring protection, one finds that it is she who is the agent of freedom, bringing release from marital enclosure, and it is the putative hero, the magical being, who is threatened by domesticity. Midway in the text the "marriage-plot" pattern alluded to above is radically reversed. It is Bob who most acutely feels entrapped, he who goes mad, suffers debilitating medical treatment, fights to regain sanity, and find his way back to family and work. The courageous wife risks endangering her treasure, his magical creativity, by subjecting him to treatment that might have destroyed his prospects for recovery. But courage and steady persistence reward her with seeing him recovered and again taking up his art. It is she who shields him, cares for her father, supports her children, makes a home, takes a job, and lives to tell the tale. Whatever stresses and losses and endangerments she suffers, she has prevailed in "releasing him to be himself." The enabler and bestower of selfhood is heroic in her own right, and in her telling of this story, we find no victims. What she conveys is the delicate, transformative equilibrium these two people negotiated, the one a magical being, the other a hero, so as to live creative lives together.

The reader may weigh her stresses and losses differently, and indeed she offers ample evidence of very bleak, even bitter, times. But it is precisely the candor of these revelations that prove so persuasive of the beatitude she pronounces upon her wifehood. One may also raise the interesting question of whether a reader's acceptance of the writer's beatific judgment may be influenced by the importance the reader accords Walter Anderson's artistic achievement. That is, does one's prior regard for the significance of his work affect the way one interprets the life narrative—one's determination of whether or not Sissy Anderson's "sacrifices" are justified? Such open-ended questions lead us somewhat beyond the text at hand, and they also point up the ways that texts always exceed the story the writer sets out to tell, especially when that storyteller aims at self-effacement.

In fact, the other inversion I want to address arises from this aspect of texts and from the nature of life writing. Put simply, the taleteller always controls the story regardless of what other persons or events she casts in leading roles. The narrator-self of *Approaching the Magic Hour* is an integral part of the story she tells, not only in the historical sense of being wife but in the rhetorical sense of being the voice of the narrative. Whatever truth we can see or infer of the experience she recounts, we see through the window she opens for us. In this regard, the teller is always positioned as the protagonist, the one who has witnessed, felt, and interpreted, and who performs the central act of memory that produces the text. And she does so from the vantage of age, understanding, and motivation that exists at the time of the writing. This is a point I have already made, but I think it is worth reiterating. It is also well to remember that the reconstruction of a life in autobiography does not so much indicate an "untruth" or distortion, certainly not necessarily so, as it does the inevitability of interpretation in anyone's report of human activity. When the reader finds such an interpretation to be engaging, persuasive, and reasonably consonant with details otherwise known, as this text surely is, one is ready to cede belief in Agnes Anderson's version of the tale.

A century and a half ago Matthew Arnold wrote a poem of a "forsaken merman," whose mortal wife leaves him in his sea home to return to the world she has left. This is the "humming world" of kinsfolk, the church, the "child with its toy," and her spinning wheel. Margaret, the merman's wife, finds life in his magical kingdom isolating and threatening, even though she is loved by the merman, in his way, and by their children. But she feels her very soul imperiled by living far away from the earthly, normal world of her kind. The merman's habitation, where "Now the great winds shorewards blow, / Now the salt tides seawards flow, / Now the wild white horses play," is a foreign place beyond her capacity for acceptance and accommodation. In Anderson's remarkable story, the reader comes not only to glimpse such a magical world, that of the artist's visioning, but to believe that a mortal woman had the capacious courage to inhabit it and the grit to hold fast.

5

Belles, Wives, and Public Lives, Part I

MARY CRAIG KIMBROUGH SINCLAIR

In the early twentieth-century South, public activists like Belle Kearney or career women like Helen Keller and Anne Walter Fearn were clearly the exceptions among southern white women. Far more typical were the husband-directed, husband-centered lives of Mary Hamilton and Agnes Anderson. Marriage was the nearly universal career for which young women were prepared by families, schools, and churches, and by their own elaborated, often romanticized expectations, formed not only by these institutions but by the fiction and popular media that portrayed courtship and wedding as the pivotal moments in a woman's life. In some respects the iconic southern belle and lady, ensconced upon a pedestal, was even more determinedly idealized in fiction and film seventy-five years after the Civil War than she had been when, purportedly, Confederate gallants rode off to defend her and their homeland against the Yankees. Not surprisingly, white women with at least middle-class opportunities were the ones who were most likely to idealize an image of the popular belle, the privileged creature who attracted men with her beauty and charm and, having her pick among aspiring suitors, could thus ascend to glowing bride.

Scarlett O'Hara of the 1936 novel *Gone with the Wind* emerged not from history, however, but from the artistic imagination of Margaret Mitchell. Scarlett is an archetype who has come to epitomize the persisting image of the young southern white woman as a beauty whose attention is focused solely upon attracting men. Of course, Mitchell also portrayed a life that demanded more intelligence and endurance than was required of the giddy belle. The stable, grounding qualities of Ellen O'Hara and Melanie Wilkes manifest the attributes of a "lady," representing moral purity, self-sacrifice, and, above all, devotion to family. Even Scarlett eventually outgrows belledom, although it has always required a stretch of the imagination to suppose that the flirtatious coquette could suddenly meld with a genteel lady—indeed Rhett Butler insists that she cannot. Nonetheless, the combination of belle and lady has proved over many years to be an unflagging image of a certain romanticized ideal of southern white womanhood, albeit an ideal firmly grounded in its incarnation of white privilege.

Why this particular image of southern womanhood, with its backward glance toward courtly love, cavaliers, and antebellum plantations should maintain its saliency so long after its mid-nineteenth-century heyday is a question one might well raise with the autobiographers who are the subjects of this chapter, women who led long lives of significant participation in the major social and political movements of their time, educated women of influence and ambition well beyond the domestic sphere. These are women who were reared in expectation of a career of marriage, who did marry influential men and shared their active public lives, and who, in fact, in several instances achieved prominence themselves. One of the more interesting aspects of their narratives is the composition or presentation of a youthful self who is identified as distinctly "southern." In portraying their younger selves, these narrators furnish the reader with many examples of what behaviors and social influences are perceived as constituting southernness, or at least constituting a white, middle- and upper-class "southern" girlhood. Even more, these life stories suggest their authors' assumptions about their and their society's ideas of what distinctive features characterize exemplary white womanhood.

Mary Craig Kimbrough Sinclair, Virginia Foster Durr, Corinne Claiborne Boggs, and Lylah Scarborough Barber were born within two generations of one another, the oldest in 1883, and the youngest in 1916. They grew up in the Deep South: Sinclair in Mississippi, Durr in Alabama, Boggs in Louisiana, and Barber in north Florida. All four moved away during their early married years, although they maintained connections with family and home. Craig Sinclair never returned for more than a few short visits to Mississippi, living in southern California and Arizona for nearly a half century. Virginia Durr, on the other hand, after nearly twenty years in Washington, D.C., during the Roosevelt and Truman years and a brief residence in Denver, returned to Montgomery. In the ensuing years she witnessed and often participated in the civil rights movement unfolding around her. Lindy Boggs left Louisiana in 1940 at the age of twenty-four to accompany her husband Hale Boggs to Washington, where he would take his seat in the Congress as representative of the Second District of his home state. After his death in 1973, she succeeded him and served in the House of Representatives until 1991. And Lylah Barber lived most of her married years in New York with her husband, sportscaster Red Barber, until his retirement and their return to Florida.

All of these women wrote autobiographies when they were in their seventies, reflecting upon the circumstances and influences that gave direction to their lives. Each of them writes of her southern beginnings as formative of her sense of self, and each tells a story of a girlhood in which the code of ladyhood was held up as a model for her to emulate. Many scholars have discussed the complex social origins and the psychological functions of the "lady" in white southern culture. Anne Firor Scott in *The Southern Lady* (1970), Anne Goodwyn Jones in *Tomorrow Is Another Day* (1981), and many others already cited have analyzed the ways in which ladyhood has served a variety of cultural and psychic functions in the society. Indeed, the effort to understand these functions has long occupied historians of the South. In 1941 W. J. Cash disparaged the windy rhetoric devoted to the antebellum lady and to her "protection" that the Confederacy had been sworn to uphold. In *Cavalier and Yankee* W. R. Taylor analyzed the nineteenth-century development of a vast and encompassing regional mythology in which the cavalier and his lady composed major identifying markers of "the South." Many analyses of white southern ladyhood have focused upon the legacy of slavery and have located the origins of an exalted, pedestaled lady in the sexual fears, envy, and guilt of white men. Their claims of protecting "their women" through aggressive actions against African Americans have often been interpreted as expressions of their fear of retribution for their sexual exploitation of black women or as envy of the physical strength and, especially, the sexual prowess and virility attributed to black men.

It has been the feminist scholars, however, who have most searchingly sought to understand what the psychic and social advantages and disadvantages have been for the women who have actually confronted and undertaken to live the lives of "ladies." What is generally agreed upon is that the demeanor of the southern belle—or the southern lady or the southern matriarch—is an enacted, performed display of a generic gendered and racialized type. Ladyhood is a culturally coded role within a patriarchal tradition, or, perhaps more rightly called, a voiced self that pays respect to a cultural ideal greatly complicated by a vexed regional history of social divisions of class, a racial caste system arising from black enslavement, and a gender system reserving fundamental legal and familial rights to men.

Although my interest in this group of autobiographies is focused primarily upon their accounts of their youth and young adulthood in the late nineteenth and early twentieth centuries, many of the features of the socializing traditions for young privileged white women clearly persist into the early twenty-first century, notwithstanding a half century of social change, including the women's movement. In the 1980s British scholar Cherry Good, asking southern women about their views of "southern ladies," found a vigorous defense of the figure. Despite the steadily growing industrialization of the South and the influx of many new residents from other parts of the country and world, Good found that the women she interviewed still located power in the image of the lady. "They clearly saw the gap between the rhetoric and the actual," she writes, "but were generally concerned to prolong the myth because of its perceived benefits" (71). The dissembling shows of deferential femininity or giddy talkativeness were useful camouflage, they thought, for the enactment of covert control they were convinced such camouflage made possible. Among the ongoing commentaries on southern womanhood, Florence King in *Southern Ladies and Gentlemen* and Shirley Abbott in *Womenfolks: Growing up Down South* are particularly notable in their humorous and telling exposures of the lady's art, and, more importantly, in their descriptions of the continuing presence in contemporary southern society of a highly defined and vigorously maintained sphere of female life.

The narratives of Sinclair, Durr, Boggs, and Barber give us many examples of the narrators' awareness of role expectations and the need for dissembling, although they also signal their understanding that "pretty-is-as-pretty-does" standards have significant limits. One of my aims in reading these books is to see how the sense of southernness is configured and understood to have shaped the writers' sense of self and their relations with others. The deciphering is doubly complicated by the heightened circumspection of writers who know that candid, revealing self-exposure in public is anathema to genteel ladyhood. The self presented in the text has always to be cautious, although there appears to be a lessening of caution when the narrative originates in conversation, as in the oral accounts of Durr and Boggs, whose words are later organized and edited with the assistance of collaborators. Still, one often detects a masked display of deference and politeness, behind which firm resolve and independence are being enacted.

The more accessible and less risky public venue for southern women writers has generally been fiction. In her study of southern women's writing during the years 1930 to 1990, Patricia Yaeger vehemently disputes the model of "the belle or female 'miniature' as the prototypical southern female figure," arguing that writers such as Eudora Welty and Alice Walker and other of their southern contemporaries have boldly portrayed female figures of powerful agency. Further, in their fiction they have exposed the ways the South has "helped encode American ways of racial knowing: of both overconceptualizing and refusing to conceptualize an obscene racial blindness" (xii). Yaeger insists upon a reading of this fiction with attention to a symbol and language system that differs from that, say, of a William Faulkner. Like Yaeger, I find this twentieth-century fiction by many black and white women writers of the South often to be fierce and angry, even threatening. And many of the autobiographical writings that are the subject-texts here issue frontal attacks upon racism and the patriarchal oppression of women. But there are also many powerful expressions of social and psychological critique in every text that are imaged obliquely in tropes and in voicings of unmistakable irony.

Anne Goodwyn Jones, in an earlier study of women writers in the South during the years 1859 to 1936 has argued that the writing of fiction served as a mask through which the white writers she discusses could obliquely express their commentary upon the ways of society and the conditions of their own upbringing and life choices. An illustration of a writer who drew heavily upon autobiographical experience for fiction is Katherine Anne Porter in her "Old Order" stories, though as Porter's biographer Joan Givner shows, the writer's elaborate fabrication of her personal biography preceded her creation of a surrogate self in her fiction. For her friends and fans, she transmuted Callie Porter, born in a two-room log house in Indian Creek, Texas, into Katherine Anne Porter, daughter of the aristocratic Old South. For her fiction, she creates Miranda Gay, a protagonist who grows from child to adult in a series of short stories in which Porter rejects and also pays homage to the rooted certainties of "the Grandmother," a woman she regards as greatly unlike her own modernist, vagabond self. Sharper even than her gaze upon the older woman, however, is her portrait of Miranda, who in her youth is given to naive romanticizing about an idealized womanhood of just the kind Yaeger calls into question. In "Old Mortality" the girlish Miranda is infatuated with an image of the belle, which she has long identified with her cousin Amy, the subject of family legends so exaggerated that Miranda suspects fabulation at work. Darlene Unrue notes that Porter in fact did draw upon family legend, that of Annie and Thomas Gay, for her creation of Amy (124).

Even as she doubts, Miranda dreams of attaining to the belle's magnificence. Beauty, above all other qualities, is the indispensable requirement. In the story Miranda is discouraged because it seems to her the romantic elegance of the belles preceding her so far outdistances her capacity to measure up that she is doomed to a feckless modern womanhood. The points of beauty by which she imagines she will be judged are intractable: "Whatever color the eyes, the hair must be dark, the darker the better; the skin must be pale and smooth. Lightness and swiftness of movement were important points. A beauty must be a good dancer, superb on horseback, with a serene manner, an amiable gaiety tempered with dignity at all hours. Beautiful teeth and hands, of course, and over and above all this, some mysterious crown of enchantment that attracted and held the heart" ("Old Mortality" 9). The older Miranda's insight is focused upon her naïve failure to see the morbidity of this figure. Porter's insight is focused upon the pernicious seductiveness of the figure, this "miniaturization" of a woman. And yet, Porter never really disclaimed the iconic figure of the belle for the self-presentation she maintained all her life. Givner observes that "with her magnolia skin, her velvety voice and white hair, she presented the perfect image of a southern belle, a member, as she styled herself, of the 'guilt-ridden white pillar crowd'" (18).

The mask of an overtly fictional character is not an option, however, for the narrator of an autobiographical text. Although the writer does indeed compose a character-self constructed for public view, she is also conscious of a level of self-exposure that she cannot avoid. The audience will inevitably read the narrator of the text and the author who is named on the title page as one and the same. It is just here at the juncture between an implied declaration of candor about the telling of the life and a felt need for discretion and concealment that we can best discern the appeal and usefulness of the belle-lady imagery. If offers a shorthand, "auto-format" device of characterization that helps fill in details of personality, motive, background, and even physical appearance. It also offers these autobiographers a role model—or figural type—that provides both definition for unwieldy life experience and some distance from the emotional intensity of actual experience. The southern girl/belle/lady figure is a character well established in the American imagination and immediately recognizable to most readers. Casting oneself or some other white female figure as a "southern beauty" or "southern lady" has served to blur class lines, softening economic disparities and other class markers in ways that tend to erase contentious divisions among white southerners. Subtly, and sometimes not so subtly, the descriptive image has also appropriated unto itself some of the aura of antebellum aristocracy and privileged whiteness. In varying degrees we find in these life narratives the identification of self with this figure, often related in a slightly ironical tone that typically arises from the aged writer's judgment of the youthful idealizing self. The skillful use of irony, in fact, allows a narrator winningly to partake of whatever cachet attaches to the image and at the same time expose it to social critique.

These texts portray many models—mothers, aunts, and others—who, like Miranda's cousin Amy, the quintessential beauty, represent the girl's notion of womanly perfection. If young, they possess beauty and engaging presence; if older, power and commanding presence as a matriarch. The ideal is remarkably consistent in these narratives, and it is largely merged in the books' opening chapters with a southern landscape that includes a plantation, black servants, and a privileged white girlhood. "I was born in the midst of vast cotton plantations. It was from them that my father's wealth came," Sinclair begins. Next door to the Kimbrough family's summer home on the Gulf Coast was the home of Varina Howell Davis, Mrs. Jefferson Davis, whose dead daughter Winnie, the "daughter of the Confederacy," furnished a story as romantic as Porter's fabled Amy Gay. Winnie's tragic tale so caught Craig Kimbrough's imagination that for a time she was inspired to become a writer, that is, until the appearance of Upton Sinclair put her back on the path of the southern belle.

Virginia Durr recalls that from her childhood perspective her grandmother Foster was "the queen bee," a woman who owned the church, owned the town, owned the plantation. In a bit of teasing self-mockery, Durr confesses that her grandmother was just the sort of woman she aspired to be—"having everyone love me, and everyone obligated to me" (8). Boggs notes that she was born in the same four-poster bed that her mother and mother's father had been born in, on Brunswick Plantation, in a big white house at the end of an avenue of live oak trees. Unlike Miranda's brunette model, her mother was nonetheless a "beauty," described as a "petite young woman of nineteen, the only blond in her family and blessed with brilliant blue eyes and the fairest skin I've ever seen" (5). Barber, too, remembers her mother's beauty, and she quotes the storied advice her paternal grandmother gave to her son, Lylah's father: "Murray, you could have married one of those suitable women of your own age, but you wanted the pretty young girl, so just get busy and make enough money for her to have a cook" (7–8). Barber's childhood is more deprived and troubled than that of the other writers discussed in this chapter, but she no less regards her background as distinctly southern, identifying the early widowhood of her mother, like that of her grandmother, as "a familiar pattern of the destinies of Southern women, destinies shaped by the Civil War, by the defeat of the Confederacy, by the bitterness of Reconstruction, and by the hard years that followed" (19). Plantations, beauties, belles, Civil War devastation, romance, and tragic glamour give color to these various portrayals of girlhood years in the South. Even after living with Upton Sinclair for forty-eight years—the man who had written the muckraking novel *The Jungle* and later, with his wife's continuous assistance, would go on to write countless books of social protest, lead public crusades in defense of the poor and disenfranchised, and run for governor of California on the Socialist ticket—Mary Craig would publish a life narrative entitled *Southern Belle.* Powerful political leader Lindy Boggs, who served in the U.S. House of Representatives for nearly twenty years, would recount her life story as *Washington Behind the Purple Veil.*

Reading these texts, one is sharply reminded of how recent is the Civil War in these narrators' tales and how stubbornly persistent is the edginess in white southerners' attitudes toward the nineteenth century. Even in recent years there are such continuing reminders as the controversies regarding the display of the Confederate flag. The ambivalent pride and defensive shame that Faulkner, Ellen Glasgow, and many other novelists have written of so profoundly are also registered in these autobiographical recollections of privileged white girls' coming-of-age years. To a considerable extent, their stories depict an innocent, girlish acceptance of southern social customs and racially separate traditions— and then reflect in later years a mature woman's understanding of the much greater complexity of southern society, which they have come in maturity to apprehend. There is no gainsaying the pleasure these writers—all of them in their seventies—take in recreating a kind of "golden" South of their youth. They suggest that the childhood left behind was connected to an idealized southern womanhood, and, though they admit to some nostalgia, they also insist their past was a fixed reality, one they are resolved to record faithfully. Lylah Barber explains that among her motives for writing is the wish to "pay tribute to the gallant women of my ancestry who endured the hardships of the Civil War and Reconstruction and survived with strength and grace." She also states her wish that her daughter "know where she came from" and that her readers be given a glimpse of a time rapidly vanishing. "I wanted to tell not only of my own experience of growing up in North Florida, but also about my family and a way of life that, as I look back from the vantage point of almost eighty years, seems as though it took place in another world, so different were its rhythms and its cadences" (xii).

The early chapters of these autobiographies are more introspective than the later chapters that in memoir fashion tend to record a flow of events and people passing through the subjects' lives. These busy, outward-turned years of later life are very much those of "relational lives" that we have seen in earlier texts.

Despite the drama and celebrity of the active adulthood, it is rather the elderly woman's reflections upon her youth that are often most engaging—her effort to establish, or at least discern, the beginnings of what would become the central thread of her "life plot."

Like Agnes Anderson, Mary Craig Kimbrough Sinclair began the work that would become *Southern Belle* not as her life story but as a biography of her famous husband. The working title she spoke of was *My Husband, Upton Sinclair.* And like the autobiographies of Kearney and Fearn, her memoir is largely focused upon others, especially in the second half of the text, in which she concentrates upon the vivid cavalcade of people and events crowding upon her and her famous husband. In the opening chapters we find the inward self most revealed, the "woman within," as the Virginia writer Ellen Glasgow would describe her own inner experience.

In *Southern Belle,* as in virtually every other autobiography, the writer decides at the outset, deliberately or intuitively, on predominating life themes that she regards as formative and that she expects to develop throughout the "plot" of her life narrative. She introduces a character whose parentage and background, values and actions constitute a psychologically credible predecessor of the kind of woman she intends to find and depict at the conclusion, a woman who can also be credibly merged with the narrator of the life story. William Wordsworth's memorable line that "the child is father of the man" is inverted in autobiographical writing, for the adult narrator creates the textual child. The clearest display of the writer's self-interpretation often occurs in the beginning pages of autobiography, for the introduction arises from and is consonant with the conclusion.

The interpretive direction that Sinclair announces is her movement from an innocent, un-self-conscious, self-absorbed time and place, depicted as a gone-with-the-wind Old South, to an enlightened position in a broader expanse of the world. Her reflecting intellect, which cues the irony, tells her the journey was inevitable and that the secure traditionalism of her youth was stifling and shallow, that it was, in fact, clearly racist and male dominated. And yet, she does not, or cannot, resolve the ambivalent conclusion that a kind of gorgeous femininity flowered there, the repudiation of which she will not countenance, as evidenced by her self-presentation as southern belle. There is finally little of definitive self-analysis, little overt "rewriting the self," as Mark Freeman describes the understanding that one may signal in autobiography. Sinclair constructs a series of engrossing, often amusing scenes, all the while keeping up an agreeable, entertaining manner before the reader, often in the early chapters a rather teasing, girlish tone obviously meant to reflect the perceptions and mannerism of the youthful age depicted. Reading the woman within requires one's reading inferentially. Whether the choice of title was her husband's or the publisher's, the authorial presence seems quite deliberately crafted in the mode of the belle-lady and, if somewhat ironically named, nonetheless aptly so.

Southern Belle, published in 1957, is a lively, fast-paced book that invokes much of the literary and social history of the first half of the twentieth century. Married in 1913 to Upton Sinclair, the author whose 1906 novel *The Jungle* had spurred federal regulation of the meat-packing industry, Craig Sinclair would share his life and work for nearly fifty years.[1] She was his collaborator, editor, financial manager, household supervisor, and wife throughout a partnership that saw the publication of nearly seventy-five books. During these years he was a celebrated figure nationally and internationally, known as a "crusader" for social justice, a "socialist," a moral idealist. In a sense she lived the sort of marriage that George Eliot's Dorothea Brooke idealized and desired but was denied in *Middlemarch,* the helpmate to a man actively engaged in bringing about greater knowledge and justice in the world. At least, this is the view that Sinclair chooses to foreground in her depiction of her journey from southern belle to the activist, enabling wife of Upton Sinclair.

Despite several expressions of reservation about too much self-exposure, the presence, the voice, of this interesting woman gives the book its vitality. The editors at Crown Publishers in 1955, when Craig Sinclair began the serious work on the memoir, urged her to write a story that focused on her own experience as well as that of her famous husband. At the time she was suffering from a serious heart condition, which led to her death in 1961. Often bedridden, she nonetheless kept up her memoir writing while giving active assistance in researching and revising to Upton's projects and organizing and "marketing" their vast collection of manuscripts, letters, and other papers, which she had laboriously conserved over the years. Before her death she negotiated the sale of the collection to Indiana University, which currently houses the papers in the Lilly Library.

In *The Autobiography of Upton Sinclair,* published after her death in 1962, Sinclair describes the physical ordeal of Craig's last years, during which she undertook to write the book at his pleading. He said he sometimes sat near her and wrote to her dictation, but most of the time she wrote lying in bed with her head propped forward, holding a pad with one hand and a pencil with the other, a tiring position on which Sinclair blamed the acute back pain she suffered during the writing. Despite her debilitating illness, the book recreates in the opening chapters the youthful spiritedness of her girlhood in Mississippi, narrated with a light self-mockery and ironic humor far removed from suffering and death. An experienced professional ever mindful of her audience, she makes her way through the event-filled life, choosing incidents and characters that will amuse and inform her readers, often fleshing out scenes with dialogue and vivid descriptive detail, and thus answering her reader's curiosity about a celebrity life—and fulfilling the book jacket's promise to deliver "the personal story of a crusader's wife."

Sinclair skillfully exploits the underlying irony of her transition from "southern belle" of a staid, traditional "Old South" family to bride of the founder of the Intercollegiate Socialist Society (later the League for Industrial Democracy). Her narration of the girlhood-courtship-marriage plot that dominates the first third of the book draws upon a long literary history of fictional heroines, which is not to say that the book is inaccurate or unconvincing. In fact, there is ample evidence in her letters to her brother Hunter Kimbrough that she went to great pains to get the facts right, writing to family members and friends to check her memory and repairing to the voluminous collection of papers to verify names, places, dates, and events. But as Rachel Brownstein observes in *Becoming a Heroine,* women have typically drawn upon female paradigms gleaned from novels to understand, explain, and give coherence to their own lives, a sensible explanatory "plot" being what most human beings seek (and construct) throughout their lives.

The heroine who emerges from the opening pages is a beautiful girl, the willful, passionate oldest child of the well-to-do Judge Allen Macaskill Kimbrough of Greenwood, Mississippi, and his adored wife, Mary Hunter Southworth. The author is reticent about her age, rarely dating the events she recounts. Her birth year is given by various "official" sources as both 1882 and 1883, the later date the one her husband alludes to in his memorial tribute to Craig in a 1962 edition of the book that he commissioned and gave to public libraries across the country. The narrating voice of the text is the mature Mary Craig K. Sinclair, who looks back at her parents and homeland with fondness and respect but also with a droll irony that produces the effect noted earlier of establishing a girlish past well distanced from her later life, thus allowing some latitude for social criticism.

Sinclair's ironic stance is particularly serviceable in her commentary about the social roles and relationships of blacks and whites in her late nineteenth-century Mississippi youth, the subject that dominates the first chapter. About the racial attitudes of her parents and their contemporaries, Craig comments that their assumption of African American subservience was "fortunate" for the plantation owner, who without their labor could not have raised his crops "in a sun that was as hot as Africa's," and "fortunate," too, for women like "Mama . . . for how could she have lived with so many babies, and so many parties to give, if there had not been Negro mammies and housegirls and cooks"? The portrait of her mother is of a girlish woman, "tender and conscientious," loving, lovable, ever a support and ally, especially in matters of romance, but a woman who had little knowledge of or interest in the social ideas and activism that would engage Craig in her later life. By contrast, the patriarchal Judge Kimbrough, though loving, was the disciplinarian, to be obeyed, not argued with. She portrays him as a learned, scholarly man, equipped by intellect and education to evaluate the socialist ideas of Upton Sinclair, but whose traditional world view and social attitudes would oppose him to her marriage, at least initially. The great distance between race relations of the 1880s and 1890s and the 1950s when Sinclair was writing the autobiography is not taken up in the early section but rather indicated by the hedging ironic tone. One thinks of the aftermath of *Brown v. Board of Education,* the court ruling in 1954 that held public school segregation to be unconstitutional, and the following year, near her Greenwood home, the murder of Emmett Till, the young black man who had come from Chicago to visit his grandfather in Mississippi and was beaten to death because his manner toward a white female clerk in a rural store had offended her husband and his kin. These years of racial upheaval in the South do not intrude upon the South of Sinclair's youth, "when the world was young," as she describes it.

Recreating her youthful self from the vantage of her mid-seventies, Craig Sinclair focuses upon two aspects of her identity that largely define the "self" that is the subject of the memoir. Although she relies upon the teasing tone to suggest the naïveté and starry-eyed ambitions of outgrown youth, she chooses details of her Mississippi girlhood and New York young adulthood deliberately to establish her preparation for wifehood and for a literary career. After three years at the Mississippi State College for Women, where she was "the first girl ever enrolled who had got a grade of 100 in the course called English," she attends the Gardner School for Young Ladies in New York, which offered "opportunities to meet the millionaires of the world's richest city." It is also at the Gardner School that she is confirmed as possessing attributes of both the belle and the "bluestocking," a term she applies only rarely to herself but that she often uses to identify a female intellectual. Mrs. Gardner commends her gracious manners, those of a "true lady," and also her mental abilities:

I was serene, my voice was low, I deferred to my elders, and while I spoke frankly, I never said anything to wound anyone's feelings. Southern young ladies had these characteristics, and for that reason she always made it a point to have several in her school. . . . It seemed that I was never to break rules, or in any way descend from a fictitious throne, so as to set an example for the Westerners. . . . Mrs. Gardner told me also that she was sure I would be diligent in my studies and have a good chance to be valedictorian of the graduating class. I was not a little awed by the dual responsibility, and fearful that I might have to walk a straighter line than I wanted to. (19)

As graduate of a prestigious finishing school and eminently marriageable, Sinclair returns to Mississippi and to a coterie of beaux who would have made Scarlett O'Hara envious. But the heartbreak of her father's intervening to end her engagement to "Jerry Winston," identified as Calhoun Wilson by biographer Leon Harris, leads her back to New York and the Gardner school for further study in literature and the art of writing. She turns determinedly toward a career as a writer, attempting as her first book the biography of Winnie Davis, whose fate she associates with her own. She describes the book as "sort of written," though stilted and lacking in "reality," in 1909, when she first met the famous writer and sought his advice about the book. The meeting took place in Battle Creek, Michigan, where she and her mother had gone to seek treatment at Dr. Kellogg's sanitarium.

At the time of their meeting, she had drafted a manuscript based on interviews with many who had known Davis, including a lengthy conversation in New York with Varina Howell Davis and in New Orleans with the widow of the Confederate general William Preston Johnson, a friend of Winnie. Sinclair's effort to write the biography so as not to offend or contradict anyone had bogged down as hopeless. She had come to question Jefferson Davis's "right" to block Winnie's marriage "simply because the man was a Yankee and unacceptable . . . to the Confederate veterans," and voiced the unthinkable, "What right had these men to control her life?" (56–59). Taking cover behind the third-person voice, she alludes here to her compromised subjectivity in a breezy tone, but it seems likely that her failure of confidence in her judgment about the major issues central to the Davis story and about a viable literary approach she might employ to produce a successful biography significantly heightened her interest in a writer whose success was manifest in his fame.

Upton's social protest novel, *The Jungle,* had attracted national and international attention, as well as the widespread admiration of socialist reformers.

Energetic and wholly self-assured in his judgments about everything, he was a man worthy in her eyes to be a husband—he loved her, and he "needed" her assistance with his literary and crusading career. As Mrs. Upton Sinclair she could enact the two roles she most admired—a supporting, inspiring wife and a muse and collaborator in a great literary enterprise.

A significant obstacle to this marriage plot was Upton's embarrassing first marriage and the scandalous divorce that had ended it. Given the Kimbrough family pride and traditionalism, this was a monumental obstacle that decades later still held some emotional pain for Craig, especially the breach with her father. The narrative voice she adopts to recount details of the courtship and marriage is distanced from the action, almost reportorial, but always assuring that a satisfying future lay ahead. Because of the widespread media coverage of Upton's divorce from Meta Fuller and the continued media attention to his marriage to Craig, she could hardly omit this dramatic material from her auto-biography. But her account is extremely circumspect and shows a sure control of the art of "spinning" a story. Meta disappears in *Southern Belle,* and there is little detail of David, Upton and Meta's son, even in the later years' narra-tive. The courtship story is narrated largely as a comedy of manners, with the mothers of the older female kin of Craig and Upton meeting to establish to ev-eryone's satisfaction the noble bloodlines of the two uniting families. The two-paragraph coverage of the wedding improbably fuses a lyrical discourse about the April jonquil beauty of the Fredericksburg farmhouse site with a humorous turn familiar in Hollywood romantic comedies. At the key moment, "Mama" Kimbrough, realizing there is no ring, tugs at her finger to produce one so the ritual can be concluded "correctly" (138).

Sinclair's determination always to put on a winning public face perhaps owes to the general southern tradition of pride—and the avoidance of shame—that Bertram Wyatt-Brown has discussed as the core concept of "southern honor." Her reticence and avoidance of public embarrassment were clearly basic lessons in her training for southern ladyhood, and the gap between her notion of han-dling personal error or embarrassment and Upton's was vast. He had published a book about his first marriage and the breakup, *Love's Pilgrimage* (1911), and in the 1962 *The Autobiography of Upton Sinclair,* published the year after Craig's death, he wrote of their very different personalities. "Craig was all caution and I was all venture. She was all reticence, and I wanted to tell of my mistakes so that others could learn to avoid them. Craig would have died before she let anyone know hers" (191).

For his 1975 biography of Upton, Leon Harris drew heavily upon interviews with David Sinclair and Craig's youngest sister Dollie (Mrs. John Kling), as well as the letters of Meta to David and others, for his sharply negative portrayal of Craig. One might suspect that the book in some respects serves as a mouthpiece for the bitterness Upton's son harbored against his stepmother, whom he blamed for his father's negligence. The tenor of Harris's judgment is indicated in his very first reference to Craig: "At what precise moment Mary Craig Kimbrough decided she would have Upton Sinclair is not clear, but soon after meeting him in Battle Creek in 1909 she began her plan to appropriate him. She worked with cool and ingratiating guile and above all with an unhurried patience and calm that contrasted strikingly with Meta's chronic near-hysteria" (125). He goes on to assert that Craig became Upton's mistress before the divorce was final and that she conceived a child by him during a stay in Europe and subsequently had an abortion (126). He cites his source as Craig's sister, who he notes also claimed that Craig and Upton had been secretly married by the time the abortion took place (374). Whatever the full truth of the courtship and marriage, Craig's decision to depict it in an expurgated and almost comically romanticized version is consistent with the lady-narrator she constructs and maintains throughout the text.

Given the prickly circumstances of this marital alliance, one might well wonder why Craig married Upton when, as she writes, she had had offers from many more appropriate suitors. Doubtless she was attracted to his considerable fame as a writer and his commitment to social progress, which gratified both her literary ambition and her desire to find a "worthy" husband. She had spent several years living in New York, trying to be a writer, exposed to young Greenwich Village artists and intellectuals whose "manners were free," as was their talk (69). She was determined to learn to work, as she told Upton, so as not to become a "parasite." She had entered a world where ideas mattered more than bloodlines, though she did not entirely disavow her southern roots. One might note that she was an aging belle; her Virginia wedding took place just four days before her thirtieth birthday. And, undeniably, even according to Harris's account, she found Upton Sinclair charming.

In many passages Craig reviews her reasons for marrying him, but they seem reasons in keeping with the reflections of the older woman, looking backward with some irony and bemusement upon her own youthful naïveté from the perspective of a long marriage. "Taking stock of my marriage," she writes, "I could write home with a clear conscience that I loved my husband and was happy. This would make up, in part at least, for the divorce and the Socialism. I did love him. He was so game, and so charitable! The world was full of pain and sorrow, but with him at my side, there was hope" (146). From the outset of their relationship she accepts the primacy of his commitment to his writing and to high-minded purpose, the quality that most inspires her love, she says. He believed "most of the things he had accepted as facts early in life. He was sure that ignorance was the source of more human misery than any other one thing. The evil qualities—selfishness, greed, vanity, cruelty—would disappear when men knew the better things of life. He wanted to persuade them that neither poverty nor war was necessary. . . . I loved Upton for this optimism—this love of life, this ability to see beauty wherever we were, whatever the circumstances" (400–401).

To her credit, Craig gives a balanced account of the rewards and costs of nearly fifty years of marriage to a man almost single-mindedly devoted to his work. Like Walter Anderson, Upton wanted no children, whose needs would distract him from his writing and crusades. Although he had gained custody of David after the divorce, his son was sent to boarding schools and, for a time, to live with the Kimbroughs in Mississippi. Craig never mentions the absence of children in her life; she seems rather to accept that her maternal role is required and satisfied by mothering Upton.

In the early years Craig found the protest marches and other "crusades" exciting, though worrisome and a bit scary. Her account of the 1914 march on behalf of Colorado miners, whose unionizing efforts had been bitterly and violently opposed by the Rockefeller-controlled Colorado Fuel and Iron Company, shows a young woman who enters the fray with considerable innocence. But with such details as her misunderstanding of the word "thug," which she hears as "slugs," the narrator continues to narrate the events of these early years with humor and a gathering sense of irony.

When she writes of the later years, such as the period of Upton's exhausting candidacy for the governorship of California, we find her tone more direct, less playful. Although she maintains her commitment to Upton's ideals through the last page of the book, her account of later years reflects a growing sentiment that supporting his crusades has demanded considerable sacrifice of her health and general well-being. "I had married him because he was a writer, and though I had gone with him, perhaps foolishly, into all his other crusades, I would never do it again" (361). Nonetheless, one comes several pages later to find an account of a cross-country lecture tour in which Craig accompanies Upton as he speaks on behalf of the economic reforms advanced in his EPIC (End Poverty in California) political race and against the rising menace of Nazi Germany, as well as in support of a variety of democratic reforms aimed at bringing about greater social justice. Although she becomes increasingly skeptical about the possibilities of transforming a wicked and misguided world into a haven of justice and knowledge, she never forsakes her husband and his work, nor does she denigrate his boyish, energetic idealism.

Craig Sinclair's judgment of her husband's character and his literary talent is quite complex. For all her admiration of his noble ideals and her frequent depiction of him in hagiographic terms, she portrays Upton as often impetuous and thoughtless—about finances, clothes, shelter, even people. He was constantly engaging in faddish diets, which she, too, sometimes tried, and in ill-considered commitments to organizations and causes. As a novelist, he was often more committed to delivering unambiguous propaganda than to creating a compelling embodiment of lived life. Given this portrayal of Upton Sinclair, one can only be mystified by Leon Harris's assertion that *Southern Belle* is principally the work of Upton. The claim is mystifying chiefly because such subtle, self-imposed irony would hardly have been Upton's style—of writing or of self-assessment—as Harris's biography makes unmistakably clear. Nor does the presence of the vivid, fleshed-out figures of the narrative, not to mention the striking absence of moral preachment, indicate Upton's authorship. There is voluminous and compelling evidence not only in the text itself but in Craig's personal correspondence during the years of the book's composition to establish her as the author. Harris bases his assumption upon finding among the Sinclair papers pages of manuscript in Upton's hand. He contradicts himself, however, on those occasions when he asserts Craig's authorship in order to question the autobiography's accuracy and candor. And he implicitly dismisses Upton's account of his occasional recording of Craig's dictation during the times her illness confined her to bed. In *Radical Innocent: Upton Sinclair* (2006), Anthony Arthur remarks upon Harris's assertion of Upton's authoring *Southern Belle,* noting for one thing her one-thousand-page manuscript at the Honnold Library in Claremont, an early draft titled *My Husband, Upton Sinclair.* Arthur also identifies some of the same "false trails" that I note, which clearly indicate the absence in Craig's text of Upton's usual self-presentation (313). A number of personal letters from Craig to her brother also include details of the stages of her writing.

Harris's claims interest me for several reasons. In the late 1970s when I first read *Southern Belle* and examined the Sinclair holdings in the Lilly Library at Indiana University, I found many pages of manuscript of Upton's novels written in Craig's handwriting and concluded, as indeed Harris, Arthur, and other scholars have observed, that the Sinclairs were collaborators in many of the books published as singly authored by Upton. It seemed to me then, as it still does, that unacknowledged credit belongs much more to Craig than to Upton.

It is worth noting to what extent Craig depicts herself in this book as a literary partner of her famous husband. She writes about "his work" as "our life," and she narrates countless episodes that reflect her self-image as that of the maternal, supporting facilitator-collaborator. But from first to last, she maintains her identity as a woman of literary bent and talent. In an early exchange with Upton when she was in New York trying to launch a writing career, she answers his comment that she "probably [has] some excellent material for a novelist," with the arch retort: "You mean for a novel, don't you?" Subsequently, in several telling paragraphs she records the complicated dynamics of how her admiration for his intellectual authority led to a submerging of her ambitions to his needs and nobler career. He had sent her book after book to instruct her in his "propaganda," "certain of the validity of his doctrines and of his ability to present them convincingly." She replied that she was spending her time on her own novel, *Sylvia,* based upon her own experiences. Then, with no discernible later-day irony, she writes of his offer "to help," of his certainty that her girlhood story would be "wonderful material for a book" but his uncertainty of her "ability to handle it." A little later she writes of their "collaboration," which produced the novel *Sylvia* and, as she says, "at my insistence" it went "out to the world as Upton's work" (78, 83, 107).

This episode shines a revealing light on Craig's assumptions about woman's role as writer and wife: a career as a writer is available to the single woman, but, as soon as she becomes a wife, her work belongs to the advancement of her husband. One needs to understand how deeply formative this attitude was in Mary Craig Kimbrough's generation of southern women. Independent work outside the home that was available and respectable for her social class lay in volunteer activity in the "Daughters" organizations, including the genealogical research that membership entailed, or in the kind of public-spirited club work that has been studied by Anne Scott and many other scholars in recent years. Craig's mother was an active member of the United Daughters of the Confederacy and a tireless worker in anti-suffrage activity in Mississippi.

Always a supporting and controlling force in Craig's youth and early adulthood, her mother's model would firmly influence Craig's self-image as a married woman. Mary Hunter Kimbrough had married a man she admired, one who could provide her a luxurious life, but one she did not love, according to Craig. She bore ten children, often traveled away from home, argued that woman's place was in the home, and opposed woman's suffrage on the grounds that a woman's right to the support of a man would be jeopardized by her demanding the vote. She embodied an exotic combination of hauteur and humility, Craig writes, a sort of southern adaptation of the Victorian lady, who was an intrepid defender of the Lost Cause, a pious evangelical Christian, and a member of the Campbellites. She was dauntless in her support of her beloved oldest child, nurturing her writing ambition after the collapse of the Jerry Winston engagement, but once Craig married Upton Sinclair, everyone understood that Craig's "work" would be the advancement of his career. After the wedding, in fact, Craig and Upton immediately set to work on a sequel to *Sylvia*, which was published as *Sylvia's Marriage*. "In Bermuda we had a book to finish," she writes. "We worked steadily and conscientiously" (146). Years later she would remark that she and Upton often could not remember whether some recalled event had actually happened to her or had been some plot detail they had made up for *Sylvia*.

Craig's distinctive contribution to the literary partnership, according to both Craig and Upton, who discusses the subject at several point in his autobiography, was her ability to add vivifying detail to the fiction, what she and he came to call "putting the clothes on Mary Burke" (197). She recounts the episode of her part in the revisions of *King Coal*, a novel about the mining camps of the West, whose heroine Mary Craig thought insufficiently characterized by Upton. "I begged to describe the poor girl," she writes, and "the phrase 'putting the clothes on Mary Burke' became my formula for what the story needed, meaning of course the psychology as well as the looks of the characters" (197).

When Macmillan turned down the novel for the same problems that she had found, Craig comments that she wrote the publisher, "saying what I thought the book needed, and asking would he read it again if Upton and I revised it together? He kindly said that he would; and so began the toughest ordeal that any woman can undergo for the love of a man." Later she records rather triumphantly that Macmillan agreed to publish the novel, sending a five hundred dollar advance (thus saving the couple from financial crisis), as well as a complimentary letter regarding the revision. "I had been the 'something' that had abolished the bridge [of financial exigency]," she records, "by the simple device of 'putting some clothes on Mary Burke.'" An interesting side note to Craig's ability to compose details that heightened the verisimilitude of Upton's social fiction is Leon Harris's rather grudging admission that "Craig's sense of what art is and is not was better than Upton's" (291), an astonishing assertion, given his earlier views.

To a young feminist reading *Southern Belle* in the twenty-first century, it may be difficult to understand Craig Sinclair's readiness to commit her energy and intellect to her husband's career, but her memoir richly illuminates the social forces and values that influenced her life choices. She was trained to be "quiet and ladylike," she says in the opening pages, and she was eager to fulfill her destiny as southern belle-lady-wife by marrying her first love. She depicts the traumatic ending of this relationship by edict of her father as a tragic disappointment, the memory of which will always haunt her. Like Winnie Davis she portrays herself as a victim of the patriarchal South. She thus poses a romantic plot of an impassioned, naive love that, denied, leads to a higher purpose and, eventually, to a noble husband. Turning away from the stereotyped path of the belle, Craig comes to question much about the South she has known, its assumptions about race and about a "woman's place," for example. Visiting a cousin attending the Finch School for Young Ladies, she is fascinated by the feminist ideas of Jessica Finch, and when a final chance for marriage to a traditional southerner shows up in New York in the form of a proposal from an old Mississippi beau, she declines the offer. As she writes later, she was coming to question whether she was any longer "a Southern woman at heart" (86).

Craig even begins to regard marriage in a new light, faced as she is with rejecting the divorced Upton or reconciling herself to accepting some new elasticity in marital vows. As she ponders the prospect of this marriage, she remembers Mrs. Jefferson Davis's warning that "once *our* women are married, they are like Sterne's starling—they cannot get out" (86). Still, Craig Sinclair was ever an accommodationist more than a radical, and so, when the offer came, she did not decline wifehood with Upton Sinclair. She incurred her father's censure but retained her mother's and the rest of the family's approval and support. Lillian Hellman wrote in the autobiographical *An Unfinished Woman* that "if you are willing to take the punishment, you are halfway through the battle" (23). Craig was at least halfway willing to take the punishment that followed upon her break with tradition.

In 1979, Craig's younger brother, Hunter Kimbrough, who was living then in Bay St. Louis, Mississippi, spoke to me on several occasions about his sister and his close association through the years with her and Upton when they lived in California and later in Arizona. He shared many of the letters Craig had written him giving details of the initiation, composition, and publication of the memoir. They reveal, for example, that the incentive for undertaking a biography of Upton (or his "autobiography"), which was her original intent, came from the positive reception of *The Cup of Fury,* the 1956 book exposing the pernicious effects of alcohol upon the lives of literary men and women the Sinclairs had known. The book had been repeatedly turned down by a dozen New York publishers when Dr. Daniel Poling, editor of the *Christian Century,* accepted it and placed it with the Channel Press, providing that the author revised the manuscript to include more human interest ("clothes on Mary Burke"). The lively revisions attracted enthusiastic reviews, particularly one by Richard Armour, and also drew the interest of Crown Publishers, who asked Upton to write an autobiography.

In several letters to Hunter Kimbrough during the summer of 1955, Craig speaks of the prospects of composing an "autobiography" or a "biography," making almost no distinction between the forms. She says, for example, "My temptation is the autobiography [Crown] wants. Upton always said he wanted me to write his biography—and of course I'm the only person who really can, as I know all about his work, having taken an active part in it for nearly half a century." A little later she wrote her brother that she was looking forward to a "breathing spell" before the *Cup of Fury's* publication—"unless," she writes, "we yield to the temptation to write the 'bio' [which she crosses out and replaces with 'auto-biography'] that Donigan [Crown editor] asks us to do."[2]

The decision to go forward with the book would prevent her from fleeing the California smog so detrimental to her health, she wrote her brother, for they would need to remain near their collection of personal papers, "which we've already had to use for research for the autobiographical material I wove into [*Cup of Fury*] to take the place of some of the alcoholics Upton had lumped into one volume.... You'll see from Donigan's letter that he is charmed by the *biographical* material—in it is everything I could dig up hastily that contained humor, such as Upton and a teenage Jewish boy (each fifteen years old), going into a literary 'partnership.' ... I could dig out many such stories of Upton—if I had strength—and this is what Donigan wants a whole book to be enlivened by." In an earlier letter she had spoken of her rewriting sections of the book, including one that she feared might be libelous and wanted to delete. But Upon thought it "the funniest and saddest story in the book and refuses to cut it out."

Clearly, the work she and Upton did on the alcohol book revived many old memories of their life together. "I went down again and again and worked in the office, and in the other storerooms, to find interesting material to use to break up the monotony of drunks, one after the other. And I found things I'd forgotten years ago." She occasionally wrote her brother for his recollections of family history or requested that he do some specific research for "the book I am writing." In July 1956 she wrote that "it is a big book and took ten months"; in fact, there is correspondence suggesting that the publisher for a time considered a two-volume edition.

In letters to her brother from 1955 to 1957 she writes extensively of her plans for the book, the contents that would recount a whole era of social and political history, and her caution not to embarrass the family with any unseemly personal revelations.

> It is all about the Delta, my childhood there and at Ashton Hall, school days in New York. . . . It is not the whole Mississippi story, and you do not come into it because you weren't born then. The next section includes you. . . . I'll send it at sometime, *if* you want to see what I've made of our old home, our parents, older brothers. . . . Everyone at home has co-operated with me, sending me material asked for. I've memorialized our dear mother in the Jefferson Davis shrine story, and I've tried to show Papa as the scholar, who knew Greek and Latin and Law, honorable man of affairs, and lovable father he was. I have not told any damaging things about anyone.

She also writes in these letters of her views regarding larger social issues, especially her anxiety about the growing tensions between ethnic and racial groups all over the world—and her fears that white ignorance and racism would exacerbate the troubles. "I've had a big job for an old woman," she concluded in a 13 March 1956 letter to Kimbrough, "but I've done a book I think has historic value, for I was born only twenty years after the [Civil] war and knew the generation which fought that war."

After she completed the manuscript, Craig was concerned that the text receive the sort of careful reading, editing, and proofing that she had always provided for Upton, and while Upton was obviously a great source of help with the matter covering the years they had spent together, she worried about getting the same assistance for the Mississippi material. Again, she called upon her brother: "I'll be glad if you can read it through carefully. . . . Upton has always had his mss. read by several people. I know no one in our family who would have any idea of how to read a ms. for errors except for you." She also mentioned that she might send the manuscript to the writer Floyd Dell, who had written *Upton Sinclair: A Study in Social Protest* in 1927. "Upton and I considered him the best literary critic in America." But she had reservations, as she wrote her brother, for Dell "knows nothing about the South and will probably be bored to death (even angry) with the Southern stuff and therefore unable to judge it reasonably."

Uncharacteristically, for the astute financial manager she was, Craig readily agreed to the contract Crown offered her—a $1,000 advance and the "customary" right to decide on editing. The decision was clear evidence of her declining health: "I could have bargained, but decided my life is too short for delays." One can only speculate about the depth of desire and the lifelong conflicting impulses for self-sacrifice and self-achievement that prompted the last line of the ten-page letter to her brother on 30 October 1956: "I want something before I leave this earth—so I'm happy about the contract."

As the book went into the final stages of production, the editors asked Upton to compose a brief introduction. Craig's account of the episode in a May 1957 letter to Hunter Kimbrough is matter of fact, suggesting little irony but rather a mild bemusement at the utterly predictable attention Upton gave in the introduction to his crusades and his life as a crusader! "Crown asked U. to write an introduction to my book—wants it to show that it is authentic fact story as he does not want to use Upton's name on the outside of the book (wants to feature Southern Belle—not crusader, I guess). Says he wants the title 'Southern Belle' by Mary Craig Sinclair (not Mrs. U.S.)." And then she adds, "I wrote the introduction as Upton's effort to write it featured our 'radical' crusader!"

The reviews of the book were mostly favorable. *Time* (18 Nov. 1957) gave it full coverage, equal in length and immediately following the opening review of James Agee's *A Death in the Family*. The reviewer called *Southern Belle* "a truly romantic as well as a wonderfully goofy story—the memoirs of a Southern belle who married a notorious radical," and pronounced it "irresistible to students of U.S. [United States] life and manners, . . . the story of Mary's life with Sinclair, that strange, admirable, preposterous figure of a vanished America—a man with every gift except humor and silence." The reviewer later observed that "she never seems to realize that the romanticism of early Socialism and that of the Old South were akin. However different the windmills they were tilting at, both Mary and Upton were American romantics." In a nearly full-page review in the *New Republic* (23 December 1957), Bruce Bliven opens by noting that "the world of Upton Sinclair's youth—a world of gentle, Utopian socialism—now seems as dead as the carrier pigeon," and, though he finds Craig's world as having "more survival value," it, too, seems "passing." Bliven comments upon the contrasting worlds of Upton and Craig, which give rise to an ambivalence that constitutes for him the major point of interest in *her* story. But overall, he reviews the book rather more as a biography of Upton than an autobiography by Craig, commenting that she barely mentions some of his "70-odd books." The pleasures it offers the reader, according to Bliven, are mainly those of a nostalgic witnessing

of "a parade of half-forgotten figures of literature, the arts and political and social reform."

Reading *Southern Belle* today does indeed open a window upon a world just
past, a world of constricted choices for women of ambition and intelligence, especially when they are beautiful, talented "belles." Determined not to become
some kind of caged southern lady, Mary Craig Kimbrough Sinclair bound herself to a husband whose commitment to writing and crusading for social reform assured that her life would never be ordinary. Anthony Arthur writes that
Upton regarded her as "the single most important person in his life"—not just
because "she devoted herself to advancing his career, that she ran their household efficiently, that she was highly intelligent, or that she had a lively sense of
humor. It was her deeply felt sense of [Upton] Sinclair's *vulnerability*" (146).

Publicly, Craig never wavered in her support of Upton nor in the pride she
took in being his wife. And yet, as the years passed, she sought to pursue her
own intellectual interests and ambitions. She undertook serious, extended research in extrasensory perception, which led her to work with William McDou-
gall at Duke University and eventually to write with Upton an account of the
research in *Mental Radio*. She also pursued an intense study of Christian Science and many other subjects of interest she shared with her husband. She was
a gifted woman who bridged traditional and modernist societies, composing
an intensely lived life from the choices she faced. Sinclair suffered a fatal stroke
just five years after her memoir was published, and she died in Pasadena, California, on 26 April 1961. According to the obituary that appeared in the *Jackson
Clarion-Ledger,* she left instructions for her return to her native state: "I want
again to be a part of the soil of Mississippi. I want to be buried there."

When the Sinclairs lived in California, Craig had for years been an avid
homebuilder, seeking a living place capacious enough to house their growing
collection of papers and provide space for office and library, as well as garden
area for flowers and fruit trees. One might well read her solution as an architectural metaphor for her strategy of yoking together the southern belle and
the hard-working collaborator of her husband in an arduous literary and social
activist life. In Pasadena she sought out pieces of old houses—five in all—that
she had moved in increments over time to the original dwelling, carpentered
together in a long, rambling structure, and finally covered overall with a coat
of pink paint. She describes it as a "dream place." It did accommodate both the
writing-crusading life and the honeysuckle and star jasmine of a Mississippi
garden, but it was situated, one has to notice, not far from the dream factory of
Hollywood.

6

Belles, Wives, and Public Lives, Part II

VIRGINIA FOSTER DURR, LINDY CLAIBORNE BOGGS, AND LYLAH SCARBOROUGH BARBER

The impetus for Virginia Durr's *Outside the Magic Circle* began with a series of interviews in the 1970s. Widely known for her public support of activities to secure voting and other civil rights for fellow southerners who were black, she was sought out by oral historians interested in recording her life story. Wife of Clifford Durr, who had served during the Roosevelt administration as head of the Reconstruction Finance Commission and later of the Federal Communications Commission (FCC), Virginia began her public activism in Washington in the 1930s, working as a volunteer in the Women's Division of the Democratic National Committee (DNC). She notes that at the time there was not a single woman from any of the southern states serving on a local or state committee. There were a few ornamental women on the National Committee—pretty women who "wore big hats and sang 'Dixie'" (101), but absence was the most obvious feature of women's role in the Democratic Party, particularly in the South.

Deciding that the poll tax was one of the major deterrents to women's voting and participating in politics, the Women's Division began an active movement to abolish the tax, a strategy that of course led as well to support of greater enfranchisement of black citizens. Durr recalls that when their efforts began to be noticed, Jim Farley, chairman of the DNC, came first to see Dorothy McAllister, head of the Women's Division, and then went to Roosevelt, demanding that he "shut up these damn women," who were beginning to cause real trouble with the southern congressional delegations (115). But Virginia Durr was never one to "shut up," and her involvement in civil rights work would continue throughout her life.

In *Carry Me Home,* a study of Birmingham, Alabama, as a climactic site of the civil rights Movement, Diane McWhorter tells a well-researched and yet personal story of a turbulent era of recent southern history that drew in Alabamians of every political stripe. McWhorter's grandfather, Hobart McWhorter had been a law partner of Clifford Durr's before his move to Washington and had even been a member of the Durr wedding party. Her grandmother Marjorie Westgate McWhorter, to whom she dedicates the book, had also known Virginia in the Junior League in Birmingham, and both shared a Wellesley background. Diane McWhorter's descriptions of Virginia Durr are provocatively ambivalent, aggrandizing her in one paragraph as "one of those larger-than-life figures who seemed marked for destiny, like her late sister's husband, Hugo Black," and then, a few sentences later, condescending about her outspokenness. She writes, "Aptly nicknamed Jinksie, Virginia had always been like a belle on phenobarbital. There had been times when Hobart gave his wife the hairy eyeball after Jinksie publicly betrayed some confidence Marjorie had shared about the law firm" (91).

McWhorter's zigzagging tone, in fact, in several respects traces Durr's own voice in the autobiography, which is by turns formal and straightforward and then, as if to reassert the ever present belle—lest some display of seriousness undercut "charm"—swerves into a mocking and effacing self-depiction. McWhorter ends the paragraph in a style typical of Durr herself, with a judgment and an anecdote that gives and takes away in equal portion—and in language suggesting both Durr's extraordinary courage and a frivolous understanding of her own courageous action. "The truths that Jinksie blurted out became morally as well as socially embarrassing once she was radicalized by Senator Robert La Follette's famous civil liberties hearings," says McWhorter, who then adds, "Shocked by the revelations about how labor organizers were 'taken care of' in her hometown of Birmingham, she had telegrammed her father's industrialist friends asking them to 'refute this unwarranted lie.' The rebuttals, of course, never came" (91–92).

Although a "belle on phenobarbital" may seem more apt of Tennessee Williams's Blanche DuBois—or even of Watergate's Martha Mitchell—than of Virginia Durr, the phrase clearly conveys McWhorter's fascination with Durr's quixotic manner of extravagant candor—or earnest flamboyance. One must imagine that, when the oral historians came to talk to Durr and husband Clifford, who in the 1950s and 1960s had assisted in the case of Rosa Parks and served as attorney for many of the civil rights activists who came to Montgomery, her lively conversation, filled with anecdotes and interpretive commentary about a life lived amid many of the major political figures and events of her era, had all the marks of a "page-turner" autobiography awaiting transcription. Indeed, editor Hollinger F. Barnard recalls that interviewers Jacquelyn Dowd Hall and Sue Thrasher of the University of North Carolina, writing of their conversations with Durr, spoke of her "painful honesty," her consummate storytelling, and her "vivid and irreverent vignettes," peopled with fully realized characters. "She was what every practitioner of oral history hopes for: a source of vivid historical detail and a master of historical interpretation" (xvi).

Published in 1985, *Outside the Magic Circle* is an edited text based upon the transcriptions of four different series of interviews that took place during the period 1975 to 1977. Barnard writes that "the book is Virginia's own telling," with two brief exceptions of the interspersed narrative from Clifford Durr's oral history interviews, which were conducted over the same period. As an "oral" autobiography, the text issues from a narrator who is very much a speaking presence, with a voice that is lively and colloquial. The specificity and directness of the narrator seem pitched to an auditor who listens, questions, and actively responds to Durr's narrative.[1] The conversational quality of the book gives even Durr's reflective and analytical comments an air of immediacy and candor. Her humor, mimicry, and insouciant asides all suggest a carefree directness that disdains caution and aims more at engaging the auditor-reader than protecting some respectable image of herself. She speaks with blithe offhandedness, for example, in her account of her family's estimations of her marriageability. She was sent off to Miss Finch's school in New York to be "polished up," she says, noting that she had overheard a family friend tell her mother that "Virginia is absolutely impossible. . . . She talks too much, she talks too loud. Her voice is too high, she asks too many questions, and she is very rawboned and near-sighted." The conclusion that she would never "marry well" unless the family arranged to "get her polished up" (30) is related by Durr in good humor, but she clearly conveys the standards by which she was judged as an adolescent being molded for the marriage market.

In editing the text, Barnard describes his role as deleting questions and comments by the interviewers, piecing together various excerpts from interviews, organizing them, combining or selecting from among repeated versions of the same story, and adding "paragraphs to tie phrases together or to identify someone Virginia has mentioned." He adds, "Virginia has worked closely in this effort, especially in correcting names and adding details" (xviii). The interweaving of a scribal style with oral utterance is skillfully done, with the more formal style subordinated to the vernacular. In her recollection of her early consciousness of class and race differences, for example, we see formal transitional sentences merging into a series of simple declarative assertions, a rhetoric that merges analysis with conversation, which produces a strikingly dramatic style.

> There was such a contrast between the life I led, a fairly secure life— although we were genteelly poor—and the view that I had of the life of the miners, the actuality of which was before my eyes but which I did not comprehend. I was told by my mother and father and everybody whom I respected and loved that these people were just that way. They were just poor white trash. If they had pellagra and worms and malaria and if they were thin and hungry and immoral, it was just because that was the way they were. It was in their blood. They were born to be poor white trash. They dipped snuff and drooled tobacco juice. If they smelt bad and were dirty, well, they liked being that way.
>
> I was told the same thing about black people. . . . We were brought up, or at least I was brought up, to believe that distribution of wealth was ordained by God. . . . It was a very comforting thought, you see, because when you saw people starving and poor and miserable, you thought, "Well, it isn't my fault. I didn't do anything to cause it. God just ordained it this way." (31–32)

Born in 1903 and so in her early seventies when she was interviewed, Durr was at a stage of her life when she was perhaps most confident, certainly vindicated in her long time support of the civil rights movement, which had for years made her the target of stringent criticism by many white southerners. Looking back upon her southern girlhood, she often adopts the lightly ironic tone that one finds in Craig Sinclair's recollections, using it to obliquely undercut the behaviors and subvert the values she describes. The narrator's voice is provocative and often, one might say, seductive, edging as it frequently does toward the tradition of the charming, unselfconscious, talkative southern female stereotype. This manner dominates the early chapters on girlhood and early adulthood, but it also shows up in later sections, as, for example, in her account of encounters with Communists and with the House Un-American Activities Committee.

> Now you've got to understand my position, which still is strange. While I was not a Communist, as long as the Communists were doing what I believed in, which was fighting the war against Hitler or fighting the poll tax, then I accepted their help. I thought that red-baiting was horrible. It ruined everything. It certainly killed the National Committee to Abolish the Poll Tax. . . . No one ever strongly urged me to join the Communist party, I must

add, because I didn't have the reputation for being discreet or keeping my mouth shut. Nobody just really begged me to join, and I never did. (194)

Durr's penchant for the unguarded utterance and particularly for the half-serious descriptions of her southern upbringing creates a perspective upon her youth that often appropriates and mimics the naïveté of her youthful self. As in the passage above regarding the miners, she often communicates her mature social critique by exposing her girlish ignorant innocence of the nature of the society she was reared in. The sharp distinctions and divisions drawn by her family and peers according to family background, wealth, schooling, gender, and, most rigidly, race, become invisible, immutable categories that she comes only gradually to recognize as constructed by human beings and not ordained by God.

The opening chapter, "Family, Nursie, the Church," introduces some of the hallmarks of white southerners' autobiographies: the recital of genealogy back to the great-grandfather, references to a plantation past (located for the Durrs in Union Springs, Alabama), accounts of former slaves, Christmas gatherings, a beautiful aunt who "was destined to be a great Southern belle," and to the privileged life of the plantation son, in this case, her father, who "was brought up to do absolutely nothing for himself." With money from the plantation estate, her father had been educated at Hampden-Sydney and then in theological studies at Princeton, Edinburgh, Heidelberg, and Berlin, though his subsequent employment as a Presbyterian minister in Memphis and Birmingham fell victim to his cosmopolitan education when he was found to be "heretical." Pressed by the church elders, he confessed his disbelief that a whale had swallowed Jonah and so was brought before the Presbytery and the Synod and then forced from the church (8 ff.).

Durr's mother Anne was a Patterson from Tennessee, daughter of Josiah, who had fought with Nathan Bedford Forrest and later served in the U.S. Congress, and niece of Malcolm Patterson, who was also elected to Congress as well as the governorship of Tennessee. Anne Patterson was a beauty reared for a life of social prominence and wealth, but her ex-minister husband eventually exhausted his plantation inheritance in support of her and their two daughters and son. Facing the bitter days of the Depression, the couple lost virtually everything but their house, coming for a time to live with Virginia and Clifford, then a young lawyer in Birmingham. It was a "horrible period," Durr recalls, when her mother's melancholia became a severe depression requiring hospitalization (81). Durr is unrelentingly candid in showing up the dark side of southern claims to aristocracy and glitter. The somber exposé is unusual, though, owing to the pain that accompanies firsthand experience. Comedy requires some emotional distance, as we see in her account of the fabled marriage of her grandfather Patterson to Josephine Rice. A great plantation house, slaves standing in double ranks from the house to the road to form a processional pathway, ancestry of fabled wealth—the grand tale all eviscerated by the discovery years later on a visit to nearby Wheeler Dam that the great house was indeed made of brick, as reported, but it had two rooms, a dogtrot, a loft, and a kitchen behind. The mansion and the multitude of slaves were "just a myth" (10).

Because of her family's waning financial resources, which only exacerbated the need to see her well married, Durr remembers her adolescence in Birmingham as a studied effort to effect her "polishing" sufficient to attract a rich husband. Her schooling at Miss Finch's in New York, and later at the Cathedral School in Washington, D.C., was a major installment in the "best investment a Southern family who had fallen on hard times could make" (31), that is, sending a daughter north in search of a Yankee millionaire. Durr's lighthearted mockery of rich-husband-hunting gives way to seriousness on several fronts, namely, the unwelcome, still nettlesome memory of dependence that it foisted upon otherwise privileged women and the humiliation for the South of having to flatter, seduce, and finally obey a northern masculinity that held the keys to the nation's treasury.

Looking back, she says that as a teenager she never objected to the system; her fear was rather that she wouldn't successfully manage it. For example, she describes the "most awful system" in Birmingham of having the hostess of a party leave on the cigar counter of a drugstore a list of the girls who had been invited. Their attendance, however, was contingent upon their success in attracting a date.

> The boys would go in and check the names of the girls they wanted to take to the event. No matter what you were invited to, whether it was a buffet supper or a picnic or anything, the boys would check the names. The boys were totally in control of the social system. If you didn't get checked, you didn't go, even if it was a private party. The hostess would make frantic efforts to try to make some boy bring you! We were in a state of absolute terror all the time because we were totally dependent on popularity with the boys. If they didn't check your name, you were disgraced.
>
> Sometimes I wasn't checked. My mother's fashionable friend Mrs. Cabaniss knew my mother was worried about me because I wasn't popular.

This was when I was only fifteen, before I went off to New York. I had a few beaus but not nearly enough to make me a belle. (48)

Durr relates a number of anecdotes about the arduous preparation for attracting a suitable husband and becoming a wife in a tone that suggests she never thought of herself as a first-team player. She was a reader, a curious, question-asking girl, and unskilled at tennis and golf. So nearsighted that she could not see the leaves on trees, she nonetheless faced a date without her glasses, her mother having hidden them, convinced they would "ruin her chances." Durr's tales remind one again of Katherine Anne Porter's characters in "Old Mortality," one of whom is the plain bespectacled Cousin Eva who, remembering the frenzied marriage market of her youth, remarks to the young Miranda, "You can't imagine what the rivalry was like" (173). Durr says starkly, "Attracting men and being attractive to men and getting a nice beau and the best marriage that we could was our only ambition and our only future, our only career" (49).

Durr's account of the husband chase is perhaps not noticeably different from elite social customs in other sections of late Victorian America, except, that is, for the regional direction that marked the belles' horizon. In *Romance of Reunion,* historian Nina Silber discusses the late nineteenth century's recurring narrative of the southern bride and northern groom who served as emblems of national reunification in the popular media and fiction. The defeated and dependent South was typically cast as a submissive female, a personification that suggested a role for the region that was acceptable to the North and yet vouchsafed the South as a partner within a familial bond. Durr explicitly draws the connection between her slightly later generation of belles who scouted for rich Yankee husbands and the various southern economic development plans that courted Yankee capital. The women and the region were responding to "market forces."

> The South was and still is, in my opinion, a colony of the North. After we were defeated in the Civil War, they bought us up for a nickel on the dollar, and they still own us. When I lived in Birmingham, it was a company town, just completely owned by Northern corporations. The owners would come down in their private railroad cars. It was like being visited by a king. Everybody would bow and scrape. The South was defeated. The whole atmosphere of the South at that time was that it was a colony. . . . Henry Grady, the Atlanta editor, had preached industrialization. Booker T. Washington at Tuskegee was preaching the same thing: Northern money, industrialize and bring in the money. (33)

Of course, Durr did not attract a northern millionaire, despite the family's enterprise in schooling her in the North. Although several possible matches sprang up during her two college years at Wellesley, her early departure intervened, the consequence of the boll weevil eating up the money for tuition. Durr's writing talent had attracted the support of an English teacher in securing her a place in the Self-Help House, which would have made the college cost affordable for the Fosters, but having a daughter in the Self-Help House was simply too humiliating for her proud father to bear. Looking backward, she speaks of how much she longed to complete her education and of her discovery at Wellesley that "women could be something," that they "didn't have to marry to be somebody" (59). She nevertheless obeyed the family, came home to Birmingham, and made her debut, which may have cost as much as college, she notes, but in her mother's eyes represented an investment promising more profit. To her family, the elite schooling was in any case mostly a stage of preparation for entering the adult upper class, and she was of an age to make the transition.

Durr's account of her courtship with Clifford Durr is delivered mostly in her breezy tone, a narrative of falling into good luck as reward for spunky rebellion. When the debut year ended with only one or two desultory proposals—"nothing that appealed to me or amounted to anything"—she was faced with a family in increasing financial straits and, as she says, with a faulty furnace, a leaky roof, and bad plumbing. Her decision to find a job was greatly resented by her parents—her father announcing that with a daughter working downtown his credit would be destroyed. But her work in a law library resulted eventually in her meeting an up-and-coming young corporate lawyer. He was a Rhodes scholar, Phi Beta Kappa, president of his fraternity at the University of Alabama, and, not to be undervalued, from a good family. Surpassing the family's expectation in marrying so well, she claims that "everyone rejoiced" when she announced her engagement to Cliff Durr.

The older Virginia who narrates this autobiography constructs a girlish and young woman self who is compliant with the pressures that her family and community exert to move her steadily and single-mindedly toward marriage. Her portrait of herself is rather teasing and droll, but in it she also invokes a culture that she exposes as essentially superficial and self-absorbed. Her mother's social aspirations and her dithering over wedding plans suggest something of Mrs. Bennett of *Pride and Prejudice*. Her father's careless obliviousness seems more decadent than charming, as, for example, during World War II when he was living with the Durrs in Washington. Virginia, faced with a depleted store of rationed heating oil, went outside to chop wood. Unlike the chivalrous Thomas

Dabney, who after his slaves were freed took on the heavy domestic work to spare his daughters' hands, Sterling Foster never rises from his chair. Durr voices his spoken comment with almost caustic irony, though perhaps with a humorous nod toward a scene between Rhett Butler and Scarlet O'Hara: "Dear, I declare, it distresses me terribly to see your hands. You know, my mother had the most beautiful white hands and your mother had such beautiful white hands. I really think that hands are the mark of a lady. Since you have to do all this work, couldn't you wear gloves?" (37).

Durr then asserts that "like my father, I was brought up as a Southerner, too, completely as a Southerner" (37), but it is clear in her tone and choice of details in Part I, "Birmingham, 1903–1933," that the southern culture of her youth was one she largely left behind in her maturity. What lay ahead for her after marriage was volunteer work with the poor through her affiliation with the Junior League and Red Cross, which opened her eyes to the terrible conditions of the Depression. Her move to Washington in 1933 when her husband joined the Roosevelt administration brought her directly into the mainstream of New Deal thinkers and doers. Her work in support of voting rights and progressive legislation, her involvement in the Southern Conference for Human Welfare, her later support of Henry Wallace as presidential nominee, and her opposition to McCarthyism all moved her steadily toward the support of civil rights in the South, which she and her husband undertook after they returned to Alabama in 1951. When she indicts the southern belle vanity of her youth, she expresses genial humor about her simplicity but acknowledges the social blindness that the narrow self-absorption led to. Her indictment includes not just the youthful Virginia but the privileged social class of her era.

> While I was being brought up to be attractive and to have a lot of beaus and get married, all around me things were happening—antilynching fights and child labor fights and the suffrage movement. It was only after I was safely married that I could really be interested in anything else. I led an egotistical, self-centered life because I was always trying to do what other people wanted me to do and make everybody love me. The consequences of not being loved were plain: you didn't get married. You got to be an old maid and that was the worst fate that could befall you. (66)

The narrator whose voice we hear in this text is a woman who lived an activist public life alongside a politically powerful husband. Her access to a larger world than that of her mother was made possible principally by way of her marriage to Clifford Durr, although Virginia Durr's intelligence, sympathy, and courage have also to be acknowledged. Her political ideology, variously expressed throughout the book, is an amalgam of the classical liberal's respect for the rights and freedom of the individual, the genteel lady's respect for honorable and ethical deportment, and the empathetic compatriot's sympathy for the oppressed and exploited—even when they are themselves oppressors and exploiters. Of those Ku Klux Klan forces who bombed homes and churches in Montgomery in the mid-1950s, she writes that she was struck by "how poor and emaciated, how scrawny they looked. They looked as if they had never had proper food. You couldn't help but feel that they had been deprived all their lives" (288). Her commitment to human rights is sweepingly ecumenical. "As I see it," she says at one point, "the discrimination against Negroes and women was all part of the exploitation of human beings by other human beings," and she argues that no group can successfully work for "sectarian rights," that the appeal for civil rights must be made on a "broader basis" (131).

On the other hand, in contradiction of her comments about the Montgomery bombers, Durr is elsewhere quick to condemn those white southerners whose sense of victimization has led them to victimize blacks. She argues that there are two strains running through the southern populace, a "pioneer strain" of "independent, proud, self-sufficient people" who can be counted upon to act honorably, even when they hold different political views, and a self-pitying strain, "who felt terribly oppressed and thought the Negroes were the ones who were keeping them from getting any land" (318). This self-pity led to a morbid hatred, in her view, that poisoned the psyche. Durr's ambivalence toward white southerners who fought against integration and the extension of civil rights for African Americans is reflected in her shifting from an ameliorating "understanding" to indignant condemnation.

Outside the Magic Circle clearly mirrors the emotional and ideological entanglements faced by white southerners when, in support of efforts to bring about racial justice, they came into fierce conflict with family members who bitterly opposed such efforts. In speaking of the apartheid era of her childhood, Durr can frame her narrative as a documentary reporting a distant past viewed through her innocent and unquestioning eyes. From this perspective she portrays the black woman Easter, who "ran" her grandmother's plantation, and "Nursie," the black woman who was "a second mother." To the child, these women, even though beloved, constituted a "different group"; they were quite simply "outside everything" (46). But dealing with more contemporaneous events calls up immediate, conflicting loyalties to family and to beliefs, and Durr's certain judgments upon her childhood experiences give way to a more temperate accommodation in which she seeks to hold on to as much good will from her extended family and Alabama as she possibly can while carrying on the civic work she is committed to.

Where one finds no ambivalence in Durr is in her accounts of those political leaders she finds dishonorable and unethical—principally, Joseph McCarthy and James Eastland. She aptly describes McCarthy's witch hunts for Communists in the government as hysteric and demagogic, but she voices her condemnation in distinctly class terms. The damning word *common,* the word that had always been reserved by her mother for the very worst class of people, is the word Durr uses repeatedly to name McCarthy's principal failing. He was "common as pig's tracks"; in fact, she found him and his hangers-on to be "liars and opportunists and common." She apologizes for her language: "I suppose I shouldn't use those terms. But they were such common, vulgar people, people you would never associate with if you could help it. And the people around them were all such common, vicious, vulgar opportunists" (206).

Similarly, Jim Eastland, senator from Mississippi and chairman of the Senate Internal Security Subcommittee, was in Durr's estimation "common." In 1954 he held hearings in New Orleans aimed at identifying Communists in the South, and Virginia was issued a subpoena to appear before the committee. Her work on behalf of outlawing the poll tax, as well as her many other activities in support of civil rights, was enough to call down Eastland's wrath. Further, she had come to view his attack upon her as a surrogate attack upon Hugo Black, husband of her sister Josephine and a member of the Supreme Court that had just issued the *Brown v. Board of Education* ruling. She is unsparing in her contempt for Eastland's conduct of the hearings. "Jim Eastland had gone to the University of Alabama and was almost my age. He came from the hill country. He was no Southern aristocrat at all. The nice girls wouldn't have anything to do with him, but he married a very nice woman." The impertinence of such a man questioning her loyalty is what nettles so: "The idea of Jim Eastland, just as common as pig's tracks . . . trying to call me to account. . . . I wasn't scared. I was just as mad as hops" (256).

After the hearings, the Durrs returned to Montgomery, Cliff exhausted and suffering from a recurrent heart condition. Virginia recalls that a few local people were "nasty" about the hearings, but most paid no attention, nobody believing, as she says, that they had "the talent to overthrow the government by force and violence" (266). The reaction of Cliff's family was one of stoic silence. At the time, the Durrs were living with his mother, who is described in a cutline accompanying her photograph as "not entirely approving" of Virginia or of the liberal social views that she and Cliff had brought with them when they returned to Alabama after the Washington years. Still, as Virginia respectfully notes, "She took us into her home when we had no place else to go" (242). His mother, aunt, and sister all expressed great concern about his health, Durr recalls, but they wholly ignored Jim Eastland and acted as if the hearing had never occurred. "That's the way Southern women have so often met a difficult situation—just acted as though it hadn't happened" (267). But she clearly implies that it is precisely her rejection of passivity and compliance with tradition that so sharply differentiates her from such women, that marks her as a different sort of southerner.

Durr's explicit assessments of her own power to effect social change, however, are harshly revealing of the diminished status of a woman who became a wife, especially a southern white woman who, with her manners and accent and outgoing talkativeness, seemed to incur even further dismissal by policy makers and powerbrokers because of the belle-lady stereotype. Of course, the most powerful wife of the times was Eleanor Roosevelt, who was bitterly reviled by many southerners for her support of social change. But even she, with her highly publicized activities and powerful access to the president, could only be tolerated by southern Democrats because she was, after all, just a wife.

Durr's commitment to social change is most dramatically and riskily expressed in her early support of the anti–poll tax legislation, in the 1947–48 Henry Wallace presidential candidacy, and, of course, in her general efforts on behalf of civil rights over many years. Just how seriously her oppositional stands were taken by southerners, President Truman, and Democrats overall is narrated with her usual blithe panache. One revealing anecdote shows her intently listening to a former State Department official, a lobbyist for international oil interests she had happened to meet on the train on her way home to Alabama. He described to her an elaborate military plan to invade Manchuria and the Urals, which had been urged upon the president, confident, as she says, "that I was just a sweet Southern girl and that surely I agreed with him" (201). More pointedly, she observes that even her joining the Wallace campaign against Truman was so lightly regarded that Truman reappointed Clifford Durr to the FCC. "In those days women were not regarded as being very important. I was Cliff's wife and Hugo's sister-in-law. On my own maybe I was a little too radical, but I had no power" (201).

If she had individual freedom at the price of having little societal power, Durr nonetheless does not underrate the significance of that freedom. Throughout the book she draws parallels and distinctions between her marriage and that of her older sister Josephine, whose jurist husband "did everything in his power to make her happy, except give her her freedom" (47). Durr remarks ruefully that Hugo Black expected his wife "to subordinate herself to his life and his ambitions. It never occurred to him otherwise." He wanted his more independent daughter to attend Sweet Briar and be like her mother, Durr adds, "a sweet Southern lady and beautiful and charming." Again, what one notes in her accounts of southern-lady role-playing, whether voluntary or pressured, is sometime resignation, more often respect, and even more often, especially when depicted as an event in the distant past, humorous irony. She is quick to renounce social pretensions and women's affectations, and on occasion she chafes over oppressive societal expectations defining a "proper wife." But she rarely if ever questions her standards of polite and considerate behavior toward other people, perhaps the hallmark of the "southern lady." Throughout the text she asserts the attributes of decency, considerateness, and graciousness as the characterizing features of the southern woman. In describing a visit to the home of Mrs. Martin Luther King, for example, she remembers admiringly just these qualities: "Mrs. King was dressed in a very pretty light summer dress. . . . She served us delicious Southern tea, iced tea and cookies. She was a gracious hostess and her house was decorated very tastefully. They had one child then, a little girl named Yolanda. Mrs. King was a perfect Southern lady" (277–78). Finally, despite her candid outspokenness, we find in her narrative a respectful reticence about family members and about the deepest and most personal experiences, such as the death of her young son, her second born. In some moments she may seem irrepressible, but one senses that the self projected in this conversational narrative is very much in control of the public presentation.

Outside the Magic Circle is arguably mistitled, for Virginia Durr never really feels herself outside the circle of those who "run the country," as she admits. Her worries at the end of the book are focused upon the waning powers of the individual and the growing hegemony of corporate America, but she holds the privileged elite responsible for this turn. "I've always felt I belonged to the ruling class. But I don't feel any more that that group is leading the country in the right way" (334). But just as she claimed to have had little political power, she modestly claims at the end of the autobiography to have had, at best, a sort of adjunct achievement to that of her husband: "I think Cliff has left a great deal. I'd say I have left a little, but Cliff has left a great deal." Her last sentences, in fact, reassert her position as wife and mother: "I was so busy all the time that I never had much time to think about any role I played in anything that happened. . . . I had the house to run. I had three children to educate, and I had to work in my husband's office from 8:30 in the morning till late at night. . . . I was just trying to get the next thing done, whether it meant getting out a brief or getting the next meal on, just trying to get through the next thing that had to be done" (337).

The initial interviews that furnished the transcriptions upon which the book is based were doubtless prompted more by Durr's reputation as a public activist than as the wife of a prominent civil rights lawyer and government official. But at the end of the day, she defines her life in terms not so much of any public role she played but rather her role in "taking care" of others—a story of self realized through relations with others. It is a familiar narrative of an activist southern wife reared with lessons of dutifulness to family, an episodic life divided between the household within and the larger world beyond.

Shortly after she retired from Congress in 1990, Lindy Boggs brought her perspective of fifty years in Washington to the telling of *Washington Through a Purple Veil*. She had served a seventeen-year tenure representing her New Orleans–area district of Louisiana, following upon the death in 1972 of her husband. Hale Boggs was first elected to Congress in 1941, twenty years later named Democratic minority whip, and then in 1971, voted majority leader of the House of Representatives. Throughout his career, Lindy had been not only a congressman's wife but an unflagging working assistant in his campaigns and political life, becoming an experienced political veteran. Although she never expected to enter politics directly, she did so after a plane crash in Alaska left her a widow with commitments to her husband's political goals and to their Louisiana constituency. Although her Claiborne heritage linked her to a line of earlier illustrious public officeholders, and even contemporaneously to Senator Claiborne Pell of Rhode Island, holding elective office herself, as she writes, was a direction she never dreamed of taking.

This autobiography is organized much like Sinclair's, Hamilton's, and Anderson's in its focus upon a life directed by a husband's work and ambitions. It is memoiristic in its attention to the narrator's relationships with other people, and one finds the "self" of the narrative to be a familiar "relational self" displayed repeatedly among earlier life writings by southern women. Of the texts read so far, *Washington Through a Purple Veil* is particularly notable for its unified tone and vocabulary, as well as its controlled, straightforward management of the life plot. Passages of self-analysis and reflection are fairly rare; Boggs's intent is to share her recollections of the people and events of her life through a narrative filled with episodes informing not just of an individual's personal

experience but of mid-to-late-twentieth-century U.S. history. Seasoned politician as she has been, she brings her political sensibility to decisions about what
and how to tell her story. In the *New York Times Book Review,* Rosellen Brown
writes that "Given Lindy Boggs's firsthand experience, she misses many opportunities for a deeper level of introspection and honesty about the costs of the
delicate dance with power she's done her whole life long." Brown finds the autobiography an "engaging, even stirring story" but one that shares too little of
the "sound and fury of pitched political battle." Brown concludes that Boggs has
cast a purple veil over even the telling of her story (33).

Lindy Boggs acknowledges the professional archivists and researchers who
assisted her in transforming her story "into a book," as well as her editors and
the collaborator, Katherine Hatch, who is cited on the title page. Perhaps owing
to this collaboration with professional writers and to her own political experience and sensibility, as well as to the repetition over the years of interviewers'
questions and her responses, Boggs's story is vivid and richly detailed but told
with some dispassionate distance. Interviewed in 2002 by Anne Price, for example, Boggs repeats many of the details from the book in the same phrases and
tone (16–18). Although lacking the flamboyance of Durr's revelations and commentary, *Washington Through a Purple Veil* reveals Boggs's recollections and
interpretations of her southern upbringing, which she narrates in an easy, affectionate remembering of her family and friends in Louisiana's Pointe Coupee
Parish, the same home parish that writer Ernest Gaines has depicted in many
of his novels and stories. Interestingly, many of the attributes of "southernness"
that Boggs identifies with her childhood, she observes as familiar characteristics of the Washington social-political circles during the years of her congressional wifehood. In fact, one might read the opening anecdote as Boggs's trope
for capturing the requisite essentials for a performance of southern lady / political wife.

Not long after arriving in Washington at age twenty-four, Boggs was asked
by her husband to come to a committee hearing on the Lend-Lease legislation,
which would furnish desperately needed aid to World War II allies. He valued her judgment and counsel and wished her to hear the full testimony. She
writes that she "threw a jacket over my sweater and skirt, and made up my face,
brushed my hair and put on high heels." Leaving her toddler Barbara and baby
Tommy with a nurse, she rushed to the hearing room and identified herself,
only to be turned away by a disbelieving clerk, whose comment was, "Oh, sure,
honey." At that point, desperate to enter the hearing room, she recalled the advice of a prominent New Orleans socialite, who had confided that "the most so-

phisticated and becoming a thing a woman could wear was a purple veil." She returned home, changed into her best outfit, a "black Davidow suit, a pretty silk blouse with my pearl circle pin, and a little black velour hat, and kid gloves." On her way back to the Capitol, she purchased a purple veil. "When I returned to the hearing room, the same clerk was guarding the door. I took off one glove and then the other with as much authority as I could muster. In my sweetest Southern accent, I said, 'I'm Mrs. Boggs. I'd like to be seated, please.'" The reader is as unsurprised by the guard's response as was the veiled Mrs. Boggs: "'Oh, yes ma'am. Come right in'" (3).

It is tempting to over read this anecdote, which richly displays gender models and role expectations in the center of national political power in 1941. Later, Boggs describes Washington at this time as "a leisurely Southern town" (74), with a rigid "calling system" required of the wives, among many other rituals and protocols, as she was to learn from trusted friends like Lady Bird Johnson, Pauline Gore, and Nancy Kefauver. Most obviously, the young woman presenting herself in a committee hearing room, even one in high heels and jacket, is not admissible to the public forum. Only when she presents herself as affluent, veiled, and politely authoritative does the "young clerk," who does not even need to be identified in the story as a male, allow her to enter.

Boggs neither reads nor adduces the incident as a feminist critique of discrimination. She interprets the story in entirely pragmatic terms, offering it as an example of how she was well served by her southern-lady knowledge of how to present herself in such a setting and so negotiate gender limitations to achieve her goal. "During the next fifty years," she says, "I often thought of the lesson I received from the purple veil story. I recognized that you played the Washington game with confidence and authority and graciousness, and so I was prepared to accept the challenges, the triumphs, and the heartaches of life in the shadow of the Capitol dome" (3). She neither gives nor acknowledges any need to explain her quiet acquiescence to a protocol, evidenced in the clerk's dismissal, that required a certain dress code for women presuming to enter a committee room of the U.S. House of Representatives. Rather, Boggs's point is that the self-fashioning is crucial to a successful performance of authority— and that such a performance succeeds when the auditor is persuaded. With a view quite like that of a Belle Kearney or Anne Walter Fearn, Boggs acquiesces to social demands that she comport herself in the manner of the lady. She deploys this conscious self-presentation, complete with costume and dialogue as a camouflage, even a decoy, according to circumstances and her needs, to help her realize her ambitions.

Ambition is a prickly word in the southern lady's lexicon, and it rarely appears in the autobiographies that are the subject of this book, although one has to observe that its manifestation is widely in evidence. One might say that undisguised ambition and self-regard are the twin evils that young white women of the Victorian and post-Victorian South are taught above all else to avoid. Boggs speaks, for example, of the "most valuable lesson" she learned from her maternal grandmother: "You can succeed in anything if you give somebody else the credit for doing it" (10). She elsewhere expresses this lesson, as in the purple veil story, as an understanding dating from her childhood that a woman's most trustworthy exercise of power is through a mode of charm ("graciousness"), subtlety (occasionally even devious manipulation), and a display of deference and concern for others ("peacemaking"). She describes how long-standing opposition to the wives' organizing an official club was finally overcome. The House minority leader and strong opponent to the club, John Sharp Williams, was one day invited to lunch by his wife, who went like Salome with an agenda. Wearing her "prettiest gown and hat and her most alluring Paris perfume," she came away with the prize she sought, Williams's approval of the wives club (91). Boggs cites the story as a political success—the deal was done with the clout available at that time and place to Mrs. Williams, who went forth as delegate for the wives.

The lessons and models of womanhood that Boggs specifies she learned from her mother are significant, demanding self-control and a willingness to attend to others' needs before one's own. Her mother's rallying strength during the 1927 flood and her ability to organize a large household, to "calmly feed large numbers of people and adjust schedules under the most disorganized conditions," were instructive examples that prepared Boggs, as she states, for "being married to Hale Boggs" (36).

It is telling that the liveliest details in the book are devoted to her girlhood and the years of her marriage rather than to her seventeen-year tenure as a congresswoman. She is more comfortable talking of others, giving credit to others; it is her *nature,* she claims, to be a smoother of ruffled feathers, "a consensus builder," one meant to be "involved" in politics, but never as the candidate (126). This nature she attributes to having been an only child, of having to be "peacemaker" among many relatives—an attribute that could as easily be characterized as "vote-getter," one might observe, though this narrator does not. She compares her relationship to her husband's political career as like that of Robert Kennedy to President John F. Kennedy—organizer, buffer against criticism, expediter for her "star" (210). Her older daughter Barbara, herself a rising political star before her untimely death from cancer, is remembered as having said she thought of her father when she "needed to do something directly and head-on" and she thought of her mother when she "wanted to accomplish something indirectly, more subtly" (235).

Lindy Boggs's life, like her life narrative, exposes the stretching required of women of the early and mid twentieth century who were wives, mothers, and public leaders. This stretch is particularly straining, it would seem, for southern white women reared in a continuing tradition that socialized women for the domestic sphere and men for the public forum. Like the Wizard of Oz, this autobiographer is revealed as working hard behind the public curtain, as mother, campaign wife, assistant, cook, decorator, hostess, beauty, and so on, only to rush from behind the curtain when necessary to construct for public view a leader's show of authority. Her younger daughter, the journalist Cokie Roberts, writes in her 1998 memoir, *We Are Our Mother's Daughters,* that her mother has not only always been able to do everything "but to do everything at the same time" (xii). Roberts's book, as well as her mother's, gives accounts of Boggs's impressive skill and energy as seamstress, sewing elaborate draperies for the household and dresses for her daughters, and as a cook, preparing the food for fifteen hundred guests invited to her daughter and Steve Roberts's wedding reception. She gives affectionate attention to her three children and later to her grandchildren, and, as Cokie Roberts mentions, she is a beauty.

As noted in the introduction, the process of composing an autobiography in which one deflects the focus from the self onto surrounding others necessarily leads to a narrative that obscures the inner self of the narrator, the reflective self, in favor of an anecdotal, dramatized revelation that calls upon the reader's inferential power. "Relationality" may be a more accurate description of one's lived life than "introspection," especially if the life is that of a woman deeply implicated in family. The resulting portrait of a relational life becomes, then, a sort of mosaic, the separate units of which are vivid but the completed figure somewhat difficult to discern. Boggs tells her reader early in the book that her expectations from childhood, reflecting the life she saw around her, were "to be a good wife and a mother, keep a pretty house, and foster and participate in some cultural outlets." Although she comments that she never expected "to live on a plantation," she nonetheless saw modeled before her a way of living that did not greatly deviate from that of a nineteenth-century wife of her race and social status. Protected and loved by her family, educated in Catholic schools, a graduate of Newcomb College, the women's division of Tulane University in New Orleans, she completed the traditional belle's apprenticeship, culminating in the crowning moment of an elaborate wedding. Her account of the courtship is surprisingly terse ("our getting together was 'just one of those things'"), perhaps because the courtship is the suitor's game and the wedding is the bride's. The lengthy text announcing the wedding plans, published in the society section of the *New Orleans Times-Picayune,* is included among the photographs in the book, along with images of family members and of Lindy from childhood onward, including one in which she appears as a member of one of the Mardi Gras courts.

There is also in this record, however, ample evidence that Boggs's girlhood not only equipped her for a traditional married life but also, with an education under the tutelage of authoritative nuns, offered her models of leadership roles for women that were fully as appropriate to female nature as wifehood—though one must infer from her story that she regarded the choice as an either-or binary for a woman. As a college student, in fact, she harbored ambitions for a professional life, an independent career. Her role model, she says, was Margaret Bourke-White, whose work as a photographer and journalist took her to "great events . . . where the action was" (45).

The account of Boggs's decision to turn away from other possibilities and toward marriage is as notable for its rich suggestion of the narrator's sense of her sphere of power (and powerlessness) as the purple veil story. It may also call to mind for many readers the memorable conclusion of Kate Chopin's novel *The Awakening.* While visiting a friend on the Mississippi Gulf Coast, Boggs decided to swim out into the Gulf one blustery day when the waves were high and threatening. Exhausted and near drowning, she was rescued by a friend who happened to see her distress. She recounts the episode as a significant turning point in her worldview, commenting that "until that day I had been daring." Her recognition of vulnerability evokes a response quite different from that of Chopin's Edna Pontellier, who refuses to bridle her desire for freedom in the face of society's and nature's arrayed forces. Boggs surveys her place in the world with equanimity: "The experience of nearly drowning fundamentally changed my behavior and attitude toward my expectations in life," she writes. "I became much more cautious, realizing that I was vulnerable" (56). The consequence was that she moved toward her love for Hale Boggs, deciding that what she most wanted was to "protect" their future together.

It would be years later that her chosen role of protecting and assisting would give way to calls for leadership and independence. This would be a time when she was no longer a wife but a widow, at first accepting Hale's seat so as to finish his agenda and then seeking election as congresswoman in her own right—

the first elected congresswoman from Louisiana. The narrator makes quite clear, however, that it was not ambition but duty that led her into the political center stage. "I never expected that I would develop my own agenda or that I would become a voice and a vote for many women during two tumultuous decades" (267). As she recalls her years in Congress, she often mentions "Southern charm" as a useful tool in crafting legislation, as, for example, in instigating the inclusion of women in the Equal Credit Opportunity Act of 1974. In the committee that marked up the bill designed to protect a person's credit eligibility from racial and age discrimination, she discreetly added "or sex or marital status" and copied the revised version for each committee member. "I strongly depended on Southern charm to get my additions included in the bill," she adds, and indeed the amendment passed by a vote of forty-seven to zero. She tags her anecdote with the modest disclaimer, however, that it wasn't she who made the difference, but rather "the fact that there was a woman at the right place at the right time to make a difference" (278).

Such disclaimers of ambitious initiative and political self-aggrandizement pervade the later chapters of the narrative, and Grandmother Rets's advice—that one can succeed at anything if you give someone else the credit for doing it—is advice Boggs puts to use time and time again. Her pride in being named first female chair of a Democratic National Convention, in 1976, for example, she explains as a satisfying fulfillment of her husband's ambition to chair the 1960 convention, which had stalled in part because of Democrats' fears that, as a Catholic, his chairmanship would draw negative attention to John Kennedy's Catholicism. On the day her appointment as convention chair was announced, she received a telephone call from President Ford. The way she relates his greeting reestablishes her narrative voice as modest and unpretentious. "Hi, honey, are you going to pick a good one for me?" The greeting is spoken (and recalled by Boggs in this text) as nothing more, or less, than a warm and gracious form of address. However much that "honey" says to readers now of gender relations in those days, particularly of such relations among persons who were socialized a half century before the 1970s women's movement, it goes unremarked by Boggs, except for her comment that "it was dear of him to congratulate me in that friendly way" (308).

The changed and changing societal roles and social identifications that most sharply draw Boggs's attention are those attaching to race. In early chapters, just as in Durr's *Outside the Magic Circle,* Boggs writes of a black nurse and a household manager who was said to have "ruled the roost" of the family home. Her language in describing Hannah Hall, "Aunt Hannah"—a term she explains as used affectionately for whites as well as for elderly black women—is deliberately controlled and even at times defensively guarded and explanatory. It is precisely on the matter of race that she cannot assume or imply "southernness" to be a reservoir of political or mannerly capital. On "southern race matters" she gives explanation and qualification, but she frequently does so by drawing upon her firsthand witness, offering her views of racial justice as grounded in her own experience—quite as Lyndon Johnson did in the 1960s in discussing voting rights and other civil rights legislation that he successfully advocated. Boggs writes, for example, that "if anyone ever needed persuading to become an integrationist, a long automobile trip with children and a black housekeeper would do it" (101). She proceeds to describe witnessing a series of humiliating denials of food and lodging to the educated, "remarkable woman" Emma Cyprian, who was employed by the Boggses. She explains the conflicted situation of moderate southerners when faced with civil rights legislation by referring to her husband's experience in Congress, describing the deal struck with black supporters who sometimes countenanced, or even supported, his oppositional votes out of fear of losing his support of other progressive social and economic issues, should he be defeated by a reactionary conservative who would use his civil rights support to smear him with an "integrationist" tag.

Her recollection of the passage of the 1965 Voting Rights Act gives her occasion, however, to recount her husband's vindication of his previous caution by manifestly supporting this civil rights legislation. She devotes nearly four pages to the telling of his support of the bill—his decision to vote for it but not take the House floor to speak for it, followed by his change of mind and the brilliant speech, quoted at some length, that he offered in response to the assertions of fellow congressman Joe Waggoner of Shreveport that everyone who wanted to vote in Louisiana could do so, with full access to registration. Lindy Boggs's dramatic telling, the degree of detail, and the references to the threatening consequences to his career and to the family's personal safety (a cross burning at their New Orleans home) all convey her pride in the principled stand Hale Boggs took. They convey as well, though more obliquely, the pride she takes in her own principled stand.

> We women in the family pushed him hard on civil rights. He led us, and then we pushed him. It wasn't just Cokie and Barbara and me, it was Hale's Mamma and my Mamma and Grandmother Rets—four generations of us. . . . I thought of Bessie Rogers [her childhood nurse], Emma Cyprian, Aunt Hannah Hall—black women who had raised me and had helped me raise

my children, women who had been prevented from voting because of their color. (202)

Although Lindy Boggs does recount in *Washington Through a Purple Veil* many of her own achievements as a congresswoman and a public activist over a great span of years, she does so in a reportorial narrative voice that is consistently explanatory and descriptive, not evaluative, and rarely introspective. It is a conversational voice, mindful of an auditor's presence, relaxed and drawing upon the empathetic identification of the auditor with the events and anecdotes related. Occasionally, she gives glimpses of a demeanor and vocabulary belonging to the woman behind the purple veil, as, for example, in her story of her own application for a bank mortgage several years after the passage of the 1974 Equal Opportunity Credit Act. Pressed by the bank officer with questions about her financial status, a requirement the officer explained as being a "federal regulation," Boggs retorted that she had authored the law that forbade just such a requirement of women and the elderly. "My dear," she told the officer, "you are not complying with the federal regulation, you are in defiance of it." Characteristically, Boggs tempers the steeliness with a sympathetic phrase, but then she repeats her point and her tone: "I felt badly because I knew it wasn't her fault—she was only saying what her supervisors had taught her—but in case she wasn't paying attention, I said distinctly, 'There can be no discrimination because of race, veteran status, age, sex, or marital status'" (314).

In recent decades the phrase "steel magnolia" or, earlier, "iron magnolia" has been widely applied to female characterizations, fictional and actual, that comprise a performance of charm, graciousness, and deference, and a veiled inner being of firm resolve, self-regard, and canny intelligence. One might well argue that the idea of a calculated, politic presentation of the self in such a manner as to secure one's personal aims owes more to Machiavelli than to gender construction in the elite white U.S. South. Saying so, however, does not lessen the examples we find in autobiographical presentations like these by Sinclair, Durr, and Boggs of the deeply internalized need for women to believe in, respect, and display selflessness and concern for others as a primary virtue of southern womanhood. Not necessarily aligned with religious belief, the traits of self-effacement, modesty, and an affiliative identity with family and friends continue to be the qualities of character that these writers implicitly acknowledge in the ways they construct their textual selves. Reading their life narratives, one finds it difficult finally to infer to what extent their lives confirm an ideal of "ladyhood" and to what extent it is the ideal that shapes and constrains their actual life choices and beliefs about what kind of self they *ought* to be. Historian Margaret Ripley Wolfe confronts the same impasse in her effort to delineate the "saga" of southern women in *Daughters of Canaan,* concluding that the symbol of the southern lady, so fixed in the southern mind and the national culture, "impedes the development of southern women" (8). However much of an impediment this cultural icon may appear to many of us who have studied its history and its consequence for southern white and black women who have had to live their lives, after all, in a highly individualistic, competitive, and male-dominated national culture, it is clear that Lindy Boggs takes a different view. For her, the cultural mores attaching to her gender, social class, race, region, and historical era have proved empowering resources, equipping her to "play the game" with "confidence, authority, and graciousness" (3). Rather than rejecting the status of a restricted womanhood of her time and place, she has pragmatically devised strategies for side-stepping obstacles, negotiating territory in the manner of the political moderate she is. Thus she has not only honored the traditional commitments to family but has balanced these with her public work on behalf of the body politic. Both have been the beneficiaries.

The author of *Lylah: A Memoir by Lylah Barber* undertook the writing of her book when she was in her late seventies, with the encouragement and support of literary scholar Louis D. Rubin Jr. and William W. Rogers, history professor at Florida State University. The memoir is notable in the context of this study for several characteristics that underscore patterns expressing southernness and woman's voice, or textualized identity, that we have seen to emerge in analyses of prior autobiographical texts by southern women. Central to *Lylah* is a conflicted embrace of family and home, configured in Part I subtitled "South," and, in contrast, her depiction of her marriage to a famous, successful husband and their privileged life, which she recounts as "North." The short final section of the book, "Home Again," depicting Lylah and Red Barber's move in retirement from New York back to Lylah's native Florida, offers little of return or cyclical completion. Unlike Sinclair, Durr, and Boggs, Barber does not derive a sense of validation and selfhood from a participation in her husband's career. At the memoir's end, her longing for security and connection and her ambition for independence and personal achievement are finally unreconciled, or, at most, implied as reconcilable only by means of a feat of imagination, a fig-tree trope with which she concludes the book.

From the outset Barber signals a kind of trespassers' guilt about writing an autobiography; in a preface she explains and defends her motives. "Why did I write this book?" she asks rhetorically, and responds with another question: "Is it because after years of being the wife of the well-known sports broadcaster Red Barber, I want to be Lylah—me—with an achievement of my own? Certainly that is part of the reason, but only a small part." As it turns out, it is rather the large part; that is, the desire to find coherence in her life, to reevaluate or "re-write" the nature of the self, as Mark Freeman has titled the process, lies at the heart of the other motives she names. She mentions "therapy," observing that the writing "has done more to rid me of the Diocesan School and of my stepfather than hours of psychoanalysis did," the urge in her old age to recollect the past, and her wish to leave a record for her daughter. But all of these motives arise from the desire to stabilize and unify a sense of self, the desire to discover "Who am I?"—Who is this separate self and what are my "achievements"? (xi).

In her re-collecting of her life experience, Barber portrays a South of her childhood in which family is all important but often proves as much a troubling affliction as a support system. Like Lindy Boggs, she suffered the early loss of her father, a rising young attorney in Jacksonsville who died when she was five years old. Although she gives accounts of affectionate ties to her younger brother and her grandmothers, her relationship with her mother was strained because of financial worries and her mother's having to work long hours away from home as a secretary in support of the family. Her maternal grandmother, "Dannie," had also faced early widowhood, as well as the loss of her firstborn, and bore the scars of those sorrows. Barber writes of three generations of widows who had to assume responsibility for a family of young children. Along with pride of family ancestry, which dominates the opening pages, she relates the intricate circumstances of these widows and of kin of several generations past, commenting that "in those harsh days the sense of family was dominant." She registers her sense of rupture from this earlier South chiefly in her accounting of the vastly reduced family of her own generation. "Still evident in the South of today is a strong sense of 'blood kinship,'" she remarks, and then immediately adds, "I have only two close kin left, my daughter, Sarah, and my brother's child, Mary Anne, who was, until her marriage, the last to bear the Scarborough name" (26).

Some of Barber's most positive memories of her childhood home are those of her Grandmother Scarborough, whose orderly household she remembers as a haven of security, a golden, prelapsarian place where she was lovingly rocked and sung to in "sad and romantic songs of the Civil War, when all the girls were young and beautiful and the men were brave, going off to the War to fight for their Land." She was dressed in her "calling on" clothes to visit her kin and was allowed to play with the black cook's children, but "never with those of a certain family in the neighborhood because they were 'poor white trash'" (14). The lessons of kinship, class, and caste seem inevitable and effortless in Barber's construction of this side of her childhood, as are the sensuous pleasures of ripe figs, cold watermelons, and a lush landscape. But like a halcyon scene invaded by an ogre, this narrative is disrupted by the appearance of an evil stepfather, a domineering, "pathologically" jealous man who eventually presents even a sexually abusive threat to his stepdaughter (53).

Barber's desire to escape her increasingly tense family situation runs steadily parallel to her longing to recover an imagined ideal of family life that she partly locates in her grandmother's household, which she knew most intimately in her childhood years, but, more importantly, that she associates with an idealized life that she believes to have been lost with the death of her father. She maintains a highly romanticized memory of him from the slight record she has—her fleeting images recalled from a time shortly before his death, a few photographs, and the family stories she has managed to accumulate. Recalling first meeting the CBS broadcaster Edward R. Murrow, she was struck with his resemblance to her cherished picture of her father. Furthermore, she writes, "Like my father he was a Southerner with the charm and courtly manners that I am certain my father had" (8).

The actual southern home that she shared with her mother and brother and later with the detested stepfather was a far cry from what she wished for. Barber's experience was of boarding schools, tense family encounters, and a growing sense that few opportunities would be available to her as an adult. Given the strict, dominating manner of her stepfather, she had little or no expectation of college and hoped for training as a secretary at a business school. When she was summarily enrolled in nursing school, a choice not her own, her departure seemed as much an eviction as a move toward independence. Nonetheless, she thrived in her nurse's training, which culminated in her being chosen for a special college program of study that sent her to Florida State College for Women in Tallahassee.

Barber retrospectively portrays herself as happiest during her college and early working years. Her tone is more joyous even than when she tells of the courtship and early marriage period. The busy excitement of moving out into the world, gaining confidence and authority, gives Barber a sense of empowerment and ambition. The moment is reminiscent of Sinclair during her New York days, Durr at Wellesley, realizing that "women didn't have to marry to be somebody," and Boggs at Tulane, imagining herself a career woman, "out where the action was." When Barber is offered a position as "Instructress of Nurses" at Riverside Hospital, she excitedly prepares for it by applying for an internship at Cook County Hospital in Chicago. Waiting for the term to begin, she takes an interim position at the University of Florida. Here she meets red-headed Walter Barber, student and part-time driver of a bakery truck, which, during one of his deliveries he manages to wreck, a calamity that brings him to the infirmary covered with cake icing, sand, and blood. Although she completes her training in Chicago as planned and returns to Florida to her new job, she has made up her mind to marry Red. She writes of her mother's determined opposition to the match and in fact acknowledges, "As I write this I am still angry" (81). Rejecting Red as an acceptable suitor because he is an impoverished student and part-time broadcaster, her mother refuses to attend the wedding service.

Barber rarely reflects upon her decision to leave the career that took nearly six years of preparation and promised a successful future. We see in her life story the typical expectation that an independent livelihood was a temporary stage for a woman, whose serious career was marriage and housewifery. "Maiden ladies," such as the two elderly sisters in whose antebellum house the newlyweds have an apartment, impress Lylah as sad figures, women who were "prevalent at that time in the Deep South," she remarks. "They lived out their lives in the homes of their married brothers and sisters, little more than housekeepers and nurses for the children of their more fortunate relatives" (84). Barber's own marriage and family responsibilities diverge markedly, however, from earlier generations of southern wives. Following her husband's career, she moves to Cincinnati and then to New York, occasionally accompanying Red on his wide travel as a sportscaster, including to the South for baseball spring training coverage.

Sarah, the Barbers' only child, was attended by a nurse and later, as a teenager, enrolled in prep school. Although her mother lived with the Barbers for a short period, Lylah's connection with family beyond Red and Sarah was far more distanced geographically and emotionally than when she lived among the Florida family of her youth. Her narrative vivifies the transition from the landed, agricultural-based economy of the South of her youth to the mobile, technologically influenced life so clearly ascendant by midcentury. But what had not changed very much for her generation—or seemed to have little chance of change for women moving into middle age—was the social mandate that a married woman's place was in the home. Even as more and more women in all regions of the country found the domestic sphere of the suburbs to be a lonely and alienating site, famously described in 1963 by Betty Friedan in *The Feminine*

Mystique, the alternative of taking up a career on one's own still seemed a fairly radical thing to do. Unlike the other wives studied here, whose stories include a vigorous partnership in husbands' careers—Barber poignantly describes feelings of emptiness that are not assuaged by family involvement or Red's career. "As I think back and write of those days," she explains, "the words keep coming into my mind, 'out of step' and 'lonely.' I was often lonely and alone. Red was gone much of the time and Sarah was away at prep school and college. I was not resentful or bitter. I understood the rules. Red was at the peak of his career as a broadcaster, and that had to come first" (182).

Barber recognizes the privileges and affluence that her husband's successful career brought into her life, indeed she acknowledges these time and time again, but this seventy-eight-year-old narrator also makes clear her yearning, as she writes in the preface, for "an achievement of my own" (xi). It is a telling feature of the narrative that, commencing with the marriage, the book's focus shifts from Lylah as a subject with autonomous agency to Mrs. Barber, the wife-supporter of Red's rising success and celebrity. Yet, unlike the narratives of Agnes Anderson and Mary Hamilton, which explicitly foreground the husband's "plot," this story struggles to advance as the narrator's own but is inexorably overshadowed in parts two and three by Red Barber's career.

The last chapters of the book take up the Barbers' retirement and return to Florida, first to Key Biscayne near Miami and then eventually back to Tallahassee. The transformation of the small town Barber had once known into a city, and of the college into a large university, are characteristic of momentous changes occurring across the South over the course of her lifetime. Barber also reflects upon race relations in the South over this same period. Recounting a trip she and Red made from Florida to Jackson, Mississippi, in 1980, she describes a stop in Selma, Alabama. There she remembers Martin Luther King's march in 1965 that they had watched in New York on television and how, as southerners, she and Red had taken "something of a beating from our northern liberal friends" (227). When they find the restrooms at a gas station hung with "Out of Order" signs, she supposes them to be a dodge to keep out black people and concludes that perhaps the times have not changed so much after all.

As with Durr and Boggs, we see in Barber's account of a post–World War II South that racial attitudes and the conditions of race relations in the South are issues that particularly confront them as white southerners in the North. Barber is quite candid about the racial apartheid of her youth, remarking that her formative years were in an environment "where the two races lived side by side," the black one, however, living largely in service to the white. In Cincinnati, with their "carefully taught Southern prejudice intact," she tells of their being seated next to a black couple at the symphony and hastily moving to the only other available seats, which were higher in the gallery and poorer seats. By the end of the concert, she remembers, she had come to realize the absurdity of her action. At that point "the child of the South" took "a first step toward becoming a citizen of the world" (98).

A more dramatic turning point in the Barbers' move away from racial prejudice comes in March 1945, when Branch Rickey informed Red that he intended to bring Jackie Robinson to play for the Brooklyn Dodgers. Red's immediate reaction was shock and then the announcement that he thought he "would have to quit." Lylah observes that he was "born in Mississippi, raised in redneck Florida, and educated at the all-male, all-white University of Florida," experiences that constitute a telling example of being "carefully taught," as the phrase was coined in the famous song from *South Pacific*. Of course, he did not quit. His "innate sense of fair play, kindness, and intelligence" took over, she writes, as well as the realization that "it was a mighty fine job he was contemplating walking away from" (159). Her own quite different reaction she attributes to her firsthand witness of responsible, skilled black men and women she had known growing up (not acknowledged, however, in the concert episode). She remembers the black nurse who cared for her while her mother was at work, a helpful black orderly at Riverside Hospital, and the chauffer-yardman Henry, who "often softened my stepfather's harshness" and even risked his job by teaching her mother how to drive a car. Rather being chagrinned by Rickey's decision to bring Robinson, Barber remembers admiring his courage. "And I knew Red would get his thinking straightened out—which he quickly did" (160).[2]

On the last page of the text, a sort of epilogue entitled "Between the Trees," Barber seeks to embody her sense of journey from a South at the beginning of the century to one near the end of it. The measure of the distance is suggested in the proximity of two fig trees, one that grew in her grandmother's yard, long since victim to "a devouring bulldozer" that made way for a "sterile asphalt" parking lot, and the other growing in the yard of a distant relation, "a second wife" connected only by marriage. Her grandmother's long vanished tree, which she remembers as a site of happiness and safety, she represents as "a child's security." The other one, alive but possessing no emotional resonance for her, she associates with "a full maturity." The implication Barber draws from her metaphor is rather more melancholy and nostalgic than acquiescent, the maturity connoting a sense of modernity's aggressions upon a beloved past—and a beloved southern way of life. But Barber constructs a beneficent childhood South only by carefully filtering memories of a troubled family and a society marred by racism and poverty. Her account of her southern upbringing makes little attempt to interpret the social forces that produced the personal experience she portrays or a way of life she idealizes.

The narrator of this autobiography seeks to show a life well and fully lived, but her voice is that of a wife who, while admiring and sharing some of the aura of a husband's celebrity, is also aware of her marginality to it. One hears in the voice more than a faint hint, if not an explicit recognition, that the world she traveled between the two fig trees offered her few paths for self-discovery or for achievement that she could claim as her own. Deep-rooted traditions governing a woman's identity as defined by her place in the family—and wifehood as an obligation to complement and support a husband's career—had provided the social framework in which she grew up, but these models had given no forecast of the more mobile and nontraditional life that lay ahead for the nation and its regions, even the South. In short, the era of her formative years was sharply at odds with that of her maturity. In his study of the generation in the South just prior to the civil rights movement, John Edgerton writes that "to be as isolated as the South was in the early years of the twentieth century was to be handicapped by short rations of economic and cultural nourishment," as well as to be "imprisoned by an ignorance" of the wider possibilities and opportunities that lay beyond the "magnolia curtain" (241).

Whereas Craig Sinclair, Virginia Durr, and Lindy Boggs were able to enter into the vital life of the nation beyond a tradition-bound southernness—to be southern belles, brides, and wives who moved from the domestic into a larger public sphere—the opportunity to do so was less acted upon or, perhaps, less available to Lylah Barber. Her fig tree metaphor of the self's passage through life, quite unlike the celebrated pear tree metaphor of self-empowerment and fulfillment that fellow Floridian Zora Neale Hurston composes so joyously in *Their Eyes Were Watching God,* is ultimately more a marker of loss than of celebration. Lylah Barber records a story of a wifehood obedient to the circumscribed domesticity she learned growing up in a traditional South. The independent self she went looking for when she was nearly eighty years old was almost invisible, but she finally caught a vision of that self as she composed her life narrative for a book that she herself made.

7

Testimonial Narratives of Racial Consciousness

KATHARINE DUPRE LUMPKIN AND LILLIAN SMITH

In preceding chapters the narratives discussed have focused primarily upon the local and the personal; that is, the narrators are revealed through associations with place, family, and work and make modest claims of asserting these lives as representational of region and era. However much they imply or even state directly that their circumstances and expected roles were shaped by the general conditions of their southern upbringing in the late nineteenth and early twentieth centuries, they construct a life narrative filled with singular recollections indicative of a person who emerges from a network of quite specific relationships. We have seen some exceptions along the way—Susan Dabney Smedes, writing as a representative witness to the hardships of Reconstruction for the dispossessed planter; Anna Julia Cooper, voicing her testimony of collective discrimination against African American women; and Belle Kearney, making the case for national temperance and woman's suffrage. But the other autobiographers have sought less to offer their life stories to their audience as case histories of a regional, gendered, racialized, or other condition—that is, as an example to clarify or document some general type or ideology—than to mirror and reveal the self who is the protagonist of the story.

Two striking examples of writers who do essay to speak of, for, and to the South appear, however, in autobiographical work published in the 1940s, Katherine DuPre Lumpkin in *The Making of a Southerner* and Lillian Smith in *Killers of the Dream*. A native of Georgia, Lumpkin had earned a doctorate in sociology from the University of Wisconsin and had written several scholarly studies of the family and of southern social conditions before turning to autobiography. Smith, better known for her fiction, had achieved wide notice if not notoriety

with her 1944 novel, *Strange Fruit,* which centered upon an interracial love affair. Making the best-seller list and adapted for the Broadway stage in 1945, it
established Smith as a determined voice in acknowledging and explaining the
connections between racism, sexuality, and violence in the South. These professional women, both born in 1897 and both discerning analysts of the Jim Crow
South where they were reared—and of its connections to slavery, Confederate
defeat, Reconstruction, and the Lost Cause effort to restore southern white legitimacy and authority—are notably unconcerned with constructing a modest,
deferential voice in their texts. They rarely invoke a fond, nostalgic tone in their
account of their early years, emphasizing rather a sober and dispassionate analysis more typical of the historian or social scientist than of a raconteur. In support of the regional critique they intend to offer, it is crucial that they establish
their credentials as authoritative witnesses of social conditions in the South.
Thus, like many of the autobiographers discussed in previous chapters, they include a detailed history of their southern families, but Lumpkin and Smith do
so with a more purposeful strategy.

The rhetorical strategy of commencing an intellectual assessment of public
issues and social practices with an extended commentary upon one's family
background and one's personal experience within the family may strike later
readers as a roundabout way to arrive at one's purpose. It is, of course, the strategy Belle Kearney employed in 1900 in *The Slaveholder's Daughter.* But Lumpkin and Smith, writing in the 1940s, employ the same kind of autobiographical
entry into their books about southern racism. The literary—or oratorical—device of establishing one's authority by invoking one's bloodline was certainly
not reserved to women, although it must be admitted that most women writers
had few alternatives. Commenting in a 1950s essay on the southerner's penchant for proposing an idea by first introducing one's family background, rhet-
orician Richard Weaver maintained that "in the South the bearer of an idea
must come vouchsafed and certified." One's show of coming from a "good family" or claim to holding high public office were reliable ways of gaining an audience. Since women were rarely public officeholders, those who wished to claim
a public audience for their writing would likely draw even more heavily upon
the good family line, as indeed Lumpkin and Smith do. Weaver's generic southerner expected an idea "to come with what the old writers on rhetoric used to
call ethical proof," although he goes on to acknowledge that the "proof" was
far less ethical than political, and that the southern inclination to rate an idea
according to the social prestige of the proponent was "one of the stifling influences in Southern culture" (21).

Lumpkin and Smith both display the credentials of coming from "good families," and they offer as the chief evidence in their case against racial injustice their personal observations beginning in childhood and their firsthand knowledge of regional history, all calculated to legitimate their analyses of southern social and economic problems. In significant ways, however, their recounting of a childhood located in a segregated South takes on the tone of a confession, or that of a witness offering corroborating testimony of endemic racism, with little of the laudatory overlay that one finds in the family portraits by Fearn, Anderson, and Sinclair. Even Kearney and Durr, who sometime take a more critical view of family, nonetheless attribute failings of parents and others more to personal, psychological causes than to moral and societal breakdowns.

Neither Lumpkin nor Smith struggles with such self-consciousness. They explain the impulse motivating their personal disclosures as a hope for racial enlightenment and call for social reform. They do not write to "tell their story"; rather, they write to indict racism and to use only as much of their personal record as is cogent and necessary to substantiate their charges and explain how they came to hold the views they do. The persona that dominates each narrative is very much the middle-aged narrator, writing in her forties, who selects details and devises a structure that can serve as convincing testimony supporting the indictment of racism and its pernicious consequences for both black and white southerners.

Fred Hobson has described these texts as "racial conversion narratives," linking them to traditions of the jeremiad of a much earlier America and to the slave narrative of the nineteenth century. Jacqueline Dowd Hall, who over the years has published the most comprehensive analysis of Lumpkin's life and writings, has characterized *The Making of a Southerner* as an autobiography of "social critique." She sees Lumpkin as bringing her personal narrative and voice to her training as a sociologist, with the effect of giving heightened emotive and political power to her analytical commentary. "Daring to speak in the first person, she tried to create a new kind of writing, a new way of interweaving memory and history, poetics and politics, without blurring the distinctions between the two" ("You Must" 462). But lying behind this new kind of writing is a social commitment, a "calling," which motivates the writer to reevaluate her experience in light of the person she understands herself to be at the time she takes up her pen. Georges Gusdorf has made a point of differentiating the organized, purposeful, introspective autobiography (characteristically male-authored) from memoir, with its outward, relational preoccupations and disconnected recollections of people, events, places, and so on. Despite Lumpkin's gender, he would call her text a classic autobiography—"the attempt and the drama of a man to reassemble himself in his own likeness at a certain moment of his history" (43).

Lumpkin creates a connected narrative designed specifically to portray an emergent self who grew up in a racially based, privileged white society coded as "southern," and who eventually came to disavow a "southernness" founded upon racism and to seek a new regional identity. Smith's *Killers of the Dream* shows a similar invocation of the younger self, an innocent former self, who is a foil to the writing narrator. This youthful person appears so as to have her earlier way of false seeing registered, rejected, then transformed, and so finally "reassembled" in an image consistent with the writing narrator.

The conviction of both Smith and Lumpkin that their past experience and their present writing voice accurately and legitimately embody the region—indeed, speak for it—is not anomalous among southern women writers of life narratives, but it is rare. With a nod to Richard King's contention that most southern women writers did not undertake to write about "the region" (with the caveat that how one defines "region" may validate or undercut King's assertion), one can agree that women writers rarely presented themselves in fiction or autobiography as the representative southerner speaking for the general society. Quite clearly, to presume such a role was antithetical to the separate woman's sphere extolled in traditionalist oratory and literature.

Throughout the twentieth century one does find, however, a variety of social critiques by southern men—and a few women—that are often grounded in personal narratives and that address the recurring issues of the South as "the nation's No. 1 economic problem," as President Franklin Roosevelt characterized it. In *I'll Take My Stand* the Nashville Agrarians famously took on the proponents of New South industrialization; John Donald Wade's essay "Life and Death of Cousin Lucius" employed personal witness in the character of Cousin Lucius as authority for a defense of a farm-based South. Notably, however, these essays largely ignore bloodline provenance and rely simply on the authors' identification as southerners to demonstrate their authority for speaking for the South. More dramatic and far more seeringly personal is Richard Wright's 1945 *Black Boy,* which aims to depict Wright's personal story as a generic maturation tale of a black boy growing to manhood in the racist South. The narrative joins a long tradition dating from the slave narrative in documenting racial oppression, with material drawn in this case from Wright's experience of having grown up in Mississippi.

Other writers and public activists responded to the extreme conditions of

Depression-era poverty and the malevolent consequences of societal divisions, a failing agrarian economy, and a general resistance to change by often grounding their commentary upon their background and personal experience. Darlene O' Dell notes the influence on Lumpkin of Jonathan Daniels's *A Southerner Discovers the South,* for example, and compares Lumpkin's treatment of the region to that by William Alexander Percy and W. J. Cash (47). Howard Odum, W. T. Couch, Rupert Vance, and many others might be cited, as Daniel Joseph Singal so well shows in his study of early twentieth-century southern intellectuals in *The War Within.* These professors at Chapel Hill, Vanderbilt, and at other southern universities, many of whom were natives of the South, drew upon their personal background no less than upon their professional training as they wrote and spoke of southern social conditions.

Katharine Lumpkin and Lillian Smith, like Virginia Durr and others, were responsive witnesses to the problems and pressures of changing social conditions at home and abroad. The emerging threat of fascism in Europe, eventuating in World War II, was the central event of the decade in which they wrote *The Making of a Southerner* and *Killers of the Dream.* Having watched the rise of Germany and Italy, with their justifications of terror and destruction leveled upon "inferior" groups, and having witnessed a growing sensitivity among the U.S. military and the citizenry on the home front toward the old segregationist practices, both women understood that the war dramatically accelerated the changing political context in which a white supremacist South could continue to enforce its domination by law, intimidation, and terror. In his 2008 *Slavery by Another Name,* Douglas Blackmon comprehensively documents the forced labor practices in the South that had been common from the Civil War to World War II, which he concludes amounted to "the re-enslavement of black Americans."

Historian Pete Daniel describes the South's situation even in the years immediately after World War II as that of a continuing "colony" of the U.S.— "another country." White southerners retained many of their Populist leanings, but these were "tinged with a colonial-like bitterness toward the power of capital" that controlled the economy. And black southerners, "segregated and exploited, lived in a colony within a colony" (151). John Egerton voices a somewhat more benign view of the war's aftermath in *Speak Against the Day: The Generation Before the Civil Rights Movement in the South.* Looking back to this era, coincident with his own early years, he writes that that the triumph of the United States in August 1945 marked the conclusion of an outdated South "with more finality than any occurrence since the end of the Civil War," opening the way for a new generation "to help lift the South out of its eighty-year nightmare of post–Civil War stagnation" (4).

The southern economic and political leadership of the past, who had represented their own private interests and the region's interests as one and the same, had of course been challenged for over a century by the testimony of African American life narratives. Richard Wright's was just one of the most vehement. There was, in fact, a growing tradition of narrative witnessing by southern writers to contradictions between sustaining elite white male power and securing the well-being of virtually everyone else. Kearney's testimony, for example, made the case powerfully for female suffrage. Drawing upon his North Carolina background and his training as a newspaperman, W. J. Cash attacked the romanticized "myth" of the plantation South in *The Mind of the South,* a text in which he virtually elides the self to create a generalized "mind" that has a body, a history, and a name of "Southerner," or, in various manifestations, "Virginian," "cracker," "mill worker," "mountaineer," and so on. Even the heirs of the old elite testified that traditional patterns of class and racial divisions were giving way under the influence of modernism. In 1941, the same year that saw the publication of Cash's text, Percy would represent his life story as witnessing the waning days of the white planter class in *Lanterns on the Levee.* It was in such company that Lumpkin and Smith would likewise put their life stories in service to a regional portrait that exposed the moral malaise and economic near-collapse of a racially segregated South.

Writing a new afterword in 1980 for a reissue of her 1946 autobiography, *The Making of a Southerner,* Katharine Lumpkin returns to the central motif of her original text, the American South as site of a racially divided society. Her foremost purpose for writing the book had been to bring her own life narrative to a study of the racial caste system as it existed in the early years of the twentieth century. As she reviews the extraordinary societal transformations that had occurred over the intervening thirty-five years—*Brown v. Board of Education,* the civil rights movement of the 1960s, the Civil Rights Act, the Voting Rights Act, and other legislation aimed at discriminatory practices—she concludes her 1980 commentary by noting the major areas in which equal rights and opportunities for black people yet remain to be addressed: housing and employment. She offers no detail whatsoever of her life during this generation of change, except to note her response to the unfolding public events of the period. The focus of her afterword, like the focus of her book, is chiefly on the history of race relations in the South, and she probes and presents her life narrative only insofar as it cogently dramatizes and explains larger social practices. As a sociologist, her "thickest" field study lies in her knowledge of her own childhood, her family, her "South," and it is largely in the spirit of the social scientist that she draws upon her personal narrative to authenticate and clarify the social practices that form the key content of her writing.

The rhetorical strategy of her book relies upon a detached narrator who proposes to relate an objective account of her childhood in Georgia and South Carolina, a story that is minimally filtered by her maturing realization over many years of the glaring contradictions between the status and values claimed by her family and community and their actual social practice. The restrained voice of the narrator and the use of details often manifestly self-contradictory produce a steady irony that pervades every aspect of the text, including the titles of chapters (designated by the author as "books") and even the overall title itself. Lumpkin repeatedly shows her reader that the "southerner" is a creature of culture, one "made," not "born," and that the white supremacist southerner is one who requires intricate conditioning because the continual separation of human beings who live within an arm's length of one another is an arduous undertaking, so wholly counter to a human being's social nature and at odds with the Christian's declared belief in brotherhood and the American's declared belief in the equality of citizenship. Acknowledging the hypocrisies and contradictions of such southernness, Lumpkin implies, can lead to a changed vision and a different kind of southerner, which are the ends she seeks.

The title of section one, "Of Bondage to Slavery," refers to the ways in which the lives of her Lumpkin male forebears, from great-grandfather William Lumpkin to her father, were bound firmly to their station as slave masters and so ironically they were held in a kind of bondage themselves. Their conviction that their "burden" was a moral enterprise as well as an economic one deepened the bondage, for the planter knew "beyond argument or question," Lumpkin writes with deadpan irony, "that his black slaves needed and deserved their slavery" (42). She proceeds in the opening chapter in a bland, documentary tone that establishes a balanced objectivity and accuracy of information about the history of her family and the region. Her account recalls that of Cash in the opening chapters of *The Mind of the South,* describing the rise of a fictional, though representative, young Irishman who came to the American South and with enterprise, hard work, good land, and slave labor rose markedly in wealth and status in his one generation.

Lumpkin's authorial strategy differs from Cash's, however, in several significant ways. Her story is rooted in the factual history of her own family and so is more personalized and authenticating. At the same time, her tone is more subdued than Cash's, more observational than assertive or argumentative. But, like Cash, Lumpkin keeps before her reader the contrast between a romanticized South of legend and the actual South of her family's experience. The home place, for example, was not "a mansion of stately pillars," but a utilitarian dwelling of the kind described in New England as a "colonial farmhouse" (8). Although the Georgia plantation of twelve thousand acres was one of Oglethorpe County's larger ones, it was still a far cry from the vast plantations of the low country with their thousands of acres and hundreds of slaves, vast spreads that were far less typical of the South than her own family's farm. Lumpkin observes that as a child she listened to her father's descriptions of the "working plantation" of his boyhood, a place where the planter's and family's labor was as essential as that of the forty or so slaves. The Lumpkins were hardly the leisured, traveled, elegantly housed planters that Katharine read about in nostalgic stories of antebellum days, but she "hardly noticed the difference," she comments. "Somehow the two pictures became blurred and blended until later years" (9).

The narrator restrains her later-year judgments of the planter-slave economy in the course of describing her family history, but she uses understatement and irony to great effect. For example, in describing her grandfather's life as a slave master, she quotes liberally from a court order directing the distribution of slaves to the heirs of her great-grandfather. The litany of names and dollar values assigned to each slave goes unremarked, except for her comment about the facile commodifying that made the distribution more efficient—"Nothing was too much for man's ingenuity apparently" (4). In her helpful introduction to the 1991 reprinted text, Darlene Clark Hine reads Lumpkin in this opening section as reflecting "the master's point of view" (ix), but Lumpkin's tone is more parodic than straightforward, conveying her critique of slavery by juxtaposing the parceling out of slaves in fifteen separate "lots" alongside a description of the "exceedingly pleasant country" that was the lot of the Lumpkin brothers who arrived in Georgia in the late eighteenth century (5).

In subsequent sections Lumpkin intensifies the irony. Describing the theological contortions that devout Christians like her Baptist grandfather had to devise to rationalize their laws governing slave marriage, she intersperses quotations from various legal statutes, adding no commentary but trusting the ironical effect to carry her point: "A slave may indeed be formally married, but so far as legal rights and obligations are concerned, it is an idle ceremony," or, "A slave has no more legal authority over his child than a cow has over her calf" (20). She notes that her grandfather, like her father, would not likely have been much troubled by such laws, dismissing them as being rarely invoked and rationalizing the need of them in "special cases." But she suggests that separated families were hardly unusual, quoting a series of excerpts from contemporaneous reward advertisements for slaves who had run away to join their families. Lumpkin draws upon U. B. Phillips and others for information about slavery in the antebellum South, along with the recollections of her father, born in 1849, and her own elaborated and imagined account of day-to-day life in middle Georgia before the Civil War. At the center of her critique of slavery in the opening section is the anomaly of her grandfather—"slaveholder, Southern Baptist, and Southern gentleman, all rolled into one" (12)—a man bound to an economic system hopelessly at odds in so many ways with his religious and moral credo. And deepening the honorable slaveholder's quandary were personal relations with slaves that daily exposed the illogicality and futility of maintaining the slave's inherent inferiority.

Grandfather Lumpkin's able and respected overseer was his slave Jerry, whose responsibility for managing the plantation stretched to every aspect of the farm and was crucial to its success. Furthermore, it was Jerry who provided the religious and moral leadership for the slaves; he was preacher and pastor on the Lumpkin place and for the surround of neighboring plantations. In the characterization of Grandfather Lumpkin and Jerry, who together so clearly embody the coexistence of piety and oppression—and reveal a propensity for sociability and hospitality alongside a serene self-confident assumption of racial superiority—the narrator portrays a society bound to a welter of irreconcilable beliefs, but that managed nonetheless to construct a veneer of stability and inevitability. The Civil War, of course, would rip off the veneer.

Lumpkin portrays her father as the bereft inheritor of a lost South whose obsession with his denied legacy dominated his life. He was Katharine's chief source of her knowledge of the past. His stories of a halcyon plantation era, his interpretation of southern honor and suffering, northern victimization, and the constant, unrelieved need to keep Negroes "in their place" formed her child's understanding of her region's history and her place in it. Despite her father's deeply personal affiliation with the Lost Cause South, when she writes of slavery or even of Reconstruction, the Ku Klux Klan, and the activity of white southerners to obstruct black enfranchisement, she does so in the manner of a scribe, distanced from the action and its consequences. "Who can say with certainty," she writes, "what went on in middle Georgia at the time this Invisible Empire was sending out its unknown men to perform its unnamed missions?" (90). Her father's version of the KKK consisted mainly of tales about "scaring" blacks who stood accused of impudently challenging white privilege or, worse, threatening white women and children. They were tales to her child's ears of a time past.

What was salient and urgent in his tale telling, however, was the centrality of the family and its values and traditions to whatever self-definition the Lumpkin child might claim. She says simply that "the 'meaning' of family was warp and woof of our heritage of ideas, and with it, of appropriate actions" (103). That "meaning" of the Lumpkins that William taught his youngest child Katharine was delivered metaphorically: the pride and honor implicit in the southern "Lost Cause" signified the nobility of the Lumpkin family and each one of its members. Self-worth was tied to family, and the Lumpkins were celebrants of an enshrined Confederacy. She quotes a familiar refrain of her father's: "Their mother teaches them their prayers. I teach them to love the Lost Cause" (121). For William Lumpkin the Lost Cause was, of course, sacred belief, and from it flowed sacred ceremonies of remembrance and rededication of patriot heirs. As earlier discussed, the ritualization of Civil War commemoration was indeed a construction of the "heirs." Charles Reagan Wilson's tracing of this ritualizing of southern history during the period 1880 to 1940 uncovers what he terms "the invention of southern tradition," designed to recuperate regional pride and identity "within a concept of the South without nationality" (4). Hall, too, notes that William Lumpkin's account of the past was "bent to the political moment" and that his vow to pass on to his children a belief in the nobility of the southern past was one way of fashioning "new selves and a new society from the materials of the old" ("You Must" 463).

When the narrator titles a pivotal section of the book "A Child Inherits a Lost Cause," with the slight change of the modifying article (*the* becomes *a*), she again signals her ironic estimate of her father's Confederate theology. His effort to inculcate Lost Cause piety proved itself to be a lost cause. Despite her older sister Elizabeth's great success as an orator extolling southern heroism and honor at Confederate veterans' reunions and other gatherings, and despite the family's continual discussion and rehearsals of southern justifications—and Yankee victimization—Katharine found when she accompanied her father to the veterans' meetings, primed to recite her poem or deliver the speech he had written for her, that there was little evidence in the audience of heroism, excitement, or even fiery rhetoric. The gatherings were drab, and the old men's droning along was interrupted only by an occasional "decorous use of numerous spittoons" (126).

Lumpkin does not place her crucial discovery of cracks in the facade of southern nobility or lies masked by "lost cause" rhetoric in her observations of old veterans' faces, however. Rather, it is a traumatic display of violence enacted by her father upon the family's black cook that most acutely exposes the racial divide defining her society and compromising its vaunted claims to heroism and nobility. It was a climactic scene of her childhood, as she describes it, one that came upon her unexpectedly as she wandered one summer morning "aimlessly out into the yard." Suddenly, a noise like "bedlam" erupted; there were terrifying screams that sent her heart pounding. By describing the emotional reception of the scene before explaining the particulars of the event, the narrator emphatically communicates the elements of surprise, fear, and horror that she felt, and, ultimately, her condemnation of her father's violent act and the values that gave rise to it. "Our little black cook, a woman small in stature though full grown, was receiving a severe thrashing. I could see her writhing under the blows of a descending stick wielded by the white master of the house. I could see her face distorted with fear and agony and his with stern rage" (132).

A first reading of this passage almost always confuses students in my classes, for they do not immediately identify "the white master" as William Lumpkin, although they infer that the employer of "our family's cook" logically is he. The disjunction between the third-person impersonal designation of the attacker and the daughter-narrator's first-person witnessing of the incident makes for an oblique sentence, to be sure, but it is emphatically telling, as students all agree upon a second reading. Lumpkin deliberately structures this scene to convey a load of information about how and why she eventually came to reject her region's and her family's racism. She has devoted several preceding chapters to tracing patriarchal history and its claims for courage and nobility, passed on to her mainly through her father. Here she reports what she herself witnessed. If we are to believe that the specificity of detail she gives in this passage has been fully retained in memory over many years, we have to infer that the experience was highly charged with emotion and, likely, that the recollection has been refreshed in her thinking about it subsequently, perhaps repeatedly, during the intervening years.

Jacqueline Hall remembers when she first met the author in the 1970s, just after Lumpkin had completed her biography of abolitionist Angelina Grimke. Lumpkin's memory of family violence seemed to have "gained in psychic charge. She spoke of the beating in a whisper," notes Hall, explicitly comparing her experience to that of Grimke. "For both women," writes Hall, "remembering was a conscious political act" ("You Must" 459). The incident of the father's attack upon the cook is widely regarded by historians and literary critics who have written about *The Making of a Southerner* as the thematic turning point in Lumpkin's life narrative. In addition to Hall's insightful commentary, Fred Hobson's reading of the autobiography as a racial conversion narrative (43 ff.) and Darlene O'Dell's analysis of the text as an exposé of a moribund "Lost Cause" that sought to rationalize white supremacy (67) give special attention to the centrality of the scene in Lumpkin's indictment of racism.

Unquestionably, Lumpkin composes the scene as pivotal in her turn away from the father and toward the different kind of southerner she would become. The middle-aged narrator's purpose as the controlling maker of the narrative is to determine what events to include in the text and how to show their connection to the views and values of the emergent self who has undertaken this autobiography. The child's experiences and emotional responses are recovered (and indeed are only recoverable) as they are mediated and articulated—*interpreted*—by the adult, whose recollection of the past is inevitably incomplete. Lumpkin is not recovering her child's world and worldview in these early pages but rather is creating, indeed is imagining, the child and young woman who logically develop into the narrator-self who writes an autobiography as social critique. As a reader of autobiography, one assumes the constant presence of the writer-narrator; unlike fiction, autobiography does not allow a full suspension of disbelief and entry into the narratized world. The author's "I" is a present and available consciousness on every page. The writer Vivian Gornick, using the term *memoir* throughout her discussions of life writing, observes that "truth in a memoir is achieved not through a recital of actual events; it is achieved when the reader comes to believe that the writer is working hard to engage with the experience at hand. What happened to the writer is not what matters; what matters is the large sense that the writer is able to *make* of what happened" (*Situation* 91). And, of course, the "making" is not the act of the child but that of the narrating writer. Gornick quotes the British writer V. K. Pritchett to good purpose: "It's all in the art. You get no credit for living."

In *The Making of a Southerner* the creation and explanation of the "I-narrator" is the very point of the story being told. For example, Lumpkin's analysis of her child-self's response to the black woman's beating is to report "mixed feelings," arising on the one hand from her wish to justify her father's actions and so avoid any experience of separation and, on the other, from her disturbing sense that she has caught him in an ignoble, brutal act. This parsing of emotion is the work of the older writer, not the child. Most simply, the recoverable incident from childhood is "I saw Father beat the cook and was disturbed." In the text, the key words impressed upon the reader are "I saw it." This moment of seeing, which she comes to regard upon reflection as the moment when she first fully understood herself as unmistakably *white* (i.e., member of the privileged caste in an apartheid society), signals a budding maturity of judgment that over time led to the woman who rejects racism and who is writing about it. But this is the judgment of hindsight, made after she assesses a collection of life incidents and decides, comparatively, upon one that is laden with personal emotion and racial strife sufficient to carry the symbolic weight necessary in an autobiographical testimony about the poisonous southernness born of racism.

In addition to racial segregation, Lumpkin takes up issues of class division, shaping her account of the family's relocation to South Carolina near the desolate Sand Hills region and the habitation of the "poor whites" to illustrate her growing awareness of stratification and the opportunities—and limitations—for self-development that social status determines. Her description of the physical characteristics of the destitute people she saw on small farms scattered around the countryside follows closely similar descriptions by Cash and John Dollard. She writes of "their pasty faces, scrawny necks, angular ill-nourished frames, straw-like hair" (151), just as Cash had written a few years earlier of "a striking lankness of frame, . . . a peculiar sallow swartness or . . . a not less sallow faded-out colorlessness of skin and hair" (25). In his 1937 *Caste and Class in a Southern Town,* Dollard notes in a rather droll tone that, "from the standpoint of social usefulness," the poor whites had "arms and legs and minimum skills, usually of the agricultural type" (75). Lumpkin's awakening to her privileged class position in comparison with these alien neighbors arises, ironically, not only because her family's property is the "big farm" of the countryside but also because, upon her father's sudden death, she and her family find themselves in a threatened and dependent financial situation. Having to do hard farm work for the first time in her life, she begins to contemplate a southern way of life very different from that of plantation romance.

The account of the father's death takes up exactly one sentence in the text, a mention so briefly and incidentally noted that it catches a reader by surprise. As many commentators have maintained, this truncated exit cue seems to signal a dismissal by Lumpkin of her father's presence and power as a shaping influence on her worldview. But it would seem that she is equally structuring this section of the text so as to show a developing realization of human vulnerability to time and the vagaries of fortune, a vulnerability that touched her own life when, absent the father's "knowing hand to guide everything," they were all thrown upon their own ignorance about how to run a farm. As with her discovery of racial caste, she has "mixed feelings" about finding class differences that separate her from other farm families who are white. Just as she had taken some comfort in the security and solidarity of whiteness when she witnessed the attack upon the cook, she finds relief in her different clothes, language, schooling, religious practice, even her sense of entitlement to give voice to her desires and opinions—as the shy, country, poor children did not. And just as she had found that earlier spectacle of oppression to be "disturbing," she describes similarly her reaction to witnessing their underprivileged state. "It was as though I had a pre-arranged advantage in a race which made me always win. I longed to hide what I knew if thereby I might escape from always having the better of them. I felt unfair and that they would think me so" (160). In this section the narrator depicts the girl Katharine as disturbed because she is increasingly aware of her personal complicity in a class hierarchy that is uncomfortably like the display of racial superiority her father had expressed upon the body of the cook.

At this point in the narrative, it is significant that the author takes up the subject of religion and the church, for the Bible-trained girl that she shows the younger Katharine to have been looked to Christian principles to elucidate her moral quandaries. Lumpkin remarks that, when she was old enough to read, she daily read the Bible aloud to her mother and memorized the New Testament, "a few verses at a time . . . until I could recite by heart far along in the book of Matthew" (163). Despite what seemed to her girl's eyes an irremediable inferiority of the poor white children in the classroom, she could expect a different relationship in church, where all souls were supplicant before the altar of God. But even in church, the ill-educated, stumbling adult readers of the Bible swelled the underprivileged group before her eyes, and she felt the surety of superiority. Their country Baptist church, with its emotional religious services and preoccupations with "sinful dancing" and other venial activities that seemed so harmless to Katharine, was finally foreign and embarrassing to her sedate "Episcopal soul." Here were white southerners who believed in miraculous conversions, had no pretentions of plantation aristocracy, and lived dirt-poor, often illiterate lives. But, finally, they were people she came to know. "It was not for nothing apparently that my would-be playmates were patently children of destitution," she writes later, "so that perforce I saw their state very intimately. Seeing it and liking them, my mind was stirred by what I saw" (183). A disturbing sense of contradiction is the significant legacy she carries away from this year in the South Carolina country. Again, it is the "seeing" with her own eyes that makes impossible for her later a complacent dismissal of "the poorer classes."

In "Sojourn in the Sand Hills" Lumpkin enlarges the discussion of her southern, white, racially proud upbringing with this account of her discovery of class division and her own discomfiting sense of class pride. It is a climactic chapter, implicating the maturing Katharine in a received tradition of southernness that she has found "disturbing" but has not yet seriously questioned. Returning to the city and preparing for college just ahead, she is furnished by her race and middle-class training with the reasonable expectation of securing a privileged, traditional adulthood. But the knowing narrator has already intimated in many ways that, despite the youthful Katharine's assumption that she can quickly put behind her the lessons of poverty and vulnerability she has learned in the sand hills, this sojourn has set her in a different direction. Together with the religious concerns that have increasingly engaged her as an adolescent, her seeing a different South from the one commemorated in Lost Cause narratives and plantation romances has readied her for a new vision. A truly spiritual conversion that leads to a search beyond the legacy of traditionalism—a religious commitment that, in fact, focuses upon the remediation of white southern pride of caste and class—informs the final sections of the text.

Lumpkin's account of her transformation from lost southerner into saved southerner follows a structure almost exactly like that of Kearney's in *A Slaveholder's Daughter*. Both writers begin with a description of family and society in which honorable natures are compromised and blighted by slavery; next, they isolate and dramatize particular incidents that illustrate the social problems that call for change; and then they identify the transforming experience that authorizes their commitment to speak publicly for that new direction. For Lumpkin, just as for Kearney, this latter is identified as a spiritual transformation. It is a godly call to a Christian mission—at its core, a religious conversion narrative. She takes her titles for the concluding sections from the opening of Chapter 21 in Revelations: "And I saw a new heaven and a new earth; for the first heaven and the first earth were passed away; and there was no more sea." Although the older author seems less inspired by religious passion than is the younger self she describes in these chapters, she nonetheless attributes her turn toward racial tolerance and her lifelong commitment to social justice to the "new message" of a social gospel that said "the day of discipleship was not past." This was a religion that spoke directly of the here and now, focused not on living for a heaven beyond the clouds but upon the immediate world one was part of. "Some might say base human nature would not change. Not the new message or the new voices. Let this religion spread, they said, and it could be potent to transform the world by changing the men who made it" (188).

Hall, Hobson, and O'Dell all discuss the relation of Lumpkin's religious belief to her revisioning of southern society, noting key passages in the text in which the narrator describes the moment of hearing the "new message," but they focus more on her subsequent commitment to social change than to this precipitating spiritual transformation—as indeed, one might argue, Lumpkin herself does. Morton Sosna and many other cultural historians writing about the South have likewise explored the deep connection between certain religious commitments, such as acceptance of the social gospel, and racial liberalism.[1] When Lumpkin undertakes to make this point, however, she has to deal with a present, writing self who no longer feels such religious passion. It is a rupture between the protagonist Katharine and the narrator unlike any we have seen earlier. This emerging figure is a Katharine who is on her way to becoming the "remade" southerner composing the book, although the religious passion that gave impetus to the new vision and moral urgency has largely faded, a point the narrator makes clear in the closing pages. Without the irony she often brings to the earlier accounts of faded southern-heritage lessons, she portrays the religious conversion with straightforward earnestness. Consistent with the plot she has mapped for this text, she depicts the spiritual conversion as a second significant turning point in the narrative.

Lumpkin pointedly constructs the sequence leading to this climax: first there is a spiritual conversion, then the revelation of a mission field. She hears the "new message" and then answers a Christian mission call. This story is a familiar one, as one sees from the body of scholarship on the social gospel movement in the early twentieth century.[2] Just as Kearney describes herself as impelled into WCTU work, Lumpkin writes of being "called," the word she uses in her text, to a YWCA leadership conference in North Carolina in 1915, when she was nineteen and a student delegate from Brenau College in Georgia. At the meeting she was forced to consider how her commitment to Christianity called into question much about the southern heritage she had been taught to revere, specifically, the claims of white supremacy and the practices of racial segregation. Over several pages she emphasizes the psychological weight of the taboo against any display of social equality between blacks and whites, thereby heightening the risk of one's challenging the practice of the racial caste system. Ultimately, she decides to act upon the new message, invoking the parable of the Good Samaritan as her model. At the conclusion of *The Making of a Southerner,* she reiterates that "under religion's felt demand I could first profane the sacred tabernacle of our racial beliefs and go on profaning it in subsequent years," and then adds, "until I no longer felt the need to lean on any kind of authority, save that of the demands of a common humanity" (238–39).

Although Lumpkin justifies her "presumptuous" rebellion against southern racism on religious grounds, she acknowledges two influences important to her intellectual and spiritual development and to her sense of confidence in her own moral judgments. There are her mother, about whom she says little earlier in the text, saving her story for its heightened effect upon the transformative moment, and a memorable college teacher, whom she describes simply as "this one man [who] was my education" (186). Her book-loving mother, educated and intellectually curious, taught her that "those who have brains are meant to use them."

Reflecting upon her mother's part in shaping her independence of mind, Lumpkin remarks upon the "anomalous" condition of the family household. Although Katharine was carefully taught that deference to men was appropriate for a woman, she was also encouraged to think and express her views on a wide range of issues. The narrator's irony edges toward sarcasm in describing the demeanor she was taught as appropriate for a girl: "In some sense it remained with us the woman's part to remain silent when men were speaking, not to pit our opinions against the more knowing male's; indeed, to look on woman as a figure on a pedestal—Southern woman, that is . . . who was meant to lean her feeble strength on the firm, solid frame of a male protector and guide" (185–86). But this "woman's place" was manifestly challenged by her mother's intelligence and participation along with her father in fostering intellectuality, spirited debate, and ambition among all the children, the girls as well as the boys.

Elizabeth Fox-Genovese has observed that Lumpkin does not explicitly emphasize her gender as a shaping force upon her southernness, "that she does not represent her identity as a woman as central to her efforts to come to terms with her past and to chart a new course" ("Between Individualism" 34). In the portrayal of her mother and the description of her own socialization as a female child, however, Lumpkin is quite direct in voicing her sense of having been consigned to a female sphere and her awareness of a contingent status that depended upon male prerogative. Still, Fox-Genovese is quite right that gender equity plays a lesser role in this text than does racial and economic equity. The narrator of *The Making of a Southerner* essays to speak for the region as a southerner, that is, a white southerner, and she speaks from a position of privilege that calls for reforms, not to benefit herself in any material way but to improve the welfare of the underprivileged and racially oppressed and to satisfy the moral integrity of other southerners like herself.

One aspect of her privileged position was her access to a college education and to a teacher who, in retrospect, she regards as formative in her intellectual development. The influential professor was, like her mother, an "anomaly" at conservative Brenau College. Although "a Southerner in his roots" and a "devout churchman, a Baptist," Lumpkin remembers him as setting no limits upon his "earnest searching," nor placing any restrictions upon others. A teacher of history, economics, and sociology, he garnered her respect for his open mindedness, his willingness to read and discuss even the "flaming modernist" Harry Emerson Fosdick, and his having "no disposition to say to his questioning student, 'It is wrong where you are heading'" (187).

Although it is as a college student that the youthful Katharine comes to a decisive acknowledgement of the discordance between old ways of southernness and her new dedication to Christian social mission, she writes also of the instructive and confirming experiences of her several years as a graduate student at Columbia University and afterwards, from 1920 to 1925, as a member of the student field staff of the YWCA. During these years she was engaged in trying to understand the social causes and economic conditions of poverty, as well as working to ameliorate them. Exploitative jobs, substandard housing, poor diets, scant education, early marriage, lives that were lived as "instruments . . . moved helplessly by a larger machine" (221) were the hard truths that Lumpkin came to know firsthand, an experience that vastly expanded her understanding of the underprivileged that had begun in the Sand Hills. The questions that most engaged her were questions of poverty, especially of the white "lower classes." Why was the South so poor? So far behind other regions of the country? The answers would eventually lead her to race, but her account of this period shows that it was questions of class that initially most challenged her.

One infers that the twenty-year interim between the core narrative and the brief 1980 epilogue entitled "Time of Change" was at least as significant as Lumpkin's childhood and young adulthood to her conceptualizing her analysis of the South as a region blighted by "bondage to slavery." But about these years she is silent. Jacquelyn Hall, who has provided the most extensive biographical commentary about this period, including writing about her own meeting and interview with Lumpkin, concludes that Lumpkin's decision to end the central narrative in the 1920s reflects her reticence about strained family relationships, as well as her long relationship with Dorothy Douglas, who was implicated in the Communist-hunts of the House Un-American Activities Committee. Hall attributes these omissions from the autobiography to a reserve born of Lumpkin's professional stance of objectivity, her concern about reactions to her politics, and her resistance to a public airing of her personal life ("Open Secrets" 119). Doubtless, she also demurred because of deep strains within the family, including a difficult relationship with her sister Grace, author of the labor novel *To Make My Bread* (1932), who turned from her early leftist politics to denunciations of the Communist Party and its partisans.[3] In fact, she was determined to employ the personal only to the extent that she could connect it overtly to the political and economic analysis that she undertook to write. The personal narrative constituted the key testimony of her primary "field" informant—herself as deep-rooted southerner.

This autobiographical text is instructive in many respects but especially so for what it shows about the use of the life story as evidentiary detail. Unlike memoirs that aim to give a fleshed-out portrayal of the life lived, *The Making of a Southerner* is a highly focused narrative. The author writes to revise regional history, to show that there was a South, or several Souths, quite different from the one she was brought up to believe in—that there was a South of fact disturbingly inconsistent with the South of myth. A student of sociology and economics, holder of a doctorate from the University of Wisconsin, she began her search for understanding by studying the depressed southern economy. Why is the South so poor? She came to her conclusion that racial division lay at the root, a conviction that came not from her transforming encounter with the social gospel but from an application of her graduate training. She lays out the case not as a call for Christian brotherly love, though she has earlier dramatized the moral grounds for that position, but as the inescapable analysis of the economist, who connects the dots between the depression of white laborers' wages and the constant, competitive availability of even more depressed black wages, powerfully enforced by the tradition of racism—thus, the "bondage to slavery."

At the conclusion, Lumpkin's text veers from the life narrative offered as evidence—as a representative, even generic, record of southern white experience—and becomes particularistic. The question is put, "Why did this southerner not "hold to things as they were"? In other words, "Why am I different?" Raising the question, of course, points up the limits of the generic self, for, approaching the conclusion of the text, the autobiographer must bind together the character portrayed and the composing self. For the most part, Lumpkin implies a connection but says little explicitly, leaving the twenty-year gap unbridged. But she does advance two partial rejoinders to the question of her "difference"; one recurs among many autobiographical texts, and the other provocatively hints more of another kind of southern mythmaking than of candid introspection. She argues, for example, much as Belle Kearney does, that her values are continuous with many of the tenets of her southern upbringing—injunctions such as "aid the weak and helpless" and "he who has brains must use them," as well as a strong religious tradition (238). Although she acknowledges that her ancestors were unquestionably culpable in fostering chattel slavery, she contends that her father's generation was demoralized by the postbellum uprooting, a chaotic condition that led such southerners to seek relief by clinging to white supremacy. His was a generation of profound contradictions and ambiguities, she maintains, which she internalized as a child.

The other explanation that she offers for her "difference" is inexorably bound to her sense of class identity. Her "kind of people," the old landed planter class, had been sadly stuck in a pernicious nostalgia, she says, and were not the beneficiaries of the New South industrialization. Those benefiting rather were the "new men" who manipulated her father's contemporaries, urging a saving of "southern civilization" mainly to preserve a cheap and stable labor force. In the preceding chapter, she subjects this kind of rationalizing to scrutiny. Speaking of the revival of the Ku Klux Klan in the 1920s, she writes that "the people I knew" would say that "the 'best people' did not support the new KKK," that the Klan was "but a simple abscess on our otherwise healthy Southern body," but she goes on to undercut such assertions and imply the complicity of whites generally: "In fact, however, the numbers grew, and so did the influence of this new order" (209). In the closing pages she takes up again the defense of "her kind of Southern people," this time with sympathy. She suggests that they were misguided by their nostalgia, weakened by internal doubts and fears, and finally displaced by outliers who assumed new leadership for "ordering society" (237). This is essentially the southern story that William Faulkner would dramatize throughout his career. He writes in the 1954 essay "Mississippi," for example, of the "economic rivalry which was to send Snopeses in droves into the Ku Klux Klan—not the old original one of the war's chaotic and desperate end which, measured against the desperate times, was at least honest and serious in its desperate aim, but into the later base one of the twenties whose only kinship to the old one was the old name" (19).

Ironically, this defense of southern honor suggests a new "lost cause" mythology—the bad whites were the violent racists, while the honorable aristocratic whites may have held conflicted views about race but nonetheless condemned violence. This will surely strike most readers as a familiar scenario. In *Framing the South,* a 2001 study of the depiction of the South in film and television, Allison Graham finds this class-based defense to be a persistent pattern in the media throughout the 1950s and 1960s and, in fact, over the following four decades. It offers a strategy for showing both an "accepting of responsibility for racism (admitting white culpability, in other words) and denying it (depicting criminality as an inherent characteristic of class rather than race)" (13).[4] Like

Virginia Durr, Lumpkin finally situates her present writer-self well outside the circle of southern-cause defenders, but she claims a connection still to certain admirable qualities she associates with her class, "her people," qualities and values that, along with study, experience, and courage to accept change, she shows as paving the way for the "remaking" of the "old" southerner she once was.

In her conclusion Lumpkin muddles her plot in a quite human, understandable way. She recuperates the father, partially, but in doing so she blunts her attack upon white responsibility for racial oppression. Both the portrait she draws of the past and the vision she has for a different future South reveal greater complexity than is encompassed by a project seeking just to indict evil and locate blame. That she falls back upon class propensities as the vehicle to identity the commitment to social justice that she respects and espouses is self-justifying, to be sure. This move in the text suggests it was possible for her to envision a day beyond racial segregation but not to envision class desegregation.

Lumpkin's overriding concern in this personal narrative is to indict the racism she witnessed as a representative white southerner and to assert what she as an individual hopes to change. Like Robert Penn Warren's Jack Burden in the closing sentence of *All the King's Men,* she walks "out of history into history and the awful responsibility of Time." There remain memories of her father, her family, and herself that are "disturbing," but these may be mediated by one's actions in the present. Memory is not static. It is, as Eudora Welty has written, "a living thing," a thing "in transit." To write as a white southerner, even as one who associates an impetus for right action and justice with class-demarcated origins, is to make memory answer to the present. In *The Making of a Southerner,* Katharine Lumpkin's southern recollections are shorn of nostalgia and replaced by a revisioned self and a re-imaged region.

Like Lumpkin, Lillian Smith had occasion to return to and reconsider her personal narrative some years after its original publication. In 1961 she revised the final chapters of *Killers of the Dream* and composed a new foreword for a revised edition of the 1949 text that Norton was preparing to publish. What the reader finds in the foreword, subtitled "A Letter to My Publisher," is an exceedingly complex presentation of the autobiographical narrator. In the foreground is an older Smith, writing just a few years before her death in 1966, a woman admittedly changed by the earlier experience of writing *Killers,* as well as by other events and experiences of the intervening years. In the middle distance is that recollected younger narrator, fired with moral outrage at the southern demons that had undermined (and continued to threaten) social justice and individual wholeness—the misguided beliefs about race and sex and sin that she had sought to expose in what she refers to as her "personal memoir." In the background is a whole cast of yet younger selves, recollected and imaginatively characterized in 1949 and then reconsidered by the composing writer in 1961.

None of this authorial and stylistic complexity escapes Lillian Smith's attentive awareness; she construes it as evidence of her own developing self-consciousness, her psychological growth. As the 1961 foreword makes explicit, the "I" self in any given text is precisely the self who is writing, one whose perceptions and priorities may differ markedly from those of an earlier self. "The writer transcends her material in the act of looking at it," she writes, "and since part of that material is herself, a metamorphosis takes place: *something happens within:* a new chaos, and then slowly, a new being" (14). What Smith identifies so clearly about the autobiographical project is its nature as an expression of mind, of imagination, rather than a recovered memory of fact. She is ever conscious that the people and events she describes from her past are "never quite facts but sometimes closer to the 'truth' than is any fact" (13). Turning to a spatial image to describe the intersection of fact and truth, past and present, which are central to a life narrative, she writes, "Writing is both horizontal and vertical exploration. It has to true itself with facts but also with feelings and symbols." And the symbols are intuited, discovered, after the fact, by the composing author.

The narrator of the 1949 text is likewise aware of the gap between the composing self and the portrayed self, but there are only a few occasions when she makes a point of it. Perhaps the single best example of her explicit analysis of the processes of her own symbol making occurs in the opening chapter, in her story of Janie, the white-skinned "colored" child who came briefly to live with her family when Lillian was a girl. The child had been seen by one of Mrs. Smith's friends "while driving over to her washerwoman." Reasoning that the white child must have been kidnapped, the ladies of the town took action to remove her to a white home—to the Smiths'. Lillian quickly formed "a childish and deeply felt bond" with Janie. Then, almost as abruptly as the child had been identified as white and wrongly placed in the black quarters, she was recast as "black," with information provided by a "colored orphanage." A mistake had been made, and Janie was returned to "Colored Town." Readers of William Faulkner's *Light in August* will doubtless find reminders of Joe Christmas's plight in Janie's story. But Smith focuses her attention not upon Janie but upon her own reaction to the race-based culture. She is shamed by it and gets no rational, satisfying answers from her parents, just the refrain, "White and colored can't live together." Smith relates the episode, much as Lumpkin does of her father's beating of the family cook, as the pivotal moment of her emotional discovery of the racial humiliation that her own white kin and kind could—and did—inflict upon black people.

Fred Hobson observes that both Smith and Lumpkin "could never bring themselves, save in a sentence or two in *Killers of the Dream* and a single scene in *The Making of a Southerner* to voice open criticism of their fathers, and more important, they never fully addressed the effect of their fathers on themselves" (51). This recurrent pattern of the narrator's ambivalence toward the authority of the parents, specifically the father, can be traced from Belle Kearney's *A Slaveholder's Daughter* onward, throughout the autobiographies discussed in this book. The dilemma faced by these southern women autobiographers is easy to discern—and well documented in feminist criticism. The cultural authority that they employ to testify to racist practice, the authority that objectifies and legitimates their testimony, derives from the word lessons bestowed by the patriarchy. Smith confronts this conflict as if it were a ghostly presence, as if in eschewing to speak for the culture, she is correcting a received memory that proved false. To "cross the double cross" of culture, Smith sets out to recover the sensory detail of her own witnessed experience and deploy that detail so that it will counter, even trump, the power of the abstract lessons of white supremacy. Despite the motive of truth telling, however, her knowledge of the ancestral legacy betrayed is never quite put aside. The passionate energy that so defines the narrator's voice throughout the book owes to her struggles to establish her bona fides, to justify her rejection of the legacy, and persuade the jury of her readers of the legitimacy—the truth—of her testimony.

In placing the dramatic Janie scene in chapter one, Smith establishes her own eyewitness authority to testify to the racism that she decries throughout the book. A reader encounters the episode as a conversion moment for the child Lillian, a life-changing moment that accounts significantly for Smith's motivation for writing. Then, on a following page, she writes of this scene: "I forgot it. For more than thirty years the experience was wiped out of my memory." Rather, it remained with her, she writes, "like a splinter," a wound that never healed. The recovery of this memory, or, more properly, its reimagination, was prompted and enabled by the writing narrator's inward search for an experience that would dramatically depict the racial caste system of Smith's youth. With the child Janie, she shows the wounding effect of irrational southern racism to her reader.

Throughout the text, the accomplished novelist ably employs imagistic, metaphoric language as a bridge between fact and symbol. She is always alert to the ways in which affective details communicate differently from expository or argumentative prose, the ways in which they make an idea "felt." In this respect, as well as in the general vocabulary of passion with which she denotes her arguments and the essayistic (rather than chronological) form of her narrative, her text is quite unlike that of Katherine Lumpkin. She is very much the psychologist probing the deep psyche of southerners, less the sociologist of institutions or the economist of regional norms. Much like W. J. Cash—and a generation before Richard King's study of the region's social structure as a "southern family romance"—she characteristically dramatizes social tensions, reifying cultural values in chapter two and personifying North and South as two brothers in chapter three.

Smith is precisely like Lumpkin, however, in adducing only that personal content that she regards as relevant to her social critique. In part one, "The Dreamers," the section in which one finds the most dramatized direct personal experience, she invokes family relationships, childhood sensory memories, and a scene from the years in which she ran a summer girls' camp to illustrate the deeply troubling ambivalence she feels, as narrator, for the race-obsessed South that produced her. Rereading the text in 1961, she explains that she has come to see the book as "brought to life . . . by young questions that begged for sane answers . . . by a need to bridge fissures, to tie belief and fact and dream and act closer together." And then she adds her "other reason": "I wrote it because I had to find out what life in a segregated culture had done to me, one person" (13).

The dreamers in this opening section are the innocents of the South who harbor an innate sense of justice and have not yet been fully initiated into the culture of hardened defenders of racial segregation. Here she first introduces the girl Lillian, growing up in Jasper, Florida, troubled by the unspoken meaning of Janie's color, and then she shows us a young woman at Smith's Laurel Falls camp in North Georgia, troubled by the portrayal of Southern Tradition in the camp's adaptation of Saint Exupéry's *The Little Prince*. The campers decide to cast the companions of "Every Child" as Conscience, Southern Tradition, Religion, and Science. The protagonist, an "earth child" who announces her desire to play with all earth's children, soon discovers the magnitude of Southern Tradition's blocking power. It outmatches Conscience, Religion, and Science.

Smith uses this parable as an explanation of how social justice is subverted in the South, of why good people acquiesce to racial injustice, and of what is required to bring about change. She frames the discourse as a lengthy dialogue with "an older girl who had spent many summers on the mountain, now ready for college in the fall." Described as "pale and tense," the young woman goes over the lessons she has learned throughout her life about segregation, beliefs painfully exposed in the campers' drama. Her judgment of the very different lessons she has learned during the summers spent on Smith's mountain is that "You've unfitted us for the South" (54).

Having played the Socratic inquisitor for much of chapter two, Smith becomes the dramatic monologist in the subsequent chapter. By dramatizing the speech, with an auditor listening and responding, she attenuates the burden she places upon the (southern) reader, who is positioned as an observer, allowed to witness a conversation, and is thus shielded from direct censure. Throughout these early chapters, Smith carefully balances her narrator's tone of confident objectivity in summarizing a southern history of racism with a tone of yesteryear's grief for a South she also loves, but loves and knows always with some twinge of guilt. Lyrical passages about the region's natural beauty and cherished sensory memories from childhood abound: "I sat there facing the girl, thinking of the old questions, the fears of childhood. But you shut the bad away and remembered only the pleasant, the games, shadows of clouds moving across sunny grass, sugar cane and boiled peanuts and figs . . . sticking banana shrubs up your nostrils for the sweet smell of it. . . . These are the things white children remembered" (71).

Scott Romine has written of Smith's narrative persona as an ironic stance, "a double-voiced discourse" sounded in "a voice of the South" alongside a personal voice that calls out the false claims of southern racism. In this passage from the text, we have a clear instance of Smith's transparent show of the sort of "nice" language that is available to conceal or, at least, ameliorate the not-nice southern scenes. As Romine notes, "By placing herself in dialogue with her former self, and by extension, the South, Smith positions herself so that she is able to deconstruct the rhetorical undergirding of Southern oppression" ("Framing" 97).

The narrator rarely underestimates the difficulty, however, of active opposition to Southern Tradition, the casting off of fathers and wrong belief. In the exchange with the young female auditor who accuses the narrator of unfitting the campers under her charge for life in the South, Smith makes a point of the painful cognitive dissonance that the young white southerner has to endure on her way to enlightened moral responsibility. The girl's judgment reflects an inward questioning of just the kind Smith has encouraged, and she portrays her with sympathy. The young woman's rueful claim that Smith has "unfitted" her to live in the South is nothing like the accusatory "Love it, or leave it" responses that would come later from readers angered by Smith's harsh pronouncements about the South. Anticipating these, she uses all her novelistic skills to deflect reader resistance—a children's play, for instance, to illustrate the principal claims of her social critique. "Out of that play came questions asked by a young girl who used a young girl's words, but no wise man of our earth could have asked more important ones" (74).

In this passage at the opening of chapter four and at many other points in the text, there are clear gestures to New Testament rhetorical models of parable and other tropes, as well as to a belief system that holds forgiveness and sacrifice to be the path to salvation. She thus further employs rhetorical amelioration to bridge differences between her and readers who may resist her message but who will almost certainly recognize its links to Christianity. "I had not tried to give her answers," she writes. "I had tried only to give her understanding of the difficulties of her elders. . . . I wanted her to begin her search for answers with sympathy for those who had not found them. I knew it would be hard enough for her who so passionately loved her ideals and a family that did not share them" (74). Smith shows that typically the ideals have proved to be the sacrificial victims. The idealistic girls who for twenty-five years had come to Laurel Falls camp, "sensitive, intelligent, eager, quick with their questions, generous and honest," were, finally, "wasted by a region that values color more than children" (75). What the narrator largely refrains from describing is the opprobrium awaiting those who, like Lillian Smith, would publicly condemn the region's racist culture. This awareness she signals in the series of citations that she quotes at the end of the chapter. From an *Atlanta Constitution* editorial, 26 September 1948, one reads that "only a fool would say the Southern pattern of separation of the races can, or should be overthrown" (78).

Killers of the Dream has been widely read and studied for over a half century by scholars of southern cultural history. At the time of its publication in 1949, it was widely reviewed by national critics.[5] Some reviewers, like Homer Rainey in the *Saturday Review of Literature,* praised its candor, but others, notably Ralph McGill in the *Atlanta Constitution,* found little to praise, reacting to the book's emotional intensity and, particularly, to Smith's Freudian analyses. Despite the mixed reviews by contemporaneous readers, *Killers of the Dream* has come to be one of the foundational studies of race identity formation in the U.S. South. Indeed, Smith's expansive reach in this book is remarkable, eluding genre categorization. In her foreword she calls it a "personal memoir" and "Every Southerner's memoir," by which she means, mainly, every white southerner's memoir. She titles part two in the first edition "The White Man's Burden Is His Own Childhood" and quickly moves the narrative voice from the dominant "I" of the first section to a "we." Rehearsing the "lessons" that were employed to socialize white children—lessons about God, one's body, sex, and white superiority—Smith becomes a representative white southerner, merged with readers like her. When she discusses the influence of the church, she is its daughter and its critic. She remembers Sunday as a "day set aside, made special, with no empty moment in it. Sunday school, morning worship, junior choir practice, and a walk in the woods to pick violets" (100). But there are also other memories: revival meetings that inflamed a southern conscience already stretched "tightly on its frame of sin and punishment and God's anger"; revivalist preachers, charismatic, "potent" men who railed against the sins of the flesh; a pall of guilt that covered the region, the expectation of punishment on earth and beyond. She calls this threatening religious landscape the "trembling earth," and she figures it as a swamp, "tangled and green, oozing snakes and alligators and water lilies and sweet-blooming bays, weaving light and shadow into awful and tender designs, splotching our lives with brightness and terror" (112). Writing about the symbolic role of the swamp in Smith's imagination, Anthony Wilson describes it as "emblematic of a lurking, subversive ambiguity" (140). Her description of the ghostly features of the swamp reminds one of scenes from Edgar Allan Poe's stories, perhaps Roderick Usher's estate, with its eerie surround and its house's dark secrets.

Smith's frequent recourse to images of swamps, shadows, ghosts, and hidden or buried matter owes much, of course, to Freudian theories of the unconscious. Further, as Darlene O'Dell has shown in her perceptive commentary on *Killers of the Dream,* Smith also invokes Ku Klux Klan nomenclature in references to ghosts, ghouls, and goblins, each of which were "names of branches within Klan hierarchy" (81). What Smith clearly believes and strains to convey to her reader is the power of the unspoken, the forgotten, and the unacknowledged to influence human behavior. In the chapter, "Three Ghost Stories," she writes of the miscegenation, both literal and emotional, that makes an ongoing hypocrisy of the white southern credo of "purity." White men's exploitation of black women, the rejection of mixed-race children, segregation's forced rupture of the affection between white child and black mother-surrogate, these were some of the ghostly aspects of the region's insistence upon separation of the races. Writing of the relation of the black body to white supremacist ideology, Jay Watson notes that "the necessary presence of the nurse's body in 'white' space could be rationalized and normalized, but the power and sufficiency of that body were far more difficult to shrug off." That white southerners "sentimentalized Mammy, relegating her to what Smith calls a 'ghost relationship,' was perhaps the only way to neutralize [her] power" (483). The guilty conscience might deny or "forget" transgressions of the credo, but the psyche (and the body), Smith holds, do not forget. The appeasement that bad conscience craves comes not in confession, however, but in the Klan, projecting repressed desire upon "guilty" black men, who are slain for their sexual threat to sacred white womanhood. "It is a complete acting out of the white man's internal guilt and his hatred of colored man and white woman" (123).

At the core of Smith's analysis of her culture's failing is a modernist's apprehension of the split between the individual and the social. For historian Daniel Singal, this analysis constituted a major assault upon "the Victorian ethos," with its splitting of mind and body (374). Racial segregation is a particularly pernicious instance of an assault upon human relatedness, but the consequences of gender segregation do not escape her censure either. The pedestaled white woman is inevitably an outlier, and she responds, variously, with powerlessness, or rage, grief, simple-mindedness, piety, or sometimes even with bullying enforcement of a "police state" home. And her separation from the larger social body is made worse by an inward separation from her own sexual needs. Feminism offers no alternative to this sorry condition, for in Smith's view feminists reject their own "womanly qualities," themselves becoming a "kind of fibroid growth of sick cells multiplying aggressiveness in an attempt at cure" (141).

Readers today may likely find Smith's chapter on women a rather fiercely drawn, disorganized, and often confusing portrait. Her assumption of essential "womanly qualities" establishes a gender separation/segregation that she ideologically opposes. Although she applauds the organization of the Association of Southern Women for the Prevention of Lynching, she describes the organizers as "lady insurrectionists." The domestic sphere to which women, especially southern white women, have been consigned, she seems to suggest, would offer maternal, sexual, and aesthetic fulfillment if it were not thwarted by patriarchal dominance. The contradictions between an assigned domestic sphere and an assumed ideal of individual expression go unremarked. There is little here of Smith's psychological probing of how the maintaining of a "separate sphere" can be accommodated with her vision of a just society.

Perhaps it is in this chapter on women that Smith is most challenged to weave together strands of personal experience, observed gendered behaviors, and idealized roles that she hopes will take form in a future generation "free of wounds" (154). For many years she maintained a close relationship with Paula

Snelling, who assisted with the Laurel Falls camp and with writing and editing projects she undertook with Smith. Although biographer Anne C. Loveland notes a general assumption by associates that theirs was a lesbian relationship, she also quotes a good friend of the two women who regarded their love as "protective," not sexual. Ironically, Smith's portrait of feminists, whom she describes as rejecting "womanly qualities," resembles a caricature of lesbians: "a grim little number, cropping their hair short, walking in heavy awkward strides, . . . not daring in the secret places of their minds to confess what they really wanted, . . . to be treated 'exactly like men.'" She adds that "there was no comfortable place for such women in the South, though a few lived in every town" (140–41).

Richard King rather guardedly speculates that Smith, in her Freudian analysis of the white child's desire for the black surrogate mother's body, reflects something of a personal inner tension arising from a sexual identity she knew was unacceptable to the general society of her day (190). This infantile desire Smith attributes to the generic white child, who, significantly, she refers to in the common practice of the day as a masculine "he." "Deep down," she writes, "he often reserves his play, his 'real' pleasure, his relaxed enjoyment of sex activities, and his fantasy, for women as much like his nurse (they may or may not have colored skin) as his later life can discover" (134). King suggests that "in championing the body and making it one of her central themes, she was undoubtedly trying to redress an imbalance in her own life" (190).

One might argue that, in connecting the sexual, the emotional, and the ideological strains of the white southern psyche, and in confronting the Victorian repression of the sexualized human being, Smith was in one respect also addressing the condition of closeted homosexuality. But, as Will Brantley has observed, agreeing with the earlier critic Margaret Sullivan, "Smith never uses allegory for its enigmatic qualities or as a way of disguising her views" (56). Perhaps, though, because Smith wanted a 1949 American audience to hear her message about race relations, she confined her focus to the axis of sexual repression and racism, without any reference to homosexual/heterosexual distinctions. One may locate an implicit argument for the legitimacy of one's sexual orientation, however it might be expressed, layered deeply in the text, but perhaps layered so deeply as not to discomfit Smith.

Margaret Rose Gladney, in "Becoming a Writer," the opening chapter of *How Am I To Be Heard: the Letters of Lillian Smith*, has generally agreed that in *Killers of the Dream* Smith's approach to her relationship with Snelling is muted. Gladney describes the relationship of the two women as profoundly influencing their lives, but she concludes that Smith "never did acknowledge fully the nature and significance of her relationship with Paula Snelling" (11). Writing a half century after the publication of *Killers of the Dream,* Fred Hobson maintains that, as bold as Smith was in exposing racial oppression, "she was not bold enough to deal publicly—in print—with her sexual orientation" (21). One has to note, however, that a widespread debate about the recognition of gay rights would not occupy the American public until years after the civil rights movement had effectively guaranteed equality of civil rights to African Americans and after the women's movement had greatly extended such rights to women. Not yet in the twenty-first century has such consensus been reached, though it may be getting closer. Homophobia is unarguably a manifestation of societal segregation, but Smith's intent is, from the outset, to focus on the deleterious effects of racism.

Brantley describes *Killers* as a "confessional tract" (38); O'Dell calls it "a ghost story," alluding to the gothic imagery and style (80); and King refers to it as an "autobiography of sorts, or better a meditation upon the intersection of personal and regional experience" (192). Rereading and revising the book in 1961, Smith calls it a "personal memoir," but one that is devoted principally to race and racial segregation in the South. She wanted her race message heard and doubtless knew that a detour into an attack on homophobia would compromise her authority before the reading public she wanted to reach. In keeping the primary motive for writing the book ascendant, she shaped the personal to serve her race critique.

Even more compelling, one has to infer, was her effort to shape her personal revelations so as to protect her family and loved ones from an exposure they would regard as a betrayal of their love and trust and that might very well result in breached relationships. On 11 October 1949, she mailed family members a copy of the book, asking that they try to understand "why I felt it must be written." She speaks of her attempt to write "as honestly as I know how to write," recognizing that "this honesty will hurt many people. I hope it does not hurt my own family too much." The tone of the letter is somber, expressing the kind of pained compulsion to speak the truth as she sees it that characterizes much of *Killers.* It is her heretical challenge of the South's "false beliefs" about racial separation that she expects to inflame "much criticism." She writes, "I hope that none of you will be too deeply embarrassed by my candor nor injured too much in you own work because of it" (*How Am I to be Heard?* 127). Close kinship connection to a race heretic was quite enough to lay upon family members, she thought, and more than sufficient to warrant the early warning and the earnest request for their forbearance.

From the opening pages of *Killers of the Dream,* Smith indicates her intention not to write her life story but to write of a personal knowledge of the white South's racism. She includes limited details about her parents, her eight siblings, her ancestors, her education, the family's Methodism, her extensive musical training, which included three years at the Peabody Conservatory in Baltimore, or the three years she spent in China. Despite the intensity of the narrative voice and the purging revelations of youthful obliviousness to false beliefs and endemic injustice, Smith withholds much of the inward life of the woman behind the typewriter, the Lillian Smith who composes in this text a self suited to her theme and credible for the story she tells. In its fealty to her theme of social justice and psychological wholeness, the narrative seems more the testament of a reliable witness giving supporting evidence in a case than the confession of a guilty sinner or lawbreaker. In "Autobiography as a Dialogue between King and Corpse," a speech delivered at the University of Florida in 1962, Smith spoke of *Killers of the Dream* as a "documentary" and as a "confession," noting that she had written as fully as possible about "one fragment" of her life—her experience as a white person in a segregated society (*Winner* 196–97). But her innocence as a child and her moral courage as a woman greatly offset a portrait of transgression. The voice of the text is that of an unimpeachable witness, a distinction that suggests "testimonial narrative" is at least one apt designation for this text, as indeed it is also for Lumpkin's.

In the final sections of the book, Smith broadens her exploration of the origins of the white southern mind, writing of the geography, of the early settlers (people "rejected of Europe"), of impoverished rural life, of class divisions that were disguised by the "Mr. Rich White" who preached to "Mr. Poor White" that white skin status was all that mattered. Thus political debate on every conceivable social and economic issue was subverted by the pledge of allegiance to white superiority. It was a stultifying bargain that perpetuated regional "waste" and backwardness. Furthermore, its effects reached to the nation's capital, with congressional white supremacists, joined by "Republican reactionaries," successfully blocking progressive legislation decade after decade.

Smith mourns the waste of creativity, talent, intelligence, and general human potential that was the legacy of the "white Christian supremacy system." Public abuse and social rejection awaited those who challenged the system—writers, musicians, journalists, jurists, and statesmen. Smith's South is the Sahara of culture that Mencken mocked, and she finds only a few writers of the preceding three decades (Thomas Wolfe, Faulkner, and Evelyn Scott) to be "of more than minor worth." In the heavily revised chapter retitled in 1961 as "Man Against the Human Being," she sharpens her scorekeeping of the social triumphs and disappointments of recent years, keeping her praise of Franklin Roosevelt and the New Deal and adding recognition of "a handful of young preachers" and a "few professors" who had worked for change. But she lambastes rationalizing liberals who would slow down the pace of change, and she attacks southern intellectuals "who should have been on the side of change and were not," particularly the Fugitive Agrarians, who in her view refused to see and condemn the spiritual blight arising not from the mechanized industrial system they had harped on but from the social system that already existed. "The basic weakness of the Fugitives' stand," she writes, "lay in their failure to recognize the massive dehumanization which had resulted from slavery and its progeny, sharecropping and segregation, and the values that permitted these brutalities of spirit. They did not see that the dehumanization they feared the machine and science would bring was a *fait accompli* in their own agrarian region" (225).[6]

Most critics who have written about *Killers of the Dream* have commented on the more hopeful tone that permeates Smith's 1961 revised conclusion. "We Are Tall Enough for Men," retitled "The Chasm and the Bridge," captures the progressive promise of change that Smith reads in the nonviolent sit-ins, the Freedom Rides of 1960–61, and in the figure of Martin Luther King, "a personable, intelligent, and deeply religious young man with nerves of iron and emotions that lie down like lambs within him" (251). She expresses hope in the "Human Being Evolving," as the painful memories she had enumerated in 1949 had begun to recede: "concentration camps and Jim Crow, firing squads and the KKK, Dachau and burning crosses . . . and the most gruesome trials that the world has known since the Inquisition" (239). Whereas the book begins with the highly personal and dramatic presentation of the self, it ends with a narrator who presents herself as a religious and philosophical seeker who can offer a testament to a worldview and belief system that she has worked out over years of social observation and personal reflection. In his study of southern liberalism and the race issue, Morton Sosna discusses Lillian Smith as a "liberal evangelist," asserting that her "moralistic outlook" led her to "an evangelical conception of an artist's role" (180).

In this passionate book, Smith clearly places the personal and the religious in the service of her vision of racial justice. But insofar as she attempts to explore and represent her own inward journey of psychological and spiritual growth—a journey that validates, by the way, her authority as a Jeremiah calling for social justice—this book perhaps comes closest of all texts included in this project to the classical Augustinian form of autobiography. It is a "conversion narrative," as Hobson has termed it—one that employs a conversion story so as to convert a readership. What psychologist Mark Freeman has written of St. Augustine's *Confessions* describes as well *Killers of the Dream*. It is dominated by "the centrality of faith," which one may read in Smith as her vision of racial separation bridged by human relatedness. As Augustine "rewrote the self," employing history and memory in a purposeful narrative, so Smith, too, devised a "converted self" that served as "a kind of central figure or pivot around which to think about human lives and human development," specifically for her, about race and region (Freeman 19). Smith's self-conscious deployment of a narrator who has had a "new vision" of "southernness" is her principal strategy for addressing the reader. This narrator is a confident representative of her place, her time, her culture, and she offers her story as a moral exemplum.

In the revised text Smith arrives at a somewhat hopeful optimism for the future through recourse to post–World War II societal changes that offer promise of a more just society, much like the hopeful view John Egerton expresses. Interestingly, like Lumpkin, she finds some fellow southerners who share her rejection of the racial *injustice* that has longed plagued the South, and she recuperates southern honor to some degree in the "plain people, men and women, rich and poor" who are "searching for the right questions" (249). But in the end, she sees still a fallen world, a South not yet redeemed, a homeland that calls upon her to tell her story.

8

Narratives of a Writing Life, Part I

ELLEN GLASGOW AND MARJORIE KINNAN RAWLINGS

Autobiographical writings by southern women novelists constitute an especially interesting group of texts, composed as they are by women who have established successful careers as professional writers by the time they come to write a self-reflexive narrative, one that features an authorial self who is writing and a protagonist self who, along with other characters, forms the central cast of the stories. Their careers of writing fiction have, of course, given them ample practice in creating narratives that link imagination to memory and past experience. Consequently, we find that, in comparison with many of the writers considered in previous chapters, novelists' approach to autobiographical writing suggests a more conscious regard of the demands of narrative and the essential constructedness of a text. These women consciously wrote for publication and were very much aware of a general public audience, including the devoted readers who had read and admired their fiction. Unlike the successful novelist Lillian Smith, whose essayistic *Killers of the Dream* employed self-narrative in the service of her indictment of southern racism, these writers' chief focus is upon the authorial self *as a writer.*

Virtually alone in having written a book-long commentary about the composition of her novels, their themes and characters, and about southern writing and the art of fiction generally, Ellen Glasgow in *A Certain Measure* assumes the authority of her "certain measure of achievement" to compose a public persona of "honest craftsman," "willful author," and "persistent novelist," as she refers to herself in the book's preface (vii). In the posthumously published *The Woman Within,* however, she composes an overtly personal narrative centered upon the "quest for independence" that she depicts as having led to much anxiety and loneliness but that finally anchored her success as a writer. Similarly, the novelists' autobiographies considered here all express in one way or another the pressures of tradition—social and literary—upon their effort to compose a self-narrative of a writer's life.

As professional writers of fiction, they are experienced and sophisticated in their approach to the textual construction of their project. They have few illusions about accessing a fixed past, as if it were a film to be replayed. They know they are composing a text, a life *narrative*. They are ever aware that they are in control of what to tell and what to leave out—that is, what "belongs" in the plot they create. Each strives to construct a convincing character who over time reasonably turns out to be the very person she in fact understands herself to be—at the time of writing. As the genre demands of every autobiographer, these women begin to fashion their stories from the endings of them, writing from and toward the conclusion. Hence, age, life and career stage, family situation, the social era in which they write, and, certainly, their motive for writing—these and many other factors all impinge greatly upon the narratives they compose.

The autobiographer who is a novelist is of course mindful that a satisfying, interesting narrative needs coherent form, sensuous detail, pace, voice. She is also aware that she is writing in a genre built upon certain traditional reader expectations. For example, one expects to read of the autobiographer's family relationships, friends, education, residences, key experiences, ambitions, successes, and failures. Having already established a circle of readers of her fiction, the writer assumes her life story will in some respect be read through the prism of her previously published work. And, almost inevitably, she will fashion life events in relation to her story of "the writing life." Finally, a woman who has published novels throughout a career is also knowledgeable about the publishing enterprise—the interest of editors and publishers in producing a book that has a foreseeable market and wide readership. Thus the literary self-consciousness that the novelist brings to the writing of a life narrative leads, unsurprisingly, to nuanced, artfully formed, lively texts that have dramatic scenes, dialogue, tensions, oppositions, meditations, resolutions, and a steady thread of character development that links episodes into a coherent narrative.

Considerable scholarly attention has been devoted to many of the texts I will mention here, notably, Will Brantley's discerning and well-researched *Feminine Sense in Southern Memoir,* a study of the autobiographies of Lillian Smith, Ellen Glasgow, Eudora Welty, Lillian Hellman, Katherine Anne Porter, and Zora Neale Hurston. Pursuing an intertextual reading of the texts, Brantley seeks to "situate these authors within a context of southern feminism and the more in-clusive discourse of modern American liberalism" (x). In regard to feminism, he discusses the writers' responses to social constructions of gender as they experienced them in a traditional culture and expressed them directly and in-directly in their autobiographies. In the South of the late nineteenth and early twentieth centuries, women who sought a writing career—or any career outside the home—needed a deep well of individualism and dissent to draw upon, as we have seen earlier in the accounts of Kearney, Fearn, Lumpkin, Smith, and oth-ers. Brantley allies the spirit of independence shown by the writers he studies with a tradition of southern liberalism. The "independence and self-reflexivity" that he identifies as central to their lives and autobiographies he adjudges to be "hallmarks of the liberal tradition" (xi).

An independent, even willful, spirit typifies most writers who write for a public audience, and for a southern woman who grew up in an era of persist-ing Victorianism to reflect—in a published text—life as she saw and truly expe-rienced it required not only a good deal of spirit but courage and considerable self-confidence. Such exposure risked the censure of family and friends and outright dismissal by a segment of the society who rejected women in authorial positions. And not to be underestimated was the mental and emotional effort of composing one's life in a way that was not only "true" to the past, "true" to the self, but mindful of a critical audience, and *artful*.

Ellen Glasgow, born in Richmond, Virginia, in 1873, daughter of a shelter-ing, traditional southern family, perhaps best illustrates the pressures of com-posing a life text written for public exposure. Her approach to the project is telling: she composed and published what she thought of as the story of her writer self in the 1943 *A Certain Measure: An Interpretation of Prose Fiction*. In it, she discussed thirteen of her widely read novels, published over a career that spanned nearly a half-century. She described thematic intentions, charac-ter development, and her determined decision to depict human beings as she had come to know them. Her sense of southernness is ever present in this book, but it is acknowledged mostly to be rejected. She does not "belong" to the South nor countenance the "evasive idealism" that permeated its romantic literary tra-dition, though Betina Entzminger rightly observes Glasgow's occasional am-bivalence toward her southern heritage. When she contrasts the contemporary era with the past in her fiction, she portrays both "the grace and dignity of the traditional southern lady and the oppression and limited resources" of her life. Alongside the lady, there is a twentieth-century woman who possesses greater freedom and self-assertiveness but in some instances may display a tendency toward vulgarity and shallowness (83). Her aim in her fiction, as Glasgow says repeatedly, is to expose romantic deceptions. Her unsparing judgment of the South as a failed venue for honest self-appraisal and serious art is almost as sharp as that of H. L. Mencken. Indeed, in the artistic credo she expresses in *A Certain Measure,* she is unequivocal and ever confident in her critical commentary of the American literary scene and her own contribution to it.

In the companion autobiography she worked on from the mid-1930s until almost 1945, the year of her death, the story of the "woman within," the narrator is more nearly an object of travail than a subject in control of a life and career. In this book the obstacles she rebels against, the impediments she suffers from, are less a recalcitrant southern literary tradition and gender prejudice than the mental residue of an unhappy childhood, disappointing romances, and ill health, especially the deafness that afflicted her from an early age. Still, the writing life is compensatory. In it, she exercises a commanding voice and, despite her many protestations of failed relationships and her sense of isolated exile, she describes, unwittingly it seems at times, supportive relationships from her earliest childhood years that nurtured her career ambitions and reinforced her self-definition.

In the last paragraphs of *The Woman Within,* Glasgow asserts a fullness of experience that has given her a richly lived life. "I have had my life. I have known ecstasy. I have known anguish. I have loved, and I have been loved. . . . I have caught a gleam, or imagined I caught a gleam, of the mystic vision." But the recollection of these experiences has brought her little joy. "Not for anything that the world could give would I consent to live over my life unchanged, or to bring back, unchanged, my youth." Her final characterization of the Ellen Glasgow of this text is a woman with an "unreconciled heart," a stoical world-weariness that is somewhat belied by the extravagant rhetoric of her summary of loves and losses. ("I have not ever stolen either the ponderable or the imponderable material of happiness.") The sentences that have little flourishing language are those associated with her writing life. "I have lived, as completely as it was possible, the life of my choice. I have been free. . . . I have done the work I wished to do for the sake of that work alone" (296).

From the first lines of the autobiography, Glasgow employs an intensely emotional language of feeling. Her mode of lyrical angst irritated a number of contemporaneous reviewers who found the final effect to be self-pitying, a sort of celebration of suffering. In her fine introduction to the 1994 edition, indispensable to an informed and balanced reading of the text, Pamela R. Matthews notes Alfred Kazin's review as illustrative of critical responses to the characterization of the autobiographer: "pitiable," "a great sufferer," "agonizingly unhappy and isolated" ("Introduction" viii). Unarguably, Glasgow's foundational image of her childhood and lifelong temperament is that of a suffering victim who perseveres against obstacles so as to give voice in her writings to fellow sufferers, who are often powerless and silenced. Her earliest recollection is that of a nightmarish fear that she is unable to communicate to her mother and "colored mammy." Her screams and struggles "tell them nothing" (4). With this dramatic image she establishes a lifelong horror of voicelessness and an empathy with human beings—and animals—who are unheard, objects of others' control. From childhood she recollects a terrified black dog chased down the street and "an old Negro, Uncle Henry, as he is . . . put into the wagon from the almshouse" (9–10). Her misery comes from her inability to intervene: "Nothing that I can do will make the world different." But, of course, Glasgow is making the point that, as the writer she will become, she will expose the cruelty and injustice to her readers and give voiced respect to the marginalized who strive and suffer.

The litany of emotional struggles continues in the narrator's portrait of her family. Along with her mother and siblings, she is subjected to an unloving father who "never committed a pleasure" (15). Rejecting all that he valued and represented, Glasgow declares she "inherited nothing from him." Rather, it was her mother to whom she owed "everything in me, mental and physical." Her father, an "unbending" Presbyterian, successful manager of the Tredegar Iron Works, mistreated his wife and children, even his children's pets. In *Ellen Glasgow: Beyond Convention,* Linda Wagner observes that the mother's mental breakdown (resulting from her discovery of her husband's black mistress), a collapse described sadly and bitterly in the autobiography, gave Glasgow even more reason to regard traditional marriage as an unequal and unfulfilling partnership (8 ff.). For all the resentments and accusations against her father, however, she inevitably invites comparison of their strong, willful spirits. Her rebellions— she became "an ardent suffragist," "a radical," a determined reader of Gibbon and Darwin—are as unbending as the pronouncements of Francis Glasgow and little resemble the gentle, passive Annie Jane Gholson Glasgow.

One constant thread throughout the text is Glasgow's love of storytelling, her fertile imagination, and her confident assurance that she was "born a novelist" (41). In her early childhood, "in collaboration with Mammy," she creates "Little Willie and his many adventures." At age seven, reveling in the writing of a poem, she is mortified to hear her "precious verses" read aloud by her sister to the "kindly ridicule and amusement" of guests in the house (23). It made a lasting impression when she discovered that a writer risks painful exposure when she dares to send her work out into the world. Spiritedness and courage, even defiance, are required, especially for the girl child—or the woman—to command the attention of a public readership. With her fiction and essays, Glasgow demonstrated all the ambition and assurance necessary to publish a shelf of books, but *The Woman Within* went to the bank vault after it was written, to be delivered to her literary executor for publication after her death. She retreated from the exposure of hearing her life story read aloud, subjected to review, comment, and possible contradiction or censure. She had had her say, having created an Ellen Glasgow from the perspective of her later life, and she left the stage, taking no questions, making no further explanations.

Although the narrator of *The Woman Within* writes forthrightly about her unhappy childhood, she is circumspect in her accounts of two disappointing romantic relationships, first with "Gerald B—" and later, an attachment spanning twenty years during her active career, with "Harold S—," her pseudonym for Henry Anderson, a successful Richmond lawyer. Will Brantley, Pamela Matthews, and other Glasgow scholars have raised questions about the existence of the unidentified "Gerald," who is described in a chapter entitled "Miracle—or Illusion?" More recently, Julius Rowan Raper, citing Francis W. Saunders's proposal that Gerald was William Riggin Travers, a wealthy New York financier, contends that scholars should not dismiss Glasgow's account but continue the search for a verifiable identification (299). One notes, however, that even the well-established relationship with Anderson is recounted in a chapter entitled "fata morgana." Though it was clearly no mirage, she writes of it with ironic bemusement: "Doesn't all experience crumble in the end to mere literary material?" (226).

The "romance chapters" of this autobiography provide interesting evidence of Glasgow's awareness of her readers—and of the expectations of a society that regarded the most meaningful pursuit for a woman to be the search for a "good husband." These sections provide some of the most suspenseful material in the text and were surely intended to appeal to a female audience. In fact, Glasgow's confessional approach to her love affairs suggests to Jill Ker Conway that she is portraying herself as a "full-fledged romantic heroine" (*When Memory* 54). Glasgow certainly heightens the romantic suspense when she writes that "month by month" she has delayed revisiting the Anderson affair but refuses finally to evade the "truth." "Fidelity to life" and "unqualified" autobiographical truth were her starting point, she writes. "From the beginning, I resolved that the appeal of this book, whether or not it was ever published, should rest upon intellectual and emotional veracity, and upon that basis alone" (214).

What runs a steadier pace than romancing in the narrator's life story, though, is her memory of close, supportive friendships with women—mother, sisters, friends. Matthews's *Ellen Glasgow and a Woman's Traditions* is particularly rich in its commentary on these friendships. And as Wagner notes, "What is particularly interesting in Glasgow's development is that it is often her experiences with women and women's needs that prompt her best work" (15). From her first tentative efforts to gain literary advice, it is sister Cary who is her chief encourager, enabler, and literary "networker"—providing fifty dollars for a consultation with a "literary adviser." What she gets from him is a leering "You are too pretty to be a novelist. Is your figure as lovely in the altogether as it is in your clothes?" (96). Later, it is Cary's "flash of inspiration" to remember a University of Virginia professor who might recommend Ellen to a publisher. The reader from Macmillan who was given the manuscript returned it with advice she did not take: "'The best advice I can give you,' he said, presumably with charming candor, 'is to stop writing, and go back to the South and have some babies'" (108).

The narrator does not stint in her recollections of bad advice, nor in her insistent comments that she has had to be her own writing instructor. In Chapter Eight, "The Search for Art," she writes of having arduously taught herself how to write in a voice and a style that her "native instinct" confirmed all along the way. Again, she insists upon the solitary pursuit of the skills and themes that would lead to the serious writing she aimed for—fiction of a kind that "no Southerner had ever written." "I would write of all the harsher realities beneath manners, beneath social customs, beneath the poetry of the past, and the romantic nostalgia of the present" (98). She would create characters who exposed the psychological injuries imposed by a rigid, often reactionary society and whose most positive, life-affirming actions would be rebellions.

Glasgow despairs of finding a southern publisher for such work as she envisioned. "Southerners did not publish, did not write, did not read. Their appetite for information was Gargantuan but personal; it was either satisfied by oratory or it was sated by gossip" (105). She remembers once an interviewer asking her what she thought the South most needed. Her answer, "Blood and irony" (104). Though disappointed with her first forays in New York, she does at last find an enthusiastic reader, and *The Descendant* is published in 1897. She was twenty-four years old.

It is inviting to regard *A Certain Measure* as Glasgow's upbeat autobiography of achievement, of a life productively, satisfyingly lived, though even in this text she tempers her affirmations with mild complaint. "If I have missed many of the external rewards of success, I have never lost the outward peace and the inward compensation that come from doing the work one wishes to do in the solitary way in which one wishes to do it" (177–78). It is inescapable to read *A Woman Within* as any but an autobiography written "in great suffering of mind and body," written for her "release of mind and heart," as she explains in her note to her literary executor. Both the printed note and a facsimile of the holograph one, dated 8 February 1944, along with "A Note by the Literary Executors," are included in the 1954 edition, forming the book's preface. This first edition also includes photographs of Glasgow's parents, brother Frank, sisters Rebe and Cary, and her childhood home on First and Cary Streets in Richmond; three images of her residence on One West Main Street in Richmond; one of her dogs; and six pictures of her from ages seven to sixty-five. These photographs, omitted from the 1994 edition, have the effect of mitigating some of the sadness of the text, though one suspects that the project of going through old photographs brought on some of the grieving that is manifested here.

The Woman Within is marked by personal losses, deaths of loved ones, declining health, and isolation exacerbated by the increasing deafness that so blighted Glasgow's capacity for friendship and social connection. Her career had provided financial security, but during the years when she first began the book, the country was in the depths of the Great Depression, an era that brought widespread deprivation, especially in the South. There was the growing unrest in Europe that led to World War II. She found little to assuage her sense of a general deterioration in the larger culture, although in the later chapters Glasgow writes of pleasurable travel to England, where she met writers she admired "without reservation." There were "unforgettable hours with Thomas Hardy, a day with Joseph Conrad and his family, dinner with the John Galsworthys, tea with Arnold Bennett," and an occasional meeting of Henry James among groups "in the best houses." She finds that "placed beside Hardy or Conrad, Henry James would have appeared, in spite of his size and his dignity, slightly foppish in manner" (206–7). In 1937, during a month in Italy as guest of an old friend, a visit to a Franciscan monastery brought deep reflection about St. Francis and Christian belief. Though responsive to the site, "still brushed by the passing, centuries ago, of that miracle—or of that illusion," she does not temper her skepticism. She asks whether St. Francis's experience of the divine was "outward or inward vision." Or, "Does it matter?" Her expression of her own religious doubt is circumspect and ambiguous, granting that the saint had perhaps "found his Christ" but adding that he may have found, instead, "the flight of the alone to the Alone" (265–66).

What Glasgow can most fully and confidently affirm in this book is her literary achievement. Singling out five novels written in the 1920s and 1930s, *Barren Ground, The Romantic Comedians, They Stooped to Folly, The Sheltered Life,* and *Vein of Iron,* she pronounces them "not only the best that was in me, but some of the best work that has been done in American fiction" (270). One has to ask how much the writer of this assertion felt the need to surround it with a narrative of lifelong suffering. She endures an unhappy childhood and patronizing dismissal of her early work. She confesses failed romantic relationships, foregoes marriage, and so, in her sixties, in poor health ("hopelessly frail"), has sufficiently masked the pride and ambition that many of her contemporaries would have considered unseemly in the 1930s and 1940s—even the 1950s, when the book was posthumously published. Rosemary M. Magee cites such a view in her introduction to *Friendship and Sympathy: Communities of Southern Women Writers.* She notes that southern women writers all "acknowledged quietly to themselves and to one another what Caroline Gordon wrote in sympathy to Katherine Anne Porter about John Crowe Ransom: 'He can't bear for women to be serious about their art'" (xvi).

Reading through a feminist lens, one comes away from Glasgow's autobiography with an impression of a writing life that was richly vital. There were many "enduring friends" she enjoyed seeing in New York—Irita Van Doren, Stark Young, Eleanor and Van Wyck Brooks, Carl Van Vechten, among others (273). Though there were lifetime friends in Richmond, it was in New York during her visits in spring and autumn that she found men and women who "spoke her language" (273). In the epilogue she writes that "two things have never failed me: my gift of friendship and my sense of laughter" (284), but she has told her reader earlier of a "deceptive gaiety" that she has adopted to camouflage a "blighted life"—an "ironic mood" and "smiling pose, which I have held, without a break or a change, for almost forty years" (139).

Whether it derives from a depressive temperament or from a felt need to present herself to her audience as a woman who has paid a dear price for the successful career that she has sought and achieved, Glasgow's personal unhappiness sets the book's dominant tone. Many caring and sustaining women appear in the narrative, but Glasgow's account of them is fairly brief and considerably less dramatic than the profiles of Gerald and Harold. Her sister Cary gave crucial encouragement at a pivotal time for Glasgow. The nurse who came during Cary's illness and death in 1911, Anne Virginia Bennett, stayed with Glasgow as "secretary and companion" until 1937. Bennett is a "dear friend" who gives unstinting support, but Glasgow remarks that "in all the years she has lived with me, she has never really regarded writing as anything more serious than 'a way.'" Bennett has always been supportive, but she has offered no companionship of the mind. "Few persons have ever felt less interest in, or respect for, the profession of letters; and, as with the other inhabitants of Richmond, some of them almost as dear to me as Anne Virginia, she has always looked with suspicion upon the 'people who write.'" Even with such companionship, what Glasgow stresses is her aloneness with her "reading and thinking" (216). Similarly, her "closest friend," Caroline Coleman, figures as a very minor character in the narrative.

Although *The Woman Within* is, for the most part, a melancholy recounting of a lifetime of wounding relationships and physical ill health, there are also clear statements of satisfaction and affirmation that attach to her writing life. In that respect, this retrospective self-fashioning portrays a narrator who throughout her life pursued a goal of producing serous fiction, one whose literary achievement in the end vindicates the expense of spirit and determined will that her art demanded.

Other southern women novelists writing autobiographical texts mid twentieth century were less likely to focus on their careers. Marjorie Kinnan Rawlings's *Cross Creek* (1942), Zora Neale Hurston's *Dust Tracks on a Road* (1942), and Bernice Kelly Harris's *Southern Savory* (1964) are narratives that depict the developing character of the narrator—the protagonist as she is composed— as a woman revealed indirectly through relationships with others. The anecdotes, scenes, and life stages recounted all point up a drive for the independence deemed necessary for the writing life, an individualism often depicted as both a need for separation to do one's writing and a sense of difference from others with whom one's life was intertwined. Still, the outlines of the independence sought and gained are defined in relationships to the family and to the local and larger communities in which the narrators have lived.

As I noted in Chapter 1, it is interesting to compare these narratives with William Faulkner's 1954 essay, "Mississippi," published in April 1954 in *Holiday* magazine. That work, too, is filled with accounts of the places and people that had composed Faulkner's life, as they had furnished the habitat of his fictional Yoknapatawpha County. What is different is Faulkner's conflation of his own life story with the history of the state and the region. His life experience is represented as the general experience of "everymississippian." His autobiographical surrogates, "the boy" and later "Mr. Bill," give focus and measure to the story of a place and an era. A native son, he writes as a legatee who has assumed his place in history as inheritor of a Mississippi that is metaphor for "the South." One does not find this assumption of southern representativeness or entitlement to the sweep of southern history in the narratives of Rawlings, Hurston, or Harris. Their stories of people and place are more immediately local and personalized. They are narratives that depict women who have to make their divided way in a daily world, separated by their careers as writers but connected to relationships they value and often make their fictional subjects.

When Marjorie Rawlings came to the writing of *Cross Creek* in 1940–41, she did so as a woman of independent means, a successful writer, albeit one who had had her share of struggle and uncertainties in establishing a literary career. She had sold her first story, "Cracker Chidlings," in 1930 for $150 and a second story, "Jacob's Ladder," for $700, both to *Scribner's* magazine. Her novels *South Moon Under* and *Golden Apples* soon followed. By the end of the decade she had published *The Yearling* (1938), a major best seller and winner of the Pulitzer Prize, and had been elected to the National Academy of Arts and Letters. Along the way she had visited and corresponded with Ellen Glasgow, a writer she greatly admired. In her later years Rawlings undertook to write a biography of the author, but she never completed it. Glasgow in fact includes in the last pages of *The Woman Within* a sympathetic letter in which Rawlings describes dreaming of Glasgow "outside in the bitter cold, cutting away ice from the roadway." In the dream, Rawlings offered that "from now on I should take care of you, and you must not do strenuous things." (294).

Some of the icy blockage in Rawlings's dream may have symbolized a pattern of literary criticism that she saw as dismissive not only of Glasgow's novels set in the South but of Rawlings's own Florida stories, classifying them as "regional literature" and thus as less than "serious" writing. In February 1940 Rawlings published in the scholarly *College English* a heated rebuttal to the patronizing use of the term by reviewers and literary critics. "The words 'regional literature' call to the average reader's mind either Middle West farm stories or stories of the South," she wrote, "and my guess is the first thought is of the latter" (382). Distinguishing between regional "writing" and regional "literature," she blasts writers who produce a regionalism that specializes in salable depictions of quaint customs and picturesque speech. In her view, they betray the people of the region, holding them up "naked, not as human beings, but as literary specimens" (384). She regards Ellen Glasgow as the preeminent "creator of the only unmistakable regional literature of the South." With a curt stab at the characterization of Glasgow as less than "distinguished" because she is "regional," she writes: "Pulitzer prizes for 'distinguished' novels are amazing anomalies when they ignore work of her literary distinction." A "regional" writer like Thomas Hardy, Glasgow is "first an artist and then a Virginian" (386).

Rawlings herself was a Florida transplant. Born in 1896, she had grown up in Washington, D.C., very much a southern city at that time, where her father was an examiner in the U.S. Patent Office. She took a degree in English at the University of Wisconsin, worked as an editor in New York City, and, in 1919, married Charles A. Rawlings. Moving to Rochester, she did some newspaper work, wrote a daily syndicated feature, "Songs of the Housewife," and worked not very successfully on her short stories. Her move to Florida in 1928, pivotal for her career, led to fiction set in the Cross Creek country, not far from Gainesville, and, with the interest and assistance of the celebrated editor Maxwell Perkins at Scribner's, to a national readership, financial independence, and the Pulitzer Prize. In *Frontier Eden: The Literary Career of Marjorie Kinnan Rawlings,* Gordon E. Bigelow writes that Rawlings "moved to Florida because she was convinced that a change in setting might provide a needed change in key for her writing." She would "exchange the city for the farm, the rigor of a northern climate for the bright sunshine of the semitropics" (10). What seems more consequential for her career, however, was less the new setting than the new confidence it brought to her.

At the time of the publication of *Cross Creek,* she had put a failed marriage behind her and had held her own for a decade as farmer of the seventy-two-acre orange grove. She had purchased the land with her share of her mother's estate, largely the proceeds from the sale of the Maryland farm her beloved father had once owned. Rawlings's biographer, Elizabeth Silverthorne, notes that this stretch of Florida was "the Florida where a man could still make a living with an axe, a gun, and a fishing line. It was the Florida of wild orange groves and Indian wars still within the memory of living people" (2). Here, Marjorie Rawlings became more than a survivor, according to Idella Parker, who had begun working for Rawlings in 1940: "She was the boss." In a conversation with Bigelow in April 1988, Parker remembered that "Old Man Wills declared that Mr. Brice was the boss until Mrs. Rawlings got there. When she got there, she took over." Parker sums up her impression: "I have never known a person like her. She loved people; she loved her work; and she did it" ("Memories" 140).

Like Isak Dinesen, Rawlings learned through physical labor to cut the frills away and go straight to the essentials, and to respect her self-sufficiency. She learned to take herself seriously as a writer, to have confidence in her power as a woman and a writer. *Cross Creek* is her account of her journey from floundering neophyte to Pulitzer Prize winner. She writes of discovering scenes and characters that galvanized her imagination, experiences she could transform into material for her art. Cross Creek gave her "a room of her own," where she could devise the necessary conditions for getting the writing done, finding the balance of solitude and people, distance and connection she needed in order to sit at her typewriter on the veranda of her farm house and do her work. Above all, during the thirteen-year interval between her coming to the Creek and her writing *Cross Creek,* she came to feel and trust her power as a shaping subject who could encompass the otherness of the world in her story. She had gained sufficient mastery to rely upon her own inward eye to construct a knowledge of the world in her account of Cross Creek.

Initially, I regarded the opening paragraph of the narrative, with its omission of an explicit I-narrator as an evasive move, an instance of a "self in hiding," to use Patricia Meyer Spacks's phrase. But I have come to read it differently. Rawlings does not name herself among the five families but adopts rather a queenly "we." The domain that is her subject in this book is one she constructs and commands. It is not a metaphor for the South like Faulkner's Yoknapatawpha but a metaphor for the setting where her own emotional and literary maturation took place:

> Cross Creek is a bend in a country road, by land, and the flowing of . . . Lochloosa Lake into Orange Lake, by water. We are four miles west of the small village of Island Grove, nine miles east of turpentine still, and on the other sides we do not count distance at all, for the two lakes and the broad marshes create an infinite space between us and the horizon. We are five white families; 'Old Boss' Brice, the Glissons, the Mackays and the Bernie Basses; and two colored families, Henry Woodward and the Mickenses. People in Island Grove consider us just a little biggety and more than a little queer. (1)

In the same decade that saw publication of *Cross Creek,* Simone de Beauvoir published her monumental history of civilization's construction of womanhood, *The Second Sex.* Central to her analysis of woman's role of subordination to man is her thesis that men, chiefly because of economic power, occupy the position of Subject, and that women, in their dependency, are forced to forego self-identity and assume the identities men construct for them. "He is the Subject . . . she is the Other" (xix). Insights and terminology that have become familiar over a half century of feminist criticism are as applicable to the conditions Rawlings faced as those Beauvoir identified in Europe. Most women coming to maturity feel themselves alone "*in the midst* of the world, but they never stand up *before* it, unique and sovereign. Everything influences [the woman] to let herself be hemmed in" (Beauvoir 792). But when Rawlings came to write *Cross Creek*, she had tested her own resources, and, finding they served, she trusted them, though she did seek Perkins's advice about the book's structure. Even so, she was ready in her own voice to say the world into being, ready to construct, to incarnate knowledge in her story. She writes as Subject; Cross Creek is the Other.

Writing Max Perkins on 15 September 1941, just after she had sent him the first draft of the book, that she did not want "anything like an autobiography" but rather "the thing objective, the only subjectivity consisting of my personal reaction to the Creek, its natural aspects and its people," she seemed to be downplaying the ego—a kind of modest display of self-consciousness. But even as she asks for the editor's advice, it is clear she does not intend to subordinate the narrator's Subject position to the Creek's "aspects and people." She writes: "If I had tried to use Martha [Mickens] as more of a hook . . . I could not use much of the subjective material that seemed to me important. . . . perhaps you may see a way in which I can make a stronger thread of the growth of my knowledge" (*Letters* 209).

The growth of Rawlings's knowledge of herself and the world she inhabits forms the vital, central topic of this narrative, with its surface text of the busy dailiness of the Creek ultimately revealing the story of a woman's becoming a Subject, enjoying a growing sense of empowerment, and confidently perfecting her art. The chapters are filled with portraits of Creek residents, of guests who have passed through the grove, of incidents that have transpired in the farming, in the neighboring, even in the contending for boss of the Creek. One reads descriptions of the hammock, of dusty roads, storms, food ways, and hyacinth drifts, but one finds that *Cross Creek* is *about* the construction of knowledge. The authors of the widely read 1986 *Women's Ways of Knowing: The Development of Self, Voice and Mind* observe that the most powerful and galvanizing insights that women in search of subjectivity, or identity and voice, may come to is the realization that "all knowledge is constructed, and the knower is an intimate part of the known. . . . To see that knowledge is a construction and that truth is a matter of the context in which it is embedded is to greatly expand the possibilities of how to think about anything, even those things we consider to be the most elementary and obvious" (Belenky et al. 137–8). Rawlings makes clear in letters to Perkins that what she is after in *Cross Creek* is showing how the self is realized in interactions with others, if indeed she can ever be sure of discovering that self. "The sense of knowing a particular place and people with a deep, almost Proustian deepness and intimacy and revelation, with my own feeling about things back of it, is what I want." She tells Perkins that composing the book is like "hard creative fiction. I can call less on facts and true details, and must project myself painfully and slowly into years and scenes and feelings that I have actually forgotten, and must re-create. I would say that I cannot do it, except that I know by working hard enough, it is possible" (*Letters* 195–96). Clearly, the book she intends to write will not take any familiar form of autobiography.

Rawlings slowly builds in the early chapters a richly detailed context of life at the Creek. She writes of Tom Glisson's house and hogs and cattle, of dense palmettos, marshes, citrus groves. There are the Townsends, happily fishing through the school and work day, the young couple who set up a home under the oak tree, fighting hunger and "antses," and the procession of employees who come and go at Rawlings's farm: dependable Martha Mickens and daughter Adrenna, the loving and unpredictable Geechee, with her taste for alcohol and shiftless men, and Raymond and Kate, last seen flapping down the road, headed for town in her flannel nightgown. These are stories of ways of life Rawlings deeply values—ways of friendship, generosity, sacrifice, as well as humor and disappointment. They express the character of the woman who wrote *The Yearling*, as she thinks of herself at the time she is writing *Cross Creek* and as she imagines herself into the future. As John Paul Eakin emphasizes in *Living Autobiographically: How We Create Identity in Narrative*, "autobiographical memory and autobiographical narrative are oriented to the future" (155).

In Chapter 17, "Our Daily Bread," the longest chapter in the book and, in many ways, the liveliest, the narrator presents herself more directly than in any prior chapter. Here she is not the creative artist producing books; rather, she is the creative cook producing "imaginative dishes," serving "good food." "Cookery is my one vanity," she writes, "and I am a slave to any guest who praises my culinary art. . . . My literary ability may safely be questioned as harshly as one will, but indifference to my table puts me in a rage" (205–6). Here she acknowledges a legacy from her mother, grandmother, and mother-in-law that gave her some knowledge of cookery but that has proved not as valuable as the art she has taught herself, along with the assistance of some valued cookbooks. She disdains the notion that expert cookery is intuitive; rather, it takes study and practice to achieve excellence—just as in writing, she notes. "The new foods that I found in Florida were a challenge," she writes, "and I have learned more about cookery in my years at the Creek than in those that preceded them" (207).

The pleasure and expertise she developed in cookery signify another direction in which she asserts a pattern of womanhood that she regards as congenial with—and expressive of—her nature. In the months following the publication of *Cross Creek,* she published *Cross Creek Cookery,* which gave the recipes for the local foods, wild game, and desserts she describes in "Our Daily Bread." Many of these are distinctly associated with the South: okra, mustard greens, mayhaw jelly, scuppernong wine, alligator and turtle dishes, sweet potatoes, and cornpone. She reports in the introduction to the *Cookery* that she received wistful letters from men in the military service who were reminded of home by her descriptions of favorite dishes. In all, she writes, "eight out of ten letters about *Cross Creek* ask for a recipe, or pass on a recipe, or speak of suffering over my chat of Cross Creek dishes" (2).

In both books, it is worth noting that the narrator is rather more an artful chef than a cook in the kitchen. Rawlings is ever wary of being trapped in traditional female roles that she regards as snares of self-sacrifice and powerlessness, roles that force a woman to resort to manipulation and "sneakiness" to effect her will. In a 1951 letter to her friend Norman Berg, recounting her annoyance with a domestic helper's young daughter, she wrote: "All my life I have hated little girls, swore that I wanted five children if they could be boys, and the more I see of this she-species, the more they annoy me." She continues with a caustic analysis of the origins of her sentiment and a brief commentary on the relation of gender to writing. "This probably goes back to my memory of myself as a nasty little hypocrite, dressed perforce in frills, and to my long fight to attain a dispassionate sexlessness in writing. . . . One's thinking is inevitably influenced and tempered by one's sex, along with one's background and conditioning and a hundred other elements. Yet I insist that there must be a plane, aesthetic, intellectual and spiritual, where there is no sex." She concludes her gender plaint with bravado: "I refuse to be *only* a biological female. If I had achieved the normal destiny of a woman, which I indeed wanted, to bear children, I might have felt differently, but flatter myself that I doubt it" (*Letters* 366–67).

Clearly, Rawlings regarded the writing career that she had pursued for years to be outside "the normal destiny of a woman." In fact, she goes on in this letter to locate a self-identity corresponding to her own nature. "Perhaps, as you suggested once, I was born half-male, understanding the true male, and resenting the—what shall I say?—well, hypocrisy, *sneakiness,* of the average woman." What Rawlings most deeply resented and found personally debilitating—and fought against, as she describes in *Cross Creek*—was what she saw as the powerlessness of the average woman, the powerlessness even of exceptional women. As she had chastised critics who did not accord Ellen Glasgow the respect her art commanded, she defended other writers—Edith Pope, Margaret Mitchell, Marcia Davenport, and Zora Neale Hurston—whose work she thought of as serious and worthy of respect.

In the final chapters of the autobiography, Rawlings draws a figure of a woman who has come into full possession of herself, of her powers as an artist; she is a seeing, knowing interpreter of the world she inhabits. She modulates her style and tone in Chapters 18 through 22, composing a more lyrical prose in her responses to the four seasons. In this section and in the final two chapters, "Hyacinth Drift" and "Who Owns Cross Creek?" she most fully foregrounds the writing self. The narrating "I" consistently is present, looking inward and outward in language of revelation and reflection. Especially in the last six chapters, one finds the "subjective material" she had described to Perkins as being important to her. Here she expresses her deepest knowledge of harmony with nature, of mortality's daunting presence, and her discoveries of timelessness, of loneliness, of independence, of uncertainty about love and talent and life choices. The knowledge that she articulates in these chapters has been gained from everything in her life that has gone before, and it is embodied as the present state of mind she brings to the writing of *Cross Creek*.

It is clear from her letters and from the text itself that Rawlings sought from the outset to write a book about a way of life and an understanding of the world that she had discovered at the Creek. But she had many misgivings about the form of such a book and its reception by readers and reviewers. Gordon Bigelow concludes that it was "as much a labor of love as anything she ever wrote, and yet she went through agonies trying to find a structural scheme and a tone which would hold such diverse elements together." Having started out with material she had been accumulating for ten years, she devoted nearly two years of intense effort and drafted four versions before she had something she was satisfied with (39).

Even after the book was published and had begun to receive the praise that would soon be widespread, Rawlings continued to anticipate and deflect criticism of the form by placing *Cross Creek* outside the genre of autobiography. She wrote Perkins: "It is gratifying to have such a generous reception for so queer a book. I still wish, in a way, that I had done an entirely serious book with the 'classic' touch—but the human stories were irresistible" (*Letters* 217). She might have said, had she written more candidly, that in her view a richly detailed human context, which is shown constantly and persistently to impinge upon and shape the self, more knowingly and truthfully portrays the artist—at least, the female artist—than does the "classical" structure that assumes a more autonomous than relational self composing a life narrative.

Certainly, a degree of autonomy is necessary to a writing life. Rawlings's economic independence and self-sufficient control of the farm were directly related to the development of her art. These allowed her to assert her shaping vision of the Creek; *she* was the seeing, gazing Subject, the Creek the malleable Other. To transpose this knowledge into narrative, she needed psychological distance and solitude for her writing, as she well understood. It is worth noting that her most productive years were the years she was unmarried. After the divorce in 1933 from Charles Rawlings, she lived on at the Creek until 1941, when she completed the *Cross Creek* manuscript, married Norton Baskin, and moved to St. Augustine. With emotional distance and an undisturbed room to write in, it was possible for Rawlings to compose the stories she most wanted to tell. It was possible for her to impose her interpretation, her shaping imagination upon the unmediated experience of daily life at Cross Creek.

Samuel Bellman (105–6) and Bigelow (80 ff.) have compared Rawlings's account of life on the Creek to *Walden*. Rawlings herself invokes Thoreau in several passages, particularly in the last chapter. But *Cross Creek* is a much more personal book than Thoreau's, more steeped in dailiness lived in a social world of human beings. Annie Dillard's *Pilgrim at Tinker Creek* might suggest a recent text for comparison, but that book, too, portrays little of human interactions. *Cross Creek* is predicated on the assumption that transcendent knowledge can only be trusted if it maintains constant intercourse with the changeable, immanent life we live as needy social animals with active intelligence and spirit. In manifesting this principle in the text, as in life, however, the narrator is constantly threatened by overpowering daily routine, such as she represents in the choking hyacinth drifts that obscure the channel she seeks in her long river journey with her friend Dessie Smith. One is reminded again of Beauvoir's observation that the most common burden for the female imagination is that of immanence, being stuck in the everyday. For Rawlings, a major challenge was in subordinating the daily life and daily bread sufficiently to see and write about the larger, transcendent patterns. In "Hyacinth Drift" she undertakes the boat trip on St. John's River in a melancholy mood, weighed down by a host of worries and obligations that she doesn't explicitly name—"all the painful circumstances of living." But the trip is restorative, enlivening: "Because I had known intimately a river, the earth pulsed under me. The Creek was home. Oleanders were sweet past bearing, and my own shabby fields, weed-tangled, were newly dear. I knew, for a moment, that the only nightmare is the masochistic human mind" (358).

The structure of *Cross Creek*—a series of character profiles, narratives of interactions between Rawlings, neighbors, and domestic and farm employees, descriptions of food preparation, reflective essays about the flora and fauna of the Creek—suggests a pattern of "memoirs," though it clearly is less about a record of past experience and associations than a representation of a way of living that expresses a wide canvas of human behavior. But the figures and settings Rawlings composes are just that—her compositions—and she wants them to be understood as such. The enormous integrity of the book owes to her portrayal of balancing forces: the implicit, powerful, dominating voice and the voice's explicit descriptions and assertions of limits, of incompleteness, of dependence upon indomitable nature. In *Cross Creek* Rawlings represents the elevation of the self to Subject and the material of the text to Other; *at the same time,* she unsparingly subverts whatever knowledge the omnipotent self can marshal, especially in the last chapter, showing that all knowledge is contingent, changeable, and contextual.

The conclusion, "Who Owns Cross Creek?" most fully expresses Rawlings's awareness of the tensions between the Subject/Self and the Other/World—and her resolute willingness to let the tensions stand, unresolved. Although she is the "boss" proprietor, the narrator proclaims in the final paragraph that it is the redbirds, more than she, who own the Creek. More revealing, she opens the chapter with a reference to Thoreau, observing that he "went off to live in the woods alone, to find out what the world was like. Now a man may learn a deal of the general from studying the specific, whereas it is impossible to know the specific by studying the general. For that reason, our philosophers [and writers?] are usually the most unpractical of men, while very simple folk may have a great deal of wisdom" (359). In its way, it is a self-canceling remark, for Rawlings is certainly not one of the simple folk, however much she may acknowledge their wisdom.

Other subversions of the intellectual's claims to wisdom follow. She tells of the celebrated relativist, Albert Einstein, who was entertained by a friend on a yacht near Miami. In a misunderstanding and ignorance of his habitat, Einstein threw out a choice morsel of prune stuffing in his roast squab, thinking it a gizzard the chef had overlooked. "All his knowledge of light and space had not fitted him to know that he would not, under any circumstances, find an appended gizzard in a roast squab served him on a yacht off Miami" (359–60). Asserting that "we at the Creek draw our conclusions about the world from our intimate knowledge of one small portion of it," she gives two pages later an example of her embarrassing ignorance of the Creek's codes. Thinking her neighbor Tom Glisson guilty of poisoning her dog and, later, of cutting her fences and maliciously trespassing, she addresses him in a curt note, "Tom Glisson. I wish to see you. Hurry up about it." His response surprised her. He was humiliated by her words, by the implicit portrait of him coded in a message that from his perspective was not only denigrating but false to the language of the Creek. "That note you sent me. I'm as white as you are. You wrote like I was a nigger" (362).

Rawlings directly addresses the presence of African Americans in a chapter entitled "Black Shadows." Although she shares little of the outrage that Katherine Lumpkin and Lillian Smith express in their indictments of southern racism, she exposes the conditions of forced servitude and economic deprivation that gave rise to many of the negative stereotypes offered as justification for racist attitudes and behaviors. Such conditions, she writes, were exacerbated by "the primitive African nature, subjected precipitously first to slavery and then to so-called civilization, the one as difficult and unjust as the other" (180). Throughout the chapter, filled with episodes recounting her experiences with farm and domestic help she employed at the farm, Rawlings's tone is that of the bemused white person whose often bumbling efforts to deal fairly with her black employees are often undercut by their violation, in her view, of a reasonable reciprocation of dependable service. She is clearly ambivalent about racial roles in this chapter, portraying humorous stories of African American wit and chicanery and then analyzing her employees' actions as originating in the caste status and the clash of African and Western cultures to which they have been subjected.

At the outset, she disavows belonging to "the race of southerners who claim to understand the Negro" but then remarks that "there are a few platitudes dear to the hearts of these [southerners] that seem reasonably accurate." What follows is a list of the negative stereotypes presumably accepted by her white neighbors at the Creek: "The Negro is just a child. The Negro is carefree and gay. The Negro is religious in an amusing way. The Negro is a congenital liar." But she follows with a summary of the African American's circumstance that anticipates Douglas Blackmon's *Slavery by Another Name*, a monumental work that tracks in great detail the virtual enslavement of black southerners in the years after the Civil War and during the years that Rawlings lived at Cross Creek. She writes, "The Negro today is paid instead of being rationed. He is left to shift for himself for the most part instead of being cared for. In the South his wages are a scandal and there is no hope of racial development until racial economics are adjusted." She identifies the negative responses to such conditions as rational defense mechanisms, obligatory and understandable. The African American "could adapt himself to the injustice of his position and to the master white race only by being childish, carefree, religious, untruthful and unreliable." His response can be further complicated, in some cases, by affection for his employers, with a consequent "mental and emotional turmoil past the comprehension of the most old-school aristocrat who ever slurred his witticisms over a mint julep" (180–81).

One cannot gainsay Rawlings's expression in *Cross Creek* of her deep affection for Martha Mickens and her daughter Adrenna. A letter to Perkins suggests that Rawlings considered at one time using Martha as a character "hook," around whom to organize the book. But her descriptions of Martha well exemplify her conflicted stance in many of her observations about race and in her responses to her black neighbors, who were often her employees. "There was an interim, as always, when old Martha came in to take care of me and to tide me over. Between all the explosions she is here, steady as a lodestar. She is utterly incompetent and serves a spoon for the eating of scrambled eggs, and her inabilities grieve her more than they do me" (189).

Rawlings intuits, if she does not consciously apprehend, that as storyteller she subverts the Creek, even destroys many truths—and myths—of its people and earth in order to give her version of it and thereby master her art. It is not surprising that Zelma Cason, a friend she describes in an account of census surveying of the Creek, was offended enough by Rawlings's depiction of her to sue for invasion of privacy. Perhaps it is more surprising that many other Creek residents did not take offense as well. Words, like photographs, can steal souls. Subject-tellers *do* invade the privacy of Others, even as they bring order and meaning to the enterprise of living. Rawlings was quite conscious that she might offend some of her "characters," writing Perkins that for the most part she had used "true names, but had tried "not to put things so that anyone's feelings would be hurt. These people are my friends and neighbors, and I would not be unkind for anything, and though they are simple folk, there is the possible libel danger to think of" (*Letters* 209–10).[1]

Narratives of "relational lives," such as most of the autobiographies discussed in this study, inevitably raise ethical issues about the portrayals of the others in the writer's life. Writers are usually circumspect in their descriptions of any person who is alive and likely to read the book. Lillian Smith wrote directly to her family to explain her intentions and motives. Many such books are written later in life, when parents and others of one's earlier years have died, but there is nevertheless an ethical standard assumed by most readers and writers that biographical depictions should be factual and, at least emotionally, candid. Paul John Eakin's excellent discussions of privacy and the ethics of life writing further explore the complex decisions to be made when one writes of others in telling one's own story—others who are private persons, not celebrities—in a book written and published for sale. Zelma Cason's suit for invasion of privacy, based on Rawlings's description of her on pages 48–49, was appealed ultimately to the Florida Supreme Court, who ruled in Cason's favor. It was a demoralizing blow to Rawlings. A landmark case on the boundaries that a private person is entitled to, it is fully covered in a monograph by Patricia Nassif Acton in *Invasion of Privacy: The Cross Creek Trial of Marjorie Kinnan Rawlings.*

In some ways the lawsuit magnifies the complexity of the autobiographer's task to compose her life in a text, when that life is ever bound up and expressed through relationships. Reading a much more recent autobiography, Mary Karr's *The Liars' Club,* Eakin relates insights that apply to the form and content of *Cross Creek:* "(1) that self content might be distributed throughout an I-narrative and not merely contained in the I-characters and I-narrators where the conventions of autobiographical discourse condition us to look for it; and (2) that 'self' is not only reported but performed, certainly by the autobiographer as she writes and perhaps to a surprising degree by the reader as he reads" (*Living* 84–85). The "we" of *Cross Creek* is a collaborative self, a performing self, and an imperial self who might have been drawn from Emily Dickinson's lexicon, one who possesses self-knowledge and lays claim to knowledge of the Other. "Perhaps it is impossible ever to say," she writes, just where one can draw a line between creation and destruction. For her, those concepts are "relative" (364). One might add that it may be impossible to say where the creation of the Subject "I" (the one who sees) and the Other objectified "she" (the one who is seen) begin and end. Storytelling or word telling always necessitates some sacrifice of individual autonomy by the writer and the written. It is a vexing bargain that Marjorie Rawlings profoundly understood, as she shows us in *Cross Creek.*

9

Narratives of a Writing Life, Part II

ZORA NEALE HURSTON AND BERNICE KELLY HARRIS

At the same time in 1941 that Rawlings was composing her book at Cross Creek, Florida native Zora Neale Hurston was writing *Dust Tracks on a Road* in California, where she was the guest of her friend Katharane Edson Mershon. This autobiography, the subject of much attention in recent years by such writers and scholars as Henry Louis Gates Jr., Maya Angelou, Alice Walker, Robert Hemenway, Francoise Lionnet, Will Brantley, and many others, is the story of a woman who celebrated an independent spirit. But, like Rawlings, she most expressively portrays the self indirectly—in a narrative filled with scenes, dialogue (often in dialect), and portraits of family, friends, lovers, employers, teachers, editors, patrons, and other writers. She demonstrates her writing life throughout by performing the same strategies that she typically employed in her fiction: linguistic facility, humor, striking descriptions of characters and settings, and a fluid mix of realism, folkways, and myths. Also like Rawlings, she wholly understands the "constructedness" of the narrator she creates for *Dust Tracks,* explaining in the opening sentences that she will provide the "material that went to make me" but that it will be the reader's task to "interpret the incidents and directions of my life" (1).

One quickly realizes, however, that the incidents point in different directions, often leaving an interpreter with unresolved contradictions. Brantley remarks upon Hurston's exuberant "vitalism," comparing her spiritedness to Walt Whitman (190). Her I-narrator is a sweeping presence who can comprehend multiple ways of seeing the world around her. Her ambivalence, if not indifference, to a racially denominated society is a sticking point for many readers today. Although she says on the first page that she was born "in a Negro town," taking pride in Eatonville, Florida, as the "first to be incorporated, the first attempt at organized self-government on the part of Negroes in America," she announces later that she has no interest in writing about the "Race Problem." "I was and am thoroughly sick of the subject" (151). Disdainful of African American writers who make a career of "race writing" and of "Race Champions" who want "noting to do with anything frankly Negroid" (169), she instead goes freely about describing people "without race prejudice," as she says, whatever the color of their skin. At times, her accounts of African Americans she encountered on ethnographic research trips recall Rawlings's references to "primitive natures." Hurston writes, for example, that "primitive minds are quick to sunshine and quick to anger. Some little word, look, or gesture can move them either to love or to sticking a knife between your ribs" (130).

Certainly, Hurston did not share the focus of Frederick Douglass or her contemporary Richard Wright. For her, speaking for "the Negro" meant acquiescing to a loss of *individual* identity, a loss that for her signaled weakness. But for Maya Angelou, writing the foreword to *Dust Tracks* a generation later, the total absence of any mention of racial incidents, even as the "southern air around her most assuredly crackled with the flames of Ku Klux Klan raiders" (x), is the manifestation of weak timidity—or worse, blatant courting of a white readership. Understandably, the character Hurston portrays as narrator in the autobiography is beset by conflicts arising from the problematic place of an African American in an era of racial division. She repeatedly emphasizes the individual she is, but the racial identification in a race-conscious—and segregated—society was also inescapable. "I maintain that I have been a Negro three times—a Negro baby, a Negro girl and a Negro woman. Still, if you have received no clear cut impression of what the Negro in America is like, then you are in the same place with me. There is no *The Negro* here" (172).

This voice demanding to be regarded as an individual, however, also spoke as an ethnographer who researched and wrote in books, articles, and this autobiography about the group folkways of rural southern African Americans. John Paul Eakin observes that the double consciousness here of the individualist writer and the observing cultural anthropologist illustrates clearly the "inadequacy of racial models of identity" in American society. One is reminded of Walker Percy's observation about the inadequacy of science to "utter a single word about the individual molecule, thing, or creature, insofar as it is an individual but only in so far as it is like other individuals" (22). Of course, Hurston is of a "Negro family," grew up in a "Negro town," as she announces in the first sentences of *Dust Tracks* so "that you may know about the time and place where

I came from, in order that you may interpret the incidents and directions of my life" (1). The childhood and adulthood that she composes in this text, however, is of a person who constantly makes herself "a crow in a pigeon's nest" (25). Like Ellen Glasgow, she writes of her early sense of herself as someone very different from others, one who has known a "cosmic loneliness" (43).

In recounting her life story, Hurston follows a traditional chronological sequence, at least through chapter eleven, "Books and Things." The later topical chapters are devoted to her views on race, friendship, romance, and religion. Like many other life narratives—Kearney's *Slaveholder's Daughter* and Lumpkin's *Making of a Southerner* come immediately to mind—the book's account of childhood focuses on parents and several incidents meant to capture and express the essential traits of the narrator's temperament and personality as these would develop over subsequent years. Hurston is her "mother's child," encouraged by her from an early age to "jump at de sun," to be a confident, ambitious, independent person—unlike the mother, who was "ninety pounds of fortitude" but died an early death and would need Zora's voice to speak for her. There are two fathers in Hurston's narrative of childhood, one a surrogate who came to her mother's aid at the time of the birth, a "white man of many acres and things" (20).[1] His mentoring advice to her as she grew up, underscoring her mother's mantra, was not to lie, not to be a "nigger," not ever to fear saying the truth.

Hurston's biological father is depicted as a man of prominence in the community and a gifted speaker, but his words to her typically were to castigate her impudence, her sassy tongue, her stiff neck. He insists she should stay in her place. Soon after her mother's death, he marries a woman Hurston portrays as an evil stepmother, and later he refuses to pay for school board and tuition. However much Hurston seeks revenge for wrongs done her in the portrait she draws of him in *Dust Tracks,* his model looms large as the progenitor of the spirited Zora Neale who emerges in this text. Foremost in his character are his love of storytelling and his gift of language. Not far behind are his love of travel, his curiosity, and his pride. Thus the writer constructs a family plot that provides the origins of the woman sitting at the typewriter in California. She writes at the end of the "I Get Born" chapter, "Some children are just bound to take after their fathers in spite of women's prayers" (23). Perhaps what is most important in this "claiming" of both parents is the point Elizabeth Fox-Genovese makes that Hurston's "primary sense of herself transcends gender" ("My Statue" 81).

The youthful incidents dramatized in the book depict a girl in love with stories, with the fairy tales and myths in the books she reads. Impressing two white women who visit her school and hear her read aloud the Pluto and Persephone myth, she is rewarded with an invitation to their hotel, where they give her treats and ask her to reprise her reading demonstration with a passage from *Scribner's Magazine*. She takes home with her a cylinder of one hundred "goldy-new pennies," and later gifts of books and clothes arrive. "I stood on the mountain" (38), she writes, recalling her youthful sense of mastery and the admiring favor that the mastery brought her.

Hurston draws upon this memory for her short story, "Drenched in Light," in which she connects the travel lust—her penchant for sitting on the gatepost and watching the world go by—with the child's gifted and charismatic attractiveness to a white woman who sees her as "drenched in light." Significantly, the performance—and validation—of the child's giftedness occur beyond the sphere of the mother. In her extensive analysis of *Dust Tracks,* Francoise Lionnet traces the introduction and development of the Persephone figure as an alter ego, the daughter separated from her mother. "The scene of the mother's death is symbolic of the daughter's responsibility to articulate her story, to exhume it from the rubble of patriarchal obfuscation" (118). But available in the patriarchal world of Hurston's youth are a rich, vibrant language and a trove of stories that likewise constitute the legacy bequeathed to her.

From her earliest years Hurston loved listening to the porch talk at Joe Clark's store, experiences she draws upon for scenes in *Their Eyes Were Watching God*. She loved to hear the "lying sessions" of a gathering of men competing with their versions of the speaking roles of "God, Devil, Brer Rabbit, Brer Fox, Sis Cat, Brer Bear, Lion, Tiger, Buzzard, and all the wood folk" (47). Her display of her own "lying" gifts is performed for the reader with a tale of how and why Sis Snail quit her husband, told as she heard it, so she asserts, in the dialect of Elijah Moseley, better know as "Lige." She further illustrates the lively imagination depicted as the métier of her childhood with a lengthy story of Miss Corn-Shuck and Mr. Sweet Smell, followed by a step-by-step recounting of a fantasy she devised of Mr. Pendir, a local man whom she turned into an alligator at night. From time to time Hurston gives free rein to diversionary narrative riffs such as these; at other moments she seems to try to harness the runaway story telling.

At one point, for example, Hurston breaks off her account of her precocious reading ability with an announcement that, at about seven years of age, she began to have visions, twelve disconnected scenes that flashed before her: "I knew that they were all true, a preview of things to come, and my soul writhed in agony and shrunk away" (41). She does occasionally call up the visions later, likely a strategy she initially intended to organize the text, which she thought at times to be rambling and disconnected. But, as for Rawlings, the overflow of people and places and episodes in Hurston's life was too voluminous and enticing to be tamed by a vision-plan.

When Hurston was nine years old, her childhood effectively ended: "Mama died at sundown and changed a world" (65). Thus begins a series of "wanderings,"[2] a move to Jacksonville for schooling, involvement in family upheavals, including a spirited fight with the stepmother, a memorable stint as a professional singer's maid, and eventually secondary and college study in Baltimore, at Howard in Washington, D.C., and finally at Barnard to study with anthropologist Franz Boas and commence a career in ethnographic research. The nurturing mother and the almost magic encirclement of her "Negro town" of Maitland had allowed Hurston's imagination and ambition to flourish, but "Jacksonville made me know," she writes, "that I was a little colored girl" (68). She also learns from the northerners in the theatrical company of her soprano employer that she is a southerner. For Hurston, what makes a southerner is language, not racial ideology. "It was not that my grammar was bad, it was the idioms. They did not know of the way an average Southern child, white or black, is raised on simile and invective. They know how to call names." Clearly, Hurston takes much delight in composing her list of illustrations of such southern expressions: "It is an everyday affair to hear somebody called a mullet-headed, mule-eared, wall-eyed, hog-nosed, 'gator-faced, shad-mouthed, screw-necked, goat-bellied, puzzle-gutted . . . unmated so-and-so!" Southerners "can tell you in simile exactly how you walk and smell," taking their "comparisons right out of the barnyard and the woods" (98–99). Hurston demonstrates before her readers' eyes that she is just such a southerner. The exuberant, inventive flair for language is perhaps the one group trait she is willing to be identified with. It is an arena for individual competition and group solidarity. It overcomes racial division, providing a common ground where talent is the source of distinction. Lionnet cogently observes that "Hurston's aim is to maintain the integrity of black culture without diluting it and to celebrate its values while remaining critical of those pressures from within the 'family' which can mutilate individual aspirations" (113).

Hurston's field research was focused on rural southern folkways, especially language. Her chapter describing research experiences is lengthy, filled with scenes such as the descriptions of Polk County, Florida, which are composed alternately in the voices of the researcher and the dialectal folk, a call-and-response pattern of leader and chorus. There are the sounds of its work songs, its "jooks" after dark, its dancing, knife fighting, its "primeval flavor." She recounts an episode when she "almost got cut to death" but was saved by an ally, "Big

Sweet." The language of the section is telling and representative of Hurston's narration throughout the text. It is that of a narrator who maintains a professional third-person discourse, employing dialogue in the dialect of the characters in the scenes, but who also appropriates and interweaves the language of the folk to give her own discourse a personalized voice and conversational tone. In this scene her landlady tells her that Big Sweet "got her foot up on somebody," and then the narrator explains: "If you are sufficiently armed—enough to stand off a panzer division—and know what to do with your weapons after you get 'em, it is all right to go to the house of your enemy, put one foot up on his steps, rest one elbow on your knee and play in the family. That is another way of saying play the dozens, which also is a way of saying lowrate your enemy's ancestors and him . . . and then go into his future as far as your imagination leads you" (136–37).

When Hurston leaves off her lengthy account of her research career and turns to her professional writing life, she is terse, uncomfortable, and even evasive. She recalls approaching the writing of *Jonah's Gourd Vine* with trepidation, for she understood that "Negroes were supposed to write about the Race Problem," and she wanted to write a different kind of book. A telling example of the rigid racial classifications of the times that attached even to books and otherwise open-minded writers is a comment by Rawlings in her essay on regional literature. She admires Hurston's novel, *Moses, Man of the Mountain,* and she is "tempted," she writes, to regard is as "literature." Comparing it to Thomas Mann's *Joseph in Egypt,* she judges that it is a "timeless legend" but, finally, a racial book, rather than regional, flowing as it does from "the luminous negro mind" (387).

In addition to her encounters with the "race book" demands, Hurston tells of her poverty and persistence in trying to find publishers for her work. There is a cliff-hanging moment when she is in debt for $18 and ousted from her rented room just before a Western Union wire brings the news that Lippincott will publish *Jonah's Gourd Vine* and pay her an advance of $200. Later, and again under considerable "internal pressure," she writes *Their Eyes Were Watching God* in seven weeks while in Haiti. That book, too, carries memories of difficulty and regret. "I wish that I could write it again. In fact, I regret all of my books." Wishing she had been wiser in the writing of them, she consoles herself that it may perhaps be "just as well to be rash and foolish. . . . If writers were too wise, perhaps no books would be written at all" (155). Abruptly, she announces, "*Dust Tracks on a Road* is being written in California where I did not expect to be at this time" (156). Yet again, the reader is to understand, she is waylaid by her host's expectations that she should want to tour the state. With broad humor mocking both the narrator's dilemma (she wants to be left to her writing but is shanghaied off to diversionary sightseeing) and Katharane Mershon's enthusiasms for her state's sites, Hurston makes an elusive—and inconclusive—end to her description of her writing career. Rather than asserting details, she demonstrates, through an assemblage of narrator voices and the sundry prose styles of the telling, the stages of experience that have brought her to the point of writing *Dust Tracks* in California in 1941.

In the later sections, Hurston turns from a generally chronological sequence to a group of topical essays that broaden the book's scope, offering a perspective upon her times. Lillian Smith, Glasgow, Rawlings, Kearney, Fearn, and Lumpkin follow a similar form. Hurston's first essayistic chapter is the piece on race, entitled "My People, My People." It is structured like a sermon that poses observations about African Americans who too often themselves show color prejudice and engage in self-defeating practices. The instances she cites are somewhat like parables, which she follows with a rueful petition for "my people." There is a tonal variation in this repeated response that is alternately chastising and empathizing. In her summing up at chapter's end, she returns to her celebration of individualism, having realized, as she says, that she "did not have to consider any racial group as a whole. God made them duck by duck and that was the only way I could see them" (171). But, of course, she does see and study groups, as her research career attests. As a writer, though, she calls upon her independence, originality, talent, and courage to be a "crow in a pigeon's nest." Lionnet describes the narrative that Hurston devises to answer to these several impulses as "autoethnography" (99).

The narrator is ambivalent about the degree to which Hurston's celebrated independence was shaped or subverted by the expectations of various patrons who helped support her during and after the years of her folklore research. She writes that she was "taken up by the Social Register crowd at Barnard" and became their "sacred cow," but she relates with affection her association with Mrs. R. Osgood Mason, whose support in the late 1920s offered not only encouragement but $200 a month for two years. "There was and is a psychic bond between us" (128), Hurston writes, invoking her present state of mind. Choosing two women as subjects for a chapter on friendship and talent, she focuses upon Fannie Hurst and Ethel Waters—one white, one black, both women she admires for their "rare talents" and for what they have meant to her "in friendship and inward experience" (173). They are "drenched in human gravy." The racial balance seems deliberate, signaling again Hurston's refusal to segregate herself as a writer concerned chiefly and narrowly with African American experience, especially that expressing outrage at social injustice.

Just as Glasgow had done, the narrator withholds the "love" section almost to the end and then in terse fashion portrays and dismisses two husbands, neither of whom is named. Herbert Sheen, wed in 1927, is simply "he," and Albert Price is "A.W.P." In this chapter, the narrator is unusually colloquial, or "speakerly," to use Henry Louis Gates Jr.'s term. She teasingly satirizes her notions of romance, and, in the end, makes clear that when a choice between marriage and career was demanded, the husband had to go. She says of her attraction to Price that she did not "just fall in love. I made a parachute jump." "Tall, dark brown, magnificently built," he suggests a model for Teacake in *Their Eyes Were Watching God*. She writes that she "tried to embalm all the tenderness of my passion for him" in that novel. "Embalm," indeed! Love on the page may be the deadest kind, but it is also the longest lasting. When she concludes the section with a semicomical listing of what she knows about love, she acknowledges that love, or, at least, the romantic mood, is transitory. The narrator humorously confesses that, under the influence of moonlight and music, she may "feel the divine urge for an hour, a day or maybe a week," but then it passes. Metaphorically, her interest returns to "corn pone and mustard greens," or a little more trenchantly, "to rubbing a paragraph with a soft cloth" (191). Finally, she would not give up her writing life when Price made it a condition of their staying married.

After discussing race, friendship, and love, Hurston turns to religion. Daughter of a preacher, she has heretofore had little to say about the topic, and in the chapter she devotes to it she is clearly more interested in the folkloristic elements of church service than in theology. She is decidedly less ideological or political than Richard Wright in his commentary in *Black Boy* on the rigid religiosity of his family members, although she is as explicit in her rejection of traditional religious creeds. She recounts her early skepticism and says that when she left off questioning to acquiesce to her parents' model, she was just saying the words, making the motions. Although her views would likely be unacceptable to many Christians who might read the book, she treats religious belief seriously, grounding her views upon her study of "the history of the great religions of the world." Finally, though, her rejections are as adamant as Wright's. "People need religion because the great masses fear life and its consequences." Prayer is for those who need it, not for her. It is a "cry of weakness." Gathering force in the final paragraph, the narrator's voice is that of the Whitmanesque celebrant of nature, of the cosmos. She is the rebel, self-assured in her position but still giving lip service, at least, to a respectful recognition of religion for "those who need it." As for her own being, however, she is "one with the infinite" and needs "no other assurance" (202–3).

The text of *Dust Tracks on a Road* that was published by J. B. Lippincott in 1942 ended with a brief chapter Hurston titled "Looking Things Over." Brantley notes that it was heavily edited and that additions in the 1984 edition represent only some of the deleted material, which is housed at Yale's Beinecke Library (189). Hence, we have an autobiography filtered through not only the perspective of the forty-year-old woman who composed it but the editing of publisher and perhaps patrons as well. That the woman was an African American writing at a time when racial segregation was widespread in the South, and racial prejudice only a little less apparent in the North, undoubtedly adds to the tensions and sharp tonal variation one finds in the text. Hurston was acutely aware that she was engaged in self-presentation before a judging audience, most of whom were white, including publisher and patrons. Like the girl Zora who so carefully presented herself to two white visitors, expecting their approval would bring acceptance, favorable attention, and even material award, she cannot escape the masking that society foists upon her. She conceals much in outright omission— her 1891 birth date, for one thing—and in humorous scenes and lively language that dissipate the sting of sharp social judgments. John Lowe has observed that the humorous diversions are unmistakable signs of her awareness of the "judgmental expectations of her readers" (192).

Although the narrator claims she would like to "rewrite the books," clearly Hurston regards them as the deepest "dust track" she has left behind, showing throughout the text that it is the writing life that has brought her the most satisfaction and happiness. Her valediction in the last paragraphs reprises the central theme of her narrative: she is a unique individual. To be sure, she is one whose "kinfolks . . . and skinfolks are dearly loved," but this affirmation does not lessen her belief that the separate self is the determinant of one's identity. From that independent perch, however, she concludes that "tears and laughter, love and hate, make up the sum of life" (255). Finally, it is the self emotionally engaged with others that Hurston most celebrates.

Cross Creek and *Dust Tracks on a Road* were both written by relatively young women, in their forties at mid career, with successful novels behind them and, presumably, many productive years ahead. Even when writing of personal hardship and inward doubts, the narrators of these texts are confident and self-assured, exhibiting not only a self that has emerged from the past but one that extends into the future. The authors at the typewriter compose these autobiographical writings in the engaging style of *The Yearling* and *Their Eyes Were*

Watching God, their most widely read novels, a style that dramatizes their relational lives with speaking characters in colloquial and dialectal language. For them, the present is rather closely connected to the past, both in years and in felt connection. I quite agree with Lionnet that in *Dust Tracks* "the tone of the work and its rhetorical strategy of exaggeration draw attention to its style and away from what it directly denotes" (100). Through such indirection Hurston escapes boundaries and certitudes that can only bind and constrain a "free spirit" and composes instead a vital, if elusive, self. She has, after all, warned her readers on page one that, if they would "interpret the incidents and directions" of her life, they will have to scout about and follow her tracks.

Bernice Kelly Harris, like Ellen Glasgow, came to the writing of her life narrative late in life, in her seventies, as she looked back upon a career essentially over. She had published her first novel, *Purslane,* in 1939, later *Portulaca, Sweet Beulah,* and others. Her autobiography, *Southern Savory,* published in 1964 by the University of North Carolina Press, like most of her fiction was closely tied to her native North Carolina. A comparison of *Cross Creek* and *Southern Savory* is instructive for what the two texts illustrate of the narrator's position in the narrative and the manner in which it is supported and constrained by the regional culture that is represented. For Rawlings, Cross Creek incidents and residents are the "material" of a story that is lively and dramatic but also lyrical and metaphorical. Accounts of census taking, cookery, or a river journey partake of the localism of the actual Cross Creek, but these also point beyond the immediate and local to other, inward experience. The extreme focus upon one sparsely populated spot of rural Florida rarely expands, however, to suggest the place is a "postage stamp" of the southern United States. Harris, too, employs fictional skills in portraying the local, but she does not often cast her impressions and reminiscences as metaphors of ineffable understandings of her own or and others' inward experience. In *Southern Savory* the narrator is rather more at the mercy of her material than master of it. The earnest narrator brings the reader along, modestly recounting a relational life in which she is only one actor, sometimes more a moderator than narrator, more Object than Subject. Evidence of her awareness of what her white, well-to-do neighbors in Seaboard, North Carolina—and her wider readership, especially in the South—would find acceptable for public exposure in print occurs especially in accounts of family, her marriage, and African American domestic employees.

In the preface Harris writes that the book records "impressions and reminiscences" of the people she has known. The narrator's presentation of self is "triangulated," one might say, taking an approach often seen in southern women's life writings. She portrays the character Bernice Kelly Harris as the curious onlooker, taking in and describing the array of incidents and persons that have shaped her life. This is a familiar memoiristic structure, with many loosely connected scenes and cameo portraits, except as these form markers in the chronology of the narrator. There are sketches of childhood days on the family farm, frequently related in a quaint, gently humorous tone. One chapter begins, "It was like an earthquake to our childhood world to find Mama crying that day," only to reveal later that Mama's upset owed to gossipy Cousin Eldora's having blabbed all over the county that Grandpa Kelly, dead for some time, had been a Republican. There are fond invocations of extended family members, landscapes, tall tale telling, church going, and schooling. Harris was an early reader, who cast herself in the roles of the heroines she read about, and dreamed of becoming a "bookwriter like Mary J. Holmes," author of books beloved by her and her friends (15, 31 ff.).

Later, in her account of her school commencement ceremony one Sunday, Harris recalls the excitement over the anticipated arrival of the governor, who was to speak, and describes members of the audience, one of whom was "the little governess from the river road." She includes the following detail with no comment whatsoever, although a reader is very much aware that she is composing the scene from her 1960s perspective. "Strumming idly on the piano, trying out its tone," the governess sings softly to herself, "Coon, coon, coon, I'd like a different shade— / Coon, coon, coon, I wish my color would fade." The narrator strictly maintains the perspective of her youth, recalling that "the mamas looked at one another, not sure it was a proper song on such a Sunday occasion. They were wondering what the children's Sunday school teacher, Miss Mattie Johns, might think of a coon-coon-coon song" (81). Harris offers no qualification of the inescapable implication that the derogatory expression for an African American, "coon," might be questionable only on Sundays and only among polite ladies.

The 1909 visitation of Halley's Comet provides a simple time marker for Harris's account of her literary study at Meredith College, where she turned from the overblown, imitative kind of poetry she had tried to write to an interest in playwriting. The influence of her professor Frederick H. Koch—"the little man in the Norfolk tweeds" who "inspired, evangelized"—was pivotal. Infected with his enthusiasm for folk drama, Bernice Kelly would take it with her to her classroom in Seaboard, where she would teach until she wed Herbert Harris in 1926. In the chapters that take up the years of her marriage, the narrator largely drops the quaintness and exposes a rueful disappointment in the marital relationship. Circumspect still in her characterization of her married self, she nonetheless sorrowfully reveals that her hope for children was denied. Indeed, she accounts for her undertaking a professional writing career as a substitute for nurturing a child.

Unlike her characterization of the governess and ladies at commencement day, her portrayal of Herbert Harris is the told from the view of the older woman, writing after his death, looking back on an unfulfilling marriage. As a bridegroom, he looked like "the businessman standing by me. He was remote too. For all his handsome wedding suit he did not look like a bridegroom. He looked Bradley and Harris. He looked cotton gin and land and timber. And he looked a little lost." After the honeymoon, they return to Seaboard, where he immediately turned his attention to a wagonload of farm supplies, forgetting Bernice and the luggage. "It was as though back in Seaboard he had momentarily forgotten he was married" (121–22). She describes an episode when the couple went to purchase furniture for their house. It is a defining snapshot of Herbert, who would persist until his death as a single-minded businessman, intent on driving the hard bargain, miserly counting every penny that his deals— and later her royalties—would bring.

In a poignant chapter set at Christmas, Harris discloses Herbert's ultimate rejection of her wish to bear a child. She describes her efforts to make the home beautiful, her delight in the carolers who come by, the feast preparations. The children singing and the snowy Christmas setting associated with a holy birth inspire her candor in voicing her dream: "To channel the savor in living, to pass beauty on from heir to heir, to pass life on" (135). Herbert's "No" is an ultimatum that blasts the silent night, as she writes, and she ends the section with the recognition that a chapter in her life had closed.

The last half of the book is devoted mainly to Harris's writing life. She announces that after the Christmas rejection she started writing, first in diary form, seeking to conceptualize the "savor" of the town she lived in. Her first portraits are of people closest at hand, the household maids in her employ. She writes of Ethel Vassar, composing dialogue in which the maid rails against the hardship and poverty of her life, complaining pointedly of the three dollars a week she earns from Mrs. Harris. But Mrs. Harris notes that "three dollars was the local top price for regular domestic help six mornings a week, and cooks were glad to get it during off-farming seasons" (139). She is often forthright in her depictions of the maids' words and circumstances but offers little or no analysis of the general conditions of race relations in her town—or in the South. In fact, the narrator typically relies on factual information and dramatized scenes for most of the textual content, giving the effect of a documentary rather than a reflective narrative. In many respects Harris is a representative white southerner of her class, time, and place—in the years recounted in this text and in the perspective she embodies in the writing of it in the 1960s. When she writes of Melissie, Ethel's older sister who came afterward to work for her, Harris shows a respect for the woman's insistence on proper boundaries between the employer and employee and her ladylike disdain of coarse language. Harris notes that "she bore with Herbert's expletives, but not with mine" (145). But in describing Melissie's curiosity about words, meanings, grammar, and well-written "condolers" to be read in her church, Harris notes that "she used my dictionary only a little less than she did my Bible." She continues, with no hint of self-consciousness, "She was as content with words as a child is with goodies" (148–49).

The developing career evolved from diary to features for newspapers to a revived interest in playwriting. For a time she conducted a playwriting class in her home for interested friends and other adults, and she began to write plays herself, at first, one-acts with protagonists based on characters from her childhood. Then, with the encouragement of Jonathan Daniels, the *Raleigh News and Observer* editor, she began to write *Purslane*. There was a motive beyond literary ambition that engaged her imagination and fired her interest in writing a novel that would give voice to her judgment of Herbert's acquisitive values. In 1938, after the death of a brother, he and his family were deeply embroiled in a lawsuit in an attempt to prevent the widow from gaining the "family property." Harris found this behavior unseemly and sordid, and she set out to write a book that would protest "the stresses and anxieties over property involving people I know." A bout of anemia had Herbert dosing her with "bootleg toddies," but she had learned, she writes, that "writing . . . was better medicine for me." Determined to affirm that "people without extensive property holding could know vast bounty," she produced *Purslane*.

Submitted to the University of North Carolina Press, the book immediately won the praise of the director W. T. Couch. The portrait of common people and the exposure of connivance in land dealings were content of the sort Couch wanted to publish. As historian David Joseph Singal notes, Couch was "a man who invited contention rather than evaded it" (273). Favorable notice in the *New York Times,* in which the reviewer compared the novel to *The Yearling,* which of course had won a Pulitzer Prize, was high acclaim, Harris thought. There were many other such reviews, such as Gerald Johnson's in the *New York Herald Tribune* and Dorothy Canfield Fisher's in *Book-of-the-Month Club News.*

Many offers for commercial publication of future work came from most of the large trade houses, William Morrow, Harcourt-Brace, Doubleday-Doran, Appleton-Century, and others. Herbert, pleased by the prospect of royalties, urged her on to a second book. She felt some obligation to place it with the UNC Press and consulted with Couch, who wanted to publish it, though he offered not to interfere with her commercial prospects. Ultimately, she submitted *Portulaca* to Doubleday after editor John Woodburn came from New York to ask directly for publishing rights.

Harris writes that the theme of the novel, like that of *Purslane,* exposed the greed of those devoted to "the religion of blood and property." Emboldened by Couch's admiration for *Purslane* and its success with readers, she struck again at materialistic values that she found hostile to her own personal happiness. In *Southern Savory* she advises "devotees" of such values to "find themselves on page 275 of *Portulaca*" (162). Perhaps her courage of conviction was somewhat supported by her knowledge that Herbert would not read the book. He had given only cursory attention to the first novel, had been bored with the reading, and so an agreement had been struck that he would not read the new novel. She worried, though, that the novel might not be "impersonal enough," that she would be "finished off" when her playwriting class and others recognized themselves in the book. But there was general approval, with, surprisingly, no repercussions. Looking back, she concludes that the town "could not have read the book" (164).

Harris's account of her launching and practice of a writing life has none of the angst of Glasgow's, Rawlings's, or Hurston's experiences. Her hardship was the marriage, and the career a solace. Her association with Jonathan Daniels, Couch, several professors at the University of North Carolina, and John Woodburn, whose friendly letters she quotes, was a source of deep satisfaction, enlivening and broadening her world. She clearly valued Woodburn's encouragement, but when he moved from Doubleday to Harcourt, she did not follow him, nor does she explain in the text her decision to stay with Doubleday and a new editor. Harris's biographer, Valerie Raleigh Yow, observes that she was disadvantaged by not having "advice and advocacy from a literary sophisticate with influence on the national level," that her career suffered from too early success. Her agent, Diarmuid Russell, routinely forwarded the new manuscripts after *Purslane* to Doubleday, who published all of them, and then he checked the contracts that came back to him, offering her little advice or advocacy (286).

Yow develops an extended comparison of the careers of Harris and Eudora Welty, whose editor was also John Woodburn and her agent, Diarmuid Russell

(285–87). She notes the sustaining close friendship of Welty and Russell, who had little direct contact with Harris. Indeed, when Harris sent the manuscript of *Southern Savory* to Russell, he did not submit it to any publisher and returned it to her, at her request. Harris wrote Clara Claasen, her editor at Doubleday, that "Mr. Russell seemed unsure that parts of the material would 'come through' for northern readers, and he mentioned a University Press as a likely publisher" (Yow 148). Russell's response to Welty and to her writing was far more enthusiastic, but, as Yow points out, there were significant differences between the two in life experience and literary sophistication. Welty was younger by eighteen years, had grown up in a book-filled house, graduated from the University of Wisconsin, moved to New York City for a time, and published her first short story in 1936 when she was twenty-seven. She met Woodburn and Russell in New York in 1940, whereas Harris, after her last novel was published, finally got to New York in 1953. One might also note that Welty never married. Whereas Welty travelled internationally and widely in the United States, Harris was bound by her farm family upbringing, an in-state education, a traditional wifehood of her time and place, and literary associations largely confined to North Carolinians.

With limited opportunities, social constraints, and a career that perhaps owed as much to a desire for escape as to literary ambition, her first novel, published when she was forty-eight years old, was in its a way a surprising turn of good fortune. With the other books that were to come, her career brought exciting years of book tours, speech making, and fan mail, an emotional validation that doubtless allayed the emptiness of the marriage. The narrator of *Southern Savory* describes her writing life with obvious pleasure. In a lengthy chapter, "Distillation," she recounts interviews in the late 1930s with farm families for the Federal Writer's Project that gave her a storehouse of characters and plots for her fiction. She constructs these as vignettes, with expressive phrases and dialogue, integrating dialectal speech of black and white farm folks of this region of the South.

Seven of Harris's interview-based portraits are collected in *Such as Us: Southern Voices of the Thirties*. Chosen for inclusion by editors Tom E. Terrill and Jerrold Hirsch, they feature a variety of folk whom Harris interviewed in the late 1930s in her area of North Carolina: an African American woman who claims to be 110 years old, alive in 1831 at the time of the Nat Turner rebellion; a wealthy landowner who bemoans his troubles with "shiftless" sharecroppers; a small acreage farmer who praises his sharecroppers; a sharecropping couple who have stories of repeated cheating by the landowners they have worked for;

and a "two-horse" farmer with "no money and no prospects." Two other portraits are of Seaboard residents, one a justice of the peace identified as Roger T. Stevenson and the other, a leader in the black community who is identified only by a first name Sam. Stevenson brags about having blocked voter registration for virtually every African American in the county. Harris concludes her profile of Stevenson with his claim of having wed many couples, but, seeing so many "sorry" and neglectful husbands, he pronounces that "more divorces" are what is needed in the county. One has to think that Harris took a bit of pleasure in highlighting this section of the interview, given her experience of a difficult marriage.

Finally, in the group of seven reprinted interviews (of the many she conducted), there is an anomalous portrait of an unemployed black man, disabled in an accident at work, who has had the advantage of one year of college study, has purchased a typewriter, and has finally gotten an artificial limb, thanks to a letter for help he wrote to President Roosevelt. The transcribed language of this man she names only as Sam is almost wholly free of dialect. The vocabulary is sophisticated; his recital of his repeated witnessing of employment discrimination is worthy of a lawyer's performance. "No good times can come to the country as long as there is so much discrimination practiced," he tells Harris (270). What is notable here is that despite Harris's direct knowledge of widespread racial discrimination, both from her own experience and from the accounts of those she interviewed in the field, for *Southern Savory* she selects from her trove of WPA files the interviews that are humorous and genial or, occasionally, that reveal sad spectacles of dire poverty. But she says little or nothing in the autobiography of the stark exposure in the interviews of rigid, even brutal racial discrimination. One has to infer that in part she is thinking of her readership and avoiding the increasing racial tensions in the South in the early 1960s.

She depicts, for example, one Mrs. Carter, who tells of meeting her husband at a "pea-popping," where she "couldn't take her eyes off him." The competition from a bevy of his girlfriends gave her grief, and she says she "shed enough tears over him to wash my dress" (188). Interestingly, the narrator is easily familiar with the stories of such families—she is at home with them—but when she constructs an interview with Sallie Jordan, a black farm woman, she is an observer and uses standard discourse with limited dialectal words or phrases. "I never saw a picture show or a circus or the ocean. But I saw a mess of water the Sunday my folks took me over to Edenton. That's the farthest I've ever been" (198). Harris moves freely in the chapter from one vignette to another, occasionally pointing out a correspondence between a person she had interviewed and a character she later created for a novel. In her telling of a final instance of such correspondence, the narrator's tone loses its lightheartedness. She relates an incident when she and Herbert had driven to the country to check on one of the Harris farms. While he was out in the field, away from her, there occurred a threatening fire, and she supposed he would be concerned for her safety. But Herbert had totally forgotten about her and then "covered up his forgetfulness with expletives about women who wouldn't stay where they were told to." It is she who is the prototype of the character later "distilled" into fiction. "Like Janey Jeems I was a little sour at his unremembrance of me." She concludes the chapter with a cautiously oblique comment: "Persons 'living and dead' are distilled into fiction. They are sometimes illumined by an identification less 'purely coincidental' than is indicated in prefaces to novels" (205).

Harris's caution about what she regards as safe and respectable for public exposure is often evident in the autobiography, especially when she writes about her marriage and the Harris family connections. As Patricia Hampl notes of such life texts, the memoir is usually less intimate than fiction, which is freer "to tell the truth derived from family secrets, from intensely personal events, from the burnt but still blooming core of the self" (203). Indeed, the autobiographical thread that Harris knits into *Purslane* is more exposed, less cautious, than the one she displays in *Summer Savory.* One may observe a reversal of this effect, however, in her depictions of African American characters in her fiction. Whatever living models she may have drawn upon, she portrays with circumspection.

Janey Jeems, published in 1946, traces the story of a black farm woman, her family, marriage, children, years of hard work, and sacrifices of self. Harris writes that she received more mail about this novel, her fifth, than for any of the earlier ones, and the questions posed were surprising. Readers wrote to ask, "Is Janey black or is she white?" Harris recalls that she was puzzled, for she had mentioned slave ancestors in the opening and at the end had had the attending doctor address Janey and her dying husband as "Aunty" and "Uncle," surely cues that could not be missed, she reasoned. On reflection, Harris takes comfort in the revelation that so many had regarded Janey and family as white Appalachian folk, confirming for her that she had written of universal, not racial experience. There is no such ambiguity in *Southern Savory,* in which the narrator always clearly identifies the color of African Americans. The preoccupation with color is, of course, revealing of the dominating role of race in the society of Harris's era—northern as well as southern. Given a white supremacist ideology that could so quickly turn to volatile action against black people, perhaps dramatizing the humanity rather than the race of Janey Jeems offered not only a safe—and oblique—approach for a white writer such as Harris, but a means, nonetheless, of embodying a rationale for social justice.

Another topic that could easily arouse the emotions of a reading audience was, of course, religion, especially southern fundamentalist religious practice, and Harris approaches it warily. In a chapter on Seaboard, "Hometown," which she warns should not be taken for one of the small towns of her fiction, she nonetheless suggests that its qualities are representative in many ways. Her principal example is of Seaboard's virtue of generosity—stories of the town's taking in stray animals and stray families—but then she portrays in a quite different tone a visiting evangelist, who comes to stir emotions and chastise sinners. The narrator's fond, empathetic tone gives way to satire as she shows a preacher "from the deep South" who comes to rail against "drinking and dancing and playing cards and attending Sunday movies and dressing immodestly." In her hometown he has very modest results for his effort. Though he may manage to get a few to come forward, most will not budge from their mahogany pews. The narrator then delivers her analysis of the developing "small rift" with an irony meant to indicate her neutrality as an observer. "A little core of fundamentalism comes through the veneer of modernism. It crystallizes into the wrath-of-God thinking"; still, she finds "the love-of-God" to be the majority thinking in her town. All those who play cards and wear shorts in public and "engage in mixed bathing at beaches" are of the "love school." Bemused at the sectarian opposition, she signifies her view of the partisanship: "There are those who see that both sides twist love and wrath according to their predilections, who believe that one is narrow only in the intolerance of the other" (216–17). The narrator is reticent about her own religious belief—or disbelief—though what she illustrates with her vignette is a portrait of self-interested shallowness that she finds among all the church revival actors she portrays. With the arrival of a truly momentous event, a hurricane, Seaboard's minds are concentrated on surviving nature's wrath, a weightier matter than religious belief, she implies.

More reviving of the town's spirit than visitations by evangelists, she suggests, have been the dramatic productions that unified Seaboard in the 1950s and early 1960s. The plays, written by her, were widely attended, even by "celebrities" from nearby Chapel Hill, Raleigh, Norfolk, and Greenville. Unlike the church "rift," the community's response to this cultural project was "generally serious and wholehearted" (217). She concludes the chapter with descriptions of church services she finds meaningful and expressive of the town's communal spirit—a christening, a funeral, and a golden wedding.

In the final sections of *Southern Savory,* Harris recounts the illnesses and deaths of her husband and her father. Herbert's declining health taxes her strength, much of it the physical strength expended in nursing him, and confines her more than ever to home. What reflection she offers upon the years of marriage is far overshadowed by the detailed account of the endless activity during the years of his long invalidism—not only the nursing, with the aid of Melissie and other domestic help, but handling visitors, food, doctor consultations, broken furnaces. In the last three years of his life, Herbert was paralyzed, cared for at home, and increasingly dependent upon Harris's presence. After the narrator states the time of his death, 13 July 1950, she follows with a brief, enigmatic reflection: "I knew there was no going or staying that we were not in together. Forever we had what we had had" (234). The heavy emotional upheaval, it turns out, lay just ahead of her, the contesting of the estate by the Harris family. The absence of a will, the complications of family partnerships, Herbert's merging of her royalties into his business income, and the vehemence of the family in protecting Harris family holdings from childless widows like Bernice all conspired to lay claim not only to business properties but to the furniture and the house that had been her home for twenty-six years.

The account of Herbert's death takes up only the first page of the chapter Harris entitles "Affirmation." It is through the writing life that she finally secures her agency—her identity, as she says. She turns back to consider her own fiction for role models who succeeded in having fulfilling lives, and she finds validation and friendship among numerous "book people"—writers, academics, readers, new friends, and old acquaintances at literary workshops, retreats, and conferences. Deep pride marks the concluding sentences of the chapter: "The largest cultural group in the state is the North Carolina Literary and Historical Association, Incorporated. I served as its president in 1961." North Carolina gave her a supportive literary circle—"The book people have served me," she writes (238)—but arguably it was also something of a limiting boundary, at least to the extent that the affirmation she sought and valued was sufficiently proffered by North Carolinians. Staying with the traditional literary forms and conventions that she had employed in *Purslane,* she was never drawn to the fictional experimentation widely occurring mid twentieth century.

Traditions, far more than new ways and styles, were what Harris valued. She concludes the autobiography by circling back to the family patterns of her youth. Caring for her ninety-seven year old father in his waning days, she cherishes the family's solidarity, the memories of times shared, and the promising future embodied in the youngest members of the extended family. At a family reunion in 1956, it is the family life, not the writing life nor propertied estates, that she regards as the legacy of consequence. The narrator's leave-taking of her story is colored by regretful nostalgia. The grandfather's monument that bespeaks past lived lives is one of stone, but another, not of stone, is that of "sons and sons' sons." Denied to her, of course, are the sons Herbert would not countenance, and the sharp disappointment flares in the end, only mildly mediated by thoughts of the extended family—and the writing life.

The protagonist that Harris composes in *Southern Savory* is a woman who expresses many of the sentiments and values typically associated with southern female tradition. She is ever aware of her family duties as daughter and wife and her desires above all to bear a child. She finds pleasure in a writing career but makes sure it is subsidiary to wifehood. She respects the boundaries between what is proper for public exposure and what should be kept private. The actions and feelings that she reports are inoffensive and unlikely to provoke any reader censure. As a single woman, she pursues an education and supports herself as a respected schoolteacher. After she marries, she is careful to gain her husband's agreement to whatever activities she undertakes outside the home. When she conducts interviews for the Federal Writers' Project, he drives her through the countryside. And when she receives royalties for her fiction, she hands the checks to him. It is a woman's sphere little changed from that of the nineteenth century.

Harris moves beyond this sphere in her fiction, voicing her knowledge of the land and people she knows firsthand, celebrating their connections to the land and the loyalties to family that typify her southern characters—white and black—but also exposing the injustice of mercenary family machinations as starkly as Lillian Hellman does in *The Little Foxes*. She shows little interest in advancing social or literary views in *Southern Savory* or in essays, unlike Hurston in *Dust Tracks on a Road,* Eudora Welty in "Must the Novelist Crusade?" or other professional writers included in this project. Born in 1891, Harris was a contemporary of Glasgow, Rawlings and Hurston, but she had no close association with any of them.[3] Hers was mostly a lonely voice in the wider national literary circle, but she found satisfaction in her writing life and validation in the acclaim it brought her. As for the traditions of her family and southern community, which were so defining of her art and life experience, one is hard pressed in the final light to tell whether these were more sustaining or enervating.

IO

Modes of Autobiographical Narrative

EUDORA WELTY, ELIZABETH SPENCER, AND ELLEN DOUGLAS

Finally, I should like to consider the narratives of three professional writers whose autobiographies represent three rather distinct modes of discourse available to the life writer undertaking to compose a textual self. This is not to propose some "pure" forms of a subgenre that are generalizable for the wide range of texts commonly labeled *autobiography* but rather to engage the variations manifest in the texts discussed in this study. In *One Writer's Beginnings* Eudora Welty constructs a childhood plot explicitly focused upon the people, places, and events that prepared her for a literary career. She writes a "directed narrative" that includes details that express her exposure to the tools of language and her cultivation of an empathetic and curious sensibility that she regards as undergirding her fiction. *One Writer's Beginnings* is a disciplined narrative that hews mainly to childhood recollections; details of later adulthood are integrated as these logically give evidence of the prior influences that have been recounted. Its limited focus proceeds from clear motives and careful selection of supporting details, such as we see in Katharine DuPre Lumpkin's and Lillian Smith's purposeful narratives of "awakenings" to racism, to Anna Julia Cooper and Belle Kearney's dedication to social reform, and to Helen Keller's recounting of her escape from dark silence into the enlightenment of language.

Elizabeth Spencer's *Landscapes of the Heart* follows a more traditional mode of autobiography, the "lifetime memoir" covering years of childhood and stretching toward the present moment of the text's composition. The narrator reveals a "relational self," a character discoverable by the reader far less in direct statements of thought and feeling than indirectly in depicted relationships with others. To give structure and coherence to the development of the protagonist-self, the narrator creates thematic threads that lead inevitably to the composing author. For example, Spencer portrays a childhood that was intellectually and emotionally nurturing, one that fostered ambition for a literary career but led to estrangement from family and region. Despite her impressive literary success and the personal fulfillment of a happy marriage, her sense of alienation is never wholly assuaged. The "wifehood narrators," Hamilton, Sinclair, Anderson, Durr, Boggs, and Barber all in more or less degree express adult selves in supportive relationships with husband and family, as well as in circumstances that show their resilience and initiative in dealing with life's twists and turns. Many of these narratives develop running plot lines that add suspense—the mysterious aristocratic background of Hamilton's husband, the unfolding tensions of living with genius in Anderson, Craig Sinclair's literary collaboration with husband Upton, Durr's growth from cultural acceptance of racism to active opposition, Boggs's transition from collaborating political wife to congresswoman, and Barber's rueful search to regain the autonomy she had possessed as a young career woman. Ellen Glasgow's and Bernice Kelly Harris's narratives both employ "lifetime" content, Glasgow focusing on the development of her career as a successful novelist who overcame an unhappy childhood and the travail in adulthood of illness, deafness, even failed romances. Harris combines a wifehood story marked by unhappiness with a career story that brought fulfillment and supportive relationships.

The episodic structure of these texts doubtless recapitulates the experience of "lived life" far more closely that does a narrative firmly issuing from a controlling topic. Moments of daily consciousness are fragmented, wildly scattered over time and place. But even an episodic text is not a life. It is a semblance—a virtual life. Philosopher Suzanne Langer considers James Joyce's episodic *Portrait of the Artist as a Young Man* as an exemplary illustration of "virtual subjectivity," a text that has "not a line of 'purely informative language,'" but is "all fiction, though it is portraiture. Literary events are *made,* not reported, just as portraits are painted, not born and raised" (257). These texts may be a far cry from Joyce's celebrated prose, but Langer's point is well taken. In a written text, especially an expressive one intended to portray the self who is writing, every element bears upon and shapes the reader's understanding. What is included, what is omitted, what is dramatized with dialogue, described in a lyrical vocabulary, or narrated tersely or volubly—or whatever effect is projected through language—these elements are all *expressive.* The mode of episodic memoiristic

narrative may be judged aesthetically sophisticated and successful, or something less, but as a construct of expressive language, it calls upon the same fac-
ulties for close reading that we bring to Joyce's *Portrait of the Artist*.

A third mode of narrative writing, more experimental than the foregoing,
may be termed a "performed text." In various ways it enacts a contestation of
the genre of autobiography. Ellen Douglas's *Truth: Four Stories I Am Finally Old
Enough to Tell* exemplifies texts that, at least in part, expose the limitations inherent in narrative self-revelation and, instead of the familiar memoir, give the
reader a lively *performance* of the self or, in the case of Douglas, a demonstration of the instability of memory, that facility of consciousness and imagination that assures us we are known subjects to ourselves. Rawlings and Hurston
perform their texts, and we read them as if we were audience to a dramatic
production. Douglas makes even more demands upon her reader's inferential
skills. She creates a narrator intent upon telling "true" life stories, uncovering
what has been hidden or unavailable to her in earlier years when she lacked the
language and experience necessary to translate action into words. This narrator's commitment to "fidelity of life" and "unqualified" autobiographical truth
is the same commitment that Glasgow pledges, but Douglas cannot escape the
skeptic's conviction that language, the medium of truth telling, makes a fiction
of the narrator. She introduces the authorial persona who, like an omniscient
narrator intruding upon a first person narrator, warns the reader not to believe
"truth" constructed by such an unreliable witness. The business of life telling in
words is ultimately a matter of literary artifice, imagination, present consciousness, and "memory"—that store of narrative fragments that one puts together,
variously, to constitute an identity. Douglas would thus have her reader close
the covers of *Truth* with a deepened respect for the fictiveness of autobiography
and the acknowledgment of one's responsibility throughout life for "rewriting"
one's past in light of every evolving increment of experience and insight.

A generation younger than Rawlings, Hurston, and Harris, Eudora Welty, born
in 1909 in Jackson, Mississippi, came to the writing of *One Writer's Beginnings* in her seventies, composing her narrative from the perspective of a long
career of successful fiction but focusing upon the years of childhood. Unlike
Glasgow and Harris, both of whom wrote life narratives for publication late in
life, Welty initially prepared a text for three public oral presentations, the William E. Massey lecture series at Harvard University in April 1983. Although she
later revised the lectures for publication, the fact that the first audience for *One
Writer's Beginnings* was one she stood before, faced directly, and read aloud to is

a forceful reminder that the narrative was a script composed for a public reading. One likely consequence of writing for such an audience is the tightening of focus and a heightening of scenes, episodes, and dramatic detail. Welty's text is a reflective recounting of childhood memories, but it is enlivened by many vivid moments that illustrate her storytelling beginnings. What she delivered in the lectures and the published book was not only an account of the influences that had inspired and prepared her to be a writer but also an illustration of the same widely admired literary craft that she evidenced in fiction. Still, the extraordinary success of the published version, which made the *New York Times* best-seller list, was something of a surprise to Welty and to the Harvard University Press.

Welty had long resisted writings about her life, either by others in biographies or by her own hand, but the invitation to inaugurate the Massey lecture series and the suggestion by her old friend Daniel Aaron that she talk about those experiences of youth that had equipped her for a literary career finally persuaded her to undertake the narrative. Earlier, she had revisited many memories of childhood and her parents when she wrote *The Optimist's Daughter* (1969; 1972), a novel that draws upon some of the same autobiographical details that she regards as significantly related to her development as a writer. There is a marked contrast, however, between the protagonist's voice in the novel and that of the writer who recounts childhood experiences in the autobiography. The character Laurel Hand is deeply engaged emotionally in unfolding family affairs, returning to her childhood home in Mount Salus, Mississippi, to face the death of her father, a vexing stepmother, and long-repressed memories of earlier sorrows—her husband's wartime death and, wrenchingly painful to Laurel, her mother's declining health, blindness, and agonizing final days. In the closing section of the novel, Laurel reconnects with (remembers) her place in the family past, bringing her mature judgment to a reinterpretation of her parents and so coming to imagine a different future for herself. In *One Writer's Beginnings* the authorial voice has from page one already assimilated the memories of childhood and parents into a plot line that eventuates in the honored writer standing before a Harvard audience.

The girl Eudora depicted in this memoir is greatly distanced from the author speaking, though she is the protagonist of the youthful events constituting most of the text. She is childlike, naïvely accepting the privileges she enjoys as daughter of loving and intellectually curious parents. "From as early as I can remember," she writes, there were gifts of books, many books—fairy tales, myths, legends—and even toys of instruction ("separately," she notes) for her and her younger brothers. Their father provided a comfortable income for the family, but Welty concludes that "they must have sacrificed" to buy her beloved series *Our Wonder World*. "I believe I'm the only child I know of who grew up with this treasure in the house." Dominating the first section is her recollection of this reading household and the books she read and that were read to her. "I live in gratitude to my parents for initiating me . . . into knowledge of the word, into reading and spelling, by way of the alphabet. They taught it to me at home in time for me to begin to read before starting to school." As a child she supposed her family's ways were as natural and usual as breathing. "You learned the alphabet as you learned to count to ten, as you learned 'Now I lay me' and the Lord's Prayer and your father's and mother's name and address and telephone number, all in case you were lost" (840–47). (One may note that the body of the sentence is voiced to recall the child's perceptions of the lessons; the tag phrase that follows invokes the authorial voice, obliquely suggesting that the alphabet is valuable even to adults who may be "lost.")

In addition to Welty's emphasis upon the literate interests of her parents are numerous reflections and narratives describing their differing personalities, which model for her a union of complementary traits that she comes to regard in later life as a joint legacy they bequeathed to her, a pattern commonly exhibited in autobiographies, as we have seen. Placing her focus upon them and the host of others who populate the text, she is freed of her dread of displaying egotism and assured by the structure she establishes of boundaries that delineate a youthful, relational self whose identity is inextricably connected to her "beginnings." From her distanced perspective, Welty writes a story that heads toward personal and professional fulfillment; her humor and lyricism suggest, even in accounts of emotional pain, that the story will end in affirmation.

In the head note that opens *One Writer's Beginnings* Welty composes a scene drawn from her early childhood that reflects the dynamism of her parents' union. Her father is shaving, preparing to leave the house for work, and her mother is frying bacon in the kitchen. The child Welty listens from the stairs, her father "whistling his phrase" and her mother trying to whistle but having finally to hum hers. The italicized paragraph introduces a moment of sensory awareness, the child's apprehension of sounds that the author, reaching back to childhood, composes as tropes for the separate natures of the parents. In several earlier essays I have considered the implications in this text of Welty's gendering of the influences of the father and the mother upon her literary vocation and life, and the observations still seem valid.[1] As she implies in the head note, she associates the father, an insurance executive, with the world of work beyond the hearth. He whistles the tune and later will purchase a typewriter for her to make her own "tunes." As a teenager she accompanies him on distant train trips, precursors of her independent journeying outward to establish a writing career. After several years at Mississippi State College for Women, she leaves Mississippi, at his insistence, to complete her education at the University of Wisconsin. Afterward, with his encouragement, she goes to New York and enrolls at Columbia for enough study in business to assure that she can find a job, be self-supporting, though her ambitions lay in the financially unpromising direction of photography and fiction.

In a poignant scene she recounts his carrying her, an infant in his arms, to the window to witness Halley's Comet's arrival in 1910, a family story passed down. She recollects stargazing with him at night. His telescope, with its brass extensions, exposed an awesome world, expansive and mysterious, with its comets and eclipses and constellations. "Bending behind me and guiding my shoulder, he positioned me at our telescope in the front yard and, with careful adjustment of the focus, brought the moon close to me" (848). Christian Welty pulled her away from the hearth, supporting, but always exposing her to a world that lay beyond the sheltering.

Chestina Welty was the keeper of the hearth, the ardent shelterer—loving and nurturing as Welty portrays her from the child's vantage. She was the constant reader, sitting down at any time of day in any room of the house to read to her daughter. Welty writes that her mother was an expressive and passionate reader, one who early had sacrificed her long hair, at the urging of the family, who thought it dissipated mental energy, for a set of Dickens novels. Her daredevil spirit perhaps incited the aversion to risk that she showed with her children, but it was a source of prideful storytelling—including a story of running into a burning house to save her Dickens. Her mother's passionate reading she describes as a surrendering to the text: "She sank as a hedonist into novels. She read Dickens in the spirit in which she would have eloped with him" (842).

Although her mother supported Welty's ambition to be a writer, she did so principally, Welty says, because she regarded it as a vocation that was "safe." Throughout *One Writer's Beginnings* it is clear that Welty finds great joy and fulfillment in the reading and writing of books, but the provocative question of whether writing is a "sheltered" or "daring" enterprise provides a line of suspense that leads to the concluding sentences of the narrative. At the end of the opening "Listening" section, she posits the role of the writer as one of "vaunting," asserting that "it is always vaunting . . . to imagine your self inside another person, but it is what a story writer does in every piece of work; it is his first step, and his last too, I suppose" (883). For her, such "vaunting" is not the safe path but the one less taken, the daring to part the curtain and make stories of lives uncovered, or guessed at. That her mother, who "could not help imposing herself between her children and whatever it was they might take it in mind to reach out for in the world" (883), regarded a writing career as an extension of a sheltered life is a view that continues to challenge the seventy-three year old author and call for rebuttal.

Welty's tendency to identify reading with the maternal world and authoring with male power is hardly surprising; it is a long established and common association in Western culture, much discussed by feminist critics and writers and evidenced by many of the texts studied here. Like so many others before her, she grounds her authorial identity in the legacy from the father, associating her journeying away from home and literary ambitions with the model of the father. But this correspondence is fraught with unease, for the leave-taking of the mother creates an unavoidable residue of guilt. A writing life is seemingly like any other choice, coming with cost as well as with profit. On her way to New York to try to interest publishers in her stories and photographs, she knows her mother is "already writing to me at her desk, telling me she missed me but only wanted what was best for me. She would not leave the house till she had my wire, sent from Penn Station the third day from now, that I had arrived safely" (916). Welty immediately compares her departure to that of her father's when he left on business trips, he the "train lover, the trip lover." She concludes that, for her, joy and guilt are inescapable consequences of independence: "The torment and the guilt—of having the loved one go, the guilt of being the . . . loved one gone . . . comes into my fiction as it did and does into my life. And most . . . of all the guilt then was because it was true: I had left to arrive at some future . . . secret joy, at what was unknown, and what was now in New York, waiting to be . . . discovered. My joy was connected with writing; that was as much as I knew" (937).

Many years later, the author describes these tensions with equanimity, unsentimentally acknowledging the demands of artistic creation, accepting with a certain Keatsian "negative capability" the guilt along with the joy. The feminist literary critic Carolyn Heilbrun has read Welty's equanimity as nostalgia camouflaging of truths she has not told. She writes that "nostalgia, particularly for childhood, is likely to be a mask for unrecognized anger." Tellingly, she attributes the masking that she argues occurs in *One Writer's Beginnings* to Welty's "southern lady" socialization, writing that "to her, this is the only proper behavior for the Mississippi lady she so proudly is" (15). Heilbrun is correct that

Welty gives few words in *One Writer's Beginnings* to expressions of anger. I venture to say that the intense emotion Heilbrun is looking for is more to be found in *The Optimist's Daughter*—the daughter's feelings of guilt, regret, anger, love, burdensome emotional ambivalence. Patricia Hampl, a Minnesotan, tells a relevant story of a novelist friend who once remarked that she could not speak "soul's truth" in a memoir and explained that autobiography offered "less intimacy than fiction" (203). Of course, whether in fiction or autobiography, there are numberless ways of inscribing "truth," as we are reminded by the narratives discussed in this study, or even by Joyce's *Portrait of the Artist*. Further, there are many levels of consideration to negotiate when one presumes to implicate others in the telling of one's story.

Welty's focused attention in the lectures at Harvard was largely directed toward what she regarded as the positive, actionable influences preparing her to be a writer. She does ponder, however, one irresolvable constraint that a writing life imposes. Art making requires social distance, a certain single-minded withholding from family and friends and even lovers, and the separateness strains relationships that are dear and leaves a residue of guilt. Many writers' narratives recount similar experience. Still, "getting one's distance" is essential to Welty's "finding a voice," as she titles the final section of the memoir. Here she figures the gaining of "distance" not only in terms of the emotional and physical separation she needed for writing but also as a coming into possession of distance— an engagement and knowledge of the world that she would form into fiction. In the second section, "Learning to See," Welty devotes most of the text to accounts of family trips to visit grandparents, her mother's in West Virginia and her father's in Ohio. These visits take the child far beyond Jackson, Mississippi, show her other places, other ways to live. She looks back upon the contrasting home places as illustrative of traits of the parents and of the regions they came from. As she once told interviewer John Griffin Jones, "My mother was a Southerner and a Democrat. My father was a Yankee and a Republican. They were very different in everything" (320–21). In an earlier essay, "The Construction of Confluence: The Female South and Eudora Welty's Art," I observed that the singleness of mind and purposive action she sees as traits of her father—and also as necessary to the psychological makeup of the creative artist—she associates with the North, whereas the singing, tale-telling uncles of West Virginia, the southerners, are sources of imaginative power.

Again, Welty asserts her legitimate claim as daughter of complementary regional influences, the practical, progressive, logical North and the fanciful, imaginative South, drawing of course upon an old and persisting psychic opposition in the American mind, one prominently exemplified in "romances of reunion" after the Civil War, as Nina Silber has noted. Taking up again the differing traits of the parents in the last part of the memoir, Welty writes that "it was my mother who emotionally and imaginatively supported me in my wish to become a writer. It was my father who gave me the first dictionary of my own, a Webster's Collegiate, inscribed on the flyleaf with my full name (he always included Alice, my middle name, after his mother) and the date, 1925. I still consult it" (925). She was sixteen years old.

Welty explores dualities and compensations as she composes the early influences that shaped her into the mature artist writing *One Writer's Beginnings*. The career has been joyful and fulfilling in many ways, but it has exacted relational costs. She makes no attempt to address the critical reception of her work, which lies beyond the boundary of "beginnings." But she does foreground scenes that suggestively question the role of the observing artist and set it in contrast to heroic endeavor. Is writing "safe"? Or is it a daring participation in life, a risky exposure of the self? The questions are dramatized, not answered, in the gripping narrative she tells near the end of the book of her father's death. Shortly after she returned from Columbia in 1931, at age twenty-two, her father was diagnosed with leukemia. As he lay on a cot, dying, her mother insisted that she would save his life with her transfused blood, just as years before he had saved her life when she was dying of septicemia.

Welty's narrative is reportorial, factually descriptive. She writes that she does not know "how much was known about compatibility of blood types then." What she knows of compatibility in 1973 as she is writing, she does not say, though it is clear to the reader that the daughter's blood was likelier to have been a match. "I was present when it was done," she writes. Welty's is the seeing eye, looking on as "a tube was simply run from her arm to his. . . . All at once his face turned dusky red all over. The doctor made a disparaging sound with his lips, the kind a woman knitting makes when she drops a stitch. What the doctor meant by it was that my father had died." The scene signifies not only the loss of the father but, in an important way, the loss of the mother: "My mother never recovered emotionally. Though she lived for over thirty years more, and suffered other bitter losses, she never stopped blaming herself. She saw this as her failure to save his life" (186–87). No doubt Welty regards her mother's action as courageous, but she also reveals another's show of courage in this scene. It is embodied in the gaze of the daughter onlooker, who is determined to *see*. Wrenchingly painful, the moment tests the onlooker's capacity for looking at life and death *whole*. Such intimate moments, even those "longed for, sudden, or even painful," as Dawn Trouard has remarked, lead to a release of power "latent in the individual." For the writer, then, the exercise of power takes the form of "symbol, act, and legacy" (x).

In *The Optimist's Daughter* Welty draws heavily upon much of the autobiographical content central to the memoir. The adult daughter remembers the parents' naming themselves the "optimist" (father) and the "pessimist" (mother), just as she describes in *One Writer's Beginnings*. In the novel it is the memory of the mother's death that is haunting. Suffering from blindness and a stroke, she says to Laurel: "You could have saved your mother's life. But you stood by and wouldn't intervene. I despair for you" (*Optimist's* 975). Laurel could not have saved her mother's life, nor could Welty have saved her father, given the medical practice of 1931. But the knowledge of one's limits does not lessen the regret, nor even the guilt, for one's impotence in facing mortality. There is a compensation for Welty, however, gazing upon the unwelcome realism of the scene, despite the painful intensity of the moment. She discovers the courage of the onlooker, which matches the heroism of intervention. Both are passionate responses to life, both are exposures to "risk." Further, when passionate observation is carried to the storytelling art, it is regenerative, both of what has been seen and known and what it instructs the artist to look for in the future. "It seems to me, writing of my parents now in my seventies, that I see continuities in their lives that weren't visible to me when they were living," she writes, and then asks, "Could it be because I can better see their lives—or any lives I know—today because I am a fiction writer?" Thus, the gains of the writing life are not just the fulfillment from the joy of writing, that practice of the art for itself. For Welty, writing fiction has developed her capacity for understanding what she sees, "an abiding respect for the unknown in a human lifetime and a sense of where to look for the threads, how to follow, how to connect, how to find in the thick of the tangle what clear line persists. The strands are all there: to the memory nothing is ever really lost" (933).

One Writer's Beginnings bears witness to an extraordinary memory. Welty returned to family photographs to jog her memory from time to time, but the detail of the narrative sequences that she recounts is extensive and vivid. There are the "talk" of her mother's friends, the play with her brothers, a talkative sewing woman, a baby's death, memorable school teachers like Miss Duling, visits to the library, her father's office, conversation around the dining table, visiting evangelists, the movies that she saw, extended descriptions of the automobile travel and the visits with family in West Virginia and Ohio, cross country train trips, college life in Mississippi and Wisconsin, the friendly support of her agent Diarmuid Russell and editor John Woodburn, and some commentary late in the book on her fiction. An overarching theme that she iterates throughout is the confluence of her beginnings—sensory, emotional, intellectual—and the later life experience and writing career that lay ahead. Her characters are not portraits of living models, she writes, but "attached to them are what I've borrowed, perhaps unconsciously, bit by bit, of persons I have seen or noticed or remembered in the flesh—a cast of countenance here, a manner of walking there, that jump to the visualizing mind when a story is underway." She adds in parentheses her friend Elizabeth Bowen's dictum that "physical detail cannot be invented. It can only be chosen" (944).

Welty's power of attentive observation gave her a trove of material for her writing. She gives ample evidence of parental and classroom lessons in *paying attention*. No reader can escape the conclusion that she was deeply schooled in paying attention. Recently, a prominent scientist, Nobel laureate Eric Kandel, has suggested a physiological connection between the unconscious processing of sensory information and memory. He states in *In Search of Memory: The Emergence of a New Science of the Mind* that one of the questions that most interests him is "how conscious attention guides the mechanisms in the brain that stabilize memory. . . . I am much taken by Crick and Koch's argument," he writes, "that selective attention is not only essential in its own right but also one of the royal roads to consciousness" (424). Welty would likely describe the relation of attentiveness to consciousness as the necessary link of seeing to writing.

At the conclusion of *One Writer's Beginnings*, Welty parses the narrative she has delivered to her Harvard audience and her later readers with a meditation upon the nature of memory. This, her approach to intellectualizing the nature and "problems" of autobiographical writing, is more oblique and more probing than the comments often made by authors of life narratives—that their memory may be weak or flawed. She never assumes or proposes that one can recreate the past in prose or memory. What is recounted is always transformed by the imagination of the writing autobiographer. She sees from the window of the present moment, formed as it has been by all that has passed before. She calls this merging of the present and the past the "greatest confluence of all." It "makes up the human memory—the individual human memory." One infers that memory is almost, perhaps entirely, congruent with identity. Individual agency, subjectivity, is enacted upon the foundation of memory. Welty implies this attribution in her claim that her memory "is the treasure most dearly regarded by me, in my life and in my work as a writer." Her passionate observations may have recorded moments past in the long-term memory bank, but when they are revisited, they are *re-imagined*, filtered through the present moment of their recall. This is Welty's "confluence." She writes, "The memory is a living thing—it too is in transit. But during its moment, all that is remembered joins, and lives—the old and the young, the past and the present, the living and the dead" (948).

Because writings—fiction or life narratives—or even everyday oral and written and gestural expressions of the self issue from memory, are enacted in the moment and expose the self's integrity and credibility, what is called for in the writer is an independent truth teller's courage. Welty speaks of having been "shy physically" and reticent about rushing into relationships, suggesting that she feared exposure. "Not rushing headlong, though I may have wanted to, but beginning to write stories about people, I drew near slowly; noting and guessing, apprehending, hoping, drawing my eventual conclusions out of my own heart. I *did* venture closer to where I wanted to go. As time and my imagination led me on, I did plunge" (862–63). Again and again, in this memoir and in essays on the writing of fiction, Welty describes the act of artistic creation as a fall, a leap, a jump, a separation from secure, familiar terrain, and then a coming back, restored.[2]

She gives one of her earliest illustrations of "plunging" in a vignette set in West Virginia. Her recollection of the scene, midway in the middle lecture "Learning to See," opens with her memory of the water, the cold, fern-scented well water that she drinks with the common dipper. Like Helen Keller at the well, Welty begins to sense a world different from the sheltered one she has known, and she describes a swelling sense of independence, a sense of daring. "What I felt I'd come here to do," she writes, "was something on my own." Walking down a mountain path with her mother and uncles, she decides (while safely within the confines of family) "to take off on a superior track" she saw for herself. She strikes out with derring-do, and then, "the next moment I was flying . . . straight down, . . . falling, rolling and tumbling, gathering dust and leaves in my clothes and hair, and I could hear a long rip coming in my skirt." She looks upward to mother and uncles, who were laughing at her. She got to her feet, rescued by one of the uncles, and rode on his shoulders back to the house. Composing this anecdote from the vantage of over sixty years, she concludes it with a wry admission—she is sure only of the risky leap she took, less sure how to figure the outcome. "I was aloft up there, hanging my head or holding it up—I can't be sure now" (900). The image surely harkens to the magnificent figural metaphor that closes *The Golden Apples* (1949), Botticelli's Perseus holding aloft the head of Medusa, a symbol suggesting a confluence of vaunter and victim, of daring and the cost of daring. Welty's West Virginia memory, still alive and available to her years afterward, is reinterpreted as a metaphor of the daring spirit that the aging author identifies as essential to the writer. She concludes in the text's last sentence that she is a "writer who came of a sheltered life," but as she has imaged in an expressive childhood scene, "a sheltered life can be a daring life as well. For all serious daring starts from within" (948).

One Writer's Beginnings is as much a serious literary project as any other Welty wrote. Its title exactly explains its focus, which is upon the shaping influences of her early years and the subsequent manifestations of the consequences for the writer she became. In the third section of the book, she discusses her writing as the active employment of the early preparation. She comments on such matters as the initial impulse for some of the stories, the relation of characterization to experience drawn from her own life, and her use of Greek mythology in *The Golden Apples*. She calls "Death of a Traveling Salesman," published in 1936, her first good story. She reads/quotes a long opening passage from the autobiographical "A Memory," and she speaks of "A Still Moment" as a fantasy set in early Mississippi history. Of the characters in *The Golden Apples,* she finds a personal connection to the piano teacher, Miss Eckhart, who "came from me," she writes. "What I have put into her is my passion for my own life work, my own art. Exposing yourself to risk is a truth Miss Eckhart and I had in common. . . . In the making of her character out of my most inward and most deeply feeling self, I would say I have found my voice in my fiction" (945–46).

Anticipating the final paragraphs of the memoir, Welty turns to *The Optimist's Daughter,* quoting from the last scenes in the novel. The action portrayed is that of Laurel Hand, recalling, reinterpreting her youthful marriage and the early wartime death of her husband Phil, her return home having brought a different perspective to the memory. One thinks of the scene as exemplifying the autobiographical stance that Welty maintains as she faces her Harvard audience. It is in remembering, and in subjecting the memory to new discovery, new understanding, new wisdom from the life lived in the interim, that one can tell the truest story.

When Eudora Welty's first collection of short stories, *A Curtain of Green,* was published in 1941, there was an aspiring young writer who took notice of this new Mississippi voice and invited her to speak to her student writing group at Belhaven College, the Presbyterian women's college that stood just across the street from Welty's Pinehurst Street residence in Jackson. The student who shyly knocked on the door to issue the invitation was an English major from Carrollton, Mississippi, Elizabeth Spencer. The two women would form a friendship they maintained until Welty's death in 2001. In the memoir Spencer published in 1998, *Landscapes of the Heart,* her affection and respect for her longtime friend are evident in the recounting of many visits and conversations over the years, occasions that offered them mutual encouragement and support.

Like Welty, Spencer was in her seventies when she wrote most of her autobiography, though she incorporates material from earlier essays and stories. The organization and focus of *Landscapes* suggest evidence of the novelist's attention to form, to a structure that brings the disparate parts into a pattern. The text is considerably longer than Welty's, and it reaches from childhood nearly to the years of the composing author's life, ending with her move to North Carolina at age sixty-five. Although Spencer develops some discernible life plots, she does not direct the narrative to a central purpose, as we have seen in texts by Welty, or in those by Lumpkin and Smith. The chronological sequence, which provides an implicit connecting thread typical of most life narratives, is segmented into three parts, each focusing upon a physical and emotional progression outward from a circumscribed beginning. It is a familiar pattern in autobiographies, but Spencer employs the spatial metaphor with unusual explicitness, invoking place designations in the book's title and the titles of the three main parts—and developing these not only as settings but as symbols that forecast, or express, a writer's life.

The authorial voice narrating the text is that of a viewer who stands at great distance from the child Elizabeth in the opening, "at age twelve, a slight little girl all but enveloped in overalls, a long-sleeved white shirt, and a big straw hat. . . ." From her writer's desk, she chooses the details that presage the independence, curiosity, and self-confidence that are the professional writer's traits. Here again, as in all autobiographies, we witness the circularity of the self writing the self recollected. It is useful to keep in mind the distinction in the text between the "autobiographical act" and the "autobiographical subject," so as to take full account of Spencer's deliberateness in her selection of life material for the memoir, her composition of landscapes that reveal the contours of her life journey *as a writer.* She chooses not to title the work an autobiography, presumably because she determines not to present an explicit portrait of the woman within; rather, she writes a "memoir," a novelistic construction of places, people, and events that conveys a world exterior to the self but that implicitly composes a life story. One aspect of the memoiristic approach is the inclusion of an index, a feature not typically found in life narratives but always welcome to literary scholars who embark on critical studies. One of the most telling features of this narrative, and integral to its development, is Spencer's composition of the southern landscape of her youth and the purposes to which she puts it in providing a credible life plot. The most significant elements of the plot are that she grew up in the South, began to write a fiction firmly located in her region, and incurred the censure of her father and, to as lesser extent, her mother, both of whom wanted a traditional life for their only daughter—wanted her to marry, have children, and maintain the respectability of the family. For a time she tried to negotiate a truce between warring factions—her family and her own determination to establish an autonomous life and a career as a writer. In the summer of 1955, she returned to the South following a sojourn in Europe, where she had largely completed work on her third book. She still hoped to make her home in the South, which in one way or another, she anticipated, would form the societal subjects of the fiction she would write.

In her introduction to a 1965 edition of *The Voice at the Back Door,* Spencer described this period of her life as a time of hope not only for her own personal prospects of accommodation with family but for the white South's prospects of peacefully acknowledging African American claims for respect and social justice. In many ways this political novel, first published in 1956 and directly addressing issues of racial oppression in a Mississippi small town, anticipated momentous change that lay just ahead for her and for the South. The 1955 visit home coincided with the social tension attendant upon the recent *Brown v. Board of Education* ruling and, even more volatile, the murder of Emmett Till, a fourteen-year-old African American boy from Chicago who had come to visit relatives living only a few miles from Carrollton. Spencer's visit ended in an explosive argument with her father about race, politics, and ultimately her own life choices. For Spencer, it was an experience of betrayal.

Rejected by a father and a fatherland that she regarded as having inculcated the very values that animated her political views—values disavowed when race relations were confronted—she felt exiled from the South she had known. Ultimately, she completed and published the novel, returned to Europe and married an Englishman, settled in Canada for many years, and published a shelf of fiction, none of which, however, would again portray the volatile politics of Mississippi hill country and Delta. In this memoir, Spencer depicts a landscape of the heart that is available to a fond, even nostalgic re-creation, a theme reviewer Mark Childress hardly gets beyond in his comments in the *New York Times Book Review;* however, her active memory of the land of her youth, the living connection with it that is alive and working in this book about her beginnings and life as a writer, is a memory informed by injury and loss.

The opening sketch of the memoir, depicting the twelve-year-old Elizabeth, boyishly prepubescent, inscribes a telling and recurrent image. The "Riding Out," emblematic of the life that lies ahead, forecasts an independence and perseverance that she will demand of herself and will demonstrate throughout her life. In the girlhood moment that Spencer portrays as the book's foundational image, the girl Elizabeth makes her way from the patriarchal Spencer household in Carrollton to the matriarchal home, a place that offers, among many bustling activities, lively book talk by uncles who are enthusiastic readers and talkers. As she departs, she is instructed to tell anyone who might stop her that she is "Mr. Spencer's daughter" and that her uncle is Joe McCain. She writes that she supposed even as a twelve-year old that there might be someone who would fail to be impressed—or daunted—by the announcement she was Luther Spencer's daughter or Joe McCain's niece. But clearly for her, the family connection conferred weighty status, protecting and constraining. In Carroll County she was a Spencer, with a mother who was a McCain. The young protagonist is a southern girl setting forth under the patriarchal protectorate of her respectable white Presbyterian family in 1930s Mississippi.

What follows this opening sketch is a series of descriptions that include familiar scenes of southern agrarian and small town life—family dinners, church going, porch talk, black workers in the field and kitchen, storytelling of the Civil War and other bygone days. She was witness to a way of life, she implies to her reader, that was not just a stereotypical pattern of white southern social mores but one individually hers, one she can describe factually, accurately, because she was there and alive to the nuances of her experience.

In the first section of the memoir, entitled "The Circled World," Spencer incorporates two autobiographical stories previously published, "The Day Before" and " A Christian Education." In both stories Spencer focuses upon her childhood encounter with the central values of her familial and community culture: education and religion. The central revelation embodied by the stories, however, turns upon the discovery that the values are anything but simplistic and unitary. "The Day Before" refers to the day before Elizabeth's first day of school, a major transition that is ritualized by the family and celebrated with gifts and encouragement by gracious elderly neighbors, Miss Henrietta Welch and Mr. Dave and Mr. Dick Welch (actual names that replaced earlier fictional versions). What Elizabeth learns in the story's compressed interim between home life and school yard is that the Welches' home, with its books and Airedale dogs and milk glass boxes with secret compartments, points to a world larger, more various, and eccentric than hers, one promising and fascinating. To be sure, there is also voiced a narrow, provincial view, that of a judgmental older child who is rejecting and contemptuous of the Welches, announcing to Elizabeth that "they feed their old dogs out of Havilland china." But Spencer implies that, on balance, the education Carrollton offered her proved to be as wide as she had sensibility to grasp; it was a place in which she learned that there were many ways to live.

Similarly, "A Christian Education" turns upon the child Elizabeth's apprehension of religion's uncertainties. The stern, rigid prohibitions of the Spencer household regarding Sunday activity have seemed absolute until one day, left in the care of her grandfather when her parents were called away by the death of a cousin, Spencer becomes a confederate with him in defying the taboo against walking to town and purchasing an ice cream cone. Her grandfather's authority as a family elder and a good man respected by everyone is unquestionable, and when he calmly acknowledges his part in the proscribed venture, offering neither apology nor explanation, Elizabeth comes to understand that there are many different ways of believing. "After this, though all went on as before, there was nothing much my parents could finally do about the church and me. They could lock the barn door, but the bright horse of freedom was already loose in my world" (22).

In the early section of the book, Spencer, native daughter, gives witness to her knowledge of a southern homeland rich and various. She wants her reader to understand that this place not only gave her a store of sensory experience but an intellectual grounding that led directly to the writer she would become. The autobiographical self here is not one who rebels *against* so much as one who *fulfills* the lessons of youth. Spencer insists, for example, the reader understand that the literary culture surrounding her was a casual, natural milieu and that the writers her McCain uncles recalled and discussed—Kipling, Scott, Stevenson, Macaulay, Browning—were familiar, not distant presences. "Stuck away in trunks in the attic in Carrollton," she writes, "school notebooks I came across when exploring were full not only of class notes but also of original verses that spoke of heroism and daring deeds. Their Latin texts with Caesar's Gallic Wars were in our bookshelves" (14). The older McCain uncles, Bill and Sidney, invoked not only a literary disposition for the heroic but an affinity for a world well beyond Carrollton, having attended West Point and Annapolis and then pursued distinguished military careers. But it is their love of books that Spencer dwells upon in the pages devoted to memories of Teoc, the McCain plantation.

Indeed, she returns again and again to the presence of books in her childhood. She writes that at Teoc "the shelves were solid in their Dickens and Thackeray and Jane Austen and Hawthorne." She speaks of *Moby Dick,* her older brother's favorite, and of *Les Miserables,* which her uncle Joe McCain insisted she read from cover to cover. She recalls rainy day conversations with him about the comparative merits of Hugo and Dickens, about his liking Darcy in *Pride and Prejudice* and thinking Becky Sharp in *Vanity Fair* "a mean little devil." Predictably, there is a memorable teacher, Miss Willie Kenan, whose encouragement and example anticipate the literary life that will eventually be Spencer's. In short, Spencer constructs a narrative of a writer's beginnings with the steady forward momentum of inevitability. Midway into the memoir, she opens a chapter with the sentence, "Carrollton should have had a great poet," and sketches then the life of a distant cousin, Lawrence Olson, a remarkable man whose giftedness marked him from youth. Despite his lifelong regard for Carrollton, for the physical beauty of the town and the countryside, and despite his early achievements as a poet and musician, World War II would lead him away from Carrollton and from a poet's life to a study of Japanese and to a career as an analyst of Japanese culture and politics. "A brilliance like his should have been the town's pride," Spencer notes, and then concludes, "I never heard that it was" (143). Olson's story is of course a precursor of Spencer's own experience of the town's—and the family's—disregard of literary achievement.

Where does the blame lie, then, Spencer asks, for missed opportunity and recognition denied in a town that demonstrably equipped its young for a writer's life as well as for any other? In Olson's case, perhaps the question cannot be bluntly pursued, for "despite his constant presence in our midst," she concedes, despite "the stamp club, the storytelling, and the music, there were never many points of meeting between the town and him, so nothing on either side really took place or was there for praise or blame" (143). But for Luther Spencer's daughter? Joe McCain's niece? Here lie deep injury and a grievance that calls out for adjudication. Spencer portrays a daughter who tries time and again to win the father's approval, a dutiful, studious, creative girl whose efforts are largely ignored and, in later years, whose literary ambitions are scorned. Recalling a period of her adolescence, Spencer writes: "My father was worried about money. My mother, I think, was worried about me. In the summer, I kept writing stories. . . . I showed things I had written to my mother and sometimes to one of my jollier uncles, but it would be many years before I found any real community, or even knew that such a thing existed" (116).

The thread of memory still actively connecting Spencer the autobiographer to the landscape of a rejecting father and an oblivious Carrollton resurrects or reinvigorates a lively pain. Here is a father's ghost that haunts still the spirit of a daughter who has had a successful life, marked by a long happy marriage and a career filled with achievement. Her self-composure, established at such cost of determination and painful separation, is revealed in this memoir as tenuous still, requiring an unremitting defense against the father's threatening will to control, his scorn of her ambition to be a writer, his parsimonious withholding of financial support (and doing so in galling contrast to his praise and financial support of her brother), his rejection of her political independence, his attack upon her every effort to pursue a life of the mind—his attempt to subvert her autonomy as an adult human being.

It is clearly her father who dominates Spencer's recollections of childhood. He calls to mind Francis Thomas Glasgow, that business-minded Presbyterian and domineering Victorian father Glasgow portrays in *The Woman Within*. Like the elder Glasgow, Luther Spencer occupies the seat of household patriarch, a man of certainties and ready opinions. In this text, the Spencers' provincialism exhibits a marked contrast to the McCains' civility and more cosmopolitan outlook. In fact, in her depiction of her father and his brothers, the memoirist composes figures in a style reminiscent of Honoré Daumier's satirical figures or Dickensian characters, as Spencer herself notes. "Consider those four men," she writes, "the Spencer fathers. If the McCains resembled Highland Scots, it would take Dickens to describe the Spencers. They had sharp noses and double chins, amiable faces but strong opinions." Unlike the McCains, "who thrived on exchange, not a one of them ever listened to the other." The Spencers' talk was much like "the chanting of some ritual in Latin, or a bunch of frogs on the edge of a pond. . . . Some voices would rise above others for a moment, then fall back into the chorus. Only one thing you could be sure of: No one ever agreed with anyone else" (54–55). A few paragraphs later she remarks upon the affection the Spencer sons all bore their mother, but the tone is querulous, edging toward what seems a mimicry of her father's language: "The main quality he admired in women was sweetness, and he always said she was the sweetest woman he had ever known" (55). Spencer recalls her father's reverent remembering of his dying mother—tubercular, dependent, resignedly submissive. The youngest son, he had accompanied her on a trip west, an unforgettable trip for him, in an effort to restore her health. "At age eighty-eight, a lone widower, mentally crippled by a series of strokes," Spencer writes, "he used to recount to me for the thousandth time how he had brushed her long hair for her, holding it over his arm until every tangle was gone, and then helped her pin it up" (56–57).

The eroticizing or fetishizing of female submissiveness is of course endemic in southern culture and literature. The coercion or appropriation of the female

body to supply the culture with its rationale for male hierarchies and dominance has been a central theme in southern cultural critiques for the past century. William Faulkner, Richard Wright, W. J. Cash, Lillian Smith, and many
others have focused attention upon the pedestaled white lady whose protection
presumably stimulated the white male libido and fostered a warrior mental-
ity. Perversely, and all too typically, the libido often worked out its gratification
upon black bodies, sexually exploiting black women and violently controlling
black men.

These connections between the will to dominance and the subjugation of
women are clearly understood by the Elizabeth Spencer who writes this book,
although her exegesis is dramatic and oblique rather than discursive or argumentative. Her tone is like that of one who is still traveling in hostile territory,
wary and camouflaged. She is still trying to understand, if not declare truce
with, the father who again and again undermines her with mixed signals, putting her in a nearly paralyzing double bind. One might argue that it seems characteristically southern of Spencer to so frequently cast her analysis of the South
and her southern roots in ambiguous, problematical images. She describes as
her earliest memory, for example, her father's encouraging words (or perhaps
his command), "Walk to me," words to a girl toddler that urge her first independent steps and bring approving applause from the grownups. But as a grownup
herself, deciding to pursue her writing full time, she meets strenuous resistance
from her father. He argues that she shouldn't give up her newspaper job because
"writing was too chancy and difficult." Further, should she fail (that is, "when
she fails"), she would have a hard time finding another job. Recounting the episode, Spencer adds, "I couldn't think like that," and then she obliquely continues: "I knew he had wanted me to accept the first marriage proposal that had
come my way, at age seventeen or thereabouts. I thought for a long time that he
was considering my happiness when he favored the match, though both Mimi
[Spencer's mother] and I told him I was not in love with that eager young man.
'What does he do?' Dad demanded. 'He wants to write,' I said. 'That boy's got
too much sense to *write*.' Dad's judgments were always ready." (194)

What calls out for notice here is the pair of connected issues that form the
link between Spencer's lived life and the authored life she chooses to narrate
in this memoir. She is a female who has been reared by a willful, determined,
meritocratic father whose model of ambition, perseverance, and ingenuity are
denied her because of her sex. She is a writer reared in a community of imaginative, literate, book-loving adults whose support of her literary ambitions are
kind but half-hearted in the case of her mother and other family members, and

angrily dismissive in the case of a father who is ever mindful of keeping his costs—and losses—low.

It is true that the dilemma Spencer faces in her youth and young adulthood is hardly atypical; in fact, it typifies the process of separation experienced by most individuals in modern western cultures. We have a shelf of books, from Freud to Lacan, to tell us so. But I would maintain that Spencer's is a particularly intense instance, owing perhaps to the thick residue of Victorian traditionalism composing the culture in which she came of age: white, elite, deep South, small town, Protestant fundamentalist, and female in a patriarchal society. Reading this life narrative, one has to feel deep regret, even despair, at a cultural system that so coerced and finally failed its most intellectually gifted daughters.

For example, when it came time to make college plans, Spencer wanted to attend the University of Mississippi, where her brother had gone, but she was sent to Belhaven College, the Presbyterian women's school that offered heavy doses of religion and training in manners for proper young ladies. Whereas one might expect the cultural premium to have been set upon braininess and righteousness, it was the "cute girls" and "Southern belles" who were admired, the ways of whom, writes Spencer, were a "blind alley" to her. "But what else did any girl in that place and time have to wish for?" she asks. At a time in young adulthood when one might expect a gathering and consolidating of the ego, a period of discovering or possessing one's subjectivity, Spencer reports experiencing herself as "an intriguing mystery," but mostly someone she "had rather not think about" (169).

The stumbling journey toward the writerly self that Spencer describes is marked at every crucial turning point by rejection from the father, followed by a period of self-doubt or illness, and finally a determined but crippled effort to move beyond the father's sphere. The publication of her first novel, *Fire in the Morning* (1948), produced "a family crisis." Angry and ashamed that she would use situations and characters suggestive of Carrollton figures, mortified that she wrote phrases like "God damn" and "Go to hell," her parents were full of denunciation. She remarks that when she called to tell them of the contract with Dodd, Mead to publish the book, the "news did not excite them. They had thought I might be engaged" (197). Looking back upon the often-troubled relation with them, Spencer identifies the publication of the book as marking "a rift in my parents' thinking about me that was never entirely mended" (200).

In her account of the years of effort leading to the publication of *Fire in the Morning,* Spencer writes of several supportive friendships in Nashville, where she was working and writing, and one significant male mentor who, like her father, gave anxiety-producing mixed signals. Her professor at Vanderbilt, Donald Davidson, one of the twelve Agrarians of *I'll Take My Stand* and a die-hard believer in southern exceptionalism, advises her she "would do better to get married" than pursue a writing career, though he does eventually congratulate her on "making the plunge" (196). Deeply ideological in his passionate defense of southern culture, even though, as critic Michael Kreyling has recently noted, he was often quite inexact in articulating what he regarded as essential southernness (8–18), Davidson impressed upon Spencer during her tenure as a graduate student—and in the several years following when she was laboring over her early writing—the importance of centering her vision upon her southern roots. Thoroughly imbibing Davidson's view, she fully expected to locate herself and her writing subjects in the South, only partially appreciating then the burden that southern traditionalism placed upon an ambitious woman. The inexorable recognition of such a burden would come, however, and with it the painful sense that leaving the South, her "home and native land" was inevitable.

After completing her master's degree at Vanderbilt, Spencer taught briefly at a junior college in Senatobia, Mississippi, where she became friends with the daughter of the college president. Spencer writes that this young woman, "more than I, was leaning outward. She revealed in confidence that though she valued family ties, she was acquiring a real dislike for Mississippi, its narrow outlook, its ignorant disdain of a larger world, the poverty of cultural interest. Many people were charming, many were endlessly laughable, but to her it was not the world she wanted to live in" (187). When the friend left a year later for work in Washington, D.C., Spencer clearly took note, though she struggled with conflicting impulses. "I did dare to hope for publication of my work, to win through to a writing life," but the ambition was coming to seem better served by leaving than staying. "And yet, to leave my home and native land seemed a sort of betrayal" (188). One may infer that such a move also represented a repudiation of Davidson's teachings—and her father's expectations that she would live a traditional life not far from Carrollton.

One is inevitably reminded in reading *Landscapes of the Heart* of the recurrent portrayals in Spencer's fiction of vexing, painful, often even frightening male figures who seek to control the lives of central female figures. Without undertaking autobiographical readings of the fiction, one can hardly fail to register in the memoir a pattern of intimidating male relationships that are mirrored in many of the novels. Even Spencer's chief supporter in sponsoring the publication of *Fire in the Morning,* David Clay, the Dodd, Mead editor who shepherded the manuscript through publication and would continue as a trusted counselor and agent through the publication of *The Light in the Piazza,* would eventually attempt to dominate her professional career, growing "crazier and crazier" as she once described him in an interview with Terry Roberts (*Conversations* 217). The figure of a mentor turned Minotaur, as I characterized the threatening male presence in my earlier study, *Elizabeth Spencer* (82–87), is especially evident in the 1965 *Knights and Dragons* and the 1967 *No Place for an Angel.* In the memoir we find antecedents of fictional male characters who express an ever-present masculine will to dominance that threatens female autonomy.

The early confrontations with her father, the ambivalent encouragement from Davidson, and, years later, the break with David Clay prove inevitably distressing and enervating. In spring 1953 as Spencer is concluding a year of teaching at the University of Mississippi, overworking to keep up her writing and depressed over the death of her beloved uncle, Joe McCain, she pays a physical price (with origins in psychic stress, one is led to suppose) for what her parents deem misguided, selfish ambition. She suffers a long, life-threatening illness that leaves her debilitated for months. Only when she leaves for Europe the following October with a Guggenheim grant in hand does she begin finally to recover her vitality and health.

Later, at the time of the hopeful 1955 homecoming from her two-year stay in Italy, the blowup with her father leads to a final turning away from Carrollton, the father, and the South and toward an altogether different life from the one she had imagined for herself. She recounts this intensely anticipated "homecoming" and her traumatic leave-taking in the last section of the memoir, like a key that answers a riddle posed by suspenseful contradictions. In so structuring the memoir, Spencer composes a narrative that offers artful coherence and emotional credibility. In her effort to tell her story of her relationship to the father—and fatherland—we see that she is asking autobiographical questions that call not only for interpretation of the self but for analysis of larger structures of society and their shaping influence upon an individual.

What Spencer reveals at the center of the conflict is the extent to which the father's selfhood/subjectivity (that of Luther Spencer, Donald Davidson, or indeed of the whole psychic structure of southern patriarchy) is founded upon her submissiveness, her self-sacrifice of autonomy, separateness, subjectivity. Her portrait of the gender relations that blocked autonomy and ambition, an insight with origins in her early experience but fully realized in this 1998 memoir, mirrors the observations of Anne Goodwyn Jones, Susan Donaldson, Michael Kreyling, and many other literary critics who have noted the male-centered construction of the "Southern Literary Renascence." Spencer portrays clearly in *Landscapes of the Heart* how deeply her experience and vision were at odds with southern white male traditionalism—familial and literary. She recounts the disheartening rejection and subsequent self-exile: "I was brought up short in every passing comment," she writes. "I might as well have been eight years old and told to go sit in a corner. Italy, an unimportant place full of Eye-talians, should not be mentioned. My work was not discussed" (287). After only two days, her blunt survey of her situation conduced to an inescapable conclusion: "*You don't belong down here anymore*" (291). Her father gave her $2,000 to go to New York, where she would complete *The Voice at the Back Door,* but he made it clear that after the money was gone, no more would be forthcoming.

The breach with the father was the ultimate testing of the young questing Elizabeth. In many ways her rite of passage is quite male-denominated. She must do battle with the male chiefs to make her own way. As Spencer herself wryly observes, even her Vanderbilt mentor Davidson never spoke to her again after *Voice at the Back Door* was published (184). In his eyes its exposure of the political structures of white supremacy, undergirded by acts of corruption and lawlessness, constituted a betrayal of the South, if not an upstart rebellion. Spencer published the novel in 1956; among American novels, it is one of the most discerning of local, county politics in the South of that era. Afterward, her work would turn away from the places of her youth. As she said of the father's $2,000, "I didn't myself know what I would do when it was spent, but whatever it was, it would be done without further reference to Luther Spencer or to Carrollton, Mississippi" (291). Like Lillian Smith, Katherine DuPre Lumpkin, and many other independent-minded southern women before her, Elizabeth Spencer had come to know the utter irreconcilability of female independence and the structure of white patriarchal supremacy that defined so much of southern society. The long-established roots of a system stretching back to the antebellum South and founded upon biblical grounds have been succinctly described by historian Eugene Genovese: "The justification of black slavery derived from the general justification of slavery, regardless of race, as ordained of God, and slavery and all class stratification derived from the prior divine command that women submit to men—racial subordination derived from class subordination, which derived from gender subordination. For the mouth of the Lord hath spoken it"(127).

As a youth, Spencer had grown up in a culture not only traditional in respect to family and religion but also bourgeois in its emphasis upon individual ambition and achievement. Equipped to pursue the writing career she sought, she discovered as an adult female a shift in this culture's gender expectations and its tolerance for female ambition. Her family's attitude, her place, her time, and her gender all militated against her reconciling or even negotiating the contradictions that came to be so clearly manifest in 1955. To a significant extent, she resolved her dilemma by shedding her "southernness." Faced with her family's censure, which to her crystallized the region's censure, she felt blocked in her effort to construct a southern imaginary congruent with her experience of gender and race in the South.

In their introduction to *Haunted Bodies: Gender and Southern Texts,* Anne Goodwyn Jones and Susan V. Donaldson describe the composite portrait of gender and southern literary history that emerges when one looks beyond the "monolithic images of the conservative, hide-bound, isolated South that we have inherited" (16). Rejecting such "monolithic images," which to her represented a false inheritance, Spencer turned away from the South literally and imaginatively. In *Self and Community in the Fiction of Elizabeth Spencer,* Terry Roberts has discussed Spencer's literary development after 1960 as representing a move toward "a different sort of 'southern' writer" (135). This shift, of course, is precisely the gesture toward an expanded and redefined image of southern regionality that Jones and Donaldson describe. It was in many ways an energizing move for Spencer, but this memoir reveals how deeply and pervasively felt has been her sense of rupture and loss.

The price Spencer paid for freeing herself from the binding constraints of a culture she found increasingly hostile was the loss of her sense of connection with her richest imaginative material—the storehouse of memories directly linked to her growing up in Mississippi. Her *Marilee* stories are comic mediations, benevolent mediations, upon what life might have been for an Elizabeth Spencer who gave in and so held on to family and homeland. In several of the interviews collected in *Conversations with Elizabeth Spencer,* as well as in *Landscapes of the Heart,* Spencer mentions Henry James's "The Jolly Corner," as if intrigued by the thought of what an alternate adult life in the South might have been like for her (200). There are also occasional intimations of regret, even guilt and self-recrimination at having perhaps capitulated to the separation from home because of weakness or not having "loved enough." At the end of "The Day Before" the autobiographical narrator, writing of her early leave-taking for school but metaphorically also of her later psychic immigration from family and Carrollton, puzzles over the contradiction between loving and leaving home: "having once started to lose them a little, I couldn't make the stream run backward, I lost them completely in the end. The little guilt, the little sadness I felt sometimes, was it because I hadn't really wanted them enough, held on tightly enough, had not, in other words, loved them?" (104).

In novels and stories after the mid-1950s, Spencer largely gives up subjects of racial conflict and settings of small towns in the throes of change, a landscape she thinks of as "southern." Among later works set in the South—*The Snare,* "The Business Venture," *The Salt Line,* and *The Night Travellers*—one finds a markedly different locale from that of the early novels. Much of this later fiction, like that placed outside the South, turns toward cosmopolitan settings and characters threatened with rootlessness and psychic vulnerability—wounded women struggling to free themselves from dominating, destructive men and moving with courage toward self-possession—Margaret Johnson in *Light in the Piazza,* Martha Ingram in *Knights and Dragons,* Catherine Sasser in *No Place for an Angel,* Julia Garrett in *The Snare,* Mary Kerr Harbison in *The Night Travellers.*

Even women like Eileen Waybridge in "The Business Venture," from *Jack of Diamonds and Other Stories,* a "twenty-eight-year-old attractive married woman with a family and friends and a nice house in Tyler, Mississippi," is caught in a "spinning world." In transit, bridging her way intuitively, she is also "spinning along with it" (156). But as Spencer writes near the conclusion of *Landscapes of the Heart,* "a spinning center that builds its own force is not sufficient to meet the human need for meaning" (326–27). Calling Eudora Welty's *Losing Battles* and William Faulkner's *The Reivers* the last "distinctly and thoroughly Southern novels," Spencer locates the grounding, "centralizing knowledge" of her fiction in "the human and humane," in "decency," and "the values of love, fairness, and justice." Such knowledge, abstracted and distilled from life experience, comes at some remove, however, from personal memory and sensory knowledge of the physical world, the knowledge we most deeply possess from our impressionable beginnings.

The memory that stands most revealed in *Landscapes of the Heart* is that of a separation from the father and home, a loss regarded by the authorial Spencer as inevitable, a fortunate banishment in some regards for it proved to be a legitimation of the courage and determination that she would draw upon throughout her career. And there was much in the writing life that has brought many satisfactions, not only in the success of her fiction, the awards and recognition, but in the many friendships and pleasurable encounters, especially the literary ones, along the way. There are the O. Henry Awards, election to the American Academy and Institute of Arts and Letters, honorary degrees, and countless invitations to read at literary conferences and university campuses. She writes of the early support of Stark Young and Robert Penn Warren, of meeting Faulkner, Allen Tate, Caroline Gordon, John Crowe Ransom, Karl Shapiro, and Saul Bellow. There are visits from Welty, Katherine Anne Porter, and Elizabeth Bowen, a trip through Italy with Alberto Moravia and others, and the many trips to Europe, one of which introduced her to John Rusher, the Englishman she married in 1956. There are long, productive years when she and Rusher lived in Montreal, and, finally, a southern homecoming of sorts. Encouraged by Louis Rubin, a professor at the University of North Carolina, to make their home in Chapel Hill, she and her husband decided to do so, but their move in 1986 was to a South different from the Carrollton, Mississippi, of her youth.

The last chapters of the book move away from the chronological sequence of the early years to places and episodes associated with these settings, often spanning many years: the Mississippi Gulf Coast, New York, Italy, North Carolina. These are the places where the author has lived out the writing life, a cosmopolitan literary life that has offered cultural support and congenial relationships. Finally, though, this autobiography is only partly the heroic, victory narrative of a woman who summoned the psychic strength to become the writer of her early ambitions. It is also an elegiac vindication of a woman's story of struggle for autonomy and self-possession in a male-dominated world. It is an elegy for a southern daughter who, in the remains of the day, appraises the birthright her homeland granted her—and the one that it denied.

In conclusion, I turn to a life narrative markedly different in form from most of those discussed above, Ellen Douglas's *Truth: Four Stories I Am Finally Old Enough to Tell,* published in 1998, the same year that marked the publication of Elizabeth Spencer's memoir. Ellen Douglas, the pen name of Josephine Haxton, is an exact contemporary of Spencer, both born in July 1921, in Mississippi of well-to-do white families long established in their several regions of the state. Douglas lived for some years during her youth in Louisiana, but her birth place and the home for generations of her family was Natchez, a Mississippi River town well known for its antebellum wealth, prominence, and stately mansions. She graduated from the University of Mississippi, having begun to write short stories as a student, and in 1945 she married and moved to her husband's home, Greenville, Mississippi. Another river town, it was known for its literary prominence as the home of William Alexander Percy, Walker Percy, Shelby Foote, journalist Hodding Carter, and many other writers. The mother of three sons, Douglas again took up writing fiction when her children were still young, publishing "On the Lake" in the *New Yorker* in 1961, followed by a novel, *A Family's Affairs,* the next year.

The publication of the novel occasioned Douglas's first encounter with the ethical issues involved when one makes public the personal relationships that involve others. She was surprised, and of course gratified, when she learned in 1962 not only that she had won the Houghton-Mifflin/Esquire Twenty-Fifth Anniversary Fellowship Award but that the award included a publishing contract. Having drawn from ample autobiographical matter in writing the novel, she was concerned that family members would be offended by the publication, perhaps even think her disloyal. "I had not really thought about the consequences of having put to use the lives of members of my family, my two aunts, in particular; I had really invaded their privacy," she recalls to interviewer Rick Feddersen. "I felt I had to ask them if they would mind, and of course, what that amounted to was blackmail. They were decent ladies and they wouldn't say no, particularly after I won the competition. So when I went down [to Natchez] to ask my aunts if it would be all right to publish it, they said . . . it was okay so long as they didn't have to read it and if I would use a pen name and not tell anybody who I was" (148–49). So she took her grandmother's name, Ellen, and, with her Scottish ancestry in mind, the surname Douglas.

One is reminded here of Lillian Smith's letter to her family before the publication of *Killers of the Dream* and the concern of writers generally about what kind of, and how much, exposure of the private life of others (or their own, for that matter) is ethical, appropriate, and "safe." Rawlings, of course, incurred a lengthy, debilitating lawsuit brought by her long-time friend Zelma Cason for invasion of her privacy with the publication of *Cross Creek.* Ellen Douglas is very much mindful of the conflict that exists between "keeping silent about the personal" and "truth-telling," the issue raised indirectly by Carolyn Heilbrun's response to *One Writer's Beginnings.* In *Truth: Four Stories I Am Finally Old Enough to Tell,* Douglas has waited not only upon her own maturity to see and interpret the past more wisely than her youth would have allowed, but she has waited to write until after those whose stories she tells have died, and so she is freed from the worry of giving offense. Writing in the introduction to a recent book on the ethics of life writing, John Paul Eakin observes that "in recent years, reflecting the circumstance of our relational identities, autobiographies have become increasingly *biographical,* featuring those others in our lives—parents, siblings, lovers, friends, and mentors—who have shaped us decisively" (*Ethics* 9). The self embedded in a social web of relationships is the characteristic stance of the narrators discussed in this present study. Socialized in a place and time that inculcated the practice in public presentations of referring to others, especially family and friends, in polite or at least bland or inoffensive detail, such narrators should hardly surprise a reader who finds "biographical indirection" in the lives they compose. Vexed by the absence or slippage of fact in her attempt to tell others' stories, Douglas strains for "truth," only to find when she questions others no less slipperiness of detail issuing from their grasp of their own lives.

In many ways the themes and preoccupations that Douglas addresses in this collection of four autobiographical stories—and in her fiction, essays, and interviews—touch upon the attributes common to all of the texts previously discussed, taking into account privacy considerations as well as attributes of form, voice, vagaries of memory, southern cultural influences, and justification or motive for writing a life narrative composed for a public audience. She focuses particularly upon the instability or fluidity of the memories that furnish detail for the stories we tell ourselves and others, the gap between the recounted material composed for a text—or for a story in any form—and its truth quotient. Insofar as past events and feelings exist in the human imaginary as clusters of images with meanings for us, it is inescapable that, as our experience and age modify what is relevant to our lives at any given moment, our interpretations of the past change over time. As Welty concludes at the end of *One Writer's Beginnings,* memory is a living thing. Memory yields constantly to change.

In a 2004 collection of essays entitled *Witnessing,* Douglas again confronts the limitations of the human ability to tell, or know, "the truth," constrained as we are—in seeming contradiction—by both the singleness of our vision and all the relational influences that have shaped (and perhaps misshaped) our perceptions. This later collection, in which she discusses the craft of writing and her own fiction, bears some resemblance to Glasgow's *A Certain Measure* and Welty's *The Eye of the Story,* texts with autobiographical references throughout, but more essayistic than narrative.

In *Truth* Douglas implicates the autobiographical narrator in four narratives that are focused upon others, thus portraying the self as enacted indirectly in relationships. She also portrays the self dramatically by bringing the authorial voice directly into the narrative. Frequently informing the reader of the difficulties of telling a "true story"—sketchy memory, gaps in one's knowledge, revised interpretations of past emotions and events—she employs a doubled voice, a doubled subjectivity. There are, of course, the stories the narrator tells of remembrances from the past, and then there is the ongoing story of the writer who is caught up in the self-conscious process of composing the authorial self who creates the narrator, the designated truth teller. Douglas weaves into her narrative her ploys to expose, if not elude, this inescapable "closed circuit." "Because the subject of autobiography is a self-representation and not the autobiographer her/himself, most contemporary critics describe this 'self' as a fiction," writes Leigh Gilmore in *Autobiographics:* "When we locate the pressure to tell the truth in the context of the fictive self accountable for producing truth, the problematical alliance between fact and fiction in autobiography begins to emerge" (121).

Douglas is indeed aware that in her truth telling about herself and the focal characters, Grant, Julia and Nellie, Hampton, and her nineteenth-century forebears in the final story, she displays the same characteristics of mind—memory and imagination—that inform her fiction. Her approach is a little like that of Rawlings in *Cross Creek,* leaning in the direction of fiction in its creation of scene, dialogue, and action that is contained within short story form. In the opening story, "Grant," she relates the last months of life of an uncle-in-law who had come to her house in Greenville to be cared for at a time when her sons were still young and living at home and she a busy wife running a household. But like Nick Carraway remembering Gatsby, the story is more deeply about the narrator's reinterpretation of the events of that earlier time, the empathy and understanding she brings to it in her old age. Her husband's uncle Ralph, whom she renames Grant in the story, "was a huge presence in our house, and he was family, but I didn't want to see him or to think about him." A widower and childless, he had come at their invitation when he became ill. The narrator, recalling that at first he took long walks every day, provides the lively details he likely encountered on the walks—"the humming, buzzing late-spring world, bees swarming around the honeysuckle vines on the back fence, towhees calling, flickers drilling for bugs in the bark of the pecan tree." She recalls, or imagines, that "one day he pointed out to me that a wren had built her nest in the potted fern by the side door." She confesses then, "I never joined him on these walks. I didn't have time" (9).

The lyrical paragraph anticipates the conclusion of the story, when she has come to occupy a later stage of life, one distant from the busy household, a time when she herself is needful of connection with the sensory world. Of course, she had been busy those months Grant lived in their house; that was the truth. But the story has changed, as the narrator has changed. Then, she had had to force herself to go to his room every day for ten-minute visits. "I felt the weight of my watch on my wrist and willed myself not to look at it, but I knew to the minute when I could leave." Writing years later about those days, she tells a different story: "There can be only one reason why I hated so deeply the ordeal of going back to visit with this lovely old Man. He was dying. His dying was a terrible disgrace, an embarrassment not to be endured. That's the story I could not tell. I abandoned him" (15).

There are other stories connected with the months of Grant's dying, that of the caretaker Rosalie, a beautiful woman, like an elegant lady on the wall of an Egyptian tomb, and the eerie appearance of a great hive of swarming bees on the night of Grant's death, which Rosalie attributes to the ignorance of the household about death rituals. "Any fool ought to know. You got to tell the bees immediately when somebody dies" (23). Juxtaposing events of "then" and "now," the narrator keeps before the reader the question of how much the contents of the memory recounted owe to the past, how much to the narrator's present meditation, informed by the twenty-odd years of lived experience following Grant's death. "Death," she writes, "has become, so to speak, family." The long walks she takes in the present time of the writing are the source of detail she draws upon to describe Grant's walks.

> Sometimes, in the morning, when the bees are just beginning to stir (I wake early these days, as old people so often do), I fill my coffee cup and stand listening in the kitchen. The boys are long gone now on their separate ways; the house is still, no longer breathing and swelling with their energy. I take my cup then and go out into the yard and listen to the raucous cries of the jay, the flicker's jackhammer drill, the *tchk, tchk* of the squirrels chasing each other through the high branches of the pecan tree. . . . I lay my hand against the bark and tell the bees that I, too, will die. I admonish them not to swarm, not to leave us, but to stay in their hollow in the pecan tree, to keep making for us all their golden, fragrant, dark, sweet honey. (24–25)

Douglas hovers over the illusion of a continuous, contained self and any notion of a fixed narrative of the past. The head note that she places just under the title of the story, "We are *forever* cleaning up our act," a quotation from Robert Stone's "The Reason for Stories," points up an important motive for writing one's life narrative. One reimagines, reinterprets the past so as to compose a text that prepares for and validates the character who is writing the text, as she regards herself in the present moment, and, presumably, as she will be in the future that lies ahead. The busy mother is another self from the older woman who takes her cup into the yard, pondering death, but still savoring the sensations of living. In telling a revised story of Grant's dying, she portrays a narrator who has come to possess a wise humility about knowing "truth." It is a repara-tive story, in its way a confessional that leaves the reader with a narrator able to reimagine the past and finally able to give a dying man the empathy she had withheld.

In one of the essays in *Witnessing,* Douglas tells an anecdote involving her friend Shelby Foote, historian of the Civil War and novelist. She recalls his saying that in the three-volume *Civil War* he included only those details for which he had primary sources, an assertion that immediately triggers for her the question of how reliable are primary sources. "I'm a primary source for all I have seen and known and heard and felt. And, believe me, I tell you now I am unreliable. I have been molded, branded, buried in 'facts' that other primary sources—my parents and my grandparents, historians, politicians, journalists, preachers—have imprinted on me, as they in turn were imprinted before me." She would wholly agree with Tzvetvan Todorov's assertion that "The self is the product of others that it, in its turn, produces" (122). Her description of a self-hood that is always enmeshed in relationships with others is succinct: "We are always pawns in someone else's game" (103).

In the second story of the collection, ostensibly focused upon her great-aunt Marian Davis, she begins in 1948, midway between the present moment of the writing and the occurrence years before of a tangled friendship and love affair involving Julia Nutt, who was her aunt's friend, and nearby neighbors Dunbar Marshall and his wife Fanny. The scene is a drive from Greenville to Natchez in the company of an elderly companion, Adah Williams, who insists upon tell-ing a Faulkneresque tale about Douglas's own family of a generation past. Not knowing that her story involves Douglas's relations, the woman presses her dra-matic account of those whom Douglas knew well and remembers. She recalls fifty years later that she, the "primary witness," was amused and a little put off that her family members were appropriated by a storyteller who knew nothing firsthand. She tried then to interrupt, to assert the facts as she recalled them, but her memory was uncertain, vague about the details that Adah Williams was so certain of. Her sketchy hold on the past that afternoon in 1948 (and perhaps still sketchier fifty years later) acquiesced to the cohesive credibility of Adah's narrative. In its confident detail, it had more "truth-power."

Douglas continues to probe the episode for what it reveals of the layers that lie between a witness and witnessed acts. Zooming forward, in a sort of post-modern testing of her own reliability for primary knowledge, she takes up a brief analysis of the car ride, acknowledging that, fifty years later, she has had to resort to imagination to portray the scene in enough detail to make it credible.

She has invented almost every feature of her and Adah's conversation—dialogue, facial expressions, emotional responses. With this frame, she puts her reader on notice that a story, even a narrative of one's own witnessed past, makes demands that stretch beyond memory's capacities, that is, if one conceives of memory as a site closed from the present. When she recounts the scene of her visit with her grandmother, from whom she sought the true story of the triangle affair, she again faces the need to invent their dialogue: "Maybe she said that and maybe she didn't. I suppose it may just be that I have the memory now of wanting to sympathize with Dunny" (49), the narrator writes.

The concept of memory as a "living thing," to recall Welty's phrase, is theorized, analyzed, and illustrated by Ellen Douglas in this collection. To demonstrate what information can escape the "contamination" of the active imagination, that is, names and dates and places, she composes a chart of the cast of characters—her grandmothers, their friends, and the three principals—and the two plantation house settings: Longwood, "Of Moorish castle design, only the first floor completed. Built in 1860–61 by Haller Nutt," and the Forest, "Burned before the Civil War, leaving only the carriage house. Built in 1793 by William Dunbar" (44). The chart may have the seeds of narrative, but it has no plot, no causality, no sensory detail, no human voices speaking. Inventing, imagining these and so giving flesh to narrative, Douglas has to acknowledge the limits of one's knowledge of past experience. For her, a presentist filter always operates; however, she regards the filtering positively, as psychological engagement that connects one to the past. One can learn from—and even revise—the past as one grows in humility and wisdom. In fact, the revised memory of Ellen Douglas in 1998 may be even "truer" to the conversation with Adah Williams than Josephine Haxton's momentary perception of it had been in 1948, Douglas having given up her claim of "reliable primary witness." At the conclusion of "Julia and Nellie," the narrator dismisses worry over the vagaries of memory. "Does it matter at all whether I recall or imagine this scene?" (81). Such a cavalier attitude about acts of recalling versus imagining would seem an almost fatal flaw for a truth-committed autobiographer. But the flaw lies in believing in the possibility of "truthy" memory, Douglas would say. One has to call upon a well-furnished and empathetic imagination to tell a true story.

She brings such an imagination to her third story, "Hampton," a narrative that further expands the narrator's reach beyond her own experience. Beginning with Uncle Grant, a story in which she is directly involved—"How could I forget what happened in my house, under my nose, to me?" (3)—she turns in "Julia and Nellie" to the era of her grandmother and then, in this third narrative, "Hampton," to an African American man who was employed by her grand-mother and great-aunt for over twenty years, from 1931 to the mid-1950s. His lifetime spanned years of racial apartheid and then the emerging civil rights movement that gained momentum after World War II. In his final years, spent in an integrated nursing home, Douglas visited him from time to time. "He had decided that he wanted to tell me about his life," perhaps, she thought, "he felt—as if the crumbling loess of our land had shifted and compacted and risen under his feet [with] the shift of power toward him and his people. His vote would count, so to speak" (92).

She reports what she hears from him, of his life as a boy, a sharecropper, of his desperate poverty and then as a servant in her grandmother's household. Employing his perspective to give meaning and historical context to the Natchez she knew as a child and young adult, she is once more stymied by the gaps in the story he tells. In an effort to give it narrative shape, she once more acquiesces to the artifice necessary to give it continuity and credibility. She is sure of her own memories, or almost sure: "Hampton's brown skin and shaven head, my great-aunt's pince-nez, her story of the flood in the rice fields, my uncle's auburn hair and high color." But, "I know that I put words in the mouths of people who did not speak them. I imagine scenes at which I was not present. I know that this is my world and no one else's—my stories, my history. Or myth, perhaps, one among the myths that form the lives of families and sometime of larger worlds." She then declares, in something of an apology to Hampton and the family forebears, "I should say, too, that everyone who cared about these events is dead. I do not believe that any living person can be hurt either by the truth or by the fiction in my stories. . . . I'm an old woman" (90).

A reader approaches life narratives with the same curiosity that one brings to any novel—what is this writer about to reveal to us? The autobiographies by novelists discussed here are partly, or largely, about how the authors came to be writers—and how the texts they compose demonstrate their deployment of their craft. Douglas's *Truth* is one of these, with a twist. Much of the surface content of this text is concerned with the craft, with the filtering, shaping, and reshaping of narrated action expressed in written words. She is dubious about pinning down what a life story is "about," and yet she tries to weave together events, to devise some sort of plot, which she knows narrative continuity depends upon. A self-referential author throughout the stories, she foregrounds her narrator's effort to devise connections that bridge gaps and imagine details. She keeps directly before the reader the "problem" for the autobiographer: artifice is necessary to tell the truth.

Toward the end of "Hampton," she writes of a long-standing interest of hers that one may read as an indication of her commitment in her life and fiction to racial justice. She is drawn to the infamous occurrence that historian Winthrop Jordan wrote of in *Tumult and Silence at Second Creek*—a reported plot, perhaps nonexistent, writes Douglas, "said to have been concocted in 1861 by slaves in Natchez . . . and the "trial" that resulted in the torture and execution of some thirty or more of the so-called plotters" (117). Douglas attempts to unravel the story in much greater detail—and come to terms with her connection to it—in the final story of the collection. In "Hampton," it has been her inability to ferret out the "plot" of all the scenes she has put together that so troubles her. What causation leads from one stage or event to the next? Hampton's lengthy reminiscences end abruptly with more gaps than revelations. "What happened to the middle of the story?" the narrator asks. She thinks that she could give her story about Hampton a direction, a plot, if she could connect two enslaved men of the Second Creek era with Hampton—John Roy Lynch, who was the slave of her great-grandparents, and Bill Postlethwaite, supposedly one of the rebelling slaves. But the pieces do not fit together; there is no evidence of any such connection. If there is one, the narrator decides, it "must be found elsewhere," presumably supplied by a novelist's imagination in a work of fiction.

In the lengthy fourth story, "Second Creek," the narrator makes a heroic attempt to search out facts that give credible evidence of what took place in May 1861 that led to the deaths of a number of Adams County slaves. In a sequence of interviews with elderly relatives and with African American elders whose family had lived in the county for generations, Douglas dramatizes again the wispy fragments of memory and momentary apprehensions and tenuous written records that the narrator has to rely upon for her search. Implicit in her effort is the conviction that "the ancestors" are part of who she is, that their stories shape her own imperfectly known world. In this regard, Douglas bears out a felt connection to family ancestry that is often characterized as a "southern" attribute. Whereas a number of the texts I have discussed include a history of ancestors—one thinks of Smedes's *Memorials of a Southern Planter,* Kearney's *A Slaveholder's Daughter,* Lumpkin's *The Making of a Southerner,* Glasgow's lengthy appendix entitled "A Dull Note for Genealogists"—*Truth* portrays a narrator actively engaging earlier generations. She first seeks information from a ninety-nine-year-old distant cousin, so deaf that written notes on a tablet must be handed to her. An extended interchange is necessary to establish the family relationship between the narrator and the aged Liza Conner Martin before questions may be posed. The narrator hopes she can get added information, old letters perhaps, that amplify the sparse, ambiguous account of the slave uprising that Martin's grandfather had written, a record housed in the archives at Louisiana State University. Once again, Douglas determines to expose the mental processes of the author, who is consciously constructing a narrator remembering an interview that took place years earlier. Douglas's authorial self intrudes upon the narrator, speaks directly to the reader, undercutting the narrator's authority by insisting upon the fallibility of memory.

> I have been debating how to make it clear, to put you on notice, so to speak, that every single detail of my story is not true. On the one hand I want you to get a sense of how I approached Liza, how she responded, what the house was like. Her surroundings. But I couldn't take notes and I don't always recall our precise words. Even the geography and the look of the house have faded a little in my memory. It's not that I wish to mislead you. The detail I fill in with—the riven cedar tree, the clawing laurel by the front window—these may be substitutes for details I've forgotten, but I'll try to give you as accurately as I can my sense of the way the interview went, where it took place, who we were. (142)

"Who we were" or "who I was" is the autobiographical contract, but Douglas insists the reader see the contract as tenuous, not really actionable, even if well intended.

In an abrupt departure, the narrator leaves the Second Creek uprising matter to write a profile of one Gold Smith Sr., "an old black man" who had hunted and worked with her father, who called him "the Elder." The narrator calls Smith "a bard." She had met him in 1958 when he had told her stories of events in his life that she had refashioned in her fiction, in particular, his memory of a white man who had seemed to come from nowhere and for a short time had "helped the people with their papers." When she had seen Gold Sr. sometime later, he had upbraided her for falsifying "the rest of that story, when you wrote it down for a book, you made it up" (153). One question she leaves for the reader to ponder is whether, in composing her version of Gold Sr.'s story, she had preserved it or destroyed it. The far more gripping issue for Douglas, though, is the inescapable invention that threads through any life narrative. For her, the lies we live by, lies we tell and hear, are forever being exposed, shaking one's hold on truth, proving how contingent truth is upon forces beyond our ken.

An ultimate demonstration of the incompleteness that marks our knowledge of close family members—and even of ourselves—constitutes the middle section of "Second Creek." Written after her mother's death, the narrator reveals the secret kept for more than sixty years that her maternal grandfather had committed suicide. He had not died of apoplexy, as the narrator had believed until she was in her fifties. Casually, she hears her sister remark one day that the widowed mother and children had moved to a relative's home after "he had killed himself" (165). Douglas writes, "For me it was as if the continental plate of our family life had moved ever so slightly, as if a crack were widening in the yard in front of the house, an earthquake beginning" (167). Questioning the family, she finds that her brother had known of the suicide, as had her older sister Anna, informed by their father, who had known the truth before he married their mother. And her mother's younger brother had known. It was he who had long ago informed Douglas's mother, who, having kept the secret for sixty years from her widowed mother and sisters, had had to listen to their "recounting again and again . . . the romance of his life—his Creole good looks, his élan, his game cocks, his charming friends, his courage, his resilience. No wonder she was deaf" (173). A new memory of her mother emerges for the narrator, who now understands why there was never a photograph of her grandfather in the house—an image of every other member of the family, but not of him. The photograph of him that the narrator remembers belonged to the grandmother and her sisters. For years she had not known this storied secret; had she known it, she could not have written of it while her mother lived. "She died believing that she took with her the knowledge that her father had chosen to kill himself rather than stay and struggle to protect the lives of his young family" (173).

When the narrator considers the momentous gap in what was known to her, in her own time, in her own family, she can hardly be surprised at the paucity of information passed down by the participants in the Second Creek massacre, by the families of the victims, or by the witnesses, such as Liza Conner Martin's grandfather, who wrote sketchily of the trial. Returning to the Second Creek manuscript in the LSU archives, she tries again—through inference and imagination—to supply what is missing from the record. But there are questions that cannot be answered. Added to all the other barriers that impede her recovery of the past, Douglas is also stymied in her search for the "true" Second Creek story by the racial divide that has so long shaped southern culture. In her effort to validate the "facts" of the nineteenth-century torture and execution of thirty or more slaves that occurred near her family home in Adams County, Mississippi, she cannot bridge the chasm between past and present in part because, as she discovers, her narrative is chiefly about whiteness—white racial secrets, denials, emotional distance. In these, she is complicit, however unknowingly, and the inescapable irony of the white liberal's effort to narrate black experience, this frustrating but necessary experience, is one that she communicates in an intimate, deeply personal narrative voice: "No devices, fictional or historical, can rescue Obey and Harry and Adam and John, Billy and George and Alfred and Dick, from silence and oblivion" (202).

In a slightly wearied, exasperated tone, the narrator declares that "it is impossible to make sense out of stories that purport to be true. Something is always missing." The intervention of identity—not only that of the composing self but all of those earlier selves—limits one's viewing area to one window. And to make those visible images cohere, "to give them form, extract their deepest meaning, one has to turn them into fiction [or narrative], find causes, or if, as is usually the case, causes are unfindable, one has to invent them" (175). What Douglas tells and shows her reader is that, in our efforts to find and name the causes of our own actions, we all become interpreters, composers of selves.

CODA

Reflections on a Literary Genre

The composition of a life in written words is a task of self-invention. For women reared in the American South over the three generations following the Civil War, the constraints upon writing a life narrative for a public audience were numerous and often acutely felt. The traditional woman's sphere, largely un-challenged in the years of their youth, proscribed female claims for recognition in public arenas. Earlier, in mid-nineteenth-century autobiographical writings, woman of the white elite upper class typically justified undertaking an autobio-graphical project as a commitment to honor ancestors, to depict the gentility of the region before the war, or to describe the experience of the war itself and the devastation left in its wake. *The Civil War Diary of Sarah Morgan, Mary Chesnut's Civil War,* and Susan Dabney Smedes's *Memorials of a Southern Planter* are all memoiristic, filled with external details of persons, places, events. Passages of self-revelation or strong emotion, such as Chesnut's rumination upon the ignominy of being a childless wife, are relatively rare. African American writers such as Harriet Jacobs focus more directly upon the protagonist-self, her struggles and emotions, for she is the embodied victim of racial oppression, as well as the emancipated victor who outwits and escapes slavery.

Motivated by a moral purpose—and thereby justified by a higher calling than self-revelation—writers like Anna Julia Cooper, Belle Kearney, and, later, Katharine DuPre Lumpkin and Lillian Smith draw upon life experience to bear witness to the white South's oppression of African Americans and, especially in Kearney's narrative, to oppose the patriarchal subjection of women. The "Lost Cause" memorializing of the Civil War by white women was especially goad-ing for Lumpkin, who was determined to register her own witness of injustice perpetrated by former Confederates, some of whom were members of her own family.

There are few autobiographies in this study in which the protagonist-narrator is explicitly characterized as closely aligned with and representative of the prevailing cultural values of the region or as one acknowledged by her mostly male contemporaries to be a deserving legatee of cultural privilege. That women reared in a patriarchal culture do not regard themselves as "representative" of the society at large comes as no surprise. But, of course, their way of seeing themselves and their world is inevitably linked to the culture. Their general practice of muting or avoiding explicit references to sexuality, for example, obviously reflects their society's disposition to respect Victorian modesty and circumspect language. Even the breezy narrative of physician Anne Fearn employs indirection and euphemisms in accounts of childbirth, sexual intercourse, gynecological ills, and bodily functions. We may also note that the defensiveness shown by some writers in justifying their reasons for writing a life narrative bespeaks the continuing influence of an old ordering of "woman's place."

What I have observed, however, is that these writers regard their stories as accounts of uniquely personal lives. They often structure lifelong stories as beginning in typical circumstances, with girlhood as a time mainly of unquestioning acceptance of the status quo. As adults, they typically shift focus from the youthful self to the social surround and narrate personal experiences that reflect a relational self connected to the outside scene and an implied self who harbors an inward spirit propelling and infusing the creative act of writing. Whatever the approach to composing the self's identity, it is rarely to call up a semblance meant to represent a constituency of like sisters.

Reading William Alexander Percy's *Lanterns on the Levee: Recollections of a Planter's Son* (1941), one notes how easily and familiarly the narrator recounts a life that *represents* an era, a region, and a family. Anne Walter Fearn and Zora Neale Hurston exhibit some of Percy's ease and self-fulfillment in their narratives, but neither assumes—in fact, both reject—the role of a representative figure of any kind, insisting rather on their difference from any type or categorical identification (woman, white, black, southern). In *Black Boy* (1945) Richard Wright, in contrast to Hurston, describes a coming-of-age story of *a* southern black boy, emphasizing through symbol and scene experiences portrayed as representative of the inculcation in young black men of the racial caste system. In contrast, Maya Angelou's *I Know Why the Caged Bird Sings* (1969) portrays the narrator Marguerite as closely identified with family and neighbors but also as a girl and young woman whose experiences are uniquely individualized.

Some female autobiographers who grew to womanhood later, in mid twentieth century, have composed even more highly individualized selves, selves in rebellion against the values of their own era and particularly opposed to constraining gender (and sexual) roles of an older tradition. Rosemary Daniell's beautiful mother in *Fatal Flowers: On Sin, Sex, and Suicide in the Deep South* (1980) is shown as suffering from the warping contradictions of the southern beauty/belle/lady code, like a later version of Aunt Amy in Katherine Anne Porter's "Old Mortality." And Daniell herself, a little like a fierce incarnation of Miranda, determines to shed the old gender encasements, those repressions of sexuality, and turn her back on female submissiveness. But even in these more recent texts, gender role traditionalism still influences self-invention, either in exerting lingering and often unconscious constraints on public exposure or, as in Daniell's narrative, motivating active, angry rebellion against a society privileging erotic female beauty while defining its fleshly expression as a violation of idealized ladyhood.

What has proved most interesting to me in this study of southern women's autobiographies is the wide window these texts open upon the larger culture. The writers may not be representative selves, but taken together their narratives vividly convey the daily and local felt life of women across the South in a great variety of life circumstances, women of different classes, races, places, ages, careers, political views, and familial roles. Their modes of telling their stories also differ, but their published texts give evidence of the considerable skill and courage necessary to a realization of the self on the printed page. For all the exposure of selves, I have also encountered myriad intimations of much lived life left out of the narratives, perhaps deemed not relevant or appropriate for public view, or repressed, or forgotten, or perhaps never registered in the memory. I have also come to view autobiography not just as a literary form but as something of a literary "venue," a site of negotiation among the principal agents— memory, unfolding identity, and the demands of inscribed narrative, that is, sequence, causality, and coherence. At such sites, writers persevere, struggling to compose texts that mirror their own lived lives.

Autobiography is the genre most at war with itself, always contending with the transformation of self into artifice, always signaling its mixed motives, gaps, indirections, and contingent reality in the thrall of language and the inescapable acculturation of the writing self. Still, for all its limitations, it may be the genre most expressive of the multiplicity of selves that complicate human identity.

Notes

CHAPTER ONE

1. In her 1933 preface Helen Davis assures the reader that her "presence does not enter the book," that her task was "removing the less interesting material and leaving in the dramatic and moving events that happened to Mary Hamilton herself, her husband, and her children." Before her death in 1992, Davis appended biographical details about herself and her family during the 1930s and added information about the then-unpublished manuscript's history. She writes that, undertaking various writing projects, she had learned of the competition sponsored by Little, Brown for a publishable manuscript, and, with Hamilton's permission, had submitted Hamilton's autobiography. It did not win the competition, but in 1935 Little, Brown did publish a novel coauthored by her and her husband Reuben Davis, *Butcher Bird,* thus confirming advice they had been given by their agent—"that publishers were at the time primarily interested in literature about southern Negroes" (xix–xxi).

2. Darlene O'Dell in *Sites of Southern Memory* analyzes the metaphor implied in Lost Cause rituals, especially those encoding an intention to restore the old order of racial caste. She argues that the autobiographies of Katharine Lumpkin, Lillian Smith, and Pauli Murray are directly pitched to expose the tropes (the sites of memory) that are intended to perpetuate white dominance.

3. Gaines Foster notes that the high honor and esteem accorded the private soldier came well after 1865. He reports that "24 percent of the statues erected before 1885 featured the Confederate soldier, compared with 62 percent in the period 1885–99 and 80 percent in 1900–12" (228, n. 43). Charles Reagan Wilson's "The Invention of Southern Tradition: The Writing and Ritualization of Southern History, 1880–1940" offers a wealth of information about the "remaking" of antebellum and Civil War history.

4. See "Between Individualism and Community: Autobiographies of Southern Women." Fox-Genovese argues that southern women, black and white, reflect in their narratives the dual claims of individualism and community, "but they have not normally seen those claims as incompatible" (36). My reading of many of the texts I discuss is that such claims are more often than not felt as conflicting and constraining. See also Fox-Genovese's "Family and Female Identity in the Ante-

bellum South," *In Joy and in Sorrow,* ed. Bleser, 115–31. This collection of essays offers a wide range of informative essays on the subject of the subtitle: *Family and Marriage in the Victorian South.*

5. See also Scott's "Women in the South: History as Fiction, Fiction as History." She notes that Woodward's *Origins of the New South,* a study of the progressive era, "a time when women were key political actors in every social reform movement throughout the South," contains only five references to women (27–28).

6. Clara Junker discusses the Chesnut autobiography as a hybrid form, a "rebellion against male conceptions of genre and gender" (18) in "Writing Herstory: Mary Chesnut's Civil War." See also Elizabeth Muhlenfeld's *Mary Boykin Chesnut: A Biography.* In her 1989 dissertation, "Rewriting the Unwritten: The Fictions of Autobiography in the Civil War Journal of Mary Chesnut," Melissa Mentzer analyzes the journal as a narrative structured to represent women's life experiences. Wendy Kurant, in "The Making of Buck Preston: Mary Boykin Chesnut, Women, and the Confederate Memorial Movement," examines the influence of Lost Cause ideology on the revised edition of Chesnut's journal published as *A Diary from Dixie.*

7. Among the many books I have found useful in thinking about the theoretical constructs of female autobiography, some I would cite as especially accessible to general readers include Judy Long's *Telling Women's Lives: Subject, Narrator, Reader, Text;* Jill Ker Conway's *When Memory Speaks: Reflections on Autobiography;* Patricia Hampl's *I Could Tell You Stories: Sojourns in the Land of Memory;* and Timothy Dow Adams's *Light Writing and Life Writing,* a study of the use of photography in autobiography. For an excellent anthology of studies of the theory and practice of women's autobiographical writing, see *Woman, Autobiography, Theory: A Reader,* edited by Sidonie Smith and Julia Watson. As noted elsewhere in the text, Paul John Eakin's work is particularly noteworthy. See *How Our Lives Become Stories* and *Living Autobiographically: How We Create Identity in Narrative.*

8. A focus upon published works inevitably introduces issues of "multiple authors' because preparation for production entails the involvement of many—editors, at the very least, and often collaborators. Even autobiographers as revisers of texts bring changes to earlier forms of their narratives, as we see with Mary Chesnut. The closest to a singularly produced text that we could identify would likely be the diary or daybook never intended for publication. Autobiographies written with an expectation of publication give us, however, an expanded view of the context of a document, notably that of the audience assumed by author and editors. All texts finally are "versions" of what the author "remembered" or "intended." See Jack Stillinger's *Multiple Authorship and the Myth of Solitary Genius,* especially the conclusion.

9. Yagoda begins his 2009 *Memoir: A History,* "In this book I use the words 'memoir' and 'autobiography'—and, on occasion, 'memoirs'—to mean more or less the same thing: a book understood by its author, its publishers, and its readers to be a factual account of the author's life" (1).

10. On the matter of regionality, contested definitions of what constitutes "South" have a long history in scholarly and popular culture. In her introduction to *Southern Women,* a collection of writings drawn mainly from the social sciences, Caroline Matheny Dillman begins with an insistence that "Southern women" has a distinctly different meaning from "women of the South," the latter phrase being the more inclusive. Whenever we say "Southern woman," she writes, "almost no one in the white educated middle-class (and upward) pictures, for instance, a female Cuban immigrant to the South, a black Southern woman or a female Jew who lives in the South. If we say 'women in the South,' such an array of women should come to mind much more readily than when we say 'Southern women.'" I take Dillman's point, but in this study of women who grew to adulthood in the late nineteenth and early twentieth centuries, it is *their* ideation and expression of *southernness,* of being both in and of the South, that is my focus.

11. See, e.g., *South to a New Place,* ed. Suzanne W. Jones and Sharon Monteith, esp. the editors' introduction, Richard Gray's foreword, and essays by Scott Romine and Barbara Ladd. See also Michael Kreyling's *Inventing Southern Literature;* Patricia Yaeger's *Dirt and Desire: Reconstructing Southern Women's Writing, 1930–1990;* and Anne G. Jones and Susan V. Donaldson's introduction, "Rethinking the South Through Gender," to their edited collection, *Haunted Bodies: Gender and Southern Texts.*

CHAPTER TWO

1. Kett notes that he cites these figures from p. 276 of Dewey Grantham's *Southern Progressivism* (171).

2. See, e.g., Constance Cary Harrison [Mrs. Burton Harrison], *Recollections Grave and Gay* (1911), a memoir mainly about the Civil War years, written for publication; see also examples of recovered holograph autobiographies, edited and published in the 1980s and 1990s: Nannie Stillwell Jackson's *Vinegar Pie and Chicken Bread,* ed. Margaret Jones Bolsterli; Annie Harper, *Annie Harper's Journal,* ed. Jeannie Marie Deen; Pauline DeCaradeuc Heyward, *A Confederate Lady Comes of Age,* ed. Mary D. Robertson; and Cornelia Jones Pond, *Recollections of a Southern Daughter,* ed. Lucinda H. MacKethan.

3. See for biographical information Mary Helen Washington's introduction to her 1988 edition of *A Voice from the South* and Charles Lemert's biographical essay, "Anna Julia Cooper: The Colored Woman's Office," in *The Voice of Anna Julia Cooper.* Two earlier biographies are Louise Daniel Hutchinson's *Anna Julia Cooper: A Voice from the South* and Leona C. Gabel's *From Slavery to the Sorbonne and Beyond: The Life and Writings of Anna J. Cooper.*

4. See Lemert's discussion of various positions scholars have taken as to whether the language of womanhood undercut Cooper's reformist position or "packaged" it in a way that would be more likely heard by a potentially hostile male audience (24 ff.).

5. It seems Kearney retained her pleasure in attractive dress. Joanne V. Hawks and Mary Carolyn Ellis report that when she first entered the Mississippi Senate chamber in 1924, she cut a "rather flamboyant figure . . . attired in a black crepe dress." Quoting from the Jackson *Clarion-Ledger,* 9 January 1924, they write that she was applauded by her colleagues and presented with a bow and a gesture of appreciation that brought up visions of "Queen Bess or Queen Anne" (85). See also for biographical information about Kearney's career Nancy Carol Tipton's 1975 MA thesis, "'It is My Duty': The Public Career of Belle Kearney," and Marjorie Spruill Wheeler's *New Women of the New South.*

6. This is the opening sentence of Welty's essay, "Words into Fiction," in *The Eye of the Story.* Here she discusses the necessity of winning the reader's belief in the validity of a work of fiction, a necessity perhaps even more true of a life narrative, one might argue. "Validity of a kind, and this is of course a subjective kind, gained in whatever way that had to be, is the quality that makes a work reliable as art" (140).

CHAPTER THREE

1. See Todorov's *Life in Common,* also discussed in previous chapters.

2. Keller published segments of the autobiography in *Ladies Home Journal* in 1902, the year of the earliest copyright. The 1903 book, dedicated to Alexander Graham Bell, was published by Doubleday. Dorothy Hermann writes of the editing assistance that John Albert Macy gave. He was "a tall, twenty-five-year-old instructor of English at Harvard and an editor of *Youth's Companion*

who was both a gifted critic and a writer. Swiftly learning the manual alphabet to communicate directly with the twenty-two-year-old Helen, he helped edit her book" (132). Of course, Keller had as well the never-ending assistance of Annie Sullivan, who married Macy in 1905.

3. Both Hermann and Lash give full accounts of the "The Frost King" episode. See Hermann 79–85, and Lash 133 ff.

4. For biographical sources, see the entry "Fearn, Anne Walter" in the 1944 edition of *The National Cyclopaedia of American Biography*. See also Jeannie B. Gardiner, "Book Ends"; Bonar Linn, Review of *My Days of Strength*; and "Dr. Annie Walter Fearn," Obituary.

CHAPTER FOUR

1. In his lengthy history of the Yazoo-Mississippi Delta, James C. Cobb has described the largely uncleared frontier in the 1880s, the decade of Hamilton's marriage, as a sparsely populated wilderness. There were only two towns between Vicksburg and Memphis with a population over one thousand. What land had been cleared lay along the bayous, lakes, and rivers. Even land that had been cleared in the antebellum era was rapidly returning to forest. Cobb writes that "the rich Delta soil was still covered in many places with blue cane 'fifteen to twenty feet high,' bears were still plentiful as the 1880s began, "and in true frontier fashion, the saloons far outnumbered the churches and schools." See *The Most Southern Place on Earth*, 78.

2. In her introduction to Nannie Stillwell Jackson's journal, Bolsterli quotes Octave Thanet's description from "Town Life in Arkansas" as a reasonably accurate portrait of Watson, the northeastern Arkansas town where Jackson lived, the same general area of Hamilton's young adulthood. "Freight came to Red Fork on steamboats and was hauled to Watson in wagons. Mail came three times a week until 1890, when daily service was introduced. The only newspaper in the country was the *Arkansas City Journal*, a four-page weekly paper" (Thanet 333). See Jackson, *Vinegar Pie and Chicken Bread*, 8. See also Bolsterli's autobiography, *Born in the Delta: Reflections on the Making of a Southern White Sensibility*, for an account of the same region.

3. See *These Are Our Lives*, the oral interviews conducted in the 1930s, written as narratives by members of the Works Progress Administration, and published in 1939 by the University of North Carolina Press. The life stories in this collection focus on plain folk, black and white, from North Carolina, Tennessee, and Georgia. In 1978 Tom E. Terrill and Jerrold Hirsch edited a second collection from the WPA file, *Such as Us: Southern Voices of the Thirties*, also published by the UNC Press. An elderly African American man living in Holly Grove, Arkansas, tells of the 1927 flood, farming conditions, and "credit" relations with landlords. His main complaint is that there are no screens for his windows (54–57).

4. The descriptions of the tenant farm women Margaret Hagood interviewed in the 1930s in the Carolina piedmont and Georgia and Alabama well reflect the conditions and habits of mind and action of Mary Hamilton's life. "Frills and furbelows, imagination and introspection, superficial and artificial pursuits have little time or place in the thinking and acting of these women. Of more importance, however, is the emotional maturity evidenced in their acceptance of economic hardship. Such acceptance can not be termed passive for it involves constant output of labor that even a subsistence living may be obtained. It is mature in the sense that activities are directed toward the objective factors of the situation—toward farm, children, home—rather than toward inner goals demanded by inferiority feelings or other internal maladjustments" (75–76). See also well-known works by Erskine Caldwell and Margaret Bourke White, *You Have Seen Their Faces* (1937), and James Agee and Walker Evans's *Let Us Now Praise Famous Men* (1941).

5. Walter Anderson began a series of written and sketched logs of his visits to Horn Island in

1944, a record he would continue to keep until his death. In 1985 the University Press of Mississippi published these in a handsome book that includes color prints and inked sketches. The editor, Redding S. Sugg Jr., estimates that overall the logs run to 350,000 words.

CHAPTER FIVE

1. For biographical information on Upton Sinclair, see his *The Autobiography of Upton Sinclair* (1962); Leon Harris, *Upton Sinclair: American Rebel* (1975); Jon A. Yoder, *Upton Sinclair* (1975); and Anthony Arthur, *Radical Innocent: Upton Sinclair* (2006).

2. All quotations from the letters come from the correspondence of Craig Sinclair to her brother Hunter Kimbrough from 1955 to 1959. Context and postmarks help date letters not otherwise dated. I indicate dates or approximate dates in the text. Copies of the original letters are in my possession. See Works Cited.

CHAPTER SIX

1. Barnard writes that in addition to the voluminous interviews conducted by Jacquelyn Hall and Sue Thrasher in 1975, Thrasher continued the interview project, taping thirty additional hours of reminiscences for the autobiography that Durr had already begun. "Sue's affection and admiration for Virginia made it possible for Virginia to talk freely. And her love of laughter prompted Virginia—who loves to laugh—to remember even the painful times with good humor (xvii).

2. Edgerton describes Robinson's move to the Dodgers, his entry into baseball's major league, as being aided by both black and white southerners. "Helped by . . . John Wright of New Orleans, who withstood the slings and arrows of bigotry alongside him, and by Montreal manager Clay Hopper, a white Mississippian, Robinson blazed a trail that brought the Dodgers organization— and the city of Daytona Beach [site of spring training camp]—into the modern era well ahead of their competitors. Play-by-play announcer Red Barber, another Southerner, also helped, as did the baseball commissioner, former (and future) Kentucky politician 'Happy Chandler,' who ignored the negative reaction of almost all the other major-league club owners and approved Rickey's plan to transfer Robinson's contract from Montreal to Brooklyn in early 1947" (421).

CHAPTER SEVEN

1. Sosna discusses Lillian Smith's liberalism as radical evangelism. He notes her "uncompromising stand against caste" and writes that what distinguished this view, held by only a minority of southern liberals, from that of most southern liberals and northern advocates of civil rights, white and black, was the emphasis on religion" (172 ff.).

2. For the widespread influence of religion on women's commitment to social justice, see, e.g., Anne Scott in *Southern Lady* (135 ff.); Dewey Grantham in *Southern Progressivism* (23–24); and Sosna. J. Wayne Flynt notes anomalies, however, that disrupt any easy linking of religion, social reform, and Progressivism, the definition of which is disputed among historians. Still, he argues that "to look at the South without discussing religion is like examining modern American culture without reference to sex: it is possible, but one certainly misses the drift of things" (135). One denominational study of women's role in social justice causes is John Patrick McDowell's *The Social Gospel in the South: The Woman's Home Mission Movement in the Methodist Episcopal Church, South, 1886–1939*.

3. See O'Dell for Katharine Lumpkin's relationship to her sister Grace (55 ff.).

4. Diane McWhorter in *Carry Me Home* and Douglas Blackmon in *Slavery by Another Name* extensively document the influence of elite white businessmen in the South in fostering racist labor practices. Both give special attention to Birmingham.

5. See Anne C. Loveland's biography *Lillian Smith* for an overview of the critical reception of *Killers of the Dream* (102–5).

6. See Roseanne V. Camacho's "Race, Region, and Gender in a Reassessment of Lillian Smith" for a discussion of the ways in which the New Critics of the 1940s and 1950s, most of whom had been involved earlier in the Fugitive poet group and the Agrarian opposition to southern industrialism, "produced a new aesthetic that allowed a generation of intellectuals to avoid the imperative for racial change" (159). Camacho examines in particular Smith's response to John Crowe Ransom.

CHAPTER EIGHT

1. Perkins seemed unconcerned about libel, but he did suggest that Rawlings omit the chapter dealing with her installation of indoor plumbing and the prior information about the outhouse. He thought its coarseness might be offensive to her fans. She did receive some angry letters from readers accusing her of being a "low, evil woman for writing about the disgusting sex relations of animals" (Silverthorne 198; 208).

CHAPTER NINE

1. Hurston's reference to "Papa Franz" at the opening of her "Research" chapter suggests that her mentoring professor at Barnard, Franz Boas, also served as something of a surrogate father.

2. Lionnet argues that Hurston includes only those private aspects of her life that have "deep symbolic and cultural value: the death of the mother and subsequent dispersion of the siblings echo the collective memory of her people's separation from Africa-as-mother and their ineluctable diaspora" (112).

3. Although in the opening chapter Harris gives the reader the impression that her birth year is 1892, the date cited by several sources is 1891. The *Dictionary of North Carolina Biography,* ed. William S. Powell, gives the date as 8 October 1891.

CHAPTER TEN

1. See Prenshaw, "The Construction of Confluence," and "Fevered Desire and Therapeutic Gaze in Welty's World."

2. Timothy Dow Adams finds this pattern embedded in the structure of *One Writer's Beginnings,* with its linear three sections that form a "continuous loop" of listening, seeing, and voicing (154). This pattern is related to the time loop endemic to autobiography, the present moment of composition offering the only portal to and from the past.

Works Cited

PRIMARY SOURCES

Anderson, Agnes Grinstead. *Approaching the Magic Hour: Memories of Walter Anderson.* Ed. Patti Carr Black. Jackson: UP of Mississippi, 1989.

Barber, Lylah Murray Scarborough. *Lylah: A Memoir by Lylah Barber.* Chapel Hill, NC: Algonquin, 1985.

Boggs, Lindy. *Washington Through a Purple Veil: Memoirs of a Southern Woman.* With Katherine Hatch. New York: Harcourt, Brace, 1994.

Chesnut, Mary. *A Diary from Dixie.* Ed. Ben Ames Williams. Boston: Houghton Mifflin, 1949.

———. *Mary Chesnut's Civil War.* Ed. C. Vann Woodward. New Haven: Yale UP, 1981.

Cooper, Anna Julia. *A Voice from the South.* 1892. Introduction by Mary Helen Washington. New York: Oxford UP, 1988.

Douglas, Ellen [Josephine Haxton]. *Conversations with Ellen Douglas.* Ed. Panthea Reid. Jackson: UP of Mississippi, 2000.

———. *Truth: Four Stories I Am Finally Old Enough to Tell.* Chapel Hill: Algonquin, 1998.

———. *Witnessing.* Jackson: UP of Mississippi, 2004.

Durr, Virginia Foster. *Outside the Magic Circle: The Autobiography of Virginia Foster Durr.* Ed. Hollinger F. Barnard. 1985. New York: Simon and Schuster Touchstone, 1987.

Faulkner, William. "Mississippi." 1954. In *Essays, Speeches, and Public Letters by William Faulkner.* Ed. James B. Meriwether. New York, Random House, 1965, 11–43.

Fearn, Anne. *My Days of Strength.* New York: Harper Bros., 1939.

Glasgow, Ellen. *A Certain Measure: An Interpretation of Prose Fiction.* New York: Harcourt, Brace, 1943.

———. *The Woman Within: The Autobiography of Ellen Glasgow.* 1954. Ed. with introduction by Pamela R. Matthews. Charlottesville: U of Virginia P, 1994.

Hamilton, Mary. *Trials of the Earth: The Autobiography of Mary Hamilton.* Ed. Helen Dick Davis. Foreword by Ellen Douglas. Jackson: UP of Mississippi, 1992.

Harris, Bernice Kelly. "No Stick-Leg," "The Landlord Has His Troubles," "Jackson Bullitt, a Small Landlord," "Aaron and Mary Matthews," "Just a Plain Two-Horse Farm," "Roger T. Stevenson, Justice of the Peace," and "Sam Set It Down." *Such As Us: Southern Voices of the Thirties.* Ed. Tom E. Terrill and Jerrold Hirsch. Chapel Hill: U of North Carolina P, 1978.

———. *Southern Savory.* Chapel Hill: U of North Carolina P, 1964.

Harrison, Constance Cary. [Mrs. Burton Harrison]. *Recollections Grave and Gay.* New York: Scribner's, 1911.

Hurston, Zora Neale. *Dust Tracks on a Road.* 1942. Foreword by Maya Angelou. Afterword by Henry Louis Gates Jr. New York: Harper Perennial, 1991.

Jacobs, Harriet. *Incidents in the Life of a Slave Girl.* Ed. L. Maria Child. 1861. Ed. with introduction by Jean Fagan Yellin. Cambridge: Harvard UP, 1987.

Kearney, Belle. *A Slaveholder's Daughter.* New York: Abbey, 1900.

Keller, Helen. *Midstream: My Later Life.* New York: Doubleday, Doran, 1929.

———. *The Story of My Life.* New York: Doubleday, Page, 1903. See digital copy of the 1903 edition at www.google.com/books.

———. *The World I Live In.* New York: Century, 1908.

Lumpkin, Katharine DuPre. *The Making of a Southerner.* 1947. Foreword by Darlene Clark Hine. Athens: U of Georgia P, 1991.

Rawlings, Marjorie Kinnan. *Cross Creek.* New York: Charles Scribner's, 1942.

———. *Cross Creek Cookery.* New York: Charles Scribner's, 1942.

———. *Selected Letters of Marjorie Kinnan Rawlings.* Ed. Gordon E. Bigelow and Laura V. Monti. Gainesville: UP of Florida, 1983.

Sinclair, Mary Craig Kimbrough. *Southern Belle: A Personal Story of a Crusader's Wife.* Introduction by Upton Sinclair. 1957. Jackson: UP of Mississippi, 1999. Afterword by Peggy Whitman Prenshaw.

———. Letters to Hunter Kimbrough. Twenty-six holograph letters. 16 May 1955 to 18 May 1957. Xerox copies from Hunter Kimbrough given to Prenshaw. March 1979.

Smedes, Susan Dabney. *Memorials of a Southern Planter.* 1887. Ed. Fletcher M. Green. Jackson: UP of Mississippi, 1981.

Smith, Lillian. *How Am I to Be Heard? Letters of Lillian Smith.* Ed. Margaret Rose Gladney. Chapel Hill: U of North Carolina P, 1993.

———. *Killers of the Dream.* 1949. Rev. 1961. With introduction by Margaret Rose Gladney. New York: Norton, 1994.

Spencer, Elizabeth. "A Business Venture." *Jack of Diamonds and Other Stories.* New York: Viking, 1988.

———. *Landscapes of the Heart.* New York: Random House, 1998.

Welty, Eudora. *Eudora Welty: Complete Novels.* New York: Library of America, 1998.

———. *Eudora Welty: Stories, Essays, Memoir.* New York: Library of America, 1998.

———. *One Writer's Beginnings.* Cambridge: Harvard UP, 1984. In *Eudora Welty: Stories, Essays, Memoir.*

———. *The Optimist's Daughter.* New York: Random House, 1972. In *Eudora Welty: Complete Novels.*

———. "Place in Fiction." *The Eye of the Story.* New York: Random House, 1978. In *Eudora Welty: Stories, Essays, Memoir.* 781–96.

———. "Words into Fiction." *The Eye of the Story.* New York: Random House, 1978. This essay is not included in the Library of America volume.

SECONDARY SOURCES

Abbott, Shirley. *Womenfolks: Growing Up Down South.* New Haven: Ticknor and Fields, 1983.

Acton, Patricia Nassif. *Invasion of Privacy: The Cross Creek Trial of Marjorie Kinnan Rawlings.* Gainesville: UP of Florida, 1988.

Adams, Timothy Dow. *Light Writing and Life Writing.* Chapel Hill: U of North Carolina P, 2000.

Anderson, Walter Inglis. *The Horn Island Logs of Walter Inglis Anderson.* Ed. with introduction by Redding S. Sugg Jr. Jackson: UP of Mississippi, 1985.

Andrews, William L. "Booker T. Washington, Belle Kearney, and the Southern Patriarchy." *Home Ground: Southern Autobiography.* Ed. J. Bill Berry. Columbia: U of Missouri P, 1991. 85–97.

Angelou, Maya. Foreword. Hurston vii–xii.

Arnold, Matthew. "The Forsaken Merman." 1849. See www.poetryfoundation.org.

Arthur, Anthony. *Radical Innocent: Upton Sinclair.* New York: Random House, 2006.

Ayers, Edward L. *The Promise of the New South: Life after Reconstruction.* New York: Oxford UP, 1992.

Barnard, Hollinger F. "Editor's Note." *Outside the Magic Circle: The Autobiography of Virginia Foster Durr.* Ed. Hollinger F. Barnard. 1985. New York, Simon and Schuster Touchstone, 1987.

Beauvoir, Simone de. *The Second Sex.* 1953. New York: Vintage, 1974.

Belenky, Mary Field, Blythe McVicker Clinchy, Nancy Rule Goldberger, and Jill Mattuck Tarule. *Women's Ways of Knowing: The Development of Self, Voice, and Mind.* New York: Basic, 1986.

Benstock, Shari, ed. *The Private Self: Theory and Practice of Women's Autobiographical Writings.* Chapel Hill: U of North Carolina P, 1988.

Berry, J. Bill, "The Southern Autobiographical Impulse." *Southern Cultures* 6:1 (2000): 7–22.

———, ed. *Located Lives: Place and Idea in Southern Autobiography.* Athens: U of Georgia P, 1990.

Bigelow, Gordon E. *Frontier Eden: The Literary Career of Marjorie Kinnan Rawlings.* Gainesville: U of Florida P, 1966.

——. "Memories of Marjorie: A Conversation with Idella Parker and Dessie Prescott." *Journal of Florida Literature* 2 (1989-90): 131-51.

Black, Patti Carr. Introduction. Anderson, *Approaching the Magic Hour* vii–xi.

Blackmon, Douglas A. *Slavery by Another Name: The Re-Enslavement of Black Americans from the Civil War to World War II.* 2008. New York: Anchor, 2009.

Bleser, Carol, ed. *In Joy and in Sorrow: Women, Family, and Marriage in the Victorian South.* Introduction by C. Vann Woodward. New York: Oxford UP, 1991.

Bliven, Bruce. "Upton Sinclair's Lady." *New Republic* 23 December 1957: 18.

Bolsterli, Margaret Jones. *Born in the Delta: Reflections on the Making of a Southern White Sensibility.* Knoxville: U of Tennessee P, 1991.

——, ed. With Introduction. *Vinegar Pie and Chicken Bread: A Woman's Diary of Life in the Rural South, 1890–1891.* By Nannie Stillwell Jackson. Fayetteville: U Arkansas P, 1982.

Brantley, Will. *Feminine Sense in Southern Memoir.* Jackson: UP of Mississippi, 1993.

Brodhead, Richard H. *Cultures of Letters: Scenes of Reading and Writing in Nineteenth-Century America.* Chicago: U of Chicago P, 1993.

Brodzki, Bella, and Celeste Schenck. *Life/Lines: Theorizing Women's Autobiography.* Foreword by Germaine Bree. Ithaca: Cornell UP, 1988.

Brown, Rosellen. "Belle of the Bayou." *New York Times Book Review* 27 November 1994: 33.

Brownstein, Rachel M. *Becoming a Heroine: Reading About Women in Novels.* New York: Viking, 1982.

Bruss, Elizabeth. *Autobiographical Acts: The Changing Situation of a Literary Genre.* Baltimore: Johns Hopkins UP, 1976.

Bynum, Victoria. *Unruly Women: The Politics of Social and Sexual Control in the Old South.* Chapel Hill: U of North Carolina P, 1992.

Camacho, Roseanne V. "Race, Region, and Gender in a Reassessment of Lillian Smith." *Southern Women: Histories and Identities.* Ed. Virginia Bernhard, Betty Brandon, Elizabeth Fox-Genovese, and Theda Perdue. Columbia: U of Missouri P, 1992. 157–76.

Campbell, Donna M. *Resisting Regionalism: Gender and Naturalism in American Fiction, 1885–1915.* Athens: Ohio UP, 1997.

Cash, W. J. *The Mind of the South.* New York: Alfred A. Knopf, 1941.

Cashin, Joan E. *A Family Venture: Men and Women on the Southern Frontier.* New York: Oxford UP, 1991.

——, ed. "Culture of Resignation." Introduction. *Our Common Affairs: Texts from Women in the Old South.* Baltimore: John Hopkins UP, 1996. 1–41.

Childress, Mark. "Southern Comfort." *New York Times Book Review* 4 January 1998: 26.

Cobb, James C. *The Most Southern Place on Earth: The Mississippi Delta and the Roots of Regional Identity*. New York: Oxford UP, 1992.

Conway, Jill Ker. *When Memory Speaks: Reflections on Autobiography*. New York: Alfred A. Knopf, 1998.

———, ed. *Written by Herself: Autobiographies of American Women: An Anthology*. New York: Vintage, 1992.

Daniel, Pete. *Standing at the Crossroads: Southern Life in the Twentieth Century*. 1986. Baltimore: Johns Hopkins UP, 1996.

Daniell, Rosemary. *Fatal Flowers: On Sin, Sex, and Suicide in the Deep South*. New York: Holt, Rinehart and Winston, 1980.

Davis, Rebecca Harding. "Here and There in the South." *Harper's New Monthly Magazine* 75 (1887): 235–46.

Dillman, Caroline Matheny, ed. *Southern Women*. New York: Hemisphere, 1988.

Dollard, John. *Caste and Class in a Southern Town*. 1937. New York: Doubleday Anchor, 1957.

Donaldson, Susan V. "Gender and the Profession of Letters in the South." Honnighausen and Lerda 35–46.

Eakin, Paul John. *The Ethics of Life Writing*. Ithaca: Cornell UP, 2004.

———. *Fictions in Autobiography: Studies in the Art of Self Invention*. Princeton: Princeton UP, 1985.

———. *How Our Lives Become Stories*. Ithaca: Cornell UP, 1999.

———. *Living Autobiographically: How We Create Identity in Narrative*. Ithaca: Cornell UP, 2008.

———. *Touching the World: Reference in Autobiography*. Princeton: Princeton UP, 1992.

Edwards, Laura F. *Gendered Strife and Confusion: The Political Culture of Reconstruction*. Urbana: U of Illinois P, 1997.

———. *Scarlett Doesn't Live Here Anymore: Southern Women in the Civil War Era*. Urbana: U of Illinois P, 2000.

Egerton, John. *Speak Against the Day: The Generation Before the Civil Rights Movement in the South*. Chapel Hill: U of North Carolina P, 1995.

Entzminger, Betina. *The Belle Gone Bad: White Southern Women Writers and the Dark Seductress*. Baton Rouge: Louisiana State UP, 2002.

Farnham, Christie Anne. *The Education of the Southern Belle: Higher Education and Socialization in the Antebellum South*. New York: New York UP, 1994.

Faust, Drew Gilpin. "Altars of Sacrifice: Confederate Women and the Narratives of War." *Journal of American History* 76.4 (1990): 1200–1228.

———. *Mother of Invention: Women of the Slaveholding South in the American Civil War*. Chapel Hill: U of North Carolina P, 1996.

———. *This Republic of Suffering: Death and the American Civil War*. New York: Alfred A. Knopf, 2008.

[Fearn]. "Dr. Annie Walter Fearn" [Obituary]. *South Reporter* [Holly Springs, Mississippi] 28 April 1939.

"Fearn, Anne Walter." *National Cyclopaedia of American Biography.* Vol. 31. New York: James T. White and Co., 1944. 381.

Feddersen, Rick. "An Interview with Ellen Douglas." *Conversations with Ellen Douglas.* Ed. Panthea Reid. Jackson: UP of Mississippi, 2000. 140–49.

Federal Writers' Project, ed. *These Are Our Lives.* As told by the people and written by members of the Federal Writers' Project of the Works Progress Administration of North Carolina, Tennessee, Georgia. 1939. New York: Norton, 1975.

Flynt, J. Wayne. "Southern Protestantism and Reform, 1890–1920." *Varieties of Southern Religious Experience.* Ed. Samuel S. Hill. Baton Rouge: Louisiana State UP, 1988. 135–57.

Foster, Gaines M. *Ghosts of the Confederacy: Defeat, the Lost Cause, and the Emergence of the New South.* New York: Oxford UP, 1987.

Fox-Genovese, Elizabeth. "Between Individualism and Community: Autobiographies of Southern Women." Berry, *Located Lives* 20–38.

———. "Family and Female Identity in the Antebellum South." Bleser 15–31.

———. *Feminism without Illusions: A Critique of Individualism.* Chapel Hill: U of North Carolina P, 1991.

———. "My Statue, My Self: Autobiographical Writings of Afro-American Women." Benstock 63–89.

Freeman, Mark. *Rewriting the Self: History, Memory, Narrative.* London: Routledge, 1993.

Friedman, Jean E. *The Enclosed Garden: Women and Community in the Evangelical South, 1830–1900.* Chapel Hill: U of North Carolina P, 1985.

Friedman, Susan Stanford. *Mappings: Feminism and the Cultural Geographies of Encounter.* Princeton: Princeton UP, 1998.

———. "Women's Autobiographical Selves: Theory and Practice." Benstock 34–62.

Gabel, Leona C. *From Slavery to the Sorbonne: The Life and Writings of Anna Julia Cooper.* Northampton, MA: Smith College Library Technical Services, 1982.

Gardiner, Jeannie B. "Book Ends." *Commercial Appeal* [Memphis] 30 April 1939.

Gardner, Sarah E. *Blood and Irony: Southern White Women's Narratives of the Civil War, 1881–1937.* Chapel Hill: U of North Carolina P, 2004.

Genovese, Eugene. "Our Family White and Black: Family and Household in the Southern Slaveholders' World View." Bleser 88–102.

Gilmore, Glenda Elizabeth. *Gender and Jim Crow: Women and the Politics of White Supremacy in North Carolina, 1896–1920.* Chapel Hill: U of North Carolina P, 1996.

Gilmore, Leigh. *Autobiographics: A Feminist Theory of Women's Self-Representation.* Ithaca: Cornell UP, 1994.

Givner, Joan. *Katherine Anne Porter: A Life.* New York: Simon and Schuster, 1982.

Gladney, Margaret Rose. "Becoming a Writer." *How Am I to Be Heard? Letters of Lillian Smith.* Ed. Margaret Rose Gladney. Chapel Hill: U of North Carolina P, 1993. 1–16.

———. Introduction. Smith, *Killers of the Dream.*

Good, Cherry. "The Southern Lady, or the Art of Dissembling." *Journal of American Studies* 23.1 (1989): 72–77.

Gooze, Marjanne E. "The Definitions of Self and Form in Feminist Autobiography Theory." *Women's Studies* 21 (1992): 411–29.

Gornick, Vivian. "Memoir: An Inward Journey Through Experience." *Chronicle of Higher Education* 3 August 2001: B7.

———. *The Situation and the Story: The Art of Personal Narrative.* New York: Farrar, Straus and Giroux, 2001.

Graham, Allison. *Framing the South: Hollywood, Television, and Race during the Civil Rights Struggle.* Baltimore: Johns Hopkins UP, 2001.

Graham, Patricia Albjerg. "Expansion and Exclusion: A History of Women in American Higher Education." *Signs* 3.4 (1978): 759–73.

Grantham, Dewey W. *Southern Progressivism: The Reconciliation of Progress and Tradition.* Knoxville: U Tennessee P, 1983.

Gray, Richard. Foreword. Jones and Monteith xiii–xxiii.

Gusdorf, Georges. "Conditions and Limits of Autobiography." Olney, *Autobiography* 28–48.

Hagood, Margaret Jarman. *Mothers of the South: Portraiture of the White Tenant Farm Woman.* 1939. New York: Norton, 1977.

Hall, Jacquelyn Dowd. "Open Secrets: Memory, Imagination, and the Refashioning of Southern Identity." *American Quarterly* 50.1 (1998): 109–24.

———. "Partial Truths." *Signs* 14.4 (1989): 902–11.

———. "'You Must Remember This': Autobiography as Social Critique." *Journal of American History* 85.2 (1998): 439–65.

Hampl, Patricia. *I Could Tell You Stories: Sojourns in the Land of Memory.* New York: Norton, 1999.

Hampsten, Elizabeth. *Read This Only to Yourself: The Private Writings of Midwestern Women, 1880–1910.* Bloomington: Indiana UP, 1882.

Harper, Annie. *Annie Harper's Journal: A Southern Mother's Legacy.* Ed. and introduction by Jeannie Marie Deen. Denton, TX: Flower Mound Writing Co., 1983.

Harris, Leon. *Upton Sinclair: American Rebel.* New York: Thomas Y. Crowell, 1975.

Hawks, Joanne V., and Mary Carolyn Ellis. "Heirs of the Southern Progressive Tradition: Women in Southern Legislatures in the 1920s." *Southern Women.* Ed. Caroline Matheny Dillman. New York: Hemisphere, 1988. 81–92.

Heilbrun, Carolyn. *Writing a Woman's Life.* New York: Norton, 1988.

Hellman, Lillian. *An Unfinished Woman: A Memoir by Lillian Hellman.* 1969. New York: Bantam, 1970.

Henry, Josephine. "The New Woman of the New South." *Arena* 11 (1895): 353–69.

Hermann, Dorothy. *Helen Keller: A Life.* Chicago: U of Chicago P, 1998.

Heyward, Pauline DeCaradeuc. *A Confederate Lady Comes of Age: The Journal of Pauline DeCaradeuc Heyward, 1863–1888.* Ed. Mary D. Robertson. Columbia: U of South Carolina P, 1991.

Hine, Darlene Clark. Foreword. Lumpkin.

Hobson, Fred. *But Now I See: The White Southern Racial Conversion Narrative.* Baton Rouge: Louisiana State UP, 1999.

Hoffmann, Leonore, and Margo Culley. *Women's Personal Narratives: Essays in Criticism and Pedagogy.* New York: Modern Language Assoc., 1985.

Honnighausen, Lothar, and Valeria Gennaro Lerda, eds. *Rewriting the South: History and Fiction.* Tubingen: Francke, 1993.

Hutchinson, Louise Daniel. *Anna Julia Cooper: A Voice from the South.* Washington: Smithsonian Institute Press, 1981.

I'll Take My Stand: The South and the Agrarian Tradition. By Twelve Southerners. 1930. New York: Harper Torchbook, 1962.

Jackson, Nannie Stillwell. *Vinegar Pie and Chicken Bread: A Woman's Diary of Life in the Rural South, 1890-1891.* Ed. with introduction by Margaret Jones Bolsterli. Fayetteville: U Arkansas P, 1982.

Jelinek, Estelle C., ed. *Women's Autobiography: Essays in Criticism.* Bloomington: Indiana UP, 1980.

Jones, Anne Goodwyn. *Tomorrow Is Another Day: The Woman Writer in the South, 1859–1936.* Baton Rouge: Louisiana State UP, 1981.

——, and Susan V. Donaldson, eds. *Haunted Bodies: Gender and Southern Texts.* Charlottesville: U of Virginia P, 1997.

Jones, Jacquelyn. "The Political Economy of Sharecropping Families: Blacks and Poor Whites in the Rural South, 1865–1915. Bleser 196–214.

Jones, John Griffin. "Eudora Welty." *Conversations with Eudora Welty.* Ed. Peggy Whitman Prenshaw. Jackson: UP of Mississippi, 1984. 316–41.

Jones, Suzanne W., and Sharon Monteith, eds. *South to a New Place: Region, Literature, Culture.* Baton Rouge: Louisiana State UP, 2002.

Junker, Clara. "Writing Herstory: Mary Chesnut's Civil War." *Southern Studies* 26.1 (1987): 18–27.

Kandel, Eric R. *In Search of Memory: The Emergence of a New Science of Mind.* New York: Norton, 2006.

Kett, Joseph F. "Women and the Progressive Impulse in Southern Education." *The Web of Southern Social Relations: Women, Family, and Education.* Ed. Walter J. Fraser Jr., R. Frank Saunders Jr., and Jon L Wakelyn. Athens: U of Georgia P, 1985. 166–80.

King, Florence. *Southern Ladies and Gentlemen.* 1975. New York: Bantam, 1976.

King, Grace. *Memories of a Southern Woman of Letters.* 1932. Freeport, NY: Books for Libraries Press, 1971.

King, Richard H. *A Southern Renaissance: The Cultural Awakening of the American South, 1930–1955.* New York: Oxford UP, 1980.

Kreyling, Michael. *Inventing Southern Literature.* Jackson: UP of Mississippi, 1998.

Kurant, Wendy. "The Making of Buck Preston: Mary Boykin Chesnut, Women, and the Confederate Memorial Movement." *Southern Quarterly* 46.4 (2009): 35–56.

Ladd, Barbara. "Dismantling the Monolith: Southern Places—Past, Present, and Future." Jones and Monteith 44–57.

Langer, Suzanne K. *Feeling and Form: A Theory of Art.* New York: Scribner's, 1953.

Lash, Joseph. *Helen and Teacher: The Story of Helen Keller and Anne Sullivan Macy.* New York: Delacorte, 1980.

Lemert, Charles. "Anna Julia Cooper: The Colored Woman's Office." *The Voice of Anna Julia Cooper.* Ed. Charles Lemert and Esme Bhan. Lanham, MD: Rowman and Littlefield, 1998.

Linn, Bonar. Rev. of *My Days of Strength.* By Anne Walter Fearn. *Commercial Appeal* [Memphis] 30 April 1939.

Lionnet, Francoise. *Autobiographical Voices: Race, Gender, Self-Portraiture.* Ithaca: Cornell UP, 1989.

Long, Judy. *Telling Womens's Lives: Subject, Narrator, Reader, Text.* New York: New York UP, 1999.

Loveland, Anne C. *Lillian Smith: A Southerner Confronting the South.* Baton Rouge: Louisiana State UP, 1986.

Lowe, John. *Jump at the Sun: Zora Neale Hurston's Cosmic Comedy.* Urbana: U of Illinois P, 1994.

MacKethan, Lucinda H. *Daughters of Time: Creating Woman's Voice in Southern Story.* Athens: U of Georgia P, 1990.

Magee, Rosemary M., ed. *Friendship and Sympathy: Communities of Southern Women Writers.* Jackson: UP of Mississippi, 1992.

Mason, Mary. "The Other Voice: Autobiographies of Women Writers." Olney, *Autobiography* 207–35.

Massé, Michelle A. *In the Name of Love: Women, Masochism and the Gothic.* Ithaca: Cornell UP, 1992.

Matthews, Pamela R. *Ellen Glasgow and a Woman's Traditions.* Charlottesville: U of Virginia P, 1994.

———. Introduction. Glasgow, *The Woman Within.*

Mattingly, Carol. *Well-Tempered Women: Nineteenth-Century Temperance Rhetoric.* Carbondale: Southern Illinois UP, 1988.

Mayo, A. D. *Southern Women in the Recent Educational Movement in the South.* 1892. Ed. with introduction by Dan T. Carter and Amy Friedlander. Baton Rouge: Louisiana State UP, 1978.

McDowell, John Patrick. *The Social Gospel in the South: The Woman's Home Mission*

Movement in the Methodist Episcopal Church, South, 1886–1939. Baton Rouge: Louisiana State UP, 1982.

McGill, Ralph. "Miss Smith and Freud." *Constitution* [Atlanta] 24 November 1949: B18.

McLemore, Richard Aubrey. *A History of Mississippi*. Vol. 2. Jackson: UP of Mississippi, 1973.

McMillen, Sally G. *Southern Women: Black and White in the Old South*. American History Series. Arlington Heights, IL: Harlan Davidson, 1992.

McWhorter, Diane. *Carry Me Home: Birmingham, Alabama: The Climactic Battle of the Civil Rights Revolution*. New York: Simon and Schuster, 2002.

Mendenhall, Marjorie Stratford. "Southern Women of a 'Lost Generation.'" *South Atlantic Quarterly* 33 (1934): 334–53. Rpt. in *Unheard Voices: The First Historians of Southern Women*. Ed. Anne Firor Scott. Charlottesville: U of Virginia P, 1993. 92–110.

Mentzer, Melissa. "Rewriting the Unwritten: The Fictions of Autobiography in the Civil War Journal of Mary Chesnut." Diss. U of Oregon. 1989.

Miller, Nancy K. "The Entangled Self: Genre Bondage in the Age of the Memoir." *PMLA* 122.2 (2007): 537–48.

Mississippi: A Guide to the Magnolia State. Comp. and written by the Federal Writers' Project of the WPA. New York: Viking, 1938.

Montgomery, Rebecca. "Lost Cause Mythology in New South Reform: Gender, Class Race, and the Politics of Patriotic Citizenship." *Negotiating Boundaries of Southern Womanhood*. Ed. Janet L. Coryell, Thomas H. Appleton Jr., Anastatia Sims, and Sandra Gioia Treadway. Columbia: U Missouri P, 2000. 174–98.

Muhlenfeld, Elizabeth. *Mary Boykin Chesnut: A Biography*. Baton Rouge: Louisiana State UP, 1981.

Newby, I. A. *Plain Folk in the New South: Social Change and Cultural Persistence, 1880–1915*. Baton Rouge: Louisiana State UP, 1989.

O'Brien, Michael, ed. *An Evening When Alone: Four Journals of Single Women in the South, 1827–67*. Charlottesville: U of Virginia P, 1993.

O'Dell, Darlene. *Sites of Southern Memory: The Autobiographies of Katharine DuPre Lumpkin, Lillian Smith, and Pauli Murray*. Charlottesville: U of Virginia P, 2001.

Olney, James, ed. *Autobiography: Essays: Theoretical and Critical*. Princeton: Princeton UP, 1980.

———. *Memory and Narrative: The Weave of Life-Writing*. Chicago: U of Chicago P, 1998.

———. *Metaphors of Self: The Meaning of Autobiography*. Princeton: Princeton UP, 1972.

Ownby, Ted. *Subduing Satan: Religion, Recreation, and Manhood in the Rural South, 1865–1920*. Chapel Hill: U of North Carolina P, 1990.

Painter, Nell Irvin. Introduction. Thomas 1–67.

Papashvily, Helen Waite. *All the Happy Endings*. New York: Harper Bros., 1956.

Percy, Walker. *The Message in the Bottle.* 1975. New York: Farrar, Straus and Giroux, 1977.

Percy, William Alexander. *Lanterns on the Levee: Recollections of a Planter's Son.* 1941. Baton Rouge: Louisiana State UP, 1973.

Perreault, Jeanne. "Southern White Women's Autobiographies: Social Equality and Social Change." *Southern Literary Journal* 31.1 (2008): 32–51.

Polk, Noel. *Faulkner and Welty and the Southern Literary Tradition.* Jackson: UP of Mississippi, 2008.

Pond, Cornelia Jones. *Recollections of a Southern Daughter.* Ed. Lucinda H. MacKethan. Athens: U of Georgia P, 1998.

Porter, Katherine Anne. "Old Mortality." *Pale Horse, Pale Rider.* New York: Harcourt Brace, 1939.

———. "The Old Order." *Leaning Tower and Other Stories.* 1944. *The Collected Stories of Katherine Anne Porter.* New York: New American Library Plume, 1970.

Powell, William S., ed. *Dictionary of North Carolina Biography.* Chapel Hill: U of North Carolina P, 1979.

Prenshaw, Peggy Whitman. "The Construction of Confluence: The Female South and Eudora Welty's Art." *The Late Novels of Eudora Welty.* Ed. Jan Nordby Gretlund and Karl-Heinz Westarp. Columbia: U of South Carolina P, 1998. 176–94.

———. *Elizabeth Spencer.* Boston: Twayne, 1985.

———. "Fevered Desire and Therapeutic Gaze in Welty's World." *Eudora Welty and Poetics of the Body.* Etudes Faulkneriennes 5. Rennes, France: Presses Universitaires de Rennes, 2005. 71–78.

Price, Anne. "Lindy." *Baton Rouge Advocate Magazine* 14 April 2002: 16–18.

Rable, George C. *Civil Wars: Women and the Crisis of Southern Nationalism.* Urbana: U of Illinois P, 1991.

Rainey, Homer. P. "The Mind of the South." *Saturday Review of Literature* 22 October 1948: 21.

Ransom, John Crowe. "Reconstructed but Unregenerate." *I'll Take My Stand* 1–27.

Raper, Julius Rowan. "The Importance of Seeking 'Gerald.'" *Mississippi Quarterly* 49 (1996): 295–300.

Reed, John Shelton. *One South: An Ethnic Approach to Regional Culture.* Baton Rouge: Louisiana State UP, 1982.

Roberts, Cokie. *We Are Our Mothers' Daughters.* New York: W. Morrow, 1998.

Roberts, Terry. *Self and Community in the Fiction of Elizabeth Spencer.* Baton Rouge: Louisiana State UP, 1994.

———. "A Whole Personality: Elizabeth Spencer." *Conversations with Elizabeth Spencer.* Ed. Peggy Whitman Prenshaw. Jackson: UP of Mississippi, 1991.

Romine, Scott. "Framing Southern Rhetoric: Lillian Smith's Narrative Persona in *Killers of the Dream.*" *South Atlantic Review* 59 (1994): 95–111.

———. "Where Is Southern Literature?" Jones and Monteith 23–43.

Scott, Anne Firor. *Making the Invisible Woman Visible.* Urbana: U of Illinois P, 1984.

——. *Natural Allies: Women's Associations in American History.* Urbana: U of Illinois P, 1992.

——. *The Southern Lady: From Pedestal to Politics, 1830–1930.* Chicago: U of Chicago P, 1970.

——. "Women in the South: History as Fiction, Fiction as History." Honnighausen and Lerda 22–33.

Seidel, Kathryn Lee. *The Southern Belle in the American Novel.* Gainesville: UP of Florida, 1985.

Sensibar, Judith L. *Faulkner and Love: The Women Who Shaped His Art.* New Haven: Yale UP, 2009.

Showalter, Elaine. *A Literature of Their Own: British Women Novelists from Bronte to Lessing.* Princeton: Princeton UP, 1977.

Shulevitz, Judith. "The Close Reader: Powers of Perception." *New York Times Book Review* 20 April 2003: 31.

Silber, Nina. *The Romance of Reunion: Northerners and the South, 1865–1900.* Chapel Hill: U of North Carolina P, 1993.

Silverthorne, Elizabeth. *Marjorie Kinnan Rawlings: Sojourner at Cross Creek.* Woodstock, NY: Overlook, 1988.

Sims, Anastatia. *The Power of Femininity in the New South: Women's Organizations and Politics in North Carolina, 1880–1930.* Columbia: U of South Carolina P, 1997.

Sinclair, Upton. *The Autobiography of Upton Sinclair.* New York: Harcourt, Brace, 1962.

Singal, Daniel Joseph. *The War Within: From Victorian to Modernist Thought in the South, 1919–1945.* Chapel Hill: U of North Carolina P, 1982.

"Small Typhoon." Rev. of *My Days of Strength,* by Anne Walter Fearn. *Time* 24 April 1939: 95–96.

Smith, Sidonie, and Julia Watson, eds. *Women, Autobiography, Theory: A Reader.* Madison: U of Wisconsin P, 1998.

Sosna, Morton. *In Search of the Silent South.* New York: Columbia UP, 1977.

Spacks, Patricia Meyer. "Selves in Hiding." Jelinek 112–32.

Spruill, Julia. *Women's Life and Work in the Southern Colonies.* Chapel Hill: U of North Carolina P, 1938.

Stillinger, Jack. *Multiple Authorship and the Myth of Solitary Genius.* New York: Oxford UP, 1991.

Stowe, Steven M. *Intimacy and Power in the Old South: Ritual in the Lives of the Planters.* Baltimore: Johns Hopkins UP, 1987.

Taylor, William R. *Cavalier and Yankee: The Old South and American National Character.* 1961. New York: Doubleday Anchor, 1963.

Thanet, Octave. "Town Life in Arkansas." *Atlantic Monthly* 68 (Sept. 1891): 332–40.

——. "Plantation Life in Arkansas." *Atlantic Monthly* 68 (July 1891): 32–49.

Thomas, Ella Gertrude Clanton. *The Secret Eye: The Journal of Ella Gertrude Clanton*

Thomas, 1848–1889. Ed. Virginia Ingraham Burr. Introduction by Nell Irvin Painter. Chapel Hill: U of North Carolina P, 1990.

Tillett, Wilbur Fisk. "Southern Womanhood as Affected by the War." *Century Magazine* 43 (1891): 8–16.

Tipton, Nancy Carol. "'It Is My Duty': The Public Career of Belle Kearney." MA thesis. U of Mississippi, 1975.

Todorov, Tzvetan. *Life in Common: An Essay in General Anthopology.* 1995. Trans. Katherine Golsan and Lucy Golsan. Lincoln: U of Nebraska P, 2001.

Trouard, Dawn, ed. "Landing in Akron." Introduction. *Eudora Welty: Eye of the Storyteller.* Kent, OH: Kent State UP, 1989. ix–xiv.

Twain, Mark. *Adventures of Huckleberry Finn.* Ed. Henry Nash Smith. 1885. Boston: Houghton Mifflin, 1958.

Unrue, Darlene Harbour. *Truth and Vision in Katherine Anne Porter's Fiction.* Athens: U of Georgia P, 1985.

"Uppie's Goddess." *Time* 18 November 1957: 118, 122–23.

"Upton Sinclair's Wife, Native of State, Dies." *Clarion-Ledger* [Jackson, Mississippi] 28 April 1961.

Wade, John Donald. "The Life and Death of Cousin Lucius." *I'll Take My Stand* 265–301.

Wagner, Linda W. *Ellen Glasgow: Beyond Convention.* Austin: U of Texas P, 1982.

Wallach, Jennifer Jensen. *"Closer to the Truth Than Any Fact": Memoir, Memory, and Jim Crow.* Athens: U of Georgia P, 2008.

Washington, Mary Helen. Introduction. Cooper xxvii–liv.

Watson, Jay. "Uncovering the Body, Discovering Ideology: Segregation and Sexual Anxiety in Lillian Smith's *Killers of the Dream*." *American Quarterly* 49.3 (1997): 470–503.

Watts, Rebecca Bridges. *Contemporary Southern Identity: Community through Controversy.* Jackson: UP of Mississippi, 2008.

Weaver, Richard M. "Aspects of the Southern Philosophy." 1953. *Southern Renascence: The Literature of the Modern South.* Ed. Louis D. Rubin Jr. and Robert D. Jacobs. Baltimore: Johns Hopkins UP, 1966.

Weintraub, Karl J. "Autobiographical and Historical Consciousness." *Critical Inquiry* 1 (1975): 821–48.

Wheeler, Marjorie Spruill. *New Women of the New South: The Leaders of the Woman Suffrage Movement in the Southern States.* New York: Oxford. 1993.

Whites, LeeAnn. *The Civil War as a Crisis in Gender: Augusta, Georgia, 1860–1890.* Athens: U of Georgia P, 1995.

Williamson, Joel. *The Crucible of Race: Black-White Relations in the American South since Emancipation.* New York: Oxford UP, 1984.

Wilson, Anthony. *Shadow and Shelter: The Swamp in Southern Culture.* Jackson: UP of Mississippi, 2006.

Wilson, Charles Reagan. "The Invention of Southern Tradition: The Writing and Ritualization of Southern History, 1880–1940." Honnighausen and Lerda 3–21.

Wilson, Edmund. *Patriotic Gore: Studies in the Literature of the American Civil War.* New York: Oxford UP, 1962.

Wolfe, Margaret Ripley. *Daughters of Canaan: A Saga of Southern Women.* Lexington: UP of Kentucky, 1995.

Woods, Katherine. "A Woman Doctor's Years in China." *New York Times Book Review* 16 April 1939: 9.

Woodward, C. Vann. Introduction. Chesnut, *Mary Chesnut's Civil War* xv–lviii.

———. *Origins of the New South.* Baton Rouge: Louisiana State UP, 1951.

Wright, Richard. *Black Boy.* 1945. New York: Harper Perennial, 1966.

Wyatt-Brown, Bertram. *Southern Honor: Ethics and Behavior in the Old South.* New York: Oxford UP, 1982.

Yaeger, Patricia. *Dirt and Desire: Reconstructing Southern Women's Writing, 1930–1990.* Chicago: U of Chicago P, 2000.

Yagoda, Ben. *Memoir: A History.* New York: Riverhead, 2009.

Yoder, Jon A. *Upton Sinclair.* 1975. New York: Frederick Ungar, 1975.

Yow, Valerie Raleigh. *Bernice Kelly Harris: A Good Life Was Writing.* Baton Rouge: Louisiana State UP, 1999.

Index

Aaron, Daniel, 257

Abbott, Shirley, 129

Acton, Patricia Nassif, 233

Adams, Timothy Dow, 296*n*7, 300*n*2

African Americans. *See* Black men; Black women; Race relations; Slavery

Agee, James, 148, 298*n*4

Agrarians. *See* Fugitive Agrarians

Alcohol use, 102–3, 106–7, 116, 146–47. *See also* Temperance movement

Anagnos, Michael, 74

Anderson, Agnes Grinstead: birth date of, 113; childhood of, 113; children of, 112, 115–16; education of, 112, 117; and feminine ideal, 117–18; journals of, 114; marriage of, 111, 113–25, 255; parents of, 113, 115, 121, 122, 124; sister of, 115, 121, 122; as teacher, 116, 122

—*Approaching the Magic Hour:* acknowledgments in, 112; Black as editor of, 111, 112; on black caretakers, 122–23; compared with other autobiographies, 112, 115, 117–18, 134, 163, 176, 181; on courtship and marriage proposal, 115, 118–21; dating of manuscript of, 111; dialogue in, 123; on husband as artist, 111, 113, 114, 116, 121–22, 255; inversions of hero's centrality to tale in, 123–25; length of, 111; on mental illness of husband, 115–16, 122, 124; on motherhood and grandmotherhood, 120; motives for writing of, 111, 112; narrator

and narrative style of, 114, 124–25; provisional readings of and questions on, 116–17, 121, 124; relational self in, 36; on sacramental and protective role of wife, 111, 121–24; on South, 114–15; as wife-narrative, 95, 96, 111–25, 176, 255

Anderson, Henry, 217

Anderson, Pat Grinstead, 115, 121, 122

Anderson, Peter, 112, 115, 121

Anderson, Walter Inglis (Bob), 111–25, 255, 298–99*n*5

Andrews, William, 63

Angelou, Maya, 234, 235, 293

Approaching the Magic Hour (Anderson). *See* Anderson, Agnes Grinstead

Armour, Richard, 146

Arnold, Matthew, 125

Arthur, Anthony, 142, 149

Augustine, Saint, 24, 26, 28–29, 211

Austen, Jane, 118

Autobiography: censorship of, 27; chronology in, 5, 300*n*2; and Civil War experience, 3, 4, 15–16, 292; coded language in, 15; compared with diary and memoir writing, 3, 22, 25–27, 30, 181, 296*n*9; conclusions on, 292–94; conversion narratives and accounts of racial discrimination, 16–17, 181, 190, 211; credibility, reliability, and facticity of, 3–4, 24–25, 283; current interest in, 3; daily life recounted in generally, 15; definition and characteristics of,

WITHDRAWN

Gramley Library
Salem Academy and College
Winston-Salem, N.C. 27108